D0712760

Composers of North America

Series Editors: John Beckwith, Sam Dennison, William C. Loring, Jr., Margery M. Lowens, Martha Furman Schleifer

1. *William Wallace Gilchrist, 1846–1916: A Moving Force in the Musical Life of Philadelphia,* by Martha Furman Schleifer, 1985
2. *Energy and Individuality in the Art of Anna Huntington, Sculptor, and Amy Beach,* Composer, by Myrna G. Eden, 1987
3. *Ruth Crawford Seeger: Memoirs, Memories, Music,* by Matilda Gaume, 1986
4. *An American Romantic-Realist Abroad: Templeton Strong and His Music,* by William C. Loring Jr., 1995
5. *Elinor Remick Warren: Her Life and Her Music,* by Virginia Bortin, 1987
6. *Horatio Parker, 1863–1919: His Life, Music, and Ideas,* by William K. Kearns, 1990
7. *Frances McCollin: Her Life and Music,* by Annette Maria DiMedio, 1990
8. *Hard Trials: The Life and Music of Harry T. Burleigh,* by Anne Key Simpson, 1990
9. *He Heard America Singing: Arthur Farwell, Composer and Crusading Music Educator,* by Evelyn Davis Culbertson, 1992
10. *Follow Me: The Life and Music of R. Nathaniel Dett,* by Anne Key Simpson, 1993
11. *Normand Lockwood: His Life and Music,* by Kay Norton, 1993
12. *Ridin' Herd to Writing Symphonies: An Autobiography,* by Radie Britain, 1995
13. *Henry Holden Huss: An American Composer's Life,* by Gary A. Greene, 1995
14. *Frederick Shepherd Converse (1871–1940): His Life and Music,* by Robert J. Garofalo, 1994
15. *John Weinzweig and His Music: The Radical Romantic of Canada,* by Elaine Keillor, 1994
16. *Amy Beach and Her Chamber Music: Biography, Documents, Style,* by Jeanell Wise Brown, 1994
17. *Music of Many Means: Sketches and Essays on the Music of Robert Erickson,* by Robert Erickson and John MacKay, 1995
18. *Divine Song on the Northeast Frontier: Maine's Sacred Tunebooks, 1800–1830,* by Linda G. Davenport, 1996
19. *George Whitefield Chadwick: His Symphonic Works,* by Bill F. Faucett, 1996

Divine Song on the Northeast Frontier

Maine's Sacred Tunebooks, 1800–1830

Linda Gilbert Davenport

Composers of North America, No. 18

The Scarecrow Press, Inc.
Lanham, Md., & London

SCARECROW PRESS, INC.

Published in the United States of America
by Scarecrow Press, Inc.
4720 Boston Way
Lanham, Maryland 20706

4 Pleydell Gardens, Folkestone
Kent CT20 2DN, England

Grateful acknowledgment is hereby made for permission to reprint the following items:
Excerpt from 1896 letter of J. T. Little. Reprinted by permission of the Castine Scientific Society.
Excerpts from the letters, tunebooks, and newspaper (*The Orb*), of Japheth Coombs Washburn. Reprinted by permission of Margaret Clifford.
Excerpt from the Constitution of the Musical Society in Falmouth, Collection S-627, Misc. Box 24/4, Maine Historical Society, Portland. Reprinted by permission of the Maine Historical Society.
Excerpt from the Ephraim Stinchfield Papers, Manuscript Collection 44, Maine Historical Society, Portland. Reprinted by permission of the Maine Historical Society.

British Library Cataloguing-in-Publication Information Available

Library of Congress Cataloging-in-Publication Data

Davenport, Linda Gilbert, 1951–
Divine song on the Northeast frontier : Main's sacred tunebooks, 1800–1830 / by Linda Gilbert Davenport.
p. cm. — (Composers of North America ; no. 18)
Revision of author's thesis (Ph.D. — University of Colorado-Boulder, 1991) under title: Maine's sacred tunebooks, 1800–1830.
Includes bibliographical references and index.
1. Tune-books—History and criticism. 2. Hymns, English—Main—19th century—History and criticism. 3. Composers—Maine. I. Title. II. Series
ML3186.D26 1996 787.27′09741′09034—dc20 95-9756 CIP MN

ISBN 0-8108-3025-6 (cloth : alk. paper)

Printed in the United States of America

♾ ™The paper used in this publication meets the minimum requirements of American National Standard for Information Sciences—Permanence of Paper for Printed Library Material, ANSI Z39.48–1984.

CONTENTS

TABLES

FIGURES

MAPS

MUSICAL EXAMPLES

SERIES EDITORS' FOREWORD

This series, Composers of North America, is designed to focus attention on the development of art music and folk music from colonial times to the present. Few of our composers of art music before 1975 had their works performed frequently during their lifetimes. Many suffered undeserved neglect.

Each volume consists of a substantial essay about the composer and a complete catalog of compositions, published and unpublished. Part I deals with the composers' lives and works in the context of the artistic thought and the musical world of their times. In Part II the goals of the composers and the critical comments by contemporaries are included, as are illustrations and musical examples. Some works which merit performance today are singled out for analysis and discussion. In Part III the catalog of the composers' output has full publication details and locations of unpublished works. We hope that this series will make readers conscious and appreciative of our North American musical heritage.

The books are also intended to help performers and teachers seeking works to use. For them we designed the Part III catalog of the composers' music to allow a quick search for works the author finds of historic or current interest to be considered for readings and hearings.

Series Editors:
Sam Dennison, William C. Loring, Jr., Margery M. Lowens,
Ezra Schabas, Martha Furman Schleifer

PREFACE

My interest in Maine's sacred music grew from a seed planted in a graduate course at the University of Colorado–Boulder. Knowing of my Maine background, music librarian and psalmody scholar Karl Kroeger suggested I explore Supply Belcher and his music for one of the short papers required for his music bibliography seminar. Although born and raised in Maine, I had never heard of Belcher, a Maine hymn-tune composer of the late eighteenth century.

Following my introductory study on Belcher, Dr. Kroeger suggested research on two even more obscure Maine psalmodists of the early nineteenth century: Abraham Maxim and Japheth Coombs Washburn. In addition to composing, both Maxim and Washburn had compiled several hymn-tune collections, or "tune-books." Further investigation revealed the existence of several other virtually unknown Maine tunebooks and compilers of the early nineteenth century. A dissertation topic perfect for me was born: "Maine's Sacred Tunebooks, 1800–1830." Not only could I satisfy my curiosity about these fellow "Mainiacs" and inform others about them, but I would have the opportunity to concentrate on sacred music, something dear to my heart as a born-again Christian (not to mention that my research trips to Maine would give me an opportunity to visit my mother, who still lives there).

My research focused on the context, compilers, and contents of all eighteen extant sacred music collections compiled in Maine between 1800 and 1830. Diaries, church records, town histories, and newspapers were utilized to establish the historical and musical contexts in which the tunebooks were written and used. Biographical data were gathered and synthesized to provide sketches of the lives of the composer-compilers. The tunebook contents were compared and contrasted, and each psalmodist's original compositions were surveyed to form preliminary conclusions about his practices. Representative pieces by the Maine psalmodists were selected for inclusion in complete musical transcription to facilitate discussion and contemporary performance of these neglected and somewhat inaccessible works.

This book represents a revision of my doctoral dissertation,* reorganized slightly to meet the parameters of Scarecrow's Composers of North America series and modified to incorporate findings on two tunebook editions (*Northern Harmony*/4 and *Temple Harmony*/3) largely unavailable during the writing of the dissertation. My hope is that Maine's early-nineteenth-century tunebooks and composer-compilers will become better known as a result of this book. Mainers and non-Mainers alike need to become aware of this largely ignored musical culture; the findings of this study have implications for understanding the nature and place of early-nineteenth-century sacred music in other rural areas of the eastern United States.

In large part, the individuals who contributed significantly to the book are those who facilitated the research and writing of the dissertation on which it was based. Foremost, of course, is Professor Karl Kroeger, who introduced me to the field of psalmody. As my dissertation advisor, he provided excellent guidance and shared generously from his personal collections. He continues to be a valued mentor and friend.

My other doctoral committee members—Professors William Kearns, Deborah Hayes, Oliver Ellsworth, Ralph Mann, and initially Steven Bruns—offered helpful suggestions from their areas of expertise prior to the completion of the dissertation. My series editor—William C. Loring, Jr.—has done the same in the transformation of the dissertation into a book. A special acknowledgment is due Professor Kearns, my pre-candidacy advisor, who served as encourager and mentor throughout my doctoral studies. His contagious enthusiasm for American music was a major factor in my becoming an Americanist.

Individuals to whom I am especially grateful for sharing invaluable information or resources include Nym Cooke, Nicholas Temperley, Mr. and Mrs. William Foster, Kathleen Martin, Nancy Merrill, Glenn Skillin, Florence Whitman, and particularly Margaret Clifford. Miss Clifford, a descendant of Japheth Coombs

*Linda Gilbert Davenport, "Maine's Sacred Tunebooks, 1800–1830: Divine Song on the Northeast Frontier" (Ph.D. dissertation, University of Colorado–Boulder, 1991).

Washburn, generously allowed me access to her personal collection of Washburn tunebooks and papers. Several Calais residents—particularly Karen Herrick of the Calais Free Library, Glendon Ayer of the Calais Masonic Lodge, and Jackie Dudley of the Second Baptist Church of Calais—were especially helpful in completing my knowledge of Washburn's years in Calais.

Besides these individuals, I am indebted to the staffs of many libraries, particularly the Maine and Massachusetts Historical Societies, Hubbard Free Library (Hallowell, Maine), Maine State Library, Maine State Law Library, Maine State Archives, Old York Historical Society, Bagaduce Music Lending Library (Blue Hill, Maine), Norlands Living History Center (Livermore Falls, Maine), the Essex Institute, and the American Antiquarian Society. Many other librarians were also very cooperative, in response to either personal visits or correspondence.

I am grateful to the University of Colorado for a doctoral fellowship my first year and for two Graduate School Dean's Small Grant Awards which helped considerably with the costs of two research trips to New England.

On a personal level, two individuals who have had important roles as listening posts and suggestion-givers throughout the preparation of both the book and dissertation warrant special mention. My mother, Nina C. Gilbert of Augusta, Maine, dropped everything to serve as personal chauffeur during my research trips to Maine and patiently accepted the little time that was allotted for "fun times" together during my visits. I am grateful to her, and to my late father, George G. Gilbert, for their unfailing belief and pride in me. I also appreciate the sacrifices made by my husband, Allen E. Davenport, C.M.L., during my doctoral studies and the writing of this book. He has patiently endured discourses on the Maine psalmodists during our morning runs together and has motivated me to press on and to finish the dissertation and book in a timely fashion.

I must also acknowledge the grace and providence of God and my Lord Jesus Christ in every step of this study and my life. "I will sing unto the Lord, for he hath dealt bountifully with me" (Psalm 13:6). To God be the glory.

Linda G. Davenport
Alton, Illinois

CHAPTER I

INTRODUCTION

At the turn of the nineteenth century, the northeast frontier was a popular destination for young adults from southern New England, particularly Massachusetts, who sought inexpensive land on which to settle. Transportation by sea made Maine particularly accessible and attractive for those without the funds for a long overland journey. Although Maine was not completely frontier territory,[1] most of the new settlers were drawn to the wooded, inland areas in central Maine, where large tracts of previously unsettled land could be acquired for a relatively small price.

The hardy new residents brought with them the Sabbath worship practices of their New England upbringing. In some areas, they met together in the town meetinghouse for "Divine Service"; in other places, they gathered informally with their neighbors in a schoolhouse, barn, or private home to hear an itinerant preacher. Regardless of the setting, "Divine Song"—that is, music sung to praise and honor God—was an important component of worship.

Printed collections called "tunebooks" provided the tunes for the singing. Unlike present-day hymnals, which furnish several stanzas of text along with each setting, early-nineteenth-century tunebooks usually contained only a single stanza of text beneath each line of music. Singers were accustomed to consulting psalters and hymnbooks (publications of texts without music) for additional stanzas or for alternate texts. Since the appropriate meter was indicated above most tunes, any other texts of the same meter could be substituted for the one printed in the tunebook.

The tunebooks typically began with several pages of instructional material, often termed a "theoretical introduction" to the rudiments of music, followed by three- and four-voice, unaccompanied choral settings of psalms and hymns.[2] Since tunes were not always linked with a single text, they were often assigned names which had no relationship to the words sung with them. Maine town names—such as Hallowell, Portland, China, and Turner—frequently appear as titles of pieces composed by Mainers.

Tunebooks were used in churches by choirs and in singing schools by students learning music reading and choral singing. Singing schools (discussed in more detail in Chapter IV) met several evenings a week for about three months, usually in the winter. They were eagerly attended by young people, who looked at them as adult-sanctioned opportunities to gather with their friends. Singing-school instructors, called "singing masters," frequently compiled collections for the use of their students and others. In addition to including their own music, they usually selected tunes by other "psalmodists" (sacred music composers) as well.[3]

Twenty-three Protestant tunebooks, listed in Table 1, were compiled in Maine prior to 1830. Twenty-one different editions were compiled by six individuals: Supply Belcher, Abraham Maxim, Charles Robbins, Japheth Coombs Washburn, Edward Hartwell, and Henry Little. The other two tunebooks were prepared by unidentified editors. This study focuses on the eighteen extant collections compiled in the nineteenth century.

Table 2 provides an introduction to the Maine compilers. Although they were Maine residents when they prepared their collections, all were born in other parts of New England, usually Massachusetts. Most had travelled as young adults to the northeast frontier in search of land and opportunity. Finding conditions there satisfactory, they remained in the area for life. Since Maine was part of Massachusetts until 1820, the Massachusetts emigrants remained under familiar jurisdiction.[4]

Before 1816, because Maine printers did not possess music type, all of the "Maine" tunebooks were printed in nearby Exeter, New Hampshire. After publisher Ezekiel Goodale of Hallowell, Maine, acquired music type in 1814, nearly all the tunebooks compiled in Maine were also printed there. In this book, the phrase "Maine tunebooks" will not be limited to Maine imprints, but will encompass publications compiled in the state (or district) but printed elsewhere. Collections which were for sale in Maine bookstores but which were neither compiled nor printed in Maine will not be considered "Maine tunebooks."

TABLE 1

Tunebooks Compiled in Maine Before 1830

Date	*Title*	*Compiler*
1794	*The Harmony of Maine*	Supply Belcher
1802	*The Oriental Harmony*	Abraham Maxim
1805	*The Columbian Harmony*	Charles Robbins
1805	*The Northern Harmony*	Abraham Maxim
1808	*The Northern Harmony/2*	Abraham Maxim
1810	* *The Northern Harmony/3*	Abraham Maxim
1813	*The Parish Harmony*	J. C. Washburn
1815	* *The Parish Harmony/2*	J. C. Washburn
1815	*The Chorister's Companion*	Edward Hartwell
1816	−*The Northern Harmony/4*	Maxim & Washburn
1817	*The Hallowell Collection of Sacred Music*	[E. Goodale?]
1817/18?	* *The Parish Harmony/3*	J. C. Washburn
1818	*The Temple Harmony*	J. C. Washburn
1819	*The Hallowell Collection/2*	[E. Goodale?]
1819	−*The Northern Harmony/5*	Abraham Maxim
1820	*The Temple Harmony/2*	J. C. Washburn
1820	*The Wesleyan Harmony*	Henry Little
1821	*The Wesleyan Harmony/2*	Henry Little
1821	*The Temple Harmony/3*	J. C. Washburn
1823	*The Temple Harmony/4*	J. C. Washburn
1824/25?	*The Temple Harmony/5*	J. C. Washburn
1826	*The Temple Harmony/6*	J. C. Washburn
1827	* *The Temple Harmony/7*	J. C. Washburn

NOTE: The tunebooks are arranged in chronological order, with an asterisk (*) next to editions not known to be extant and a minus sign (−) for those existing only in incomplete copies. Second editions are indicated by /2 after the title, third editions by /3, etc.

Beyond the scope of this book is the sacred music of two Maine religious groups: Shakers and Catholics.[5] The ritualistic Shaker music was of a different sort than that published in conventional New England tunebooks. Catholic services did not include the hymn- and psalm-singing so integral to Protestant worship.

An explanation may be in order regarding the beginning and ending dates chosen for this book. Many recent scholarly works in other disciplines have focused on Maine in the years between 1783 and 1820, certainly an important period in Maine history.[6] The most fruitful years of tunebook production in Maine, though,

TABLE 2

Compilers of Maine Tunebooks Published Before 1830

Compiler	*Native State*	*Occupation*	*Maine Town*	*Tunebooks*
*Supply Belcher (1751–1836)	MA	Tavern-keeper, teacher, J.P., legislator	Farmington	*The Harmony of Maine* (1794)
*Edward Hartwell (1747–1844)	MA	Ferryboat operator, farmer	Bloomfield (*now* Skowhegan)	*The Chorister's Companion* (1815)
Henry Little (1788–1878)	NH	Clerk, trader, postmaster	Bucksport	*The Wesleyan Harmony,* 2 editions (1820, 1821)
*Abraham Maxim (1773–1829)	MA	Teacher, farmer	Turner	*The Oriental Harmony* (1802) *The Northern Harmony,* 5 editions (1805–1819)
*Charles Robbins (1782–1842)	MA	Cabinetmaker, tavern-keeper	Winthrop	*The Columbian Harmony* (1805)
*Japheth Coombs Washburn (1780–1850)	MA	Store-owner, trader, J.P., postmaster, legislator, newspaper publisher	China	*The Parish Harmony* (1813) *The Northern Harmony,* 4th ed. (1816; co-compiled with Maxim) *The Temple Harmony,* 7 editions (1818–1827)
Possible Compiler (not named on title pages)				
Ezekiel Goodale (1780–1828)	MA	Publisher, bookstore owner	Hallowell	*The Hallowell Collection,* 2 editions (1817, 1819)

NOTE: An asterisk (*) denotes those who were composers as well as compilers. The second column names the state (Massachusetts or New Hampshire) in which they were born. The fourth lists the Maine town in which they were living when their tunebooks were published. See Map 1 for town locations.

were 1800 to 1830. Prior to 1800, only one collection by a Maine resident had been published: *The Harmony of Maine* (1794) by Supply Belcher. Since Belcher and his music have already been discussed in other studies,[7] this book provides just an overview of his work and concentrates instead on the period beginning with 1800. The ending year of 1830 allows the inclusion of all the tunebook editions compiled by Mainers Abraham Maxim and Japheth Coombs Washburn.

Songs of Sion (1830),[8] the next Maine tunebook to be published, represents a new phase of sacred tunebook publication in Maine. It consists almost exclusively of European tunes, supplemented by unattributed tunes not found in the earlier Maine tunebooks. The tunebook and its compilers seem to have little relationship to the collections and psalmodists listed in Table 1, so it will not be included. Accordingly, this book extends from 1800 to—but not through—1830.[9]

The Need for This Book

New England psalmody has received much scholarly attention in the last half of the twentieth century. Some studies have focused on the lives and works of individual psalmodists, including William Billings,[10] Oliver Holden,[11] Jeremiah Ingalls,[12] Stephen Jenks,[13] Andrew Law,[14] Justin Morgan,[15] and Daniel Read,[16] to name just a few. One of the most recent has synthesized data relating to a number of psalmodists to suggest interrelationships among them.[17] Another study has been devoted to a single collection, *The Worcester Collection,* and the changes in psalmody which its various editions reveal.[18] The genres of anthem[19] and fuging-tune[20] have been the topics of books, while landmark dissertations by Allen Britton[21] and Alan Buechner[22] earlier in the century have provided the foundation of our knowledge of theoretical introductions and the singing school. *The Core Repertory of Early American Psalmody,* a scholarly edition of the 101 sacred pieces most often printed in America between 1698 and 1810, is a valuable resource for performers as well as scholars.[23]

The 1990s will surely be remembered for the publication of the final volume of the complete-works edition of William Billings, America's premier psalmodist,[24] and the long-awaited sacred music imprint bibliography by Britton, Lowens, and Crawford.[25] The

Hymn Tune Index produced under the direction of Nicholas Temperley at the University of Illinois provides scholars with another type of bibliographic control.

While all these studies have greatly increased our knowledge of New England psalmody, little attention has been focused on sacred music in rural areas, particularly Maine, New Hampshire, and Vermont. Although sacred music was important throughout New England, it took on special significance in frontier areas, where art music concerts were a rarity. Religious music was the popular music of the day, the type with which most residents were familiar. Area studies on the sacred music of the northern New England states are needed to determine if there were significant differences between urban and rural sacred music practices and to suggest possible explanations for any variants.

With its ties to urban Massachusetts, rural Maine is an ideal focus for the study of rural/urban contrasts. The large number of tunebooks compiled in Maine in the first decades of the nineteenth century provide rich sources for a study of the changing repertory. The Maine compilers themselves are appropriate subjects for a study of interrelationships among psalmodists because they were contemporaries who lived in the same general area and apparently knew of one another's work. Findings about Maine's sacred music may have implications for understanding the nature and place of sacred music in other rural areas of the eastern United States.

Edwards's *Music and Musicians of Maine,* written in 1928, remains the standard work on Maine's musical past.[26] While a work of such scope is bound to have some inaccuracies of detail, Edwards provides information not available elsewhere on organizations and individuals active in music in Maine. His book does not deal with the music itself, however.

More recent is Ronald Cole's 1975 dissertation, which surveys the secular and sacred music of Portland, Maine's largest nineteenth-century city.[27] Based largely on newspapers and church records, Cole's chapter on sacred music presents a fairly comprehensive picture of church music in Portland. Cole also discusses several Portland singing societies (the Handel Society of Maine and the Beethoven Society) which performed sacred music. The music of early Portland has also been the topic of an article by Donald Sears.[28]

Most of the sacred music collections which were compiled in Maine in the early nineteenth century, however, did not originate in Portland or other established, southern Maine towns, but in the rural towns of burgeoning central Maine—such as Turner, China, Hallowell, Winthrop, and Skowhegan—and in the river town of Bucksport. Boston sacred music collections, easily obtained by merchants in the older coastal towns, may have been quite adequate for the needs of southern Maine citizens who supported the Congregational establishment and were culturally allied with Massachusetts urban society. They were apparently less satisfactory for evangelical believers in the small Maine towns on the growing edge of the frontier.[29]

The nineteenth-century Maine psalmodists who compiled tunebooks for these rural settlers are virtually unknown, even in Maine, although Maine's principal eighteenth-century psalmodist,[30] Supply Belcher, has been the topic of several extended studies.[31] Belcher is the only Maine psalmodist to receive even passing mention in the standard American music texts,[32] in part because he was an imaginative composer whose tunebook includes a notable number of secular texts. In addition, he was a somewhat colorful figure because of the epithet he acquired; he was known as "the Handel of Maine."[33] His musical career was at its height in the late eighteenth century, when native psalmody was in full bloom.

Of the Maine psalmodists whose collections were published in the early nineteenth century, when sacred music by Americans was beginning to decline in favor, only Abraham Maxim is included in the biographical sketches in Metcalf's *American Writers and Compilers of Sacred Music*[34] and Cheney's *American Singing Book*.[35] The recent Lowens-Britton-Crawford bibliography provides accurate, brief biographical sketches of Maxim, as well as Maine residents Supply Belcher and Charles Robbins.[36] Since the listings encompass only tunebooks which were printed by 1810, however, the publications and lives of the later Maine compilers (Japheth Coombs Washburn, Edward Hartwell, and Henry Little) are not included. To find information on them, one must look in town history books or family genealogies, which frequently contain little information pertaining to their musical careers.[37]

Just as Belcher is Maine's only recognized psalmodist, Belcher's collection, *The Harmony of Maine,* is the only Maine tunebook of the late eighteenth or early nineteenth centuries to be known by most music scholars, largely because it is available in a modern reprint.[38] Few copies of the other Maine tunebooks are extant. Patrons of libraries owning the American Antiquarian Society/Readex Microprint Series of Early American Imprints Before 1820 can easily examine microprint copies of some of the rare Maine collections.[39] One must look elsewhere, however, for several of the pre-1820 editions as well as all of the post-1820 editions.[40] Several Maine tunebooks may be viewed only in person, since no reproductions are obtainable for them.[41] In view of the scattered locations of the Maine tunebooks, there is a need for a study providing an overview of these collections and a guide to where they may be found. Part II of this book supplies the overview, while Part III assists the reader in locating copies of the tunebooks for further study or performance.

Methods Used

To understand the sacred music milieu in early-nineteenth-century Maine, I examined diaries, church records, town histories, newspapers, orations, and other primary sources from Maine for mentions of sacred music. Special attention was paid to materials dealing with the central Maine towns in which the compilers lived. To obtain biographical information on these psalmodists, I consulted town records and census listings. In the case of Washburn, I also studied personal papers preserved by his descendant, Margaret Clifford.

While the diaries and church records surveyed seldom contained relevant information, Maine town histories frequently did. Their authors were often late-nineteenth-century residents who mentioned church music issues pertaining to local churches and sometimes shared personal memories of events earlier in the century. Hallowell (Maine) newspapers were another particularly fruitful source. Because many of the Maine tunebooks were published in Hallowell, they were frequently advertised there; bookstore ads provided information about the sizes, prices, and publication dates of most of the collections. Many of the other central Maine towns in which the psalmodists lived did not yet have their own local newspapers.

Historical societies and libraries in Maine, and major libraries elsewhere, were combed for extant Maine tunebooks. Information about each tune in these collections was entered into a data base, which provided the basis for comparative analysis of the repertory.[42]

Organization of This Book

This book is organized into three major sections: The Composer-Compilers and Their Milieu, Tunebook Contents, and Catalog of Music. The first part is further subdivided into Cultural Context and Biographies of the Composer-Compilers.

Part I.A discusses the historical and musical context of the tunebooks. Chapter II surveys Maine's political and religious culture in the first three decades of the nineteenth century, while Chapters III and IV address music in Maine churches, singing schools, and musical societies, the primary settings in which the collections were employed. Chapter V, based largely on newspaper advertisements, suggests which tunebooks from Maine and elsewhere were available in the state during the period.

Part I.B provides biographical information on the compilers themselves. The antecedent roles of Maine's eighteenth-century psalmodists—Supply Belcher and James Lyon—are explored in Chapter VI. Abraham Maxim and Japheth Coombs Washburn, compilers of several tunebooks each and arguably the most important of the Maine psalmodists, are allotted separate chapters (Chapters VII and VIII, respectively). The other compilers (Edward Hartwell, Charles Robbins, Henry Little, Ezekiel Goodale, and the unidentified compilers of *The Hallowell Collection of Sacred Music*) are discussed in less depth in a single chapter (Chapter IX).

Part II surveys the contents of the eighteen extant editions. Compared and contrasted are their prefaces (Chapter X), theoretical introductions (Chapter XI), and overall repertory (Chapter XII). Changing trends in Maine's sacred music are identified, and the Maine tunebooks are compared with other New England collections of the time. Chapter XIII provides an introduction to the sacred tunes composed by Maine residents Maxim, Washburn, Hartwell, and Robbins by discussing representative tunes written by each. Also included are complete musical transcriptions (on two staves) of these eleven Maine tunes, facilitating performance, if desired. The concluding chapter (Chapter XIV), a summation of Parts I and II, compares sacred music in Maine and Massachusetts during the period and surveys some of the important tunebooks and sacred music trends of the two decades or so after 1830.

Part III features an index to the tunes composed by the Maine compilers. Also listed are the locations of extant Maine tunebook copies. To assist those interested in eighteenth-century Maine psalmody, the scope of Part III has been extended back to 1794 to encompass Belcher's works. Following Part III are the End Papers: Notes by Chapters, Bibliography, and Index.

The Genres of Psalmody

Throughout this study, reference will frequently be made to the various types of psalm- and hymn-tune settings contained in tunebooks of the eighteenth and nineteenth centuries, using the standard terms employed in studies of early American psalmody. Complete musical examples of three of the types can be found in Chapter XIII.

The five genres of psalmody are the plain tune, tune with extension, fuging-tune, set-piece, and anthem. The first three—plain tune, tune with extension, and fuging-tune—are strophic, while the others—set-piece and anthem—are through-composed.

The plain tune, the simplest type of strophic psalm- or hymn-tune, sets one, or sometimes two, stanzas of text. The musical structure is strictly controlled by the meter of the text: one line of text is set to one line of music, with no textual or musical repetition of words or phrases. Plain tunes are not necessarily limited to block chords; each voice can be somewhat melismatic as long as the melismas do not extend the length of the piece beyond a syllabic setting.

The tune with extension is a slightly more elaborate setting of a psalm or hymn in which the text does not completely determine the musical structure. In such tunes, some words or phrases are repeated or extended beyond the scope of a syllabic setting.

The fuging-tune is a psalm- or hymn-tune setting containing one or more sections in which voices enter successively, producing textual overlap. Fuging-tunes often begin and end homophonically, but have a middle section with several independent entries.

Since fuging-tunes are not fugues in the classical sense, the entrances are more loosely related than the subjects and answers in traditional fugues.

The two types of through-composed pieces (set-pieces and anthems) are usually of extended length. Historians designate as set-pieces settings of metrical poetic texts, and as anthems, settings of Biblical prose. This distinction was not always made by composers, who sometimes called a piece an anthem even though its text consisted of poetry rather than prose. Set-pieces and anthems are the most varied of the forms, frequently containing word repetitions, melismas, and changes of mood, meter, dynamics, tempo, and/or texture between contrasting sections within a piece.[43]

PART I.
THE COMPOSER-COMPILERS AND THEIR MILIEU

A. The Cultural Context

CHAPTER II

THE MAINE CONTEXT

Frontier Settlement

At the beginning of the Revolutionary War, settlement in Maine was limited primarily to the southwestern tip, the Kennebec River valley in central Maine, and narrow strips of land along the coast. As might be expected, Maine's oldest communities were located in the southwestern coastal areas closest to Massachusetts, which governed the District of Maine.[1]

Previously unsettled areas of the district drew many settlers in the years following the end of the American Revolution, causing Maine's population to quadruple between 1784 and 1820.[2] As later settlers arrived, the edge of the inhabited area expanded in a northeasterly direction. One of the most popular destinations for new settlement in Maine in the late eighteenth and early nineteenth centuries was an inland area in central Maine or "mid-Maine," roughly between the Androscoggin River on the west and the Penobscot River on the east.[3] Map 1, based on an 1829 map by Moses Greenleaf, shows the northern limits of settlement in 1778, 1800, and 1820.

Prevented from carrying on external commerce by British warships during the Revolution, some former residents of coastal Maine moved inland where there was better soil, plentiful game, and less chance of a British raid. After the war, they were joined by New England families who were suffering the effects of the postwar depression and who thought the backcountry lands were free for the taking.[4] Returning soldiers took advantage of an act granting two hundred acres on the eastern frontier to men who had served three years in the Revolutionary War.[5]

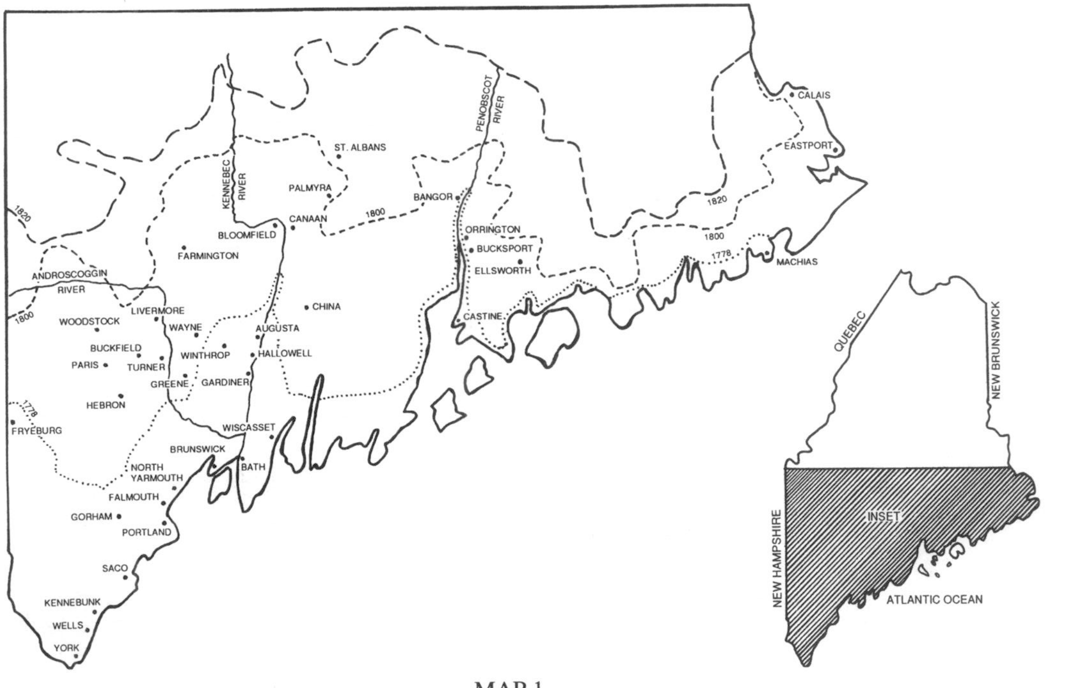

MAP 1

NORTHERN LIMITS OF SETTLEMENT IN MAINE, 1778–1820

Adapted from Moses Greenleaf, *Map of the Inhabited part of the State of Maine, exhibiting the progress of its settlement since the year 1778* . . . (1829) [Maine State Library map #MA829GR001].

The northern limits of settlements in:

. . . . 1778 (except for a few detached settlements higher up the Kennebec and Androscoggin)

– – – – – 1800

— — — 1820 (except the few at Houlton and New Limerick, and the settlement at Madawaska)

In the late eighteenth century, land was extremely important to most Americans, who lived by farming. For farm families, success depended on accumulating enough land to provide plots for their sons when they came of age. As the population in the older towns in New England grew, however, less land was available. Young men, faced with the unpleasant alternative of becoming unlanded wage laborers or tenant farmers in their hometowns, were attracted to the frontier because it offered the promise of plentiful land and the potential for autonomy as a small farmer.[6]

In many cases, those who came to Maine (or the "Eastern Country," as it was called) were not the prosperous but the poor. Those with financial means were attracted to more promising frontier lands in Vermont or western New York. Maine had the disadvantages of "thin, stony soil, long, cold winters, deadly Indian wars, and conflicting land titles," even late in the eighteenth century.[7] Poor families in southeastern New England, though, could not afford the long trek to better frontier lands, but could get to Maine by sea relatively quickly and inexpensively. Alan Taylor has determined that most of the residents of a selected area of mid-Maine in 1800 came from "hard-pressed families" from eastern Massachusetts and New Hampshire. They had not migrated from the more prosperous major ports of southern New England, but from small towns on or near the coast.[8]

The men who compiled tunebooks in Maine between 1800 and 1830 appear to fit the profile of the "typical" Maine immigrant of the late eighteenth century, although little is known of their parents' economic status. Nearly all of them grew up in small Massachusetts towns not far from the coast.[9] They emigrated to Maine after the Revolutionary War, settling in the inland or river towns whose modern names are Turner, China, Winthrop, Skowhegan, Hallowell, and Bucksport.[10]

The life of inland settlers in mid-Maine was one of many hardships as they tried to eke out an existence in an area with a short growing season and many predators.[11] The tracts being offered were previously unsettled, wooded lands which needed to be cleared and planted. The vast majority of settlers were subsistence farmers, whose expectations did not far exceed the goal of making enough profit to obtain more land and pay taxes.[12]

The isolated nature of frontier existence served to reinforce the independent nature which had caused many of the new arrivals to migrate to the frontier in the first place. While interdependence and mutuality were a part of the frontier experience,[13] the settlers were forced to become self-sufficient and reliant on their families to a degree unprecedented in the southern New England towns of their origins.[14] The traditional political and religious institutions they knew in the older, established areas of New England were not yet organized on the frontier; churches and towns were organized gradually as the number of settlements in a given area warranted them.

Some of the settlers on the frontier had immigrated out of a desire to be free from a church and state they found oppressive. The frontier offered an escape from the political, religious, and social controls imposed by southern New England culture.[15] Such constraints were incompatible with the ideals of freedom and equality for which many of them had recently fought.[16] The typical settler on the Maine frontier left behind an established order, symbolized by Congregational beliefs and Federalist politics, and openly embraced a more egalitarian society, linked with the Democratic-Republican party and evangelical beliefs.[17]

In some parts of the Maine frontier, settlers found themselves in ideological opposition to the wealthy land proprietors who considered it their paternalistic duty to direct the process of settlement and to promote social order by centralizing power.[18] As recipients of grants made by the royal governors, these elite land proprietors owned huge tracts of Maine land. Conflicts between the proprietors and squatters were frequently resolved by the forcible eviction of squatters unable or unwilling to pay for their land, although resistance was sometimes offered by groups of settlers disguised as Indian bands.[19]

Religion

Buoyed by America's recent success in throwing off the yoke of Great Britain, frontier residents were not afraid to question authority, whether political or religious. In the religious realm, they were easily persuaded by itinerant preachers to abandon Congregationalism, the state-mandated religion, for new belief systems, resulting in the formation of many splinter sects, including Separate and Freewill Baptists, Methodists, Universalists, and Shakers.

Only a few Presbyterian, Episcopal, and Catholic churches existed in Maine between 1780 and 1820.[20]

Congregationalism had been the dominant religion in Maine at the beginning of the American Revolution. By the laws of Massachusetts, which governed the District of Maine, citizens were required to pay taxes to support the building of a meetinghouse and the sustenance of a learned, orthodox minister. The Revolutionary War had created a scarcity of college-educated clergy, the pool from which Congregational ministers were drawn. Qualified candidates, limited in number, were often loathe to accept a position and accompanying hardships in a struggling Maine frontier town when an easier life was offered in one of southern New England's more established towns. The result was that many Maine towns had neither a church nor a minister. Congregationalism was largely confined to the more prosperous and populated commercial towns on the coast and in the river valleys.[21]

Members of the Congregational churches which did exist in the late eighteenth century were sometimes doctrinally divided into "Old Lights" and "New Lights," due to the Great Awakening of the 1730s and 1740s.[22] In some parts of New England, radical New Lights withdrew from their town parishes and formed independent churches, called Separate or Strict Congregational.[23] In Maine, Congregational ministers were often able to placate the various factions within the church and prevent complete schisms.[24]

The "New Light Stir," a sweeping revival which took place between 1774 and 1784, also weakened the position of the Congregational church. Itinerant preachers from several radical and dissenting sects—including Freewill Baptists, Universalists, and Shakers—made missionary trips to the frontier settlements of Maine, resulting in numerous conversions. Their visionary preaching and emphasis on personal religious experience was similar in style to that of the leaders of the earlier Great Awakening. Unlike the leaders of the Great Awakening (who were often settled ministers and authorized Congregational itinerants), the leaders of the New Light Stir were opposed to the religious establishment and its traditional teachings. Sects whose theology differed from that of the Standing Order sprang up in Maine's backcountry during the Stir.[25]

The New Light Stir was an important factor in the establishment of the Separate and Freewill Baptists in Maine. While sharing a belief in adult rather than infant baptism, the two groups had different doctrinal positions and origins. The Separate Baptists, Calvinistic in their beliefs about predestination and election, evolved from the Separate Congregationalists. The Freewill Baptists were followers of visionary leader Benjamin Randel of New Durham, New Hampshire; Randel rejected the Calvinist doctrines of predestination and election.[26]

Two other denominations—Shakerism and Methodism—were introduced into Maine largely as a result of the revivals of the 1790s. The Shaker faith originated with Mother Ann Lee, who promoted her radical new gospel that sexual intercourse was the original sin, and celibacy the only remedy.[27] Methodism, founded by John Wesley, held to an Arminian theology, as did the Freewill Baptists.[28] A Second Great Awakening, from 1802 to 1807, resulted in tremendous growth for Separate Baptists and Methodists and provided an opening for Universalists[29] and an indigenous sect called the Christian Connection.

Although revivals were curtailed by the War of 1812, Freewill Baptists and Methodists continued to grow in number after 1815.[30] The growth of the Baptist and Methodist churches was paralleled by a growth in the Democratic-Republican party. The leaders of the latter obtained passage of the Toleration Act, which was of particular benefit to those not of the Congregational faith.[31] In spite of an evangelistic effort, the Congregationalist Standing Order was not able to make up lost ground. The number of Congregational churches grew during the period, but the increase did not keep pace with overall population growth, which nearly doubled between 1800 and 1820. While there were still a significant number of Congregational churches in the old colonial counties (York, Cumberland, and Lincoln) in 1820, Baptist and Methodist churches outnumbered Congregational churches in the inland and eastern counties.[32]

Part of the eagerness with which the various sects were embraced can be traced to the fact that many of those who emigrated to the frontier were New Lights, whose dissatisfaction with the Standing Order was part of the reason they sought opportunity in a new area.[33] The belief systems promoted by the itinerant evangelical preachers, who poured into the newly settled regions, were compatible with the frontier culture and helped the new settlers cope with their unprecedented circumstances. Belief in a better world to come made transitory, temporal hardships on earth easier to bear.

With so many religious sects springing up in the backcountry at the same time that tunebooks were being compiled there, one might think that the latter were written to provide the non-Congregational groups with collections containing texts appropriate to their doctrinal positions. Among the Maine compilers Maxim was a Universalist, Washburn a Baptist, and Little a Methodist.[34] Their tunebooks do not, however, appear to be intended for a single denomination; on the contrary, the compilers stressed the applicability of their tunebooks to all denominations. Even Little's *Wesleyan Harmony,* which includes tunes to fit the unusual meters in the Methodist Hymn Book and which was written specifically for Methodist societies, was advertised as appropriate for all denominations.

The majority of the texts in the Maxim and Washburn tunebooks appear to be by Isaac Watts, the eighteenth-century English minister and hymn writer whose religious poems were extremely popular in both England and America.[35] The almost universal appeal of his lyrics among Protestant denominations made them appropriate texts to feature in tunebooks intended for various churches. Singers belonging to religious groups that found these texts incompatible with their doctrines could turn to their denomination's hymnal and substitute other words for those printed in the tunebook.[36] In general, the growth of new religious sects in Maine's backcountry does not seem to have had a significant impact on the tunebooks compiled there.

Politics, Economics, and Tunebooks

During the late eighteenth and early nineteenth centuries, when religious beliefs were in a period of great flux, Maine's economy was also unstable, largely due to restrictions on the shipping trade. The prosperity of many Maine residents, particularly those living in coastal or major river-valley towns, depended on a thriving shipping business and on the profitable selling abroad of Maine's chief exports: lumber products and fish. In towns such as these, the economy was based on lumbering and the allied industries of shipping and shipbuilding, rather than subsistence farming.[37] The southern Maine coastal towns served as market towns for the agricultural produce of the inland towns and profited from the lumbering of the interior.[38] Inland farmers who sold timber from their property to merchants in the shipping towns also had a stake in the success of shipping.[39] The 1790s were economically good for many in Maine because of the neutral trade diverted to the United States by the Napoleonic Wars.[40]

One tunebook was composed by a Mainer during this era: *The Harmony of Maine* by Farmington resident Supply Belcher in 1794. The dearth of other original works during the 1790s may have been caused, at least partly, by the intensive activity of taming the wilderness; those who would later compile tunebooks were perhaps too preoccupied with other matters to have time for musical pursuits. After the turn of the century, having completed the initial tasks of settlement, Maine residents Abraham Maxim and Charles Robbins responded to the growing number of singing schools by compiling sacred music collections for school and church use.[41]

Maine's economy, though, was soon to take a nosedive as President Jefferson initiated an embargo in late 1807 which made it illegal for American vessels to clear from an American port for a foreign destination.[42] Although some smuggling took place, most merchant shippers obeyed the law and suffered great losses. By the time the Embargo Act was repealed in March 1809, 60 percent of the people of Maine's coastal towns were unemployed, and a soup line for the needy had been established in Portland, where embargo-related losses totalled over a million dollars.[43] Even after the lifting of the embargo, the shipping business was restricted, due to a Non-Intercourse Act which outlawed trade with Great Britain and France.

The situation did not improve with the declaration of war on Great Britain in 1812. Again, Maine shipping interests were directly affected. The war was not popular in New England; Mainers, in particular, were aggravated by the Massachusetts government's lack of action to protect Maine citizens from British occupation.[44]

Between 1807, the start of the embargo, and 1815, the end of the war,[45] only three Maine tunebooks were published.[46] One of them, Washburn's *Parish Harmony,* was written specifically to accommodate small congregations that could not afford the larger and more expensive tunebooks then available.[47] In view of the economic situation at the time, there clearly was a need for a collection such as his.

With the war over in 1815, shipping resumed, although not to its former level. British restrictions prevented American ships from carrying on their formerly profitable trade with the British West Indies.[48] The year 1816 was a particularly hard one for farmers, with crippling frost in each of the twelve months. The prospect of better lands on the western frontier prompted "Ohio fever," an exodus of many New Englanders to Ohio and other western lands.[49] As many as twenty thousand Mainers left between 1810 and 1820. Hardships from the war, cold weather, and asking prices of more than two dollars an acre for marginal lands caused settlers to seek new opportunities in the supposedly greener pastures of Ohio and western New York.[50]

In spite of the negative aspects of life in Maine in that period, the twelve years beginning with 1815 saw the greatest production of tunebooks by Maine compilers: five different tunebooks, published in a total of fourteen editions.[51] Those Mainers who chose to stay rather than leave for possibly better lands were probably those who were achieving some measure of success where they were and thus could afford such items as tunebooks. The number of musically literate Mainers (and thus, potential tunebook purchasers) was probably greater than ever since more people had been able to attend singing school.

Still, musical rather than economic considerations may have been the most significant motivation for the new collections. Due to a reform movement which reached Maine between approximately 1815 and 1820, simpler tunes by European composers were now considered more suitable for worship than those which had dominated the earlier Maine tunebooks; therefore, collections of a different type were needed.[52]

In 1820, Maine finally gained independence from Massachusetts and was established as a separate state, concluding the long struggle for separation that had begun in 1785. Although many Mainers had emigrated from Massachusetts, they had grown to feel that their best interests were frequently not being served by governmental officials in Boston.[53] In the numerous separation votes over the years, residents of coastal towns almost always voted against separation, while those in inland areas supported it, considering the rule of Massachusetts oppressive. The coastal resistance was partly due to the federal "Coasting Law," whose provisions favored Maine shippers as long as Maine remained part of Massachusetts. The passage of a revised coasting bill in March 1819 removed this stumbling block and was a strong force in swinging the vote of the coastal communities toward separation.[54]

The separation itself probably had few if any effects on Maine sacred music. However, the independent spirit which caused some Mainers to pursue political autonomy over a thirty-five-year period may also have contributed to their persistence in publishing and singing certain types of sacred tunes a decade after they had been devalued by Massachusetts reformers.[55]

Summary

The new inland communities established in Maine in the late eighteenth and early nineteenth centuries tended to be populated by independent, self-sufficient settlers, who managed to exist by subsistence farming. They led lives quite different from residents of the older, established towns in coastal southern Maine. The prevailing religious and political views of the two groups also differed. Inland settlers were likely to be evangelicals and Democratic-Republicans; the coastal residents, like the majority of Massachusetts citizens, were predominantly Congregationalists and Federalists.[56] The former group supported separation from Massachusetts; the latter opposed it for many years.

Most of the tunebooks compiled in Maine during the first three decades of the nineteenth century were written by psalmodists living in inland areas. While there is no evidence that the tunebooks were produced in response to the growth of new religious sects in the backcountry areas, the compilers did react to the poverty experienced by many new settlers; they prepared smaller, less expensive tunebooks. These collections contained various types of tunes no longer considered appropriate for worship in urban Massachusetts.

CHAPTER III

MUSIC IN MAINE CHURCHES

For most New Englanders of the late eighteenth and early nineteenth centuries, the Sabbath was a day to be spent going to "meeting." Residents of many of the older, southern Maine towns attended services led by the town's learned, Congregational minister in the local meetinghouse, often built in the eighteenth century. In the newer Maine settlements where a town meetinghouse had not yet been erected, services were sometimes held in a schoolhouse, a barn, or in someone's home.[1] Even the lack of a preacher did not deter rural believers from meeting together to pray, read Bible passages or a sermon, and sing psalms or hymns.[2] The worship services held in the early days of settlement in Frankfort (later Winterport), Maine, were probably typical of those in many rural Maine villages:

> A church or minister were not needed for public worship: at some house or sometimes in a barn, the people gathered to hear the exhortations of a native preacher; and if the expected missionary were detained by wind or weather, the assembled company sang hymns, read the Scripture and dispersed to their homes.[3]

The Purpose of Psalmody

Musicians and ministers were in agreement about the purpose of psalmody (the singing of psalms and hymns) in worship and the attitude with which it should be approached by singers. Maine composer Supply Belcher expressed a common sentiment in the following statement:

> And as the primary and genuine intention of Psalm Singing is to praise the King of Heaven, he [Belcher] most earnestly wishes that as often as it is attempted, it may be attended to with a becoming decency and reverence.[4]

Although music was intended for God's praise, in a church setting it was also performed "for the benefit of the congregation, and to the edification of Christians," according to Ammi Mitchell in an address delivered in North Yarmouth, a southern Maine town, in 1812.[5] Some of the benefits for believers were summarized by Rev. Daniel Dana in an address delivered in nearby New Hampshire in 1813: psalmody solemnized the mind, detached thoughts from earth, roused feelings of piety and devotion, and impressed truths on the mind.[6]

Different Types of Services

In eighteenth- and early-nineteenth-century New England, worship services usually lasted all day, with a noon intermission.[7] According to Congregational historian Calvin Clark, the forenoon service at a Congregational church typically began with a prayer (possibly fifteen minutes or more in length), followed by the reading of a passage from Scripture, and then the singing of a psalm or hymn by the congregation after it had been read by the minister.[8] Next came the sermon, which lasted for an hour or so. Concluding the morning service was another sung psalm or hymn, a shorter prayer, and the benediction.[9] The afternoon service, while containing basically the same elements, featured a different sermon, Scripture passage, and music.[10]

The musical portions of the service, then, consisted of the singing of two or three metrical psalms and hymns in the morning and a similar number in the afternoon.[11] Services for special occasions, such as Fast Day, Thanksgiving, or an ordination, included additional musical selections.[12] Regardless of the type of service, the sequence of activities seems to have been planned to provide diversity; the minister's spoken portions (principally the prayer and sermon) alternated with musical segments.

Services of such revival-inspired denominations as the Methodists, Baptists, and Universalists seem to have contained the same basic items as Congregational services: praying, singing, and preaching. While the order may have been different, a similar alternation between periods of speaking and singing appears to have been common. G. T. Ridlon's fictionalized account of "a gineral [*sic*] meetin'" at a rural, evangelical Maine church in the early nineteenth century describes one of the evening worship sessions.[13] Included were a hymn, a prayer, another hymn, and a sermon. Although the order is similar to that described by Samuel Gilman for a New Hampshire village church, c. 1805, the degree of congregational participation was greater at Ridlon's church than at Gilman's, both musically and otherwise. Not only did many of those described by Ridlon sing along with the choir, they also groaned, sighed, and spoke out loud with ejaculations such as "Lard, help," "Du, Lard," and "Hev marcy."[14]

Even less staid and more spontaneous were the services held by some of the sects formed in Maine in the early nineteenth century. Certainly this was the case at the meetings organized by Jacob Cochran (or Cochrane), a visionary and dictatorial leader who founded "Cochranism" and amassed at least two thousand followers in southwestern Maine in 1816 and 1817.[15] Although the ostensible order of his services was prayer, singing, reading of the Scriptures (frequently omitted), a brief exhortation by Cochran and other brethren, and then trances, the general scene was chaotic confusion with the intermingling of shouts, groans, jumping, and clapping.[16] The musical portion of one of Cochran's 1818 meetings in Kennebunk, Maine, was described in the following way by an admittedly biased onlooker (a Free Baptist preacher):

> They soon struck a lively tune and sung words and in [a]while others fell to dancing and jumping while others shouted amen or Glory to God and Glory to Jesus. The jumping, dancing, singing, and shouting, however it was to them was an awful jargon to me. After this exercise had lasted until they were nearly out of breath they would rest a few minutes and then renew the same exercise with more vehemence than ever and then at the close of every singing and dancing exercise they would let out a general shout which I doubt not may be heard miles.[17]

That the singing, dancing, jumping, and swooning are reminiscent of Shaker practices is not surprising, considering that Cochran's hometown of Enfield, New Hampshire, was the location of a Shaker community. Butler notes that Cochran borrowed freely from the worship practices of the Shakers and Freewill Baptists.[18]

A shrewd man, Cochran used music to enliven the meetings and to rouse his disciples to greater heights of excitement. Early in his ministry, he replaced the solemn metrical psalm- and hymn-tunes "with a quick, lively music of the most exhilarating airs," perhaps secular tunes.[19] One of the "lively little airs" most remembered by those familiar with his music had the following text:

Come you who love the Lord indeed
Glory, glory hallelujah—
Who are from sin and bondage freed
Glory hallelujah.[20]

Like many camp-meeting or revival hymns, the song had a refrain which made it easy for participants to join in without any prior familiarity with the text.

Songs resembling those sung at camp meetings were also sung at the revival services held by an unrelated group in the Skowhegan area (not yet called Skowhegan).[21] Unlike the frontier camp meetings held out-of-doors in Kentucky,[22] the central Maine meetings, conducted jointly by a local minister and a visiting preacher of the Christian Band denomination in 1818, were held in schoolhouses and private homes beginning at evening candlelight and lasting as long as there were people present. Instead of "giving out" the hymns (probably referring to "lining out," a practice described later in this chapter), Elder Merrill, the local preacher, would simply begin to sing a hymn and the others would follow. His wife's strong voice and distinct articulation probably aided newcomers in singing unfamiliar songs.[23]

Eben Weston, a participant at the services, noted that the hymns came from a small book of what were called "Pennyroyal Hymns."[24] His remark that "they were new and peculiar as were the tunes"[25] suggests that neither the words nor the music were part of the church music repertory known to him. Nevertheless, since certain songs were repeated at nearly every meeting, they were easily learned. One, a dialogue between the minister and an impenitent person, may have been a leader-and-response song in which the audience answered the phrase sung by the preacher or song leader.[26] Another had several repeated text phrases, a feature facilitating participation. The text was sung to BLUEBIRD,[27] a tune from a music book for the fife, suggesting that the tune was a secular melody. Secular tunes were frequently sung with new words at camp meetings.[28]

Still another revival hymn mentioned by Weston had simpler, less cultivated words, as follows:

> My wife has got religion, and I have got it too; And we love one another as little children do.[29]

Tunes of this type, which substitute other "family words" such as "my brother" in later verses, were also common at camp meetings because once the tune to the first verse was learned, the song could be extended indefinitely by the substitution of other family words.[30]

Although the revival services described by Weston were a special series of meetings and not a weekly event, worship services led by itinerant preachers in the frontier areas of Maine may have included the singing of similar types of songs. At least one of the circuit-riding preachers, Methodist Jesse Lee, whose Maine trips began in 1793, was said to have been a good singer; he was probably quite capable of leading the worshippers in song. In his travels on horseback, "he went among strangers, preaching, singing and praying, in barns, schoolhouses, or in the open air, wherever he could obtain an audience; forming classes whenever two or three were willing to unite with the society."[31] The songs he sang may have had repeated phrases or choruses which were easily mastered, allowing those who had never heard the songs before to join in after hearing only a stanza or two. The use of a secular melody familiar to those present may also have facilitated participation.

While meetings like those led by Cochran and revival services similar to those attended by Weston may not have been a widespread phenomenon, the reader should be aware that a variety of types of worship were practiced in Maine in the early nineteenth century, even though extant records about them may be rather scanty. For some groups, such as the Cochranites, our meager knowledge of their musical practices is based on eyewitness accounts which provide only a general idea of their form of worship. We also have little information about the informal rural meetings held in barns, schools, homes, and out-of-doors at the arrival of a circuit-riding itinerant preacher.

On the other hand, the careful records which were kept by various established churches, largely Congregational, furnish specific information about church votes affecting music. Focusing on the practices suggested by these records may give an incomplete picture of Maine church music in all its variations. The balance of this chapter will concentrate primarily on documented musical customs of certain Maine churches because information is available about them; however, the reader should keep in mind that the musical practices of other Maine religious bodies (for which records are not extant) may have been somewhat different.

Special Services and Ceremonies

The public services which were held on special occasions—such as Thanksgiving Day, Fast Day, Christmas, Easter, ordinations, church dedications, and funerals—differed from regular Sunday services in often featuring an anthem in addition to the usual psalms and hymns.[32] Anthems, which often had texts relating to the occasion on which they were performed, were extended, through-composed settings of prose (usually Scriptural); they were characterized by sectional contrasts in elements such as meter, tempo, and texture. As pieces which were more complex than psalm and hymn tunes, they were performed by the trained singers (the choir) without congregational participation.

William Bentley's account of Thanksgiving services in Salem, Massachusetts, in 1798 suggests that the anthem was performed near the end of the service, following the sermon and collection.[33] The meeting described by Bentley also featured some independent instrumental music, played on several string and wind instruments, at the beginning of the service, before the second prayer, and during the collection. The use of a "band of instruments" for special observances probably occurred slightly later in Maine churches, since instruments were only gradually introduced there, usually after 1800.[34]

The relative paucity of anthems in Maine tunebooks compared to other New England collections suggests that anthems may have been sung less frequently in Maine's smaller inland communities (where the books were compiled) than in other parts of New England. For example, Washburn's *Parish Harmony,* intended particularly for rural churches, includes but a single anthem (for Thanksgiving).[35] Anthems also comprise a very small part of the tunebooks of Abraham Maxim, who lived in the community of Turner. His first tunebook includes two anthems (an all-purpose anthem of praise and a Thanksgiving anthem); his second adds an Easter anthem.[36]

The later Maine tunebooks contain more anthems. The sixth edition of Washburn's *Temple Harmony* (1826), for example, publishes twelve "anthems and select pieces," including anthems for Thanksgiving, dedications, and funerals.[37] The greater number of anthems in later volumes may suggest that choirs were more capable of singing anthems as more people had been trained at singing school. Nevertheless, even in the 1820s, anthems seem to have been reserved mainly for special occasions.[38]

Extant broadside programs and newspaper accounts of church dedications and ordination ceremonies in Maine indicate that musical selections were also more numerous on these programs than in regular Sunday worship services. For example, the music included as part of the ordination services of Rev. Mr. Adams in Camden, Maine, in 1828, encompassed three anthems and a chorus.[39] Similarly, three anthems and one hymn were included at the service to ordain Rev. George Shepard in Hallowell in 1828.[40] For these ceremonies, one of the anthems was positioned at the very beginning of the service, another near the end, shortly before the benediction. Musical selections were equally numerous in church dedication services of the 1820s.[41]

The programming of three anthems but only one hymn or chorus suggests that congregational participation in the music of special services, if not regular services, may have been quite limited by the late 1820s. The choir alone would have sung the anthems. The hymn probably provided the "audience" with an opportunity to have a part in the service. OLD HUNDRED was frequently the tune selected for the hymn, perhaps because of its familiarity to most of those attending and its slow, dignified character, befitting a solemn occasion.[42] Twentieth-century churchgoers still sing OLD HUNDRED—as a doxology with the text "Praise God from whom all blessings flow."

Sacred music was also performed for various public ceremonies associated with Masonic lodges. Newspaper accounts sometimes provide quite detailed information about the musical portion of the programs. One example is the installation at the Bethlehem Lodge in Augusta on June 24, 1822.[43] The music was performed by the choir of Mr. Tappan's Parish, the South Parish Congregational Church. The sixty or so singers were led by a clarinet and supported by some flutes, a bassoon, and a violoncello. As in the ordination services, three of the musical selections were anthems, the other was a psalm tune. The majority of the pieces, then, were probably not regularly performed in church, although they were suitable for singing at the special "exhibitions of sacred music" or "Oratorios" which were held at the meetinghouse.[44]

Still another public occasion for the performance of sacred music was the Fourth of July. The musical portions of the Fourth of July celebration in Augusta in 1810, for example, consisted of an Ode to Independence, sung by a choir of singers, some "sacred music" following the prayer, and "a national song, set to some lofty strains of vocal and instrumental music."[45] Although this ceremony took place at the courthouse, similar celebrations were often held in the local meetinghouse, the principal building large enough to accommodate those attending.

Social and Family Worship

Sacred music was used not just in public worship and ceremonies, but also in social worship and family worship, according to the address by Ammi Mitchell.[46] As an example of social worship, he cites a group of musical friends who have gathered together in a "chamber" and who sing together; for family worship, he points to families who pray and sing together during their morning or evening devotions.

The diary of Samuel Longfellow of Maine shows that the latter practice was a reality for some families. His family's Sunday evening devotions always included the singing of one or more simple, familiar hymns: "'St. Martin's,' 'Dundee,' 'Brattle Street,' or some other generally chosen from the Bridgewater Collection."[47] Another example can be found in the journal of Rev. Paul Coffin, who made several missionary tours of Maine. A 1796 entry notes that he boarded one night with the Withams, a serious family: "Family worship, consisting of reading, singing, and praying, was performed with much solemnity and religious thanksgiving."[48]

Lining Out and the Establishment of Choirs

In the latter part of the eighteenth century, many (perhaps most) Maine churches did not have choirs. The psalms and hymns performed during regular Sabbath meetings were sung by the congregation with the help of a practice called "lining out." A deacon or other designated person would read one or two lines at a time of the psalm or hymn and then lead the congregation in singing what had been read. Lining out was widespread in New England. The practice had begun in colonial America as a temporary solution in congregations where psalmbooks were scarce or many members could not read. Having a deacon line out the hymn facilitated singing by all present.[49]

The practice of lining out was gradually phased out for two principal reasons: printed texts and music became more available, and many church members became musically literate through singing schools. After attending singing school, the graduates frequently formed themselves into a choir to provide leadership for the church music. Such choirs were loathe to have their singing interrupted by the deacon's lining out.[50]

Church choirs were established somewhat later in Maine than in Massachusetts, Connecticut, and some parts of New Hampshire. While some New England churches had choirs as early as the 1760s, Maine churches, with a few exceptions, did not include choirs until the 1780s or even later.[51] The later formation of singing schools in Maine, compared to other areas of New England, probably contributed significantly to the later organization of choirs in Maine and the continuation of lining out to a later date. Singing schools began in Massachusetts in the 1720s, but the first Maine singing schools may have been organized as late as the 1780s.[52] Until there were trained singers who could guide the congregational singing, lining out served a useful purpose, particularly since few churches had organs.

The First Parish Church of Falmouth (now Portland) was ahead of many other Maine churches in eliminating lining out in the 1750s.[53] Three decades later (in the mid-1780s), several other Maine parishes, including Wells and Brunswick, were embroiled in controversy about whether to continue singing by rote or to adopt the procedure of singing by note or "by rule." In Wells, a compromise was reached in 1787: lining out would continue in the forenoon, singing verse by verse would be done in the afternoon. Similar solutions were reached in other New England churches.[54] In Brunswick, though, the First Parish decided in 1786 to continue lining out "until all had had time to furnish themselves with books."[55]

The Brunswick vote suggests that psalters or hymnbooks were not owned by all, even late in the eighteenth century.[56] Although such large parishes as the First Parish in Falmouth could afford to buy books in quantity, the situation was different in smaller parishes, especially in the newly settled, rural areas. The advertisement in Japheth Coombs Washburn's *Parish Harmony* (1813) notes that some country societies found it difficult to purchase music books because of the expense. Washburn's solution was to publish a small, more inexpensive volume so that these groups could be "more generally furnished with books."[57]

By about 1800, choirs were probably fairly common among the Maine churches (largely Congregational) which met for worship in meetinghouses. Since singing schools began to be held in many different parts of the state after the turn of the century, the pool of potential choir members was ever increasing. In addition, the descriptions of many meetinghouses indicate that certain pews, "singers' seats," were set aside for the choir.

Singers' Seats

Once choirs were formed, the singers requested permission to sit together in church, and seats were usually allocated for them, although not always immediately. For example, in Brunswick, a proposal to set off a part of the gallery in the west meetinghouse for the use of the singers was defeated by town vote in 1768.[58]

The location of the singers' seats varied. At the Greene, Maine, meetinghouse, for example, the singers occupied one of the "plank seats" located in the center of the house on the main floor.[59] A more typical plan, though, was for choir members to sit in one of the galleries which were often built around three sides of a meetinghouse. At the original Old South Congregational Church in Hallowell,[60] for example, the singers sat in the east gallery, opposite the pulpit, in two rows which reached from the north to the south galleries. A partition separated the women, who occupied the north side, from the men.[61] The singing gallery at the Court Street meetinghouse in Castine, a coastal Maine town, was described in a letter written by one of the choir members:

> There were two rows of seats in the singing gallery, the partition between which was double, a space of some 12 or 15 inches between the two walls, the top being covered with a broad cap upon which to place a singing book. . . . The front

> seats were a step lower down than the back, but the partition was high enough to accommodate the singers' books in the back seats, but brought the back of the front seat so high as to greatly inconvenience those on the front seats.[62]

Although the members of some New England churches disagreed on where the singers should sit (main floor or gallery),[63] several Maine churches had another problem: not enough room in the singers' seats for all who wished to occupy them. The First Parish Church in York, for example, voted in 1799 to allow the singers "liberty to use the seat next adjoining the present singing seat, till it is wanted for some other purpose."[64] A year later, they came up with a more permanent solution by voting to sell the singing seats "below in the meeting house" and to build singing seats "above in the gallery."[65]

A similar problem in Gorham resulted in a quite unusual solution. In 1820 or so, singing schools were so much in fashion in this southern Maine town that the singers' seats could not hold all the trained musicians. After much dissension, singers belonging to the town's Haydn singing society obtained possession of the seats. The excluded singers, many of the town's oldest and best singers and members of the rival Handel singing society, simply arranged to have another meetinghouse built by subscription. The ousted singers occupied the singer' seats of the "Free Meeting House" (built in 1821), regardless of whether the preacher of the day was Universalist, Methodist, or Baptist.[66]

One inference which can be drawn from this ecumenical arrangement is that the tune repertories of the three denominations must not have been significantly different. Although it is likely that the doctrinal emphasis of the hymns chosen by the Universalist minister varied from those selected by the Baptist minister, the same tunes could be used for both; a Common Meter text, for example, could be sung to a Common Meter tune, regardless of the subject matter.[67] The fact that tunebooks were usually written for the use of several denominations suggests that the texts chosen frequently concerned doctrines held in common by different sects.

Congregational Participation in Singing

Although the skill level of Maine choirs may have varied significantly from church to church, the singers often worked hard to perform as well as their abilities would allow. The Old South Congregational Choir in Hallowell was described as "well-trained"[68] and was considered "one of the most effective choirs in the country" in the early nineteenth century.[69] The choir at the East Winthrop meetinghouse practiced diligently the summer of 1823, maintaining "frequent and regular" rehearsals so that the singing at the dedication service in November would be "of the highest order."[70] Some Maine choirs, like the fictional New Hampshire country church choir described by Gilman, may have held "singing meetings" in private homes two or three evenings a week "for the purpose of practice and improvement."[71]

Typically, as choirs became more proficient, their role in "Divine Service" expanded from simply providing leadership for the singing to performing more complicated tunes (such as fuging-tunes, set-pieces and anthems) which were beyond the ability of the average churchgoer.[72] Congregational singing usually became less frequent or even nonexistent as choirs became more dominant. Consequently, tunebooks such as those compiled in Maine were used largely by the choir members, rather than the congregation as a whole.[73]

Congregational participation in singing appears to be one area in which groups such as the Methodists, like the unnamed denomination described by Ridlon, differed from the Congregationalists. Samuel Gilman, writing in the first person as a fictional New Hampshire Congregational choir leader, noted a bit enviously that the Methodists and strict Presbyterians had no separate choirs.[74] Instead, the worshippers all participated in the singing, not worshipping God "by proxy," as was true of congregations where the singing of praise was delegated to a choir. He continues:

> I have often witnessed a congregation of one thousand Methodists, as they rose simultaneously from their seats, and following the officiating minister, who gave out the hymn in portions of two lines, joined all together in some simple air, which expressed the very soul of natural music. I could see no lips closed as far as I could direct my vision, nor could I hear one note of discord uttered.[75]

Although lining out was being phased out in Congregational churches, partly because choirs made the practice unnecessary,

Gilman's remarks suggest that lining out may have continued longer among the Methodists, who did not favor choirs.[76]

The Introduction of Musical Instruments

Church choirs, important in the elimination of lining out, may also have been responsible for the introduction of instruments into the singing gallery in the late eighteenth and early nineteenth centuries. Accustomed to the support of the "bass viol" at singing school, singers promoted its use in a similar role at church.[77] While the organ would have been an ideal accompanying instrument, organs were too expensive for most Maine churches until the 1820s.[78] Consequently, various string and wind instruments served to double the vocal lines and help the singers stay on pitch. As was true elsewhere in New England, church members often opposed the use of instruments in church because of their secular associations.[79]

The sequence of events relating to the introduction of instruments at the East Winthrop meetinghouse seems fairly typical. Parlin recalls that at first they sang with no instruments, the leader "setting the tune" with a pitch pipe: providing the starting pitch for each of the voice parts after sounding the keynote of the tune. When instruments were introduced to assist the singing, "there was much contention." He continues:

> Some thought it sacrilegious, especially to use a demoralized fiddle, one on which dancing tunes had been played, while others, less conservative, would consent to the introduction of instruments provided none but good, moral, virtuous violins were employed, or other instruments of like moral character, that moved in the best of society, had kept good hours and company and whose strings had vibrated to nothing faster or more joyous than Old Hundred or other psalm tunes of solemn sound.[80]

Musical instruments seem not to have been played in Maine churches until some time after the Revolutionary War.[81] Once instruments were introduced, the first to be used in most churches was often the "bass viol," the usual New England term in the early nineteenth century for a violoncello.[82] In Augusta, for example, a bass viol, purchased in 1802, was the first musical instrument used in public worship in that town.[83] In Lebanon, a bass viol was introduced in the church in 1805, amid vigorous opposition.[84] A bass viol was used so regularly at the meetinghouse in Castine that it had its own storage space, a locked cupboard, built into the partition between the double row of singers' seats; the bass viol was placed there between services.[85] While the bass viol had been played in some Massachusetts churches in the 1780s,[86] the later appearance of the instrument in Maine churches may have been due to the later organization of Maine church choirs.

Other Maine churches were even slower to accept instrumental performance in their services. As late as circa 1821, an attempt to introduce the bass viol into the meetinghouse in Brunswick failed.[87] In Portland, a church split resulted from a dispute involving the instrument; some members of the Casco Street Church seceded "in pious disapproval of the Bass Viol in the church" and formed a new church, the Christian Temple.[88] Not until 1831 did the Freewill Baptist Society of Brunswick and Freeport approve the use of the bass viol to accompany their singing.[89]

As a topic of contemporary interest, the matter of whether instruments should be used in church had been frequently dealt with in Massachusetts orations and pamphlets of the mid-eighteenth century. The issue was apparently already of some concern in Maine by 1800, when Samuel Emerson, a Kennebunk medical doctor and skilled musician, delivered an address in Portland. He could find no Scriptural justification for objecting to the use of musical instruments in religious worship; however, he recognized that the misuse of some instruments had lessened their dignity.[90]

Another southern Maine doctor, Ammi R. Mitchell, in the address mentioned earlier, held a similar opinion. While acknowledging that "a too great use of Instruments" in public worship "is generally painful to serious minds," he did not suggest that they be completely banished from the House of God. After wrestling with the Scriptural basis for and against, he concluded:

> However after all, as they are no where forbidden in the Scriptures, we cannot help feeling, that the *expediency* of instruments, depends greatly on their quality, and *the use made of them*. A viol on the bass is certainly beneficial, and some other instruments may be also, if they are skillfully managed, on suitable occasions.[91]

The "other instruments," introduced somewhat later, included wind instruments. Nathaniel Gould names the flute, clarinet, and bassoon (and less commonly, the oboe) as instruments frequently introduced into churches once the bass viol had been accepted.[92] His remarks seem to be supported, for the most part, by our knowledge of instruments in the Portland churches.

Rev. Elijah Kellogg, the first pastor of the Second Parish Church (founded in 1787) of Portland, recalled that no instruments except the bass viol were used at first. Later, his father, "who had been a drum major during the Revolutionary War and was extremely fond of instrumental music," introduced a cornet and clarinet to supplement the bass viol.[93] Based on expenditure records of the First Parish Church, also in Portland, the instruments used there included one or more stringed instruments and clarinet in 1801, bassoon by 1811, and flute and violin in 1815.[94] A flute also accompanied Supply Belcher's choir in Farmington at the old Center Meetinghouse.[95]

Organs began to be used in Maine churches somewhat later than the bass viol and assorted wind and stringed instruments. The presence of organs in two Portland churches—St. Paul's Episcopal Church and the Second Parish Church—as early as 1798 was exceptional. Other Portland churches did not install organs until the 1820s and 1830s.[96] Elsewhere in southern Maine, the Second Parish Church in Wells procured a small organ by subscription in 1810, replacing it with a bigger and better organ in 1827.[97] Churches acquiring their first organs in the late 1820s and early 1830s included those in Gorham (1828)[98] and Brunswick (1835).[99] The church in Eastport (First Church, Unitarian) boasted the first church organ used in public worship in eastern Maine (1831).[100]

Several central Maine churches bought organs in the early 1820s. Not surprisingly, these churches were well-endowed Congregational organizations in the large river towns, not fledgling groups in the newer interior settlements. The purchase of an organ by the South Parish Church in Augusta in 1822 resulted from a desire to improve the church music; similar sentiments led to the hiring of Mr. Holland, a music professor from Massachusetts, as choir leader at about the same time. As was typical, once the organ was installed, the bass viol, which had previously served as the only accompaniment, was set aside.[101] Not to be outdone, the

Old South Congregational Church in neighboring Hallowell acquired an organ the following year (1823). While not large, the organ was considered of appropriate size to "properly guide the different parts of the band [of singers] and support them, which is the real province of the organ."[102]

Fewer church members seem to have objected to organs than to bass viols. By the time organs were purchased in the 1820s and 1830s, churchgoers had probably become accustomed (or resigned) to the use of instruments in church. In addition, they may have welcomed the organ as a substitute for the multitude of instruments then in use, since the other instruments were frequently eliminated once an organ was purchased.[103]

Lest we assume, however, that members were uniformly supportive of instruments by the 1830s or later, we should note the remarks of a Brunswick church member who opposed a motion to pay the organist fifty dollars in 1840:

> I don't wish to wound the feelings of any one. I have felt very unpleasant ever since the organ came into the meeting-house. It is not acceptable to God. It is very offensive. It begins to make a noise after the hymn is read,—before they begin to sing. It has a very *immoral tendency*. It keeps our minds from other things.[104]

His opinions repeat the old refrain which was voiced in connection with the bass viol; however, he must have been in the minority since no one else objected and the motion passed.

The Church Music Repertory

According to Edwards, the number of tunes which could be sung by a congregation in Saco, circa 1730, might have ranged from five to maybe ten (the latter in a congregation with "accomplished singers").[105] A remark by Charles Robbins in the preface to *Columbian Harmony* (1805) suggests that the church repertory in the early nineteenth century may also have been somewhat limited. His wish is that

> our worshipping assemblies of different denominations may be better supplied hereafter than they have been heretofore, by introducing some new pieces of music (if any can be

> found of merit) instead of wearying the audience by performing continually a set number of ancient pieces.[106]

Although Robbins is not necessarily implying that the number of frequently performed tunes was as small as ten, he suggests that the usual practice in churches then (as now) was to sing old favorites again and again in preference to learning new pieces.

In East Winthrop, some of the old favorites sung in the early days of the church, according to Parlin, were OLD HUNDRED, ST. MARTIN, MEAR, and BROAD IS THE ROAD.[107] All four are tunes in the "Core Repertory of Early American Psalmody," the 101 sacred pieces identified by Richard Crawford as having been printed most frequently in American tunebooks between 1698 and 1810.[108] Judging from the number of printings they received in Maine tunebooks, the four tunes favored in East Winthrop were popular elsewhere in Maine as well as in other parts of the country.

Although most of the tunebooks which were compiled in Maine after 1793 were multi-function works, used by both singing schools and "religious societies," their contents suggest the type of music which was being sung in Maine churches. For example, the large number of fuging-tunes and pieces by American composers in the earliest nineteenth-century Maine collections implies that tunes of these types may have been important components of the repertory early in the period; plain tunes and pieces by Europeans, which make up a much smaller part of the early publications, were probably sung less frequently, both in church and in singing schools.[109]

The type of music considered appropriate for church use did not remain constant throughout the period, however. As will be discussed in more detail later, the Maine tunebooks show a definite trend away from American tunes, particularly fuging-tunes, as the period progressed. A reform movement, begun in Massachusetts around 1805 and initially promoted by the organizers of the Middlesex and Salem Societies, appears to have reached southern Maine by 1812 and central Maine several years later.[110] The reformers were successful in reviving the use of simpler, European pieces ("ancient tunes," as they were called) which could be sung by the congregation, not just the choir, and in restoring solemnity and dignity to the musical portions of the service.

Evidence that the reform movement had spread to southern

Maine by at least 1812 is provided by the remarks of Ammi Mitchell in his address on sacred music in North Yarmouth in that year. He expressed pleasure in the fact that fuging-tunes seemed to be going out of use in divine worship and praised *The Middlesex Collection* (a reform collection),[111] describing it as "a book in which there is not a single fuge [fuging-tune], for church music, and stands without a rival among musical connoisseurs."[112] Reformers considered fuging-tunes to be unsatisfactory for worship because the overlapping texts made it difficult for worshippers to understand the words.

Mitchell's comments probably did not represent the sentiments and worship practices of inland Maine residents in 1812, though, judging by the number of fuging-tunes contained in the 1813 *Parish Harmony,* a central Maine tunebook. The compilation of several reform collections in central Maine, beginning in 1817, however, suggests that the reform movement had gained some followers there several years later. The compilers of *The Hallowell Collection of Sacred Music* (1817) rejected almost all American tunes and fuging-tunes, selecting instead those which were generally simple, dignified, and "pathetic" in style. "Light and flimsy airs" were also rejected.[113] Judging from the changing repertory in the Maine tunebooks, the more lively, boisterous fuging-tunes were probably replaced by more sedate, dignified plain tunes in Maine churches by 1815 or so (earlier in southern Maine). The continued publication of fuging-tunes to a limited extent in other Maine collections of the 1820s suggests that such tunes continued to be sung, but probably outside of church.

Church singers were often less than eager to replace the American pieces and fuging-tunes they knew and loved with the slow, older European tunes which were now said to be purer and better adapted for worship.[114] Many Maine choirs may have experienced dissension in the ranks similar to the split over repertory described in Gilman's *Memoirs of a New England Village Choir.*[115] In his fictionalized New Hampshire choir, a compromise was reached in which the five tunes sung on the Sabbath would consist of "two fugues [fuging-tunes], two of the slow ancient airs, and one of a different description from either."[116]

Gilman's account suggests that the persistence and persuasion of a single choir member who had been exposed to reform sentiments in "one of our seaport towns" could lead to the introduction of the older, "purer" repertory in a northern New England church.[117] In an actual situation in Woodstock, Vermont, "Mr. Duren," who arrived in town around 1821, seems to have been responsible for promoting changes in the style of the church music:

> There is reason to believe that this gentleman brought with him the cultivation of the "newer" style of church music so eagerly promoted on the eastern seaboard, that is, the careful harmonizations that Lowell Mason had made popular and the slower more dignified renditions of the tunes.[118]

Similarly, the reform movement may have spread to Maine churches through the influence of individuals whose southern New England contacts familiarized them with the changes taking place in the church music there. The adoption of the reform position in southern Maine earlier than in central Maine may be related, at least partly, to the better access which the port towns had to Boston. In general, inland Maine residents, because of their relative isolation, may have persisted in singing American tunes and fuging-tunes in church slightly later than their New England neighbors.

Summary

Maine churches seem to have been much like their sister churches throughout New England in experiencing internal division and dissension as each new change in church music was proposed. Lining out was eliminated; newly formed choirs were accommodated; musical instruments were introduced; and an older, more solemn style of church music was revived—but acceptance of these innovations did not usually come easily. Church records and town histories allow us to pinpoint dates for some of the turning points in some places; however, the changes took place at different times in different towns, making generalizations for the whole region of Maine imprecise.

As might be expected, the sequence of events often took place slightly later in the towns of inland Maine, where settlement had taken place later, than in the well-established towns in southern Maine. After the turn of the nineteenth century, though, the interest in and opportunity for music had spread throughout the region to the extent that the smaller towns were not far behind Portland in, for example, introducing musical instruments into church services. The reform movement which had affected Massachusetts churches in the middle of the first decade seems to have impacted Maine about seven to ten years later.

In general, there is little or no evidence to suggest that church music in Maine differed significantly from church music elsewhere in New England; however, the worship experiences of believers were not uniform, but reflected the doctrines and practices of various denominations and sects.

CHAPTER IV

MUSIC IN MAINE SINGING SCHOOLS AND MUSICAL SOCIETIES

Singing Schools

Unlike twentieth-century hymnals, whose use is largely limited to church services, nineteenth-century tunebooks had an additional function as textbooks for singing schools where music reading was taught. Most collections included psalm- and hymn-tunes of varying difficulties, suitable for beginners as well as more advanced singers, and an introductory section on the rudiments of music. Since a major goal of the schools was to improve congregational singing, students practiced their music reading by singing tunes likely to be performed in church.

Irving Lowens suggests that, in many cases, early American tunebooks were actually intended for singing schools and musical societies rather than churches.[1] The title pages of many of the Maine tunebooks promote their use for both settings. The title page of Maxim's *Northern Harmony* is typical in indicating that the book was "Calculated for the Use of Singing Schools, and Religious Societies."[2]

The first New England singing schools were formed in Massachusetts in the 1720s by clergymen dissatisfied with the state of congregational singing in their churches.[3] Their success soon led to the formation of similar schools throughout New England. In the District of Maine, singing instruction is known to have begun by at least the late eighteenth century. Among the earliest references to such activity are the diary entries of the Rev. Messrs. Deane and Smith, who report the excitement caused in their church, the First Parish of Falmouth (now Portland), by the arrival of a singing teacher in 1785.[4] Between 1785 and 1830, at least twenty-two singing schools were advertised in Portland newspapers.[5] Additional schools may have been publicized in other ways. For example, schools sponsored by churches were probably advertised by word of mouth within the congregation; notice of other schools may have been posted on handbills in public places.

Singing schools were held by at least the 1790s in the inland areas settled later than Portland. Supply Belcher probably published *The Harmony of Maine* (1794) for use in his singing school in Farmington, where he had moved in 1791. He is known to have taught singing schools,[6] and the title page of his book indicates that it was "for the use of singing schools and musical societies."[7] Another late-eighteenth-century singing school reference from central Maine can be found in the diary of a Hallowell midwife, Martha Ballard, who notes her son's attendance at singing school in 1798.[8] A singing master is mentioned by a travelling preacher, Rev. Paul Coffin, in his diary account of a 1797 visit to Pittston, Maine.[9]

While some singing schools were held in Maine prior to 1800, they apparently became more numerous after the turn of the century, when there was an increased interest in music, according to Edwards.[10] Cole's list of singing schools advertised in Portland newspapers seems to support Edwards's claim: none is listed until December 1799, followed by one nearly every year for the next decade.[11] The increase in the number of tunebooks compiled in Maine during the first twenty-five years of the nineteenth century is probably related to the growth in the number of singing schools during the same period.

Several sources confirm the use of Maine tunebooks in Maine singing schools. For example, *The Hallowell Collection,* second edition, was the suggested singing book for students of Charles Dingley's 1824 "School for instruction in the Theory and Practice of Vocal Music" in Hallowell.[12] Handwritten notations on an extant copy of Japheth Coombs Washburn's *Temple Harmony,* second edition (1820), suggest that it was used in a Maine singing school the same year it was published.[13] The tunebooks by Abraham Maxim were probably compiled for the singing schools he taught in Turner and Palmyra, Maine.[14] His *Northern Harmony* went through five editions, perhaps from the need to provide new music for later singing school classes. Macdougall suggests that successful singing masters often needed to compile new collections to provide their classes with a variety of study materials for a second or succeeding session.[15]

Maine tunebooks were not the only ones used in Maine singing schools, of course.[16] For example, an anthology compiled in Massachusetts, *The Middlesex Collection,*[17] was recommended as "the most approved book now in use" for those planning to attend William Davis's 1812 singing school in Portland.[18] The numerous editions of *The Village Harmony*[19] and the *Bridgewater Collection*[20] were popular in Maine churches and singing schools throughout the period.

Singing schools were organized and supported in different ways. They were sometimes sponsored by parish churches, who offered them free of charge to their members with the expectation of improved singing in church. In other cases, the instruction was subsidized by public funds allocated by the town.[21] A third, and perhaps most common, way of supporting a singing school was through subscription. A committee would circulate subscription papers and make arrangements for the school once the pledges were sufficient to cover the expenses of hiring a singing master and hall.[22] The instructor was frequently a local resident, although itinerant singing masters were sometimes engaged.[23] The sessions were held wherever space was available in a town, frequently in a schoolhouse or meetinghouse, but sometimes in the hall of a tavern.[24] Most schools met several evenings a week during two or three winter months.[25]

Singing schools held in Hallowell, Maine, from 1817 to 1819 exemplify several different means of support. The singing school attended by William Sewall in 1817 may have been subsidized at least partially by members of the community, since he helped collect on the subscriptions after the school was over.[26] The costs of the school taught by Mr. Tenny (or Tenney) in 1818 were borne by the students: two dollars per quarter, half payable in advance.[27] Although he advertised that his school would not begin until twenty-five persons had subscribed, he had no trouble in obtaining enough students, perhaps because he had taught a school in Hallowell the previous winter.[28] The school began two weeks after the initial ad.[29] The following winter, a free singing school was contemplated by S. Tenney (probably the same person) and P. Stickney. A local newspaper ad announced that they hoped to offer the instruction to all persons over twelve years of age who would attend and be committed to making improvement in the art of singing.[30] The school may have been sponsored by the Old South Congregational Church, the church in which both men were active, or possibly the town of Hallowell.

Singing schools had a social as well as educational function. They were often organized at the behest of children "who were anxious for an opportunity of meeting their associates."[31] Singing school provided the students, often in their early to mid-teens, with a community-sanctioned opportunity for getting together with their peers in the evening.[32] W. Harrison Parlin, a nineteenth-century East Winthrop resident, suggests that one of the reasons young people in those days took up vocal music was that there were few competing entertainments:

> In the absence of anything more enticing, a large proportion of them cultivated vocal music as an accomplishment, a pastime, and as a duty to both God and man. If blessed with musical gifts they felt under obligation to improve and use them; and if the church choir called for their services their views of duty caused them to do what they could. Thus, stimulated by both inclination and duty, quite a practical knowledge of the science was obtained; at least they could "find the mi" in any key and "call the notes."[33]

Parlin's account refers to two of the rudiments learned in singing schools: the location of the syllable mi in various keys and the names or syllables of the notes. The theoretical introductions of the Maine tunebooks include these items as well as others and suggest what the usual course of study may have been. Since they present the same fundamentals in essentially the same order as other New England tunebooks, the instructional sequence may have been rather standardized.

Scholars were first introduced to the gamut (or scale) of music, learning the letter names corresponding to the lines and spaces of the various staffs in use.[34] They also were taught to "call out" the notes, using the four-syllable solmization system (fa, sol, law or la, mi) then in use.[35] Then they were ready to learn about rhythmic notation. The six notes and corresponding rests were introduced and the relationships among them described. The different moods or modes of time were explained, and students were taught how to beat time in each.[36] Interspersed between these two topics (note values and modes of time) in most of the books was an explanation of various musical symbols, such as repeat signs; flats, sharps, and naturals; bar lines; slurs; dots; and ornamentation signs. After learning about the modes of time, students were taught how to determine whether a tune was in a major or minor key. A final text section often offered suggestions relating to singing and choir decorum.

The first session of a New Hampshire singing school held in 1788 is delightfully described by Moses Cheney and quoted at length by Alan Buechner.[37] On this first evening, the master introduced certain rules of music, including the location of the syllable mi in various keys and the letter names of the lines and spaces of the staff. Then he had all of the students sing individually after him, making their voices rise and fall as his did, singing a scale up and down. By "testing" the scholars' voices, the master could determine their potential as singers and assign the appropriate voice part for each. The high and low female parts were called treble and counter; the high and low male parts were tenor and bass.[38] The rest of the evening was spent learning tunes, the master teaching each of the voice parts by rote.

While rote singing may have been necessary to maintain the interest and attention of the scholars until they learned how to read for themselves, the theoretical introductions omit any such suggestion in their ideal sequence for learning to read music. The compilers advised that the first step was to memorize all the material on the rudiments of music. With that task completed, the beginner could begin to practice singing various intervals while following musical notation. Most tunebooks included "Lessons for Tuning the Voice" for this purpose. Next, a simple tune could be sung, substituting the fasola syllables for the words. Once the pitch and rhythm were correctly performed, the tune could be sung with words.

Although some tunebooks divide the theoretical introduction into numbered lessons,[39] several topics or lessons may have been presented in a single evening, due to the desirability of covering all the basics early in the school. According to Gould, rudiments had to be learned quickly, for once singing began (often by the third evening), it became difficult to interest students in returning to the dull rudiments.[40] One Portland singing school taught all the fundamentals in the first week and did not allow those without previous training to be admitted after that time.[41] To facilitate mastery of the basics, however, other teachers may have extended the lessons somewhat longer.

The final session of a singing school was an important event. Parish-sponsored singing schools frequently concluded with a singing lecture, which combined a choral concert with a formal lecture, often by the parish minister. The sermon would often close with words of praise and encouragement to the students.[42] Independently sponsored singing schools usually concluded with a "singing exhibition," a public concert.[43]

In either case, the performance allowed the students to make their public debut as singers and to show the community what they had learned. In addition, the program was an opportunity for them to perform selections which were too elaborate or too secular for Sabbath worship services. Several of the pieces in Maine psalmodist Edward Hartwell's *Chorister's Companion* would have been quite appropriate for such an occasion: two works entitled ODE ON MUSIC and an ode subtitled "Introductory to a Sacred Concert."[44]

Since a three-month singing school was hardly long enough for a student to become musically proficient, singing-school graduates often went on to attend another singing school in a succeeding year.[45] In fact, attendance at several singing schools was the means by which many future singing masters learned their trade. Moses Cheney, for example, attended singing school nearly every winter from age twelve to age twenty-one, and then became a teacher himself.[46] Two of Maine's singing-school instructors, Supply Belcher and Abraham Maxim, appear to have received their training through studies with William Billings, the best-known singing master of late-eighteenth-century Massachusetts.[47]

Having completed singing school, new graduates had presumably acquired at least rudimentary knowledge of music, preparing them to join their church choir. If a choir did not exist, they would meet to choose a leader or leaders and organize a choir.[48] Something of the sort seems to have taken place at the conclusion of an 1817 singing school in Hallowell. At a meeting held four days after the singing school exhibition, the "Singing Society" (a commonly used term for a choir)[49] met and elected Mr. Tenny as "Chorister." As the leading singer, he would be responsible for choosing the tune to which the psalm or hymn was sung in church and would provide the singers with their starting pitches.[50] Chosen by popular vote from among the ranks of the singers, choristers continued to sing while directing the other vocalists.[51]

Although our discussion of singing schools has focused on those held in Hallowell and Portland—bustling river and coastal towns in the early nineteenth century—those formed in rural areas of Maine were fairly similar, at least in outward organization. A diary kept by farmer Elijah Fisher of Livermore contains references to several of his children attending singing schools from 1818 to 1819 and 1820.[52] The Fisher children would have been in their late teens or twenties at the time, making them slightly older than the average student.[53] The lack of parental participation is consistent with the youth orientation of most singing schools.

In spite of Livermore's small size, two singing schools were held in the winter of 1818/19, and two of Fisher's children attended both.[54] The schools were held during the winter months, from December to March, the least active months for farmers. The one taught by Mr. Joseph Merrill met at "Mr. Brittons old store" twice a week, beginning the first week of December 1818; the other, taught by Mr. Dillnor, was held at the East "S-H" (schoolhouse), beginning the last week in January 1819. The following year's sessions concluded with a "singing meeting" on Sunday evening, March 12, 1820.[55]

Although not a great deal is known about Maine's singing-school instructors, including Merrill and Dillnor, it appears that teaching music was a secondary profession for many of them, as it was for most of their New England colleagues.[56] Merrill, for example, was probably the Livermore farmer of that name.[57] Being a singing master was a seasonal (December to March) position for which the pay was not substantial. Unless one travelled widely and pushed hard, one could not live on singing-school fees alone; compiling and publishing tunebooks was one way to obtain additional income.

The Maine singing masters had various primary occupations. Cole notes that Nathaniel Ilsley, who opened a singing school in Portland in 1827, was a cabinetmaker there for a time.[58] Another singing master, Dr. Samuel Emerson, was a medical doctor and occasional orator.[59] Hallowell singing master Samuel Tenney was a shoe- and bootmaker and merchant.[60] Buechner notes that Yankee singing masters often taught both common schools and singing schools;[61] such was the case with Maine psalmodists Supply Belcher and Abraham Maxim.

On the other hand, Mr. Holland, an instructor of vocal sacred music in Augusta in the 1820s, advertised himself as a "Professor of Music" and apparently concentrated on music as his sole profession. In addition to teaching classes on the elements of vocal music, he was a church choir director (at Rev. Mr. Tappan's meetinghouse) and taught "young gentlemen" how to play the pianoforte, the German flute, and the "Clarionett."[62]

Musical Societies

After young people learned the basics of note reading at singing school, they often joined a musical organization where they could practice and improve their choral skills. In addition to church choirs (sometimes called "singing societies"), communitywide musical societies also existed.[63] For example, following the completion of the singing school he attended in 1817, Hallowell resident William Sewall occasionally mentions in his diary that he attended "singing school society" or "singing society" some evenings. Since the groups only rarely met at the meetinghouse, they may not have been affiliated with a particular church.[64] Unlike singing school, which was usually limited to winter months, the singing society also met in spring, summer, and fall.[65]

In Massachusetts proper, community musical societies were organized as early as the 1770s.[66] In Maine, one of the earliest musical societies may have been the "Musical Society in Falmouth," which was formed on September 1, 1807. The society's constitution provides the only extant clues to the nature of the group. Article 9 states:

> Every member shall attend private meetings, for the improvement of singing, every first and third Tuesday in every month at the place appointed by the society.[67]

The President of the group instructed the members "in the art of singing" at private meetings. Three other officers, called "Criticks," observed and commented on members' performances immediately after they sang.[68] Members of the all-male group[69] took an oath that they would not reveal anything they had seen in the society and would not make known to any person, except another member, what was disclosed to them at the meetings. Secrecy was probably maintained to preserve the dignity and reputation of the members, who may have feared that their singing (whether good or bad) would be the subject of gossip in the community.

Another early musical society of which little is known is the "Beneficent Musical Society," founded in the Falmouth/Yarmouth area (southern Maine) in August 1810.[70] The society, which included both men and women, had been formed partly to promote harmony among singers and uniformity in the mode of singing. In his address delivered to celebrate the society's second anniversary in 1812, Ammi Mitchell praised the members for their ability to distinguish "between mere noise and real music."[71]

The type of music sung by the society may be suggested by the advertisement which appeared on the back cover of the printed version of the anniversary address:

> The Lock Hospital, The Salem, The Newburyport, The Bridgewater, and The Middlesex Collections of Sacred Music, may be had at the Bookstore of Hyde, Lord, and Co., Portland.

The Middlesex Collection, which was highly praised by Mitchell in his address,[72] has been mentioned previously as the recommended tunebook for a Portland singing school held in 1812. Both *The Middlesex Collection* and *The Salem Collection*[73] were precedent-setting reform collections, emphasizing European tunes in a simple style as more appropriate for public worship than American fuging-tunes.[74]

The aims of the Beneficent Musical Society may have been similar to those of the Rockingham Sacred Music Society, organized in nearby New Hampshire in 1813. The New Hampshire group was formed to promote the use of appropriate music in worship and to raise the style of psalmody performance, which had become corrupt in many congregations.[75] Based on Mitchell's comments in his address to the Beneficent Musical Society, the Maine singing society may have been the product of a similar desire to improve church music in southern Maine. Comparable organizations were not formed in central Maine for another decade, though, suggesting that inland residents were slower to adopt reform sentiments.

Another musical society formed only a few months after the Beneficent Musical Society was the Hans Gram (or Hans-Gram)

Musical Society of Fryeburg, Maine. According to Edwards, the organization, which was formed on October 10, 1810, had as its nucleus the group of singers at the town meetinghouse. The Hans Gram Musical Society successfully presented a number of concerts in the next few years after its founding.[76]

At the first anniversary of the society in 1811, Oliver Bray delivered an address, *An Oration on Music,* in which he was sharply critical of the many American teachers and composers lacking knowledge, genius, and taste who had arisen within the previous thirty years.[77] He considered their fuging-tunes to be chaotic and a "promiscuous jargon of sound and sentiment."[78] Even more blasphemous in his eyes, however, was the use of secular march or dance tunes in worship, a sin committed "by Billings and other modern Pretenders."[79] While he conceded that there were some recent American composers of genius and taste, his allegiance clearly belonged to "Handel and other eminent masters."[80]

Although Bray's views may not have been shared by all his listeners, the fact that the society was named for Hans Gram, a Danish-American composer skilled in the European musical tradition, suggests that the society's founders were more supportive of European than American music.[81] European music was probably a mainstay of the society's repertory. Those inviting Bray to speak were presumably aware of, and supportive of, his views; if they had differing opinions, they probably would not have selected him or had his oration printed.

In February 1814, a musical society that would later be associated with one of the Maine tunebooks was formed. The society was the Handel Society of Maine, the tunebook was *The Hallowell Collection of Sacred Music* (1817, 1819), and the link between them was the organization's endorsement of both editions of the tunebook. A reform collection in the tradition of *The Middlesex Collection, The Hallowell Collection* consists almost entirely of older plain tunes by English composers and only a small number of fuging-tunes. The endorsement, signed by officers of the Handel Society, reads:

> We the Subscribers have perused "The Hallowell Collection of Sacred Music," and most cheerfully recommend it as a volume containing a rich variety of excellent tunes, judiciously selected and arranged; well calculated to improve the musical taste of our country and aid the devotional exercises of our Churches.[82]

The society's approval of a tunebook designed to improve musical taste is consistent with the members' initial object in associating: "to promote a taste for correct, refined & Classical & Church Musick."[83] The contents of the collection as well as the title of the society suggest that the Handel Society, like the Beneficent Musical Society and the Hans Gram Society, probably sang mostly European pieces. While the ideals and name of the Maine society appear similar to those of the famous Handel and Haydn Society of Boston, the Maine organization cannot have been modelled on the Boston one because the latter was not formed until April 1815. One of the Handel societies in New Hampshire may have been the inspiration for the Maine society.[84]

The only known performance of the Handel Society was advertised in the *Portland Gazette* of February 20, 1815: a public concert of sacred music to benefit the Female Charitable Society. Notices of semiannual meetings, held either in Portland or at Bowdoin College in Brunswick, have been found through 1816,[85] and the organization may have continued through at least 1819, judging from the endorsements of *The Hallowell Collection of Sacred Music* by officers of the society.[86] Whether the society ever sang from *The Hallowell Collection,* however, is unknown.

Unlike Maine musical societies whose membership came from a limited geographical area, perhaps even a single town, the Handel Society of Maine attempted to encompass the whole District of Maine, as suggested by the fact that the four vice presidents elected at the first meeting were from four different counties.[87] Assuming that Handel Society members also lived in various parts of Maine, the districtwide emphasis may have hastened the demise of the organization. Some members may have had to travel long distances, often on poor roads and perhaps in bad weather, to attend meetings in Portland and Brunswick. Participation in such a group, however, may have encouraged members to form similar singing societies in their own area. Cole considers the Handel Society of Maine to have been a major factor in the formation of other musical societies in Maine during the next decade.[88] For example, the Hancock Musical Association (in eastern Maine) is believed to have been organized in 1816.[89]

The musical societies enumerated so far seem to have been rather short-lived, and little is known about them. More is known, however, about the Beethoven Musical Society, which was active in Portland from 1819 or 1820 to 1826 and may have been the first musical society in America to bear Beethoven's name. The history of this organization has been described in some detail by Ira Berry (a member of the society),[90] Edwards,[91] Cole,[92] and Donald Sears.[93]

Berry contrasts the type of music cultivated by the Beethoven Society ("a high order of music") with the type of sacred music generally practiced at the time ("common psalmody, with an anthem on Fast and Thanksgiving days"). Like many other musical societies in Massachusetts,[94] the society "adapted for study" various books published under the patronage of the Handel and Haydn Society: *The Old Colony Collection of Anthems* in two volumes and *Handel and Haydn Society Collection of Sacred Music,* vol. I. Some members also had copies of Handel's *Messiah* and Haydn's *Creation* oratorios.[95] The few surviving programs (in newspapers) indicate that works of Handel, Haydn, Mozart, and Beethoven were well represented.[96] The concerts were often advertised as "Oratorio," although it is not thought that the society ever performed a complete standard oratorio.[97] The term "oratorio" frequently referred to concerts featuring soloists and chorus performing sacred music selections, some of which were oratorio excerpts.

In addition to the use of Boston Handel and Haydn Society publications, another link with the contemporary Boston organization was the participation in Portland of Mr. and Mrs. Louis Ostinelli. He had been the first violinist of the Handel and Haydn Society in Boston; she was the organist. After their move to Portland in 1822, they performed in the same capacities with the Beethoven Society.[98]

Residents of Augusta were also treated to performances by the Ostinellis in two "oratorios" held in Augusta in September 1822: one directed by and for the benefit of Mr. Holland, a music professor who had recently settled in Augusta from New Bedford, Massachusetts, and the other to benefit the Ostinellis.[99] Both performances were held at Rev. Mr. Tappan's meetinghouse in Augusta. The choir does not appear to have been an ongoing musical society as such. Rather, it consisted of members of Rev. Tappan's Society (the Congregational Church in Augusta), assisted by a few members of the Congregational and Baptist Society choirs of nearby Hallowell.[100]

The extant programs for the oratorio concerts in both Portland

and Augusta suggest that the repertory differed from that found in the contemporaneous Maine tunebooks. While the latter contained some adaptations of melodies by the European masters, they were mostly short hymn-tune-like settings, rather than arias, recitatives, or choruses from oratorios.

Figure 1 shows the program of an Augusta Oratorio concert of 1822. Since the majority of the selections can be found in music books said to have been owned by Beethoven Society members, the Augusta and Portland groups may have possessed similar scores and performed many of the same selections. For example, several excerpts are from Handel's *Messiah* and Haydn's *Creation,* scores possessed by Beethoven Society members.[101] Almost

ORDER OF PERFORMANCE.

Part I.

Organ	Voluntary.
Recitative—"Thus saith the Lord of Hosts,"	
Air—"But who may abide the day of his coming."	Handel.
Chorus—"And the glory of the Lord shall be revealed."	Handel.
Solo and Chorus—"Hark! the Vesper Hymn."	
Anthem—"I waited patiently on the Lord."	Chappel.
Air—"He shall feed his flock."	Handel.
Chorus—"Break forth into joy."	do.
Anthem—"Lord of all power and might."	Rev. Dr. Mason.
Chorus—"Hallelujah."	Handel.

Part II

Organ	Voluntary.
Song of Rejoicing—"Strike the Cymbal."	Pucitta.
Anthem—"Child of Mortality."	Bray.
Meriam's Song—"Sound the loud Timbrel."	Avison.
Recitative—"And God said, let the earth,"	
Air—"Now heav'n in fullest glory shone,"	Haydn.
Chorus—"We praise thee, O God,"	Handel.
Chorus—"To Thee, Cherubim and Seraphim."	Handel.
Hymn for Divine Inspiration.	Whittaker.
Chorus—"Worthy is the Lamb,"	Handel.

FIGURE 1. AUGUSTA ORATORIO PROGRAM, SEPTEMBER 19, 1822 (as printed in the *Hallowell Gazette,* IX/38 [September 18, 1822], p. 3).

all the others appear in the two volumes of the *Old Colony Collection,* a musical source for the Portland society's programs.[102]

The success of the Augusta concerts in the fall of 1822 and "the improving taste of Sacred Music on the Kennebec" apparently led several central Maine gentlemen to contemplate forming an amateur association "to practice music of the higher style of composition," particularly the works of Handel and Haydn.[103] While there is no indication that such an organization, apparently to be modelled after the Boston Handel and Haydn Society, became a reality, another central Maine society with an interest in sacred music held occasional meetings in 1822. Notices for the "Kennebec and Somerset Society for Improvement in Sacred Music" appear sporadically in the *Hallowell Gazette* in 1822; however, there are no indications that this society was a performing organization.[104]

The formation, or projected formation, of these societies suggests that there was an interest in improving sacred music in the Augusta-Hallowell area in the early 1820s. Members of the new central Maine organizations apparently shared the reform sentiments which had led to the formation of the Middlesex and Salem Societies in Massachusetts around 1805 and the Beneficent Musical Society in the Portland area in 1810. Paralleling the spread of the reform movement to inland Maine was a change in the music selected for tunebooks by central Maine compilers in the 1820s. The tunes appear to have been chosen with improvement in mind; a greater proportion of the pieces are by eminent European masters, considered to be superior to American psalmodists.[105]

Various other ongoing musical societies were formed in southern Maine in the 1820s. Those mentioned by Edwards include a Handel Society and a Haydn Society in Gorham, a Handel Society of Bath, a Hayden (*sic*) Society and later a Mozart Society in Brunswick, a Philo Harmonic Society in New Gloucester, and a Handel and Haydn Society in Portland.[106] Significantly, all of the towns represented are within about twenty-five miles of Portland. Portland's Beethoven Society may have served as a model for some of these other organizations.

Summary

To help delineate the various types of groups that met for instruction in singing during the first three decades of the nineteenth century in Maine, we may refer to an ad announcing the return to Augusta of Mr. Holland, "Professor of Music," in early 1824. In the notice, Holland proposed teaching a private class (not exceeding twenty) in "the Elements of Vocal Music, on the most approved principles" at his residence two evenings a week. Presumably, this would be similar to a singing school, where individuals, not necessarily known to one another, would gather for instruction.

Holland further offered his professional services to neighboring towns or villages as follows:

> either in forming choirs in the first rudiments of Psalmody, or to such as have already attained a proficiency in that Art, to instruct them in the higher species of Sacred Music, viz. the compositions of Handel, Haydn, Mozart &c.[107]

Here he suggests that he could form a choir, or direct an already existing one, to sing either basic psalmody (psalm- and hymn-tunes) or sacred art music by the European masters. In both cases, the choirs would presumably meet on a regular, continuing basis. The latter, if not the former, would constitute what might be called a "musical society" or "singing society."

These three categories seem to epitomize the various stages of activity in sacred music in Maine in the period from 1800 to 1830: 1) instruction of individuals in group sessions, 2) choirs trained in the basics of psalmody, and 3) choirs performing sacred art music.

These developments were paralleled by the production of Maine tunebooks during the same period. At the turn of the nineteenth century, singing schools were beginning to be formed in numerous towns throughout the District of Maine. In response to the need, tunebooks were imported from other parts of New England or compiled in Maine. The students thus instructed used their newly acquired knowledge to sing in church choirs where psalm- and hymn-tunes (and an occasional anthem or set-piece) were the order of the day. During the period 1815–1820, more collections were compiled in Maine than at any other time.

Not content to practice psalmody, though, some amateur musicians banded together to perform excerpts from extended sacred works by the European masters. The musical societies thus formed were often named for major European composers. As these societies began to flourish in the 1820s and 1830s, the Maine tunebooks of sacred music were replaced by Boston collections (such as *The Boston Handel and Haydn Society Collection*) for use in public concerts. After 1820, the number of collections compiled in Maine dwindled dramatically. The preference for music in the European tradition caused the tunes of the amateur Maine psalmodists to be superseded and forgotten, except in nostalgic "Old Folks" concerts and retrospective collections.[108]

CHAPTER V

TUNEBOOKS AVAILABLE IN MAINE

Although tunebooks compiled in Maine are the focus of this book, they were not the only ones used by Maine churches, singing schools, and musical societies between 1800 and 1830. Other New England collections were frequently advertised in Maine newspapers. To ignore these tunebooks completely might falsely imply that Mainers were limited to "homegrown" products. A more accurate picture is provided when Maine tunebooks are considered within the larger context of sacred music publications available in the area. To assess their relative importance, we must also know how widely available the Maine collections were outside their towns of origin.

While it would be helpful to know which publications were actually purchased and utilized, such data are extremely scarce. Maine church records of the period, for example, seldom mention tunebooks by name. Since the collections were frequently purchased by individuals rather than church parishes, they are seldom listed in church financial records.[1] Consequently, my survey of tunebooks available in Maine between 1800 and 1830 relies primarily on newspaper advertisements as sources. Newspapers published in Portland and Hallowell are of particular interest because they indicate which collections were for sale in these two important towns.[2]

In the early nineteenth century, Portland and Hallowell were the principal market towns and bookselling centers of southern and central Maine, respectively. They were also the first Maine towns to have their own newspapers, beginning in 1785 for Portland and 1794 for Hallowell.[3] Portland bookstore advertisements show which tunebooks could be purchased by southern Maine residents in Portland, a major seaport and Maine's largest town.[4] Hallowell bookstore advertisements suggest which sacred music collections were readily available to residents of the newer inland settlements surrounding Hallowell, a bustling Kennebec River town.[5]

Since newspapers in only a limited number of towns were scanned (see note 2 for list), this chronological overview is representative, not comprehensive. Nevertheless, indications are that bookstores in other parts of the state carried many of the same sacred music collections as those in Hallowell and Portland. Map 2 indicates the location of the Maine towns mentioned in this chapter; Map 3 shows Maine in relation to New England and New Brunswick, pinpointing several non-Maine towns where tunebooks were published.

Since newspaper ads indicate only which books were available for purchase, not whether they were actually sold, one must use them cautiously as sources. Nevertheless, one may fairly assume that books whose titles recur in ads through the years (as later editions were published) must have sold well enough for booksellers to continue to stock them.[6] Two such books were *Village Harmony* and the *Bridgewater Collection.*

At least after 1800, if not before, one of the most popular tunebooks in Maine seems to have been *Village Harmony.*[7] Ads for its numerous editions appear in Hallowell and Portland newspapers throughout the period. First published in 1795, the tunebook continued through a seventeenth edition, published in 1821. Although no compiler's name is printed on the title page, the book's publisher, Henry Ranlet of Exeter, New Hampshire, appears to have been actively involved in the compilation, at least through the seventh edition (1806).[8] Ranlet was also the publisher of several of the early-nineteenth-century Maine tunebooks.[9]

The first ten editions of *Village Harmony* (through 1810) were "formula" tunebooks, following the very successful model of *The Worcester Collection* (1786–1803) in featuring a small number of new tunes, a large number of the most popular (i.e., "Core Repertory") tunes, a mixture of both American and non-American compositions, and an eclectic blend of styles designed to appeal to a variety of singers.[10] By 1810, American tunes became less numerous in *Village Harmony* editions as older, European pieces took their place, the result of the reform movement in church music.[11]

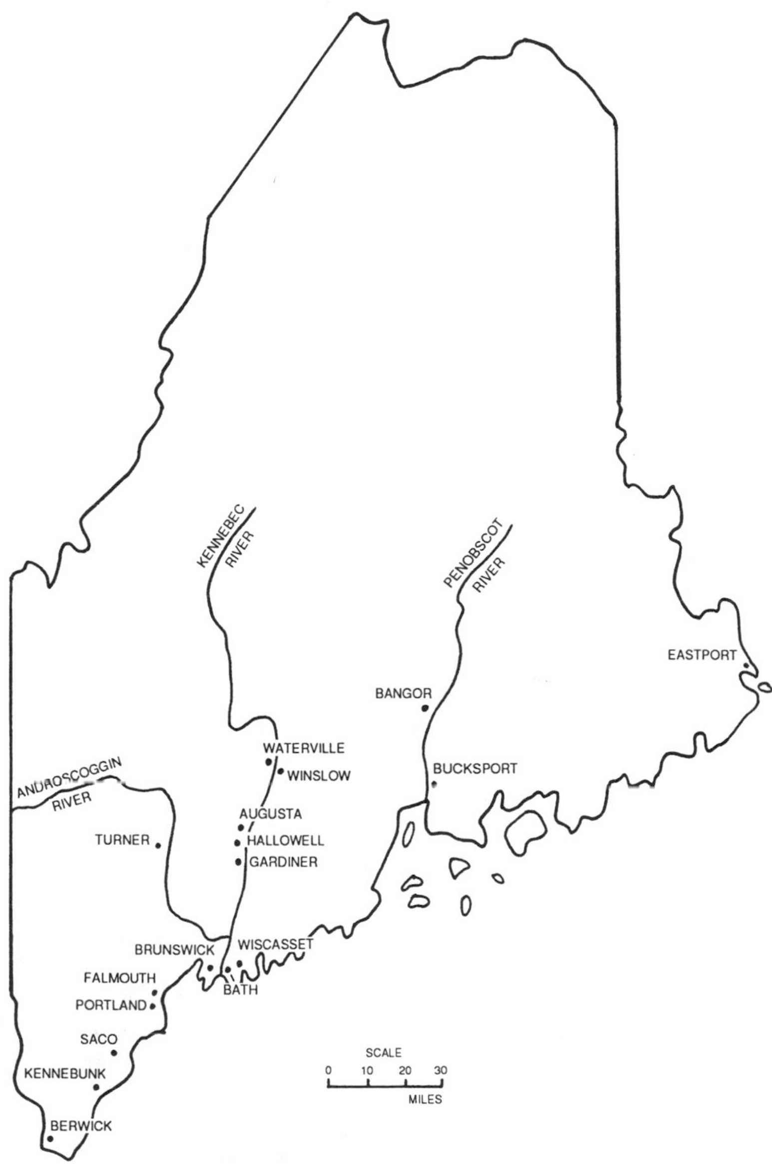

MAP 2. SELECTED MAINE TOWNS IN 1820

MAP 3. MAINE AND ITS NEIGHBORS

Another popular tunebook whose many editions were advertised in Portland and Hallowell throughout the period was the *Bridgewater Collection,* first published in 1802 as *The Columbian and European Harmony: or Bridgewater Collection.*[12] The *Bridgewater Collection,* printed in Boston, continued through a twenty-seventh edition (1839). Like *Village Harmony,* the *Bridgewater Collection* was a leading New England eclectic tunebook; however, European pieces were always more predominant in the *Bridgewater Collection* than in *Village Harmony*. American tunes comprise less than a quarter of the tunes in the first two editions of the *Bridgewater Collection* (1802, 1804), less than 10 percent of the third edition (1810),[13] and are nonexistent in the ninth edition (1821).[14] The *Bridgewater Collection* was especially popular in Maine in the 1820s. One reason may have been that one of its principal competitors, *Village Harmony,* was not published after 1821. An even more significant factor in the later success of the *Bridgewater Collection* may have been that Maine singers were more accepting of European sacred music (found in abundance in the *Bridgewater Collection*) by the 1820s.[15]

Further evidence of the popularity of both the *Bridgewater Collection* and *Village Harmony* in Maine is the fact that they were advertised in Portland and Hallowell as being sold by the hundred, dozen, or single.[16] In contrast, ads for tunebooks compiled in Maine provide a price only for a single copy and per dozen, not per hundred. Statements that a tunebook would be sold "by the hundred" may reflect the realities of urban sales or simply the optimistic hopes of a publisher. While the *Bridgewater Collection* and *Village Harmony* were probably only rarely sold in quantities as large as a hundred in rural Maine, such statements imply that the scenario was not unthinkable.

Those who emigrated to Maine in the late eighteenth century may have brought tunebooks with them. Those needing to purchase one could choose from several collections. Since Massachusetts goods could easily be shipped to Maine ports, it is not surprising that tunebooks from Massachusetts, rather than from other areas, were advertised in Portland newspapers between 1785 and 1800. They included *Federal Harmony, The Worcester Collection of Sacred Harmony,* John Norman's *Massachusetts Harmony,* and music by the well-known Massachusetts composers William Billings and Samuel Holyoke.[17] Supply Belcher's *Harmony of Maine,* compiled in Maine but published in Boston, was advertised in Portland in 1796, two years after its publication.[18]

In 1801, a sacred music collection was compiled in neighboring St. John, New Brunswick, and printed in Exeter, New Hampshire. Later editions of this tunebook, Stephen Humbert's *Union Harmony,* were published in 1816, 1831, and 1840.[19] *Union Harmony* appears to have received only limited, if any, distribution in Maine, however, in spite of the proximity of St. John to eastern Maine ports (see Map 3).[20]

Subscriber lists confirm that a few Maine residents were among the purchasers of other collections also published in Exeter, New Hampshire, or in Boston in the late eighteenth and early nineteenth centuries. When tunebooks were sold by subscription, subscription papers were circulated prior to its printing. Those wishing to purchase a copy would subscribe their name, signifying their intentions. Sometimes the list of subscribers would be printed at the end of the book. The subscribers to Samuel Holyoke's *Harmonia Americana* (Boston, 1791) or his *Columbian Repository* (Exeter, [1803]) included a single resident from each of the Maine towns of Portland, Falmouth, Turner, Winslow, and Wiscasset, and three from Berwick. One Brunswick and two Portland residents subscribed to Gottlieb Graupner's *Monitor* (Boston, 1806).[21]

Of these eleven subscribers, all but two lived on or near the coast in southern or south-central Maine (see Map 2 for locations). Only two (those from Turner and Winslow) resided in inland areas; one of these two was composer "Abram" Maxim of Turner. As a musician who had lived in Maine for only a few years, Maxim naturally wanted to keep up with the latest music publications. One might expect that coastal residents, who were closer to both Boston and Exeter than most inland residents, were in a better position to learn about and subscribe for various publications. In at least one case, however, subscription agents were appointed in the larger inland river towns (Hallowell and Bangor) as well.[22]

Among the collections advertised in Portland in the early years of the nineteenth century (1803–1806) are two by William Cooper: *Original Sacred Music* (1803) and *The Beauties of Church Music; and the Sure Guide to the Art of Singing* (1804).[23] In the preface to the latter collection, Cooper expresses his preference for the older type of church music, the kind in use before 1775; accordingly, the collection contains nearly twice as many European as American tunes.[24] Cooper, who taught a singing school in Portland in 1807 and 1808,[25] may have been a Portland native, although he seems to have lived in Boston for much of his adult life.[26]

From the *Gazette of Maine,* a newspaper which began publication in Buckstown (later to become Bucksport) in 1805, we can note the sacred music books stocked by a new bookstore in a smaller, newer town in eastern Maine. As a river town not far from the coast, Buckstown had good access to Boston, where many of the store's goods had been selected. Tunebooks for sale at the bookstore of "Brown's and Pilsbury" in October 1805 included Holyoke's *Columbian Repository* ([1803]), Cooper's *Beauties of Church Music* (1804), Emes's *Harmony,*[27] Jacob French's *Har-*

mony of Harmony (1802), and Elias Mann's *Northampton Collection of Music* (1797, 1802). All except *Columbian Repository* and possibly Emes's *Harmony* were printed in Massachusetts. Since the bookstore had recently opened and was the first such store in the area, we do not know which, if any, of the offered works sold well.[28]

Perhaps not surprisingly, the 1805 Buckstown ad does not mention any collections compiled by Mainers, not even Belcher's *Harmony of Maine,* published in 1794 in Boston. Belcher's book was not so new as the books listed, most of which had been published within the previous five years; in addition, eclectic collections, containing tunes by various composers, were probably in more demand than a tunebook containing the tunes of a single composer (Belcher). Still, more recent collections compiled by Mainers and published in Exeter, New Hampshire, in 1802 or 1805 are not listed either.[29] Although Portland booksellers had copies of the Maine tunebooks soon after they were published, the relatively small distance between Exeter and Portland and the much larger distance between Exeter and Buckstown may have been a factor.[30]

The ads of Portland booksellers Thomas Clark and Isaac Adams show that the Maine tunebooks by Maxim and Robbins were stocked in Portland in 1805. Still, these newly published collections faced stiff competition from other more established works. For example, Robbins's *Columbian Harmony* was advertised in the same ad and for the same price as *The Columbian and European Harmony; or, Bridgwater* [sic] *Collection of Sacred Music* and the sixth edition of *Village Harmony* ("corrected and improved"). The fourth edition of Andrew Law's *The Art of Singing,* a three-part book, was offered in the ad for a slightly lower price.[31] As an unknown quantity, Robbins's book was likely to be less attractive than the others. Singers belonging to choirs already using an edition of *Village Harmony* would probably choose that work over Robbins's tunebook so that they would have access to as many as possible of the same tunes as fellow choir members. Successive editions of *Village Harmony* often had much in common with each other, even to tunes being placed on the same pages.

Although we do not know what music books Ezekiel Goodale carried in his Hallowell Bookstore in 1805,[32] it seems likely that he would have carried at least a few copies of the Robbins and Maxim tunebooks, compiled in the central Maine towns of Winthrop and Turner.[33] His was the only bookstore in the area at the time. Isaac Adams of Portland is, however, the only Maine bookseller specifically listed on the title page of the second edition of Maxim's *Northern Harmony,* published in Exeter in 1808. Because he sold *Village Harmony,*[34] printed by the same firm as *Northern Harmony,* Goodale must have had the business contacts to obtain the latter and probably stocked the Maine tunebooks because of their local interest.

The period from 1806 to 1810 in Massachusetts proper saw the compilation and publication of reform collections, reflecting a change in urban taste toward simpler tunes by European authors for church use. By at least 1812, some of the reform collections were available and in use in Portland, Maine's most urban area. In that year, the bookstore of Hyde, Lord, and Co. offered for sale two of the early reform tunebooks, *The Salem Collection* (1805, 1806) and *The Middlesex Collection* (1807, 1808), as well as several other collections.[35]

Significantly, the Hyde, Lord, and Co. ad makes no mention of any of the tunebooks compiled in Maine in the previous decade (Maxim's *Northern Harmony* and *Oriental Harmony* and Robbins's *Columbian Harmony*). The large proportion of American tunes and fuging-tunes in the Maine tunebooks probably made them less attractive to the more culturally aware members of Portland's elite, who maintained ties with Boston and were clearly aware of the changes in sacred music taking place there.[36]

Massachusetts reform tunebooks such as *The Middlesex Collection* and *The Salem Collection* are not listed in the Hallowell bookstore ads which appear in the *Hallowell Gazette,* published from 1814 to 1827, although they may have been available upon special order. In central Maine, where a preference for fuging-tunes and tunes by Americans seems to have continued longer than in Massachusetts proper and perhaps Portland, there was probably less interest in the reform tunebooks in the second decade of the nineteenth century. Even by around 1817, when European tunes and plain tunes were becoming a larger component of the tunebooks compiled in central Maine, the reform tunebooks, containing virtually no American tunes, may have been too limited in variety to suit central Maine taste. The later editions of

Village Harmony, as well as most of the Maine collections through the early 1820s, continued to include at least some American tunes.

One of the first tunebooks advertised by Ezekiel Goodale and his Hallowell Bookstore in 1814 when his weekly newspaper, the *Hallowell Gazette,* began publication was John Hubbard's *Sacred Music.*[37] The collection, touted as "containing thirty-two Anthems," may have been useful for singers who had occasion to sing anthems, since many of the Maine tunebooks contained few of these extended pieces. As mentioned previously, Washburn's *Parish Harmony* (1813), carried by Goodale in late 1814, contained only one anthem.

In the fall of 1816, Goodale began printing the first of many music books. All of the subsequent tunebooks compiled by Mainers were published by his firm or by the firms formed by his former partners, Franklin Glazier and Andrew Masters, after his retirement in 1824.[38] Once Goodale started publishing tunebooks in 1816, he naturally promoted his own books, as well as the two non-Maine tunebooks which seem to have been in greatest demand: *Village Harmony* and *Bridgewater Collection.*[39] The fact that Goodale's stock of sacred collections was not limited to the ones he printed, however, implies that even in central Maine, there was a continued demand for other collections.

Confirmation that central Maine singers around 1820 did not limit themselves to central Maine tunebooks is provided by an invoice found among the records of the Old South Congregational Church in Hallowell.[40] Although several of the church's members may have assisted in the compilation of *The Hallowell Collection* (1817),[41] the church purchased a dozen copies of *Village Harmony* in 1819.[42] *The Hallowell Collection,* with its near exclusion of American tunes and fuging-tunes, may have been ahead of the tastes in sacred music in Hallowell. Besides containing some American tunes and fuging-tunes for those who still enjoyed them, *Village Harmony* had the advantage of name recognition and a reputation acquired over two decades of publication.

Although Goodale's stock may have been weighted toward the books he published, an 1819 ad in Eastport (a town on the very easternmost edge of Maine) suggests that stores in Maine towns a considerable distance away carried a similar inventory of sacred music collections, including some of the tunebooks published in

Maine. The list of books available at the Eastport Book and Stationary (*sic*) Store in August 1819 included "rules for singing, Hallowell singing books 75 cts. Village Harmony (15th last and best edition) 1 dollar."[43] The "Hallowell singing books" were probably not limited to *The Hallowell Collection* (1817, 1819), but may also have included several of the "singing books" published by Goodale in Hallowell, such as Washburn's *Temple Harmony* (first published in 1818) and late editions of *Northern Harmony* (1816, 1819). These three Hallowell tunebooks were also advertised in Portland in 1819 and 1820, indicating that they were distributed in southern as well as central and eastern Maine.

In publishing several Maine compilations in the period around 1820, Goodale and his partners must have overestimated the number of copies which would be sold. In the fall of both 1822 and 1824, they held sales "at prices greatly reduced" to eliminate the "large stock of Sacred Music" on hand.[44] Because of its significance, the ad for the 1824 sale is quoted in its entirety (Figure 2). Since new tunebooks often came on the market in late fall (just in time for the winter singing schools), they apparently needed to move the old stock to make room for the new.

The ads for the tunebook clearance sales in both 1822 and 1824 are quite similar, although the 1822 ads do not list the quantity available of each title. Other than *Village Harmony,* all the tunebooks listed were tunebooks published by the Hallowell firm. The same editions are advertised at the same prices in both years, with one exception: the 1822 ad also included the fifth edition of *Northern Harmony* at a price of $8.50 per dozen.[45] The omission of *Northern Harmony* from the 1824 ad indicates that Glazier and Co. sold all the copies of that tunebook, but was less successful at selling the other tunebooks. The fact that the "greatly reduced prices" of 1822 were not reduced further in 1824 suggests that the 1822 prices were as low as the bookseller would go.

Without knowing how many copies of each edition the store may have had to begin with, one cannot draw too many conclusions about the quantities listed in the ad. Nevertheless, the fact that comparatively few copies of *Village Harmony* and the first edition of *Temple Harmony* remained would lead one to believe that they had sold well in the past. We have already noted the popularity of *Village Harmony* throughout the period. *Temple Harmony* was published in seven editions, suggesting that it also en-

SINGING-BOOKS—cheap!

GLAZIER & CO., PRINTERS AND BOOKSELLERS, No. 1 Kennebec-row, Hallowell, having on hand a large stock of SACRED MUSIC, consisting of a sufficient variety to suit the taste of the various Musical Societies, offer the remainder of their editions of the following works, at the prices annexed.

30 dozen HALLOWELL COLLECTION, 1st edition published 1817, 200 pages, at $5.00 per dozen [orig. price: $7.50 per dozen],

10 doz., do., 2d edition published 1819, 210 pages, at $5.50 per dozen [orig. price: $7.50 per dozen].

8 doz., TEMPLE HARMONY, 1st ed. published 1818, 304 pages, at $6.00 per dozen.

15 doz., do., 2d edition published 1820, 312 pages, at $7.00 per dozen.

15 doz., do., 3d edition published 1821, 152 pages, at $4.00 per doz.

40 doz. WESLEYAN HARMONY, 1st ed. published 1820, 130 pages, at $3.50 per doz. [orig. price: 62–1/2 cents, single, which is $7.50 per dozen].

40 doz. do., 2d edition, published 1821, 142 pages, at $4.00 per dozen.

6 doz. VILLAGE HARMONY, 16th edition published 1819, 350 pages, at $8.50 per doz.

Catalogues of the Tunes contained in each book, with the names of their Authors annexed, may be had at the Bookstore, gratis.

Sept. 15.

FIGURE 2. ADVERTISEMENT FOR GLAZIER & CO. TUNEBOOK SALE, 1824
SOURCE: *Hallowell Gazette,* XI/37 (September 15, 1824), p. 3. The original selling prices, provided in brackets, were not shown in the ad but were obtained from earlier newspaper advertisements.

joyed a good deal of public support. Another conclusion one might draw from the ad is that the least expensive books (usually the ones with the fewest pages) did not necessarily sell the most copies. The bookstore still had eighty dozen copies of the two editions of *Wesleyan Harmony,* one of the most inexpensive items on the list, but only six dozen copies of *Village Harmony,* the most expensive.

One of the new books which Glazier and Company's clearance sale made room for was the fourteenth edition of the *Bridgewater Collection,* which arrived in Hallowell in November 1824, following its publication in Boston.[46] Sales must have been good because just two months later, an ad announced that the store had received "a further supply."[47] A little over a year later, the same bookstore ran an ad stating that twenty-two dozen copies of the *Bridgewater Collection* had just been received.[48] Having stocked the collection for a number of years, the Hallowell booksellers must have been confident that they could sell such a sizable number of copies. Hallowell's population in 1820 was only 2,919, but potential purchasers would have included residents of surrounding towns.

By the 1820s, and probably before, the *Bridgewater Collection* was also for sale at bookstores which had opened in all the major towns throughout the state. An 1823 ad for the *Bridgewater Collection,* for example, indicates that the twelfth edition was "For sale by the Booksellers, in Portland, Saco, Brunswick, Waterville, Hallowell, Bangor, Bucksport, Wiscasset, Bath, &c."[49] These locations include towns from southern, central, and eastern Maine.

A subscriber list is printed in one Maine tunebook of the early 1820s—Henry Little's *Wesleyan Harmony*—allowing us to observe the geographical distribution of the pledged purchasers. Not surprisingly, the greatest number of copies were subscribed for locally, where the compiler was known and where he could exert a personal influence. Residents of Little's town, Bucksport, account for almost a quarter of the 564 subscribed copies, with the surrounding towns in Hancock and adjacent Penobscot County also providing a good number of subscriptions. Also included are towns on the south-central Maine coast and in central Maine, where the book was published.

Significantly, certain counties in southern, western, and extreme eastern Maine are not represented at all,[50] although residents of those areas may have purchased copies after the book was published. Since this was Little's first compilation, some Mainers may have hesitated to sign up for an unseen tunebook by an unknown compiler. As might be expected, the proportion of subscribers from outside the state was small.[51] Since the book was especially tailored for Methodist societies, it is likely that a large number of the subscribers, especially the out-of-staters, were Methodists.

Although subscriber lists are unavailable for the other collections compiled in Maine, it is likely that the geographical distribution of sales, especially for first-time compilers, may have shown similar trends: a greater number of copies sold in the immediate area, proportionately fewer copies sold further away. In the case of such veteran compilers as Maxim and Washburn, who published a number of tunebooks over the years, one might expect that they were more successful at selling later editions outside of their immediate area as more people became familiar with their works.

As 1830 approached, two of the Maine collections published ten or more years earlier were still for sale by their publisher in Hallowell and by a bookseller in nearby Gardiner.[52] *The Hallowell Collection* and *Wesleyan Harmony* may have retained their popularity because they contained predominantly European compositions, which were even more in vogue than in the previous decade. A more realistic explanation may be that because they did not sell well, copies were still gathering dust in bookstores ten years after publication.

In addition to these Maine collections and the ever-popular *Bridgewater Collection* and *Village Harmony,* the music books advertised by the Hallowell and Gardiner booksellers in the late 1820s included the *Handel and Haydn Collection,*[53] the *Stoughton Collection* ("new, and much improved"),[54] and *Gould's Anthems.* All three collections were particularly suitable for the many amateur musical societies formed throughout Maine in the 1820s.

Although two of the tunebooks compiled in Maine (*Temple Harmony* and *Northern Harmony*) were advertised in Portland in January 1823,[55] the Maine tunebooks seem to have been displaced by Boston tunebooks in Portland as the decade continued. Several of the Maine collections contained predominantly European tunes, but the harmonizations were probably not considered acceptable to Portland followers of "scientific" musical ideals. The conception of music as both a science and an art was particularly fashionable in the 1820s. Older American hymn-tune settings were looked down upon because they were not based on principles of musical "science" (i.e., European common-practice harmony). Newer harmonizations (by Mason, Hastings, and others) which followed these principles were considered more "scientific."

As early as 1822, most of the tunebooks advertised in Portland were not of Maine origin: *Boston Handel and Haydn Society Collection, Bridgewater Collection of Sacred Music, Hubbard's Thirty Anthems,* and *Newport Collection.*[56] A Portland ad in December 1829 noted the recent arrival of the nineteenth edition of the *Bridgewater Collection* and the last edition of the *Handel and Haydn Collection.*[57] The latter was one of the music books used by the Beethoven Society in Portland.[58] Members of the society, active in the early 1820s, also sang music contained in the two volumes of the *Old Colony Collection of Anthems*.[59]

Summary

The tunebooks compiled in central Maine were not limited to that area, but were available in bookstores in other parts of the state as well. Besides the Maine tunebooks, the tunebooks most frequently advertised in Maine between 1800 and 1830 were tunebooks published in the closest New England states of New Hampshire and Massachusetts. Geographical proximity to these areas, coupled with the political ties between Maine and Massachusetts, undoubtedly contributed to the ease with which they were obtained. Tunebooks compiled in other parts of New England and in New Brunswick appear to have been less readily available.

Various editions of the eclectic collections, *Village Harmony* and the *Bridgewater Collection,* were available in Maine bookstores throughout the period. Unlike the Massachusetts reform collections which were restricted to "ancient tunes," *Village Harmony* contained a mixture of tunes which must have been especially pleasing to rural Mainers, who apparently continued to enjoy American tunes and fuging-tunes later than singers in other areas. Massachusetts reform collections were known and adopted in Portland as early as 1812, perhaps reflecting the closer ties between Boston and Portland than between Boston and the inland areas.

Although the *Bridgewater Collection* was sold throughout the period, the height of its popularity seems to have been in the 1820s, after *Village Harmony* ceased to be published and rural residents had come to accept a European-dominated repertory. As the "scientific music" movement gained strength near the end of the period, the *Handel and Haydn Society Collection* made inroads in the tunebook market, not only in Portland but in central Maine and probably other parts of the state as well.

B. Biographies of the Composer-Compilers

CHAPTER VI

EIGHTEENTH-CENTURY MAINE ANTECEDENTS: JAMES LYON AND SUPPLY BELCHER

Although the publication of tunebooks by Maine compilers did not begin in earnest until the nineteenth century, tunebooks by two residents of the District of Maine were published in the eighteenth century. One of these psalmodists, James Lyon, was not, however, actually living in Maine when he compiled his tunebook. His *Urania* was published in 1761; he did not settle in Machias, Maine, for another decade. Still, some of his later tunes (such as PSALM 17TH and FRIENDSHIP), which appeared in various American tunebooks in the last few decades of the eighteenth century, were probably composed in Maine. Therefore, he may be considered a "Maine" psalmodist. Nevertheless, the distinction of being the first Maine resident to compose or compile a published sacred music collection belongs to Supply Belcher of Farmington, Maine. His tunebook, *The Harmony of Maine,* was published in 1794, the year James Lyon died.

James Lyon (1735–1794): His Maine Connection

Nearly all the biographical information known about James Lyon is contained in Oscar Sonneck's classic monograph, *Francis Hopkinson and James Lyon.*[1] A New Jersey native, Lyon received an A.B. degree from the College of New Jersey (Princeton) in 1759 and an A.M. degree in 1762. A short time later, he was licensed to preach by the Presbyterian Synod of New Jersey. For the rest of his life, he was first and foremost a minister. His calling took him initially to Nova Scotia (in 1765) and then to Machias, Maine (in 1772).[2] He served as a pastor in Machias (except for absences in 1773 and 1783–1785) until his death in 1794.[3]

When the Revolutionary War began a few years after Lyon settled in Machias, he became chairman of the town's Committee of Safety and Correspondence, formed to deal with the dangers of the British. In that capacity, he corresponded with the Massachusetts legislature about war-related activities and difficulties in Machias. He also wrote a letter to George Washington, in which he volunteered (as a person thoroughly familiar with Nova Scotia) to lead an expedition to capture Nova Scotia from the British; his offer was not accepted.[4]

As for *Urania,* the tunebook Lyon compiled in his pre-Machias days, it is considered significant primarily because of its size and repertory, compared to other tunebooks of the time:

> Far larger than any earlier American tunebook, it was also the first to contain English fuging-tunes and anthems and the first to identify native compositions.[5]

Following a theoretical introduction on the rudiments of music are seventy psalm-tunes, twelve anthems, and fourteen hymn settings. Unlike its American predecessors, the collection consists of tunes set primarily for four voices, rather than two or three. Although most of the tunes had been previously published in British collections, Lyon sometimes altered them with embellishments or an added voice.

Lyon identified six tunes in *Urania* as "new" (never before published). Sonneck believed all six of these tunes were original compositions by Lyon.[6] Crawford's opinion is that Lyon may have written four of them, but probably not the fifth and "surely not" the sixth.[7]

By 1774, Lyon seems to have written a new tunebook, containing many of his own tunes, and was in the process of getting it published, according to an entry in the diary of Philip Vickers Fithian, an acquaintance of Lyon's in Virginia. No such tunebook is known to exist, however.[8] Still, several original Lyon tunes, not included in *Urania,* appeared in later American tunebooks: A MARRIAGE HYMN in Daniel Bayley's *New Universal Harmony* (1773); PSALM 17TH in Jocelin's *Chorister's Companion,* second edition (1788); PSALM 19TH in Bayley's *New Royal Harmony* (c.

1778); and FRIENDSHIP, performed by the Uranian Academy in Philadelphia in 1787, published in Elias Mann's *Massachusetts Collection of Sacred Harmony* (1807).[9] These four tunes, plus the four tunes of probable Lyon provenance in *Urania,* are believed to be his only extant tunes.

Although Lyon lived in Maine for two decades, neither his tunebook nor his tunes seem to have had a direct influence on Maine tunebook compilers. Maine tunebooks contain none of the six "new" tunes from *Urania* or any other tune attributed to Lyon. While the Maine collections include some of the English tunes found in *Urania,* the versions are not similar enough to conclude that the latter was the direct source.[10] In most cases, the Maine compilers probably obtained the tunes from later eighteenth-century collections rather than from *Urania.*

Urania may have been used in Maine, even though the subscriber list does not specifically include anyone identified as a resident of "the Province of Maine" (which was not yet "the District of Maine"). At the very least, Lyon probably brought some copies of *Urania* with him to Machias for use in his parish there. With his interest in music, he would certainly have been concerned about the quality of music in the worship services he led. "A man of strong intellect, broad-minded yet not a little aggressive,"[11] he may even have taken a leading role in teaching some of his parishioners to read music, although there is no evidence that he organized or taught a singing school. He was a zealous laborer with his religious society and in his community until his last illness.[12]

Elsewhere in Maine, his tunebook may have been neglected because it was published well before there was a substantial population in Maine, let alone a musically literate one. A decade after *Urania* was published, the entire population of the Province of Maine was less than thirty thousand. Not until the beginning of the nineteenth century, when Maine's population had increased fivefold, did singing schools become widespread throughout Maine, resulting in an increased demand for tunebooks. By 1800, Lyon was dead, and his tunebook, published forty years earlier, may have been considered an antique relic of a bygone age. Compilations which were particularly popular in Maine were the new, eclectic tunebooks like *Village Harmony,* containing a large number of American tunes. The earlier *Urania,* with its emphasis on

European tunes, contained no pieces by the American psalmodists whose works became so popular in the late eighteenth century.

Supply Belcher (1751–1836)

One of the newer tunebooks available in the last part of the eighteenth century was *The Harmony of Maine* (1794), the first tunebook by a Maine composer. This publication included not just a large number of American tunes, but *only* American tunes, all composed by Supply Belcher himself. Part III provides an index of the tunes.

Like many of the new settlers of frontier Maine, Belcher was born in Massachusetts proper but relocated to Maine after the American Revolution. Born in 1751 in Stoughton, Massachusetts (near Boston), he is said to have "received a superior English education,"[13] although few specifics of his training are known. For several years, he owned Belcher's Tavern, a favorite gathering place for local musicians in Stoughton. According to Metcalf, he was a member of the Stoughton Musical Society.[14] In 1785, he and his family (a wife and children, eventually to number ten) moved to the part of Hallowell, Maine, which is now Augusta. Six years later, they relocated to an area which was to become Farmington, Maine. He lived there until his death on June 9, 1836.[15]

Squire Belcher, as he was called, became one of Farmington's most prominent citizens. He served as its first town clerk, as a selectman, and as representative to the state legislature. He was known in Farmington primarily as a musician and teacher, however. He played the violin, sang, and organized and directed the town's first choir.[16] A Hallowell newspaper article once referred to him as "the Handell [*sic*] of Maine."[17]

Because Belcher's music has been analyzed by other writers,[18] his tunebook will not be examined here in depth. Nevertheless, we must consider how it may have influenced the later Maine collections. Were they modelled after it? Did they include any of his tunes? An examination of the early-nineteenth-century Maine tunebooks reveals that nearly all of them include at least one of Belcher's tunes, but that they differ from *The Harmony of Maine* in certain other respects.

Like the collections of William Billings, who may have been Belcher's teacher in Massachusetts,[19] Belcher's tunebook consists solely of his own compositions. This model was followed in the very next tunebook put together by a Maine resident: *Oriental Harmony* (1802), which was limited to the tunes of Abraham Maxim. Apparently the single-composer format was not considered a particularly viable one by the later Maine compilers, though, because their works all contained tunes from a variety of composers. Abraham Maxim's next tunebook, *Northern Harmony* (five editions, 1805–1819), for example, included other tunes in addition to his own.

There are several possible explanations of why the later Maine tunebooks were not single-composer works, as Belcher's was. In the first place, the composer-compiler would have to compose a fairly large number of tunes to have enough for a reasonably sized tunebook. While Abraham Maxim was up to the challenge, the other nineteenth-century Maine composers seem to have been less prolific. If so, a tunebook containing only their own tunes would have been rather small. Belcher wrote at least 75 tunes and Maxim 127, but the known pieces of the other Maine compilers number approximately 47 for both Robbins and Washburn and 25 for Hartwell. There is always the possibility, however, that they wrote other tunes which were not published.

Another reason that most of the post-Belcher Maine compilers avoided the single-composer format may have been that it was less marketable. Particularly after the turn of the nineteenth century, the tunebooks which sold well were large, eclectic anthologies, which included new tunes interspersed with longtime favorites.[20] Although this did not deter compilers such as Moors, Newhall, and others from publishing single-composer collections elsewhere, the nineteenth-century Maine psalmodists, for whatever reason, chose not to do so.

While Belcher did not include tunes by a variety of composers, he did attempt to meet a variety of needs with his tunebook. In that respect, he was similar to most other New England psalmodists. *The Harmony of Maine* was geared to the needs of both singing schools and churches. In addition, Belcher, as a singing school teacher himself, realized the importance of including tunes suitable for various levels of difficulty: "a number of easy and natural Airs, for the benefit of learners, and a variety of others, for the amusement of those who have made some proficiency."[21] True to his expressed design, a third of Belcher's book is made up of simple, plain tunes (suitable for beginners) and more than a third consists of fuging-tunes, whose overlapping entries made them challenging to the more advanced singers. Most of the later Maine tunebook compilers also tried to provide tunes for a variety of tastes and abilities.

A comparison with Maxim's *Oriental Harmony,* the next Maine tunebook to be published (1802) and the only other single-composer tunebook, is instructive. Belcher's favorite form, constituting the largest portion of his book, was the fuging-tune; Maxim's most prevalent genre was the tune with extension, although his later tunebooks, like Belcher's work, include a large number of fuging-tunes. The genre was particularly popular in the late eighteenth century among the New England tunesmiths but came under increasing criticism in the early nineteenth century. Anthems, the most difficult form of psalmody to write and sing, make up only a small portion of both collections, perhaps reflecting the limited opportunities for their performance in Maine.[22] Set-pieces, which were also frequently associated with particular occasions, are more numerous than anthems in Belcher's tunebook but are not included at all in Maxim's.[23] An imaginative composer, Belcher may have enjoyed writing extended pieces, such as set-pieces and anthems, because of the wider range of possibilities which could be explored in their contrasting sections.

Unlike *Oriental Harmony* and the later Maine tunebooks, which were published either in Exeter, New Hampshire, or in Hallowell, Maine, *The Harmony of Maine* was published in Boston by the well-known firm of Thomas and Andrews. Henry Ranlet, whose Exeter, New Hampshire, firm printed Maxim's *Oriental Harmony,* did not have music type in 1794, when *The Harmony of Maine* was printed.[24]

Like the later Maine tunebooks, *The Harmony of Maine* contains a theoretical introduction. Belcher's introduction is identical to that found in the first five editions of *The Worcester Collection of Sacred Music,* some of which were published by the same firm as *The Harmony of Maine.*[25] Although it is not certain who compiled the theoretical introduction, Karl Kroeger suggests that "it is altogether possible that Thomas himself may have been the principal compiler."[26] The later Maine compilers, with the possible exception of Charles Robbins, do not seem to have modelled their rudiments sections on Belcher's, although they include many of the same topics.[27]

Like many tunebooks of the 1790s, Belcher's collection includes at least one tune (THE POWER OF MUSIC) with a secular rather than a sacred text. Sonneck and Upton suggest that a total of eight songs in the collection are secular.[28] Although several of the eight refer to "the beloved," they are not necessarily secular love songs as they may appear at face value. Their Song of Solomon texts may be understood on a deeper level as allegorical references to Christ and the Church. While THE POWER OF MUSIC and perhaps the tunes with quasi-secular texts may not have been completely suitable for worship, they would have been entirely appropriate for singing school use.

One of the later Maine tunebooks, *The Chorister's Companion* (1815), the compilation of Edward Hartwell, also includes some tunes with secular texts. Hartwell did not necessarily model his tunebook after Belcher's; in fact, he may not have even known of Belcher's collection. He is one of the few Maine compilers who does not include a single Belcher tune in his publication.

The only other Maine psalmodist who did not include any Belcher tunes in his tunebook was Henry Little (*Wesleyan Harmony,* 1820, 1821). The exclusion of Belcher tunes by Hartwell and Little can be at least partly explained by their purposeful omission of fuging-tunes and their deliberate inclusion of older tunes by "the most celebrated authors."[29] Hartwell, for example, selected "many ancient, European pieces, whose antiquity and intrinsic excellence are too well known to need eulogy here."[30] Nearly half of the Belcher tunes in *The Harmony of Maine* were fuging-tunes, so they would have been automatically excluded from consideration. In addition, Belcher, although well known in Hallowell, would hardly have qualified as a "celebrated" author, and his tunes were not old enough to have stood the test of time and criticism, one of Little's criteria.

The other Maine tunebook compilers of the first three decades of the nineteenth century did include at least a few Belcher tunes, as shown in Part III. One of the most surprising findings is that the Belcher tunes printed in the Maine collections did not necessarily come from *The Harmony of Maine*. In fact, none of the seven Belcher tunes contained in Charles Robbins's *Columbian Harmony* (1805) had been printed in Belcher's own tunebook. Although *The Harmony of Maine* does include a tune entitled ADVENT, Robbins attributes a completely different tune, also called ADVENT, to Belcher.

What was Robbins's source for these seven Belcher tunes? At least one of the seven, ORDINATION ANTHEM (said to have been performed in Hallowell and Augusta), was known to have been printed by Thomas and Andrews in 1797. This publication, of which no copies are known, also included "a number of other fuging pieces never before published."[31] It seems unlikely that this separate publication was Robbins's only source for the Belcher tunes since four of the seven he printed were not fuging-tunes. ORDINATION ANTHEM and TOPSHAM (along with the Belcher tune, PITTSTON) had been included in another Thomas and Andrews publication of 1797: the sixth edition of *The Worcester Collection of Sacred Harmony*.[32] Since Robbins prints only two of the three and includes five other tunes not in *The Worcester Collection,* however, the latter cannot have been his only source, either. It is not implausible that Robbins may have become acquainted with Belcher from attending his singing school.[33] On the other hand, Robbins may simply have asked Belcher, as Maine's most famous psalmodist, to furnish some tunes for a new Maine collection.

Several later Maine collections include a smaller number of Belcher tunes. Not surprisingly, the Belcher tunes chosen in each case correspond closely with the ideals of the respective compilers. Abraham Maxim, whose preference for fuging-tunes is apparent from the large number included in his tunebooks, favored Belcher's music in this genre; all five Belcher pieces included in Maxim's *Northern Harmony* are fuging-tunes. On the other hand, the compilers of *The Hallowell Collection of Sacred Music* considered simple, dignified tunes by European composers to be the only type appropriate for worship; accordingly, they included some of Belcher's simpler tunes. That they would include any of his tunes at all surely indicates that he was still esteemed in Hallowell.[34]

None of the Belcher tunes in *The Hallowell Collection* appeared in either *The Harmony of Maine* or the earlier Maine tunebooks. They may have been newly composed for the compilation; at any rate, they seem to have been provided by Belcher directly to the compilers upon their request. It must have been an honor for Belcher to be included, by implication, as one of the "authors of well known eminence" represented in the collection.[35]

Belcher's tunes do not seem to have been especially popular with compiler Japheth Coombs Washburn. He apparently liked CONVERSION, choosing to include it in *Parish Harmony* (1813), the first two editions of *Temple Harmony* (1818 and 1820), and *Northern Harmony,* fourth edition (1816), which he co-wrote with Maxim. CONVERSION is a rather straightforward, fourteen-measure fuging-tune whose stepwise and simple triadic melodic movement would make it an ideal "first" fuging-tune for a singing school. CANTON, a tune with extension, set to a Particular Meter text, is another Belcher tune which Washburn included in the first two editions of *Temple Harmony*.[36] One suspects that Washburn's source for CANTON was the first edition of *The Hallowell Collection,* published just a year before his *Temple Harmony.* In the fourth through sixth editions of *Temple Harmony* (1823–1826), Washburn allocated more space to European tunes than American, and in the process he eliminated Belcher tunes completely.

Belcher's tunes did not completely disappear in later years, but were included in several retrospective collections of the 1830s and 1840s which featured tunes by Billings and his contemporaries.[37] For example, *Ancient Harmony Revived,* published in Hallowell, Maine, includes four Belcher tunes in its second edition (1848).[38] Two tunes are also attributed to Belcher in the *Stoughton Musical Society's Centennial Collection* of 1878.[39] Belcher was probably included because of his reputation as an early American psalmodist, not just because he was a Stoughton native.

In conclusion, while the tunes of James Lyon had a limited impact in Maine, partly because there were fewer of them and they were composed well before the heyday of Maine psalmody, some of Supply Belcher's were included in nearly all the Maine tunebooks of the early nineteenth century and in several of the retrospective collections published later in the century. Only one Maine tunebook followed Belcher's model of a single-composer collection; however, the later ones were similar to his (and to most other tunebooks of the period) in containing a varied assortment of tunes, suitable for both churches and singing schools.

CHAPTER VII

ABRAHAM MAXIM

Abraham Maxim was a "typical" late-eighteenth-century immigrant to Maine. Like many others, he was raised in a large family in a small southeastern Massachusetts town. When he came of age, he was attracted by the land and opportunities available on the northeastern frontier. He settled in an inland area of Maine, where he married and raised a large family of his own. As his children began to reach maturity, he moved further inland to obtain a new plot of land on which to establish them with their own farms. Unlike most other Maine immigrants, though, Maxim had special skills and interest in music.

Abraham Maxim was born on January 3, 1773, in Plympton (now Carver), Massachusetts.[1] Plympton was a town of about seventeen hundred residents at the time.[2] His parents had grown up in the same area: his father, John "Muxham,"[3] was from Plympton; his mother, the former Martha Norris, was from nearby Wareham.[4] They had married on July 29, 1767 at the First Church of Wareham, where Martha had been baptized as an infant.[5] Their children included five sons and three daughters.[6] Although some of the children later left the area for greater opportunities, John and Martha Muxham probably remained in the Carver area throughout their lives.[7]

As the second son, Abraham Maxim was undoubtedly expected to assist his father and brothers in the various chores associated with farm life in rural New England. From early youth, however, he was noted for his love of singing and an unusual fondness for music which sometimes hindered his usefulness on the farm. When involved in composing, which he began while still young, he was oblivious to everything else and "would be as likely to take a basket to bring water from the well, as a pail."[8] Several of the tunes he composed in Carver were later printed in tunebooks he prepared in Maine.[9]

Of his training, we learn from Simeon Cheney that "he studied music a while with William Billings, in Boston."[10] Although Boston was a considerable distance (approximately thirty-three miles) from Plympton, Maxim may have attended some sessions of a Billings singing school while in Boston to help market farm goods or obtain needed supplies. Trips all the way to Boston just to attend singing school alone would not have been practical. Another possibility is that Billings held a singing school in Plympton, although there is no documentation that he did. Even if Maxim did study with Billings, "a while" may refer to just a few meetings. Regardless of how limited the sessions were, Maxim may have wanted to claim Billings, the best-known American singing-school figure of the 1780s, as his teacher.

In recalling Maxim's musical background, Flora Barry, his grandniece, noted that "for the day in which he lived, he acquired a thorough knowledge of its principles."[11] Most American psalm-tune composers of the eighteenth century had only limited musical training, often confined to little more than singing-school attendance, "a study of the music and rules for composition in British and American tunebooks, and practical musical experience."[12]

There is no reason to suspect that Maxim's training was any more extensive. An examination of his compositions[13] suggests that he probably acquired much of his musical knowledge from personal study of tunebooks and from the practical experience of composing tunes similar to those he observed in the tunebooks. His family may have been too poor to afford private music lessons for the children, even if qualified teachers were available.[14]

His published tunes are limited primarily to the less complicated genres of plain tunes, tunes with extension, and fuging-tunes.[15] He appears to have published only a few anthems and set-pieces, extended pieces which were more difficult to write.[16] His tunes, like those of most Yankee psalmodists, appear to follow the contrapuntal rules of William Tans'ur, rather than the principles of European tonal harmony.[17]

In addition to singing and composing, Maxim's musical abilities extended to playing at least one musical instrument: the bass viol.[18] He is known to have performed on it at social gatherings such as "music parties," and probably was called upon to play it to support the psalm-singing in church.[19] His skill at the bass viol may also have been utilized when he later became a choir leader: choristers sometimes led the singing while playing the bass viol, or at the very least, used it to set the opening pitches for the singers. One of Maxim's siblings, John Jr., played the violin. Perhaps other family members were also musical, at least enough to "try out" the tunes he composed as a boy.

Sometime after Maxim came of age, he moved to Turner, Maine, probably in the 1790s.[20] Although there is no information available as to what prompted the move, it seems likely that he needed his own land on which to farm once he reached the age to set up his own household. In southeastern Massachusetts, where families had been farming and subdividing the family plot for their children for several generations, land was becoming scarce. In the District of Maine, however, land was plentiful and cheap. Maxim, one of the many young people from Massachusetts who journeyed to Maine to take advantage of the opportunities there, probably did not head off for the region alone.[21] The usual practice was for several brothers or other relatives (sometimes neighbors) to move to the frontier together, sometimes after one of them had first investigated the area.

Turner is located in western Maine, more than thirty miles north of the nearest coastline and about forty miles due north of Portland. A travelling missionary who visited the town in 1796 remarked on its flourishing agriculture.[22] Like many other inland settlements in Maine, Turner experienced growth in the late eighteenth century. The town's population, tallied as 356 in 1790, had doubled by 1800.[23]

Although Maxim was probably one of Turner's residents by 1800, Massachusetts and Maine records of the 1800 census neither confirm nor deny that he was even in Maine by that year.[24] One of the first official verifications of his settlement in Turner is the record of his marriage there in 1801 to Anna Merrill, a Turner native:

> Abraham Mackham [*sic*] and Anna Merrill both of Turner were joined in marriage Sept. the 11th 1801 by Ichabod Bonney Esq.[25]

Maxim's bride, seven years younger than he, was the daughter of Jabez and Hannah (Sawyer) Merrill. Her paternal grandfather was Deacon Daniel Merrill, a venerable member of the community.

Deacon Merrill had come to Turner in 1776 from New Gloucester, Maine, where he had served as deacon in the first church there. He led informal worship services in Turner before a formal church was organized in the town.[26]

Prior to his marriage at age twenty-eight, Maxim had experienced at least one unsuccessful love affair. Following a "serious disappointment in love," he planned to commit suicide, according to a story recounted by his grandniece, Flora Barry, in an 1894 Boston newspaper article.[27] She claimed that Maxim, planning to end his life, set off with a rope into the deep forest between the Owl's Head and Streaked Mountain in Paris, Maine. While sitting down in a deserted logging camp, he heard the plaintive song of a sparrow whose nest had been disturbed. Inspired, he decided to leave some lines which might be read by his lost lover; he wrote the following lines (verse 4 of Isaac Watts's Psalm 102) on a piece of birch bark:

As on some lonely building top
The sparrow tells her moan,
Far from the tents of joy and hope,
I'll sit and grieve alone.

After setting the poem to an appropriately plaintive melody in minor, he became so involved in fitting the other vocal parts to the tune (later to be called HALLOWELL) that he forgot his troubles. When he had completed the arrangement to his satisfaction, he was eager to hear how it would sound as performed by "his competent choir." "His love of life returned," and he decided not to commit suicide after all. Throwing away his rope, he headed home "and became a very popular and useful man."[28] The story, if true, suggests that he already was directing a choir at the time, which must have been in the 1790s, after his move to Maine and before his marriage in 1801.

Less than a year after his marriage, Maxim's first tunebook, *Oriental Harmony,* was published by Henry Ranlet of Exeter, New Hampshire. The preface is dated "Turner, July, 1802." Maxim had probably been preparing the tunebook during the winter and early spring months, while there was a lull in farm activities. Unlike his later collections, *Oriental Harmony* contains only Maxim's music: thirty-seven hymn- or psalm-tunes and two anthems, following the customary "rudiments of music" section.

Since Maxim had been composing for some time, some of the tunes were probably composed in Massachusetts and perhaps renamed to reflect his Maine surroundings.[29]

Maxim may have had the collection published for use in a singing school which he instructed. Although he is known to have taught singing schools, specific dates for them have not been determined. The fact that he wrote a tunebook "designed chiefly for the use of singing schools, and worshipping assemblies" in 1802 may suggest that he had already begun teaching in Maine by that date.[30]

The nature of his next tunebook, *Northern Harmony,* published three years later in 1805, implies that Maxim may have learned some things about marketability from his first venture.[31] *Northern Harmony,* which has nearly three times as many pages as *Oriental Harmony,* is not limited to Maxim tunes, but contains those by other composers as well. Still, he apparently contributed thirty-four new tunes of his own to *Northern Harmony,* a fact which suggests that he continued to be active as a composer during the three years since *Oriental Harmony* was published.[32]

A second edition of *Northern Harmony,* published in 1808, contains fifty-four more pages. Nearly half of the fifty-one additional tunes were by Maxim himself; these twenty-two tunes had not been published in his previous publications, suggesting his continued compositional activity between the years 1805 and 1808.[33] Maxim made a point of noting that "the additional Music is mostly *American,* from an idea that the European Music, is less agreeable to the American ear, than her own."[34]

In Massachusetts proper, reform collections were beginning to exclude American tunes from their repertories.[35] Maxim's American tunes and patriotic sentiments, however, were probably well received by independent-minded fellow Mainers. Through his teaching, Maxim was aware of the musical preferences of area residents and probably geared his tunebooks to their interests. That he succeeded in meeting their needs is suggested by the fact that *Northern Harmony* was published in a total of five editions, extending over a fourteen-year period.

Meanwhile, in the years between the publications of the first and second editions of *Northern Harmony,* Maxim became a father for the first time. Abraham and Anna Maxim eventually had a total of ten children, with eight of them surviving infancy.[36] Since Cheney refers to Maxim's sons and daughters as "singing children," the family may have enjoyed evenings of music making together. Characterized as "a very cheerful, happy man," Maxim had the temperament to encourage his children in their musical efforts.[37]

In addition to teaching singing schools, Maxim is said to have taught "reading schools" in Turner.[38] Both types of schools would have occupied his time for only a few months in the winter. Singing schools were most commonly scheduled for the months from November to February. "Reading schools," or "common schools" as they were usually called, were held for a few weeks or months in the summer and winter. Men frequently taught only during the winter terms, carrying on farm work during the late spring, summer, and early fall. Young ladies most often took over teaching responsibilities for the summer sessions, which were attended only by younger children.[39]

Although some of the teachers were college educated, there is no indication that Maxim was so trained. His education was probably limited to whatever common school instruction he received as a boy in Plympton. Formal schooling for most New Englanders—particularly those living in rural areas—was limited to summer and winter terms (five or six months a year) up to the age of ten or twelve and winter terms for several more years.[40] Such training, combined with a great deal of reading (resulting from his "natural taste for literature"),[41] may have been all the preparation Maxim had for teaching. The subjects he taught in Turner probably consisted of spelling, geography, handwriting, arithmetic, and reading.[42]

Although there is no direct evidence that Maxim spent his summers in farm work, it is doubtful whether teaching and compiling alone would have been sufficiently remunerative to support his family of ten. Especially in a rural area like Turner, a trade (such as music) needed to be combined with other activities, often subsistence farming, to provide enough to live on. Such, at least, was the advice offered in 1827 by Zadoc Long of Buckfield (the town just west of Turner) to his brother-in-law, Isaac Ellis, who was thinking of becoming a shoemaker in Turner:

> I have made enquiries respecting Turner as being an eligible place for another shoemaker, but cannot ascertain as you would find sufficient encouragement there. You must be aware that no such town in the country will afford a man

> much of an income who relies solely upon his trade. In the country he must unite with it other advantages such as speculation or cultivating the soil to render his gains ample. As your wife is willing and anxious to live on a farm and to assist you all in her power by the labor of her hands, it might be well for you to procure a snug little place where you can till the ground, raise some stock, have a small dairy, do something at your trade, and try if you cannot make several things work together to produce a competence.[43]

Abraham Maxim had the assistance of a wife, as well as numerous children, to help him with the farm activities. The combination of composing, compiling, teaching, and farming were most likely sufficient for Maxim "to produce a competence."

These activities, plus the responsibilities of a large family, may have prevented Maxim from taking an active role in town government. Turner town meeting records from 1800 to 1829 do not mention Maxim as having served as an elected or appointed town official. French's *History of Turner,* published in 1887, has only one reference to Maxim: as a petition signer.[44]

The petition suggests Maxim's probable religious affiliation in Turner was Universalist. Although he most likely attended Plympton's "Standing Order" Congregational church as a boy,[45] the petition he signed in Turner requested the incorporation of a religious parish named "The First Universal Gospel Parish in Turner."[46] The petition, directed to the Massachusetts General Court and dated December 24, 1803, was also signed by Maxim's father-in-law, Jabez Merrill, and fifty other male inhabitants of Turner.[47]

Like the residents of many frontier towns in Maine, those in Turner were not unanimous in their support of the state-mandated church.[48] Maine's inland areas, which were slower to establish a local Congregational church and minister (partly due to ministerial shortages after the Revolution), were popular preaching grounds for itinerant evangelists of Methodist, Baptist, and Universalist persuasion. These denominations attracted many converts in newly settled areas of Maine during the first few decades of the nineteenth century. Maxim's apparent alliance with the Universalists rather than the Congregationalists is not surprising, but was in keeping with the typical frontier desire to be independent of the establishment.

The townspeople of Turner had previously been split by the formation of a Baptist society in 1792. Some felt that the society had only been formed so its members could avoid financing the town's tax-supported minister; similar suspicions were voiced about the incipient Universalists. The journal of Rev. Paul Coffin, whose missionary tours of Maine included a stop in Turner, describes the unfortunate religious state of the town in 1796:

> This town is twenty-five years old and yields to few inland towns in America for its agriculture. Yet 'tis dispirited in religion, tired of its minister, and vexed by a party of Baptists and its own covetousness. Such are the circumstances of this lovely town! The sight of it will make a man wish it virtuous and mentally improved. Indeed he is loth to believe it is not so.[49]

In spite of the objections of some residents, the act of incorporation for the Universalist Society was passed on February 16, 1805.[50] While the Universalists employed a number of preachers in the first few decades of the nineteenth century, they met mostly in homes until they built their own church in 1825 (a couple of years before Maxim left the area).[51]

Beyond his signature on the initial petition, the extent of Maxim's involvement with the Turner Universalist Society cannot be determined, since the extant church records date only from the late nineteenth century. However, his publication in 1818 of a hymnbook for "the Church Universal"—a book which included texts by such Universalist writers as H. Ballou—suggests that he still inclined toward Universalist beliefs, or at least that he perceived a need among the Universalists for their own hymnbook.[52] Although Abraham Maxim's name does not appear on the title page, he deposited the book with the Clerk of the District Court of Maine to obtain copyright, claiming to be its proprietor.[53]

The book, which contains texts only, is entitled *The Gospel Hymn-Book; Being a Selection of Hymns Composed by Different Authors Designed for the use of the Church Universal; and adapted to Public and Private Devotion.* The preface clearly emphasizes the Universalist doctrine that *all* mankind will be restored to holiness and happiness in a future state and that salvation will be brought "unto all the human race without one solitary exception."[54]

With such a hymnbook, the Universalists in Turner and other areas could adapt Universalist texts (in keeping with their doctrinal positions) to tunes in whatever tunebooks they may have been using. Regardless of his personal religious beliefs, Maxim, like other compilers, undoubtedly sought to make his sacred music collections suitable for the use of all denominations. By publishing a small, denomination-specific hymnbook for the Universalists, he could provide them with suitable texts without jeopardizing the sales of his tunebooks to a number of different religious societies.

Prior to publishing *The Gospel Hymn-Book,* Maxim had prepared two additional editions of *Northern Harmony;* both were "corrected, improved and enlarged." The third edition was published in 1810, the fourth in 1816. The latter included Japheth C. Washburn's name on the title page along with Maxim's.[55]

Maxim and Washburn (who is the subject of Chapter VIII) lived fairly close to one another at several times in their lives. Both were born and raised in Plymouth County, Massachusetts. Maxim and Washburn's father were both born in what was to become Carver. Washburn himself was born and apparently grew up in Rochester, Massachusetts, just a short distance away. There is even a possibility that Washburn and Maxim may have been distantly related.[56]

An even more likely time for acquaintance may have been after they both moved to Maine. Maxim and Washburn had settled respectively in Turner and Wayne before 1800. Since the towns were less than ten miles apart, it is possible that Washburn received some musical instruction from Maxim, either in a singing school or on an individual basis. Maxim, who was approximately seven years older than Washburn, was old enough to be his singing-school teacher.

Perhaps the most conclusive evidence of an early acquaintance between the men is the fact that Washburn's first four published tunes received their initial printings in Maxim's tunebooks: NEW-MILFORD and NEW-PLYMOUTH in the 1805 first edition of *Northern Harmony,* PASSION and WATERFORD in the 1808 second edition. All four tunes are marked "Original," a term often used to designate a tune's first printing.

Although Washburn left Wayne in 1803 or 1804 for Fairfax (later to become China), about thirty-five miles northeast, he must have kept in contact with Maxim, at least to some extent. Washburn's first published compilation, *Parish Harmony* (1813), includes a never-before published Maxim tune (NORTH-HAMPTON) as well as two Maxim tunes (MACHIAS and TURNER) previously printed in both *Oriental Harmony* and *Northern Harmony*. Curiously, the new Maxim tune, NORTH-HAMPTON, does not appear in any of Maxim's own tunebooks which are extant.

Washburn became the joint compiler with Maxim of the fourth edition of *Northern Harmony* (published in 1816) a few years after his *Parish Harmony* was printed. Since the third edition of *Northern Harmony* is not extant and the two extant copies of the fourth edition are incomplete,[57] Washburn's role cannot be definitively determined. Many of the fourth edition's fifty additional pages contain European tunes.[58] Still, the tunebook features at least seventeen previously unpublished tunes by Washburn, eighteen by Maxim.[59]

Maxim probably did not ask Washburn to be his co-compiler because he needed help in composing or choosing new tunes for the fourth edition. He compiled tunebooks alone both before and after the joint edition. More likely he anticipated that the inclusion of Washburn's name on the title page would increase sales, especially in the area where Washburn lived (later to become "China"). A justice of the peace and town official, Washburn was a man of some influence and status in his community. As a successful store-owner, he also had the means of promoting and disseminating his tunebooks locally and probably contributed some capital toward the joint publication.[60] He even had contacts in Boston through his service in the House of Representatives of the Massachusetts General Court, and could perhaps arrange for some distribution in that area.[61] Maxim had a smaller sphere of influence, limited perhaps to his singing-school students in the Turner area and whatever sales could be arranged by his Exeter (New Hampshire) publisher.[62]

Whatever the reasons for the partnership, Maxim and Washburn collaborated on only one edition. Two years later, Washburn compiled another tunebook on his own: the successful *Temple Harmony,* published in seven editions beginning in 1818. In 1819, Maxim followed with the fifth and final published edition of *Northern Harmony,* compiled without Washburn and touted on the title page as "corrected, improved, and enlarged."[63] He had used the same phrase for the third and fourth editions of *Northern Harmony,* apparently to assure purchasers that each new edition was bigger and better than previous ones.

Even though they went on to edit tunebooks independently, there appears to have been no ill will between the onetime collaborators. In his preface to *Temple Harmony* (1818), Washburn states that since his "connection" with Abraham Maxim had been dissolved, he was authorized to publish all the tunes from *Northern Harmony*. Had there been animosity between the two, such permission would probably not have been granted. Although he indicated in the preface that he had eliminated "about thirty tunes" from the joint edition, the actual count was at least seventy.[64] Still, difference of opinion regarding selection is not likely to have been the reason they went their separate ways. Their subsequent independent editions are strikingly similar, to the point that they even contain large "chunks" of pages which correspond exactly.[65]

One of the Maxim tunes contained within the identical *Temple Harmony/Northern Harmony* sections is WOODSTOCK. Although Maxim is said to have written the song to celebrate the wedding of Abigail Whitman of Buckfield, Maine, to Capt. Jonathan Cole of Woodstock, Maine, the tune had already been published two years before the wedding.[66] Even if the tune was not newly composed for the occasion, the legend that the song "was subsequently sung with great unction by the wedding guests"[67] may be true. The account highlights the participatory nature of psalmody: the tune was sung *by* the wedding guests, not *to* the wedding guests.

According to Cheney, Maxim moved in December 1827 to Palmyra, Maine, where he farmed and taught for only about sixteen months before he died.[68] Palmyra is about sixty miles northeast of Turner and further inland. Because Turner was becoming more crowded[69] and Maxim's oldest children were coming of age (the eldest was twenty-one years old in 1827), it is likely that he moved so that he could provide them with their own plots of land.

At the time Maxim moved to Palmyra, it was still a relatively new settlement. First settled around 1800 and incorporated in 1807, its population by 1820 was only 336, slightly less than Turner's population in 1790.[70] Since Palmyra was further from the coast than Turner, land may also have been cheaper there. In addition, Maxim's land in Turner may have become depleted from nearly thirty years of planting; the untilled soil in Palmyra held the promise of greater productivity.

Histories relating to the area and census records confirm that the four Maxim sons made the trip to Palmyra with their parents; three of them are listed as heads of families there in 1840.[71] At least three of the four daughters probably moved to Palmyra with their parents, too. The two youngest ones, Clarissa and Nancy, would have been only five and eight years of age in December 1827, the date of the move. Daughter Sophorona Maxim married Snow Keene, who had also moved to Palmyra in 1827.[72] The other Maxim daughter, Clementina, would have been twenty years old in 1827; although she may have travelled to Palmyra with the rest of the family, she was old enough to have married and stayed in the Turner area.

We know little about Maxim's life in Palmyra other than the fact that he farmed and continued to teach. Palmyra was first and foremost a farming community. Even in 1883, half a century later, nearly all the residents of Palmyra were listed in the town directory as "farmers."[73] How much land Maxim owned and how it was distributed after his death cannot be determined, since his name is not found in the Somerset County Registry of Deeds or in probate records.

Abraham Maxim apparently attained a certain reputation in Palmyra for his musical activities, even though his life there was brief. *The East Somerset County Register, 1911–12* notes that he was "a well known hymn writer and taught singing school in Palmyra years ago."[74]

By 1820, Palmyra had several church groups, but none of the Universalist persuasion: the Baptists met in the "Ell,"[75] the Christian Church in the South Union School, and the Methodists were organizing for the first time. The first religious meetings in town were held in homes and later in schools until churches were built.[76] His son Sullivan's known affiliation with the Baptists—he became a Baptist minister a decade after his father's death—may or may not imply that Abraham Maxim joined with the Baptists.[77]

Abraham Maxim died suddenly of apoplexy one night "just after leaving his singing school, at the age of fifty-six."[78] He supposedly "dropped dead in the Road with MS copy of his 6th Ed. [of *Northern Harmony*] in his pocket," according to information written by Williams Latham (1803–1883) inside a copy of *Northern Harmony,* second edition, now in the possession of the Massachusetts Historical Society.[79] Latham had purchased the tunebook from Abraham's brother, John Maxim. According to Latham, Abraham Maxim died on March 28, 1829, and his wife died forty-seven years later, a few days short of her ninety-sixth birthday.[80]

Although there is no evidence to support Latham's statement that Maxim had a new edition of *Northern Harmony* in manuscript and "ready for the press [in] 1826," there is no reason to doubt it, either. It would have been surprising if Maxim had not composed any new tunes since the fifth edition of *Northern Harmony* was published in 1819. In addition, he may have wanted to prepare a new tunebook suitable for the singing school he taught in Palmyra. With all the interest in "scientific" music, promoted by Mason, Hastings, and others, Maxim may have wanted to update his tunebook to reflect the European music preferences of Americans in the 1820s.[81]

Although Abraham Maxim is known by only a few music scholars today, he was recognized as a well-known hymn writer, at least in parts of New England, well into the nineteenth century.[82] Nineteenth-century historian William Lapham refers to Maxim as a "well-known musical composer . . . whose 'Turner,' 'Hallowell,' 'Hebron' &c., have been sung at almost every fireside in the land."[83] The unidentified writer of a *Boston Transcript* article noted that Maxim "became an eminent composer" and was "the author of many of the most popular melodies now known as Continentals" (melodies firmly established throughout the country by their long use).[84] The tune HALLOWELL, sung by both choir and class, was said to have been "the most popular tune in the singing-books" in years gone by: "when our grandsires and their dames were young," according to this 1894 writer, who claimed that Maxim's tunes were among the most popular melodies not only in his own state, but "throughout the Union."[85]

While these writers may be overstating the popularity of Maxim's tunes, several of them were included in later nineteenth-century retrospective collections: HALLOWELL in *Ancient Harmony Revived,* sixth edition (1855), and TURNER, BUCKFIELD, and PORTLAND in *Father Kemp's Old Folks Concert Music* (1860), for example.[86] Edwards notes that some of Maxim's tunes appeared on programs of the Old Stoughton Musical Society as late as 1926.[87]

Although his tunebook collections did not achieve the widespread popularity of *Village Harmony* or the *Bridgewater Collection, Northern Harmony* must have had sufficient local success to warrant the issuance of five editions. Most of the other Maine tunebooks of the time (with the exception of Washburn's *Temple Harmony*) appeared, at most, in only two editions.

In addition to his reputation as a composer and compiler, Maxim has a legacy as a teacher. He is said to have been a cheerful, happy man, with a love of music since childhood. Surely his enthusiasm inspired at least some of his students. There is a strong likelihood that he was a mentor to Japheth Coombs Washburn in his musical endeavors, and he probably guided many others whose sole musical activity was singing or whose tunes were never published.[88]

As a teacher and frontier resident, Maxim was in a good position to know the musical needs and interests of his fellow settlers in inland Maine. His life was probably not unlike the lives of many other rural Maine citizens in the early nineteenth century. Because he was not in the public eye in an official capacity as Japheth Coombs Washburn was, we know fewer specifics about his life; farming and teaching school are professions which leave scant trace on the public record. The available evidence suggests that he led a rather ordinary existence, supporting his family and indulging in his favorite pastime: music. His experiences permitted him to write tunes and compile collections which were compatible with central Maine preferences.

CHAPTER VIII

JAPHETH COOMBS WASHBURN

Like Abraham Maxim, Japheth Coombs Washburn was born in Plymouth County, Massachusetts, and emigrated to the Maine frontier in the 1790s. He, too, had a large family, composed music, and compiled collections; however, in other respects, his life was quite different from Maxim's. Far from being an ordinary farmer, Washburn made his living by buying and selling real estate and merchandise. He was an active community leader who served as postmaster, town clerk, justice of the peace, and representative to the Massachusetts General Court. Music was just one of his many interests.

His parents were also natives of Plymouth County in southeastern Massachusetts. His father, Japheth Washburn,[1] was born on September 11, 1746, in Carver (then Plympton), where Abraham Maxim was born twenty-seven years later. This Japheth (the father of Japheth Coombs Washburn) was the ninth of ten children born to Ephraim and Mary (Polen) Washburn.[2] Japheth's wife, the former Priscilla Coombs, was born in nearby Rochester, Massachusetts, on November 1, 1745.[3] They were married on September 28, 1768.[4]

Contrary to custom, they established their home in her hometown (Rochester) rather than his.[5] Normally a married son would set up his farm on part of his father's land; however, by the time Japheth, one of the youngest sons, reached maturity, there may not have been enough left of the family land in Carver to distribute any to him.

Less than a year after his marriage, Japheth Washburn (the father) appeared before John Fearing, His Majesty's Justice of the Peace, for breaking the Sabbath. The entry in Fearing's records reads as follows, using original spelling and punctuation:

> May th 10 Day 1769 then Parsonly appeared Japhath washburn and acknowledged himself Gilty of a Breach of Sabbath In traveling From my hous onto Zaphanier Bumps on the 16 Day of april on a arond To Git Benjamin Benson to worck for him and he hath paid Ten Shillings as a Fine To me John Fearing Justis of peace.[6]

Although the transgression was minor, the incident suggests that Japheth Washburn was a pragmatic man whose actions, on occasion, were guided by circumstances, rather than the letter of the law. Years later, his son, Japheth Coombs Washburn, would also be judged guilty—by his church peers—of actions falling short of Biblical standards.

As a loyal patriot, Japheth (the father) served in the American Revolution as a minuteman in Capt. Edward Hammond's Company on April 19, 1775.[7] By that time, he and Priscilla had become parents of a daughter and a son, with another son on the way: Polly, born March 9, 1770; Zalmuna (male), September 11, 1772; and Abisha (male), June 8, 1775.[8] Their later children included two more daughters—Chloe, born June 28, 1777, and Priscilla, born April 18, 1786—as well as a third son, Japheth Coombs Washburn, who was the fifth of the six children.[9]

J. C. Washburn, as he was sometimes called, was born on January 20, 1780, in Rochester, Massachusetts.[10] Although nothing is known about his childhood, he probably grew up on a farm, where he was expected to help his father and brothers. His education may have consisted of attendance at common school for several months in the winter until his teenage years. His boyhood was probably much like that of many other eighteenth-century New England farm boys, including Abraham Maxim, who grew up in Carver (then Plympton), less than ten miles away.

After the Revolutionary War, many residents of the Buzzard's Bay region in Massachusetts left the area for other places, including the "frontier": regions such as Ohio and the District of Maine.[11] The Washburns were among those who ventured north to Maine in the last decade or so of the eighteenth century, probably drawn by the appeal of inexpensive land which could be passed on to the sons, who reached maturity in the early 1790s.

The Washburns settled in central Maine in the rapidly growing small town of Wayne in Kennebec County.[12] They undoubtedly chose the town on the recommendation of Japheth's sister Lydia, who had settled in Wayne with her husband, Samuel Norris, in 1784 or 1785.[13] Frontier settlers often chose to establish homes where they had relatives who could serve as a support system during their early days in a new area.

Although it is uncertain exactly when their emigration took place, the 1798 direct tax valuation establishes Japheth Washburn (the father) as the owner of a dwelling and thirty acres of land in Wayne, Maine, in that year, suggesting an arrival by the mid-1790s.[14] The 1800 census implies that both Japheth and Priscilla and probably all six children were in Maine by then, based on the listing of the household headed by "Japhet Washburn" of Kennebec County, Maine.[15] All three Washburn sons set up their own households in Wayne: Zalmuna by 1797 (when his first child was born), Abisha and Japheth C. in the following decade.[16]

Japheth C. purchased a small tract of land in Wayne on March 25, 1802,[17] probably in preparation for his marriage on April 18, 1802, to Mrs. Betsy (or Betsey) Lowney of neighboring Monmouth, Maine.[18] By July, a house frame had been put up on his lot; the dwelling was apparently substantially complete by winter.[19] The Washburns' first child, daughter Abra Lowney, was born the following year (February 14, 1803).[20]

Although the 1802 land deeds identify him as a yeoman, several 1803 land documents refer to him as a trader, suggesting that he may have begun a small mercantile business in Wayne.[21] It is unclear where he got the capital to begin in business, although young businessmen frequently began their careers by signing notes to creditors.[22] His father and brothers were farmers.[23]

What made him turn to a completely different occupation? Perhaps as the youngest son, he may have been in a similar situation to his father when he reached maturity: perhaps the family property had been divided among his older siblings with little left for him. Without land to farm on, he needed to find another occupation. Another possibility is that he had little taste for farming and had the wits and inclination to do something else. Many of his adult activities witness to his independent nature, his apparent desire for recognition, and his willingness to take risks. A career in business meshed perfectly with his personal characteristics.

Sometime during his early years in Wayne (probably between 1800 and 1804), Japheth probably attended a singing school taught by Abraham Maxim, who lived in nearby Turner.[24] He may have learned to compose through the instruction of Maxim, who published two tunes by Washburn in the first edition of *Northern Harmony* (1805) and two additional ones in the second edition (1808). Washburn's older brother Abisha may also have studied under Maxim; years later, when be began publishing tunebooks, Japheth included a tune called WAYNE by an "A. Washburn," most likely his brother.[25]

Japheth C. Washburn served in an official capacity in Wayne as early as August 1801, when he was elected town constable, a position he seems to have retained through March 1804.[26] As a young man of twenty-one, he was already taking an active role in government and would continue to do so well into his fifties.

Sometime in 1803 or 1804,[27] Japheth, Betsy, and infant daughter Abra moved approximately thirty-five miles northeast to Fairfax (later to become China), Maine,[28] where their second child, Oliver Wendell Washburn, was born on October 17, 1804. After they settled in Fairfax, Betsy gave birth to four more children: Rowland Freeman Washburn, born October 5, 1806; Elvira Almeda Washburn, July 9, 1808; William Vinal Vaughan Washburn, July 11, 1810; and Harrison Gray Otis Washburn, March 12, 1812.[29]

Japheth C. Washburn and his young family were among the earliest settlers at the north end of Twelve-Mile Pond (now China Lake), the area now called China Village. Washburn's move to Fairfax seems to have prepared the way for his brothers and parents to relocate to the area.[30] Having lived in Wayne for only about five years, Washburn may have been drawn by the prospect of less competition in Fairfax, which was still largely wilderness; settlement in that locale had only begun in the mid-1770s.

In 1804, soon after his arrival, Japheth Coombs Washburn opened a store, the first at the north end of the lake. Although he ran into difficulty early—his store burned down in December 1806—he persevered and built another one across the street.[31] The store must have done well, because by around 1812 he had the funds to open a new, related business while continuing to operate the store: he started the first tavern in the north end of town. The tavern also burned, although the date is uncertain.[32] Washburn's businesses also included a potash works, established sometime prior to 1818.[33]

As a merchant, he served as a middleman between the small

producers who were his neighbors and the external markets and supplies of trade goods which they needed.[34] Men in his profession, a small minority in any town, were viewed as a mixed blessing by the farmer-producers who made up the majority: although merchants were necessary and could stimulate the growth of a community, they could also be economic parasites, due to their position as nonproducers.[35] Still, Washburn seems to have earned the respect of his fellow townspeople through his hard work, perseverance, and contributions to the community. He also seems to have made a good profit.[36]

A later ad for his store suggests the type of stock he carried:

> an extensive assortment of GOODS; comprising as great a variety as is offered at any store in the county. Among which are, W.I. GOODS & GROCERIES; HARD, HOLLOW, CROCKERY & GLASS WARE; EUROPEAN, INDIA & AMERICAN GOODS; DRUGS & MEDICINES; DYE-STUFFS, OIL & PAINTS; BOOKS & STATIONARY, &c. &c. &c. All of which may be purchased upon accommodating terms.[37]

In the course of supplying his store with an assortment of books, he may have had the opportunity to view new music books as well. Even a glance at their contents would have revealed that European tunes were becoming more prevalent in many collections published by 1810 or later. He may have had the new trends in mind when he compiled his first tunebook, *Parish Harmony,* in 1813. The collection, which contained more European tunes than earlier Maine tunebooks, was sold at his store, as were his later publications.[38]

In addition to selling merchandise, Washburn frequently engaged in real estate transactions. Between 1802 and 1835, he was the grantee of twenty-seven land deeds and the grantor of twenty-six, in Kennebec County.[39] Although the monetary value of the typical transaction was fairly small, as was his profit margin, the frequency suggests that Washburn was engaged in land speculation, at least on a minor level.

In addition to being one of a small number of traders in town, Washburn was among the few who were appointed by the Governor and Council as a justice of the peace, suggesting that he must have had some contacts in the political establishment. Washburn may have been commissioned as early as 1803.[40] His post required him to keep the peace in his community and bring law violators to justice.

There were drawbacks to the prestigious position: it was not a lucrative office, and justices of the peace were sometimes put in the unenviable position of mediator between their neighbors and governmental authority.[41] More often, though, Washburn's duties consisted simply of performing marriages and issuing warrants for meetings. One of the fringe benefits was the coupling of the courtesy title "Esquire" to his name: Japheth C. Washburn, Esq.[42]

Perhaps because of his position as justice of the peace, he was sometimes appointed by the county probate court judge as a commissioner to examine the claims of creditors to local residents' estates.[43] The position of commissioner was apparently a fairly common sideline for gentlemen in that day: Squire Supply Belcher, another Maine tunebook compiler and also a justice of the peace, served as a commissioner in Farmington (his town of residence) from time to time.[44]

In addition to his selection as a justice of the peace, Washburn also received an appointment as postmaster of his town. Both positions were granted, at least theoretically, only to men who had integrity (and probably some connections in government). A justice of the peace was appointed for a seven-year term, with the expectation that he would "behave well" during that time.[45] A postmaster was presumed to be "a man accurate and punctual in business and of perfect Integrity, who would probably give extra Satisfaction to the people of [a community]."[46] Such a man, we assume, was Washburn.

He was the first postmaster for the post office established in Harlem on April 20, 1810. Following the incorporation of China, which included parts of Harlem, he became China's first postmaster on June 25, 1818; the town's first post office was in his store.[47] In discussing Harlem's early mail service, Grow describes the role of Washburn and his children as follows:

> At the north end of China Lake, for some years Japheth C. Washburn took care of mail. Sometime before 1810 his daughter Abra (later Mrs. Thomas Burrill) and son Oliver Wendell began carrying the mail once a week from Getchell's Corners (in Vassalboro) to Japheth's store. They trav-

> eled through the woods on horseback; Abra was about ten years old then, Oliver two years younger.[48]

The early Maine postmasters were the leading citizens of their towns and were usually prominent politically.[49] Washburn was no exception. On November 7, 1808, he was one of a group of Federal Republicans from Fairfax who voiced their disapproval of the national embargo laws, then almost a year old, as "highly injurious to our interests, and derogatory to the nation."[50]

As secretary, J. C. Washburne (*sic*) recorded the group's resolutions, later printed in the *Gazette of Maine* (Buckstown). Determined to support officials who would restore their former rights and privileges, those present were also prepared "to gird on our swords to defend our Independence and Liberties against any foreign invasion."[51] Too young to have served in the Revolution, Washburn strongly supported the principles for which his father had fought.

From 1812 to 1814, Washburn was Fairfax's representative to the state legislature, the Massachusetts General Court. He represented Harlem in the 1817–1818 term, China in the following two terms (1818–1820).[52] His most memorable act as a legislator was naming the town of China in 1818. In a letter written later to A. H. Abbott, who had apparently inquired about the early history of the town, he explains his role:

> I was in the Legislature of Mass. when China was incorporated—drew the Bill with the name *Bloomville*. The member from Bloomfield [another town in Maine] fearing it might cause the miscarriage of letters, I searched for a name which should not interfere with any Post Town. China being, with me, a favorite name, and there not being a post Town of the name in the U.S., *China* was substituted, and to which I have never heard an objection.[53]

William Bailey, in his history of the China Baptist Church, indicates that Washburn probably meant China was a favorite "tune" (rather than "name") since "*China* was his favorite hymn."[54]

Although Washburn did not become wealthy from his five terms in the legislature,[55] his position allowed him to spend several extended periods in Boston: monthlong legislative sessions were usually held at least twice a year.[56] While in Boston, Washburn certainly attended church services—it would have been impolitic not to—and probably heard sacred music sung from the latest tunebooks. He may also have attended art music concerts, a rarity in inland Maine.[57] After several years in the backwoods of Maine, exposure to Boston's musical culture may have rekindled his interest in music and his creative energy: the years from 1813 to 1827 were his most active as a composer and compiler.

In addition to exposing him to Boston music, his legislative stints must also have acquainted him with Boston musicians, particularly Oliver Holden, whose first term as a representative to the Massachusetts General Court coincided with Washburn's penultimate term (1818–19).[58] Although Holden was Washburn's senior by fifteen years, the two men had a great deal in common besides their musical pursuits. Both owned stores and were involved in extensive land dealings. Both were justices of the peace and active public officials in their respective towns. Perhaps most significantly, they had a brotherly bond through their Masonic and Baptist affiliations. Although there is no confirmation of a relationship between the men, Holden, an experienced psalmodist and singing-school teacher with many compositions and compilations to his credit, may have served as a mentor and musical advisor to the less experienced Washburn.[59] Washburn may also have met Nahum Mitchell, who was a fellow member of the Massachusetts House of Representatives during Washburn's first term (1812–13); Mitchell is believed to have been one of the compilers of the *Bridgewater Collection.*[60]

Regardless of which psalmodists Washburn may have met in the Boston area, his residence there during legislative sessions permitted him liaisons and musical experiences not accessible to fellow Maine composers. Abraham Maxim's teaching and farming responsibilities, for example, probably restricted him from making any extended trips outside his immediate area, once he moved to Maine.

In 1813, after he had been a legislator for a year and a half, Washburn published at his own expense his first sacred music collection of psalm- and hymn-tunes by various composers: *Parish Harmony*.[61] As a successful merchant who knew his intended market (singing schools and societies who could not afford the expense of larger volumes), he promoted the small size and price of *Parish Harmony*. At fifty cents a copy, it was about half the price of many tunebooks on the market.[62] Washburn augmented the book with nineteen additional tunes for an 1815 printing and twenty-four more pages for a late 1817 (or early 1818) third edition.[63]

At about the same time that he was enlarging *Parish Harmony,* he collaborated with Abraham Maxim on the fourth edition of Maxim's *Northern Harmony,* published in 1816.[64] Soon after, he began compiling another tunebook, called *Temple Harmony,* which was first published in the fall of 1818, during his fourth term as a legislator.

The five years between the publication of *Parish Harmony* (1813) and the first edition of *Temple Harmony* (1818) were his most prolific years as a hymn-tune composer. Prior to 1814, only fourteen tunes by Washburn had been published in tunebooks by Maine compilers.[65] Nineteen new Washburn tunes, seventeen of them marked "Original" to indicate first printing, appear in the 1816 *Northern Harmony* edition co-edited by Washburn and Maxim. Two years later, Washburn included at least fourteen additional tunes of his own (eight marked "Original") in the first edition of *Temple Harmony* (1818). The later extant editions of *Temple Harmony,* published in the 1820s, do not contain any additional tunes attributed to Washburn, implying that he may have stopped composing by 1820 or so.[66] (See Part III for a complete listing of his works.)

Only one of his published tunes, the set-piece VASSALBOROUGH, is an extended piece of the set-piece or anthem type, which were more difficult to write than psalm-tunes. Washburn's avoidance of these forms is not surprising since his principal teacher or mentor, Abraham Maxim, wrote only a handful of works in these categories and probably did not attempt to teach his students how to write in genres he himself had not mastered. Reflecting the trends of Maine psalmody in the second decade of the nineteenth century, half of the Washburn tunes published before 1815 were fuging-tunes, but most of those published after 1815 were plain tunes.[67]

Washburn's flurry of activity in composing and compiling sacred music, beginning around 1812, may have been partly inspired by his sojourns in Boston as a legislative representative, but another equally important factor may have been his spiritual awakening: he was baptized and added to the local Baptist church in October 1811,[68] and received as a member in July 1814.[69] Although he had probably attended church since childhood, the fact that he was baptized as an adult of thirty-one suggests a recent conversion experience.[70]

His profession of faith may have been accompanied by a greater interest in spiritual matters; perhaps he wanted to spend more time setting favorite sacred texts to music and producing collections of tunes which could be sung to God's glory. The publication date of his first tunebook (1813) and his most prolific period as a composer (1813–1818) are consistent with such a scenario.[71]

Although the records of Washburn's church, the First Baptist Church of China, do not indicate whether his tunebooks were used there, they may have been utilized by the choir, if not the congregation. *Parish Harmony,* in particular, was tailor-made for small country churches unable to afford larger books, churches where anthems were of limited usefulness.[72]

Washburn's grandson, Willis W. Washburn, in his "Reminiscences of the Old Church," contributes the following information about the music:

> The hymn books contained no music, as the congregation did not sing with the choir. The leader of the choir would select a suitable tune for the hymn.[73]

As one of the more musically knowledgeable local residents, Washburn may have been the leader of the church choir, at least occasionally.[74] Then as now, each member of the congregation was probably expected to use his or her God-given talents to benefit the others in the body of believers.

Regardless of whether he led the choir, Washburn was a busy man, and the year of 1818 was an especially momentous one for him. He participated in the naming and incorporating of China through his position as representative to the Massachusetts legislature. He became China's official postmaster. The first edition of his second tunebook, *Temple Harmony,* was published. He also became a widower.

Betsy, his wife of nearly sixteen years, died on April 13, 1818, at the age of thirty-six. Left with five surviving children, ages six to fifteen, to raise, he did not remain single for long. On September 17, 1818, he married Sarah Blish (born July 13, 1798), eighteen years his junior.[75] Sarah was to bear him four more children, all born in China.[76]

Sarah's presence relieved Washburn of having to manage his large household alone. At the same time, there were undoubtedly many adjustments to be made by all concerned as the responsibility of caring for five stepchildren (and soon her own infants, as well) was thrust upon the twenty-year-old Sarah, only five years older than stepdaughter Abra.

The early years of his marriage to Sarah coincided with Washburn's most active period in town government. He signed the warrant for China's first town meeting (held on March 2, 1818) in his capacity as a Kennebec County justice of the peace and was elected the town clerk at that meeting.[77] He continued as town clerk through 1821, and from 1830 through 1836.[78] He also served as a town selectman for three years, beginning in 1819, and was a member of numerous committees.[79]

Washburn's public involvements also included membership on the town's select school committee and on the board of trustees of China Academy.[80] His role in the educational system of China bears comparison with Abraham Maxim's in Turner. Although both men were actively involved with general education in their towns, Maxim actually taught, while Washburn appears to have served primarily in an oversight or administrative capacity. Maxim's occupation did not enhance his community standing: teaching was a rather low-status profession.[81] On the other hand, Washburn's position as secretary of the trustees of China Academy must have been of some prestige.

Not only was Washburn a trustee of the academy (at least in 1819 and from 1822 to 1827),[82] he is said to have "hewn the first timber" for the school's first building.[83] He also obtained a bell for the academy from Thomas L. Winthrop, former lieutenant governor of Massachusetts, "as a *present*—then worth $78": evidence of his continued connections with important political leaders.[84] His personal commitment to the academy extended to sending two of his sons there as students and boarding three of the female students in his home.[85]

Although he continued some of his activities, such as his trusteeship with China Academy, through the 1820s, Washburn seems to have realigned his priorities in the early years of the decade. After his term ended in February 1820, he did not serve again in the state legislature. His role in town government also flagged in the 1820s: although he continued to serve in minor capacities, his last term as selectman was in 1821, and he ceased being town clerk from 1821 until 1830.[86]

Perhaps he experienced what today would be called a mid-life crisis (he was forty in 1820); or perhaps his new wife, just becoming accustomed to her new burdens as wife and mother, was not so supportive of his political activity (and the absences they sometimes required) as his first wife had been. On the other hand, maybe Washburn simply tired of politics, and as a man of many interests, shifted his energies to other areas.

One continued interest was tunebook compilation. Although his composing seems to have ceased by 1820, he revised *Temple Harmony* for six editions which were published in the 1820s.[87] The tunebook must have been very successful to have been published in so many editions—more than any of the other Maine tunebooks, including Maxim's, and more than most others except the eclectic collections like *Village Harmony* and the *Bridgewater Collection.*

Although tunebooks were used for both singing schools and churches, the fact that Washburn published a new edition of *Temple Harmony* nearly every fall for a decade (1818–1827) suggests that he may have taught singing school during this period and that the new editions were timed to be newly published for the next singing school.[88] His position as legislative representative required his continual presence in Boston for much of January and February of 1813, 1814, 1818, 1819, and 1820. These Boston residences may have prevented him from teaching singing schools in Maine during these years, unless the schools started in October and finished in December or early January.[89]

During the 1820s, however, he was finally home in Maine during the winter months. Enthused by his exposure to music in Boston, he may have been eager not only to compose and compile tunes, but to hear his tunes performed and to pass on his knowledge to the residents of China and surrounding towns. Information written in a copy of the second edition of *Temple Harmony* indicates that it was carried to singing school by a seventeen-year-old girl in 1820, the same year it was published.[90] Washburn may have been the teacher of the singing school.

We know that Washburn taught music because his son-in-law, Thomas Burrill, included this information in a biographical sketch of Washburn: "He was a well known teacher and composer of music."[91] Other historical accounts of China and its residents make no reference to his musical activities. One reason may be that his documented service in the public sector, where more permanent records were kept, overshadowed his musical ventures.[92]

In addition, his musical endeavors were of comparatively limited duration in China: perhaps from 1813 to 1827 (the first and last publication years of his tunebooks). For the first decade after his arrival in China in 1803–4, he was probably occupied with clearing land, building a house and store, establishing his business, and raising his family. With his reputation and business firmly established by around 1820, he probably had more leisure to pursue music as an avocation, compiling tunebooks and possibly teaching singing school. After a devastating fire to his uninsured store in December 1826 destroyed his financial security, however, he probably found it necessary to focus on providing for his family, with the result that music became a lower priority in his life.

At the time of the fire, on Christmas Eve 1826, the store contained about seven thousand dollars worth of books, notes and other securities, joint property with Gustavus Benson, his former co-partner, as well as four thousand dollars worth of goods owned by Washburn.[93] The value of his property at the time of the fire, his third and most devastating one, suggests he had become a fairly well-to-do storekeeper.

The *Hallowell Gazette*'s account of the fire, which spread to several neighboring offices, includes the following:

> On Sunday night last, the store of Japheth C. Washburn, in China, with all its contents, was consumed by fire, in consequence of the bursting of a bottle of spirits of turpentine. The books and notes were all lost. The store had just been filled with a large stock of goods for the winter; and no insurance had been effected upon it.[94]

An article several days later in Hallowell's other weekly newspaper, the *American Advocate,* notes that "the flames were kindled so suddenly that there was no opportunity to remove any thing from the store."[95] One of the ironic aspects of the situation was that Washburn had recently made arrangements to insure his store and goods, and they would have been covered in a few days.[96]

A group of China citizens met after the fire and drafted a circular to be distributed around the town to solicit contributions for Washburn and Benson. The appeal, which describes Washburn's unfortunate experiences with fires, emphasizes Washburn's past industriousness and persistence. It explains that at age twenty-one, he had been "reduced to poverty and distress" by fire, but that in six years, "by a course of industry and rigid application to business" he had accumulated an estate worth about fifteen hundred dollars, consisting of a store, stock of goods, and house, when calamity (another fire) struck. This second fire came at a time "when this part of the country was so thinly settled that little or no effort could be made to extinguish the fire" and both store and house and all their contents were completely destroyed. Nevertheless, Washburn had made no appeal to his creditors to relinquish him from his debts but had worked diligently to pay them off.[97]

In fact, the circular continues, "a course of the most unremitted industry and strict economy, practised for a great number of years, had established him in circumstances of comparative ease and independence, when, for the third time, at an advanced period of life, with a numerous family, mostly dependent on him for support," fire struck again, reducing him to "absolute poverty."[98]

The circular's concluding assessment of Washburn suggests the high esteem in which he was held in China:

> Japheth C. Washburn, Esq. is a gentleman of high respectability and a valuable citizen; and there yet may be seen, in this place, many monuments of his enterprise and public spirit.[99]

As mentioned earlier, the fire, and accompanying life-style changes, may have contributed to the demise of his compilation activities. Washburn's accumulation of wealth, which allowed him to live in "comparative ease and independence" in the 1820s, had probably given him the leisure to engage in tunebook compilation; however, his reduction to "absolute poverty" in 1827 changed things considerably. Copies of the sixth edition of *Temple Harmony* had just come off the press a month before the fire;[100] those which Washburn had in his store were, of course, destroyed. A seventh edition, published the following year, was apparently his last tunebook.[101]

The upheaval which the fire caused in his life may also have exacerbated Washburn's difficulties with his church, difficulties which had begun a few years before the fire. Records pertaining to his early years in the church do not hint of future troubles. In September 1815, for example, he was one of three delegates sent from the church in Fairfax to a meeting of the Lincoln Association [of Baptist Churches], held at St. George, Maine. He even wrote the "Circular Letter"—an epistle of encouragement and exhortation—which is included in the printed pamphlet of the proceedings.[102] Several years later, in 1820, he was chosen to be on an ordination arrangements committee.[103] By the mid-1820s, though, his name was beginning to appear in the church records for reasons of discipline. Like other church bodies in those days, the collective membership of Washburn's church took an active role in overseeing the moral well-being of its members. Washburn's church frequently dispatched committees to call on those deemed errant for poor attendance, excessive drinking, or interpersonal difficulties.

The first situation concerning Washburn seems to have been some difficulties between him and Benjamin Libbey, Jr., caused by their use of "harsh" and "angry" words to each other. Church members took up the matter at a meeting in August 1824, but an outside council (consisting of elders and brethren from neighboring churches) was eventually called in, eight months later, to help settle the continuing difficulties.[104]

Although the dispute with Libbey did not jeopardize his church membership, over the next eight years, J. C. Washburn was dismissed from membership on several occasions, but was always allowed later to rejoin the fellowship.[105] Most often, the dismissals concerned Washburn's disagreements with another individual, and he was allowed to rejoin once he had confessed his wrongdoing. Sometimes other factors were involved. In May 1827, for example, the church was displeased with the manner in which he had returned to the meetinghouse and taken part in worship, contrary to a church vote; part of their ire stemmed from his assistance in setting up another meeting in town, following a voluntary withdrawal from the Baptist church. On another occasion, the members felt he had been drinking intoxicating liquors to excess. The periods of his exclusion from fellowship ranged from as little as eight months to as much as two years and five months at a time.

His frequent dismissals do not appear to have altered permanently members' opinions of him: he continued to be selected for various posts when he was a member in good standing. In November 1831, for example, he was chosen to be one of the messengers to a quarterly conference, and in February 1832, he was elected clerk pro tem and the member of a committee.[106]

Church members often seemed reluctant to deal with matters concerning Washburn, sometimes postponing consideration of such issues for several meetings. Exclusion from membership seems to have been their action of last resort after considerable conversations with him to no effect. The fact that he kept rejoining the church after his dismissals—and the fact that the church allowed him to rejoin—suggest mutual benefit.

What do these incidents suggest about Washburn's character and personality? First of all, his church dismissals mostly stemmed from interpersonal difficulties and do not necessarily reflect negatively on his personal faith. Second, while the incidents suggest an argumentative and stubborn nature, there may have been extenuating circumstances.[107] Third, a positive side of his stubbornness is that he was self-assured enough to follow his own conscience—and not be boxed in by the demands of his church—if he felt justified in his position. Finally, he was honest enough to admit on more than one occasion that he had been wrong.

These traits probably carried over to his musical activities. As a person of strong independence, Washburn probably composed tunes which pleased him personally and seemed right to him, regardless of whether they followed all the "rules" or pleased other people. He may have chosen tunes for his compilations on a similar basis, although, had he not kept public preferences in mind, his tunebooks would probably not have gone through multiple editions.

During the late 1820s, when Washburn was having difficulty pleasing his fellow church members, he may have found relief in the fellowship of his lodge brothers. He may have been the first resident Mason in town, and he was one of the founding members of China's Masonic Lodge (Central Lodge), chartered in 1824.[108]

Not content to be just a member of the lodge, Washburn served in a number of leadership roles. He provided the meeting place (the hall over his store) for the first organizational meeting in December 1823 and for subsequent meetings until his store burned down three years later.[109] Once Central Lodge was established, he was elected its first treasurer (1824). In succeeding years, he was elected to other important posts, including Senior Warden in 1825[110] and Master (the highest local officer) in 1826.[111]

Music was typically a part of certain Masonic rituals, including installation ceremonies. For example, when Washburn was installed as Master on July 19, 1826, a procession which had formed at the Masons' Hall "moved to the meetinghouse preceded by a band of music."[112] The lodge minutes do not indicate, however, that Washburn took any particular role in the musical activities. A professional Masonic lecturer, Brother Samuel Vudder,[113] a Pennsylvania native hired by the lodge to instruct the members—many of whom were "inexperienced craftsmen in the work of the Masonic temple"—was the one who introduced singing into the activities of Central Lodge. One of the hymns he taught them began "When shall we three meet like then"; it was "much admired" by the members.[114]

One of the appeals of Masonry for Washburn may have been the opportunity it gave him to achieve distinction as a lodge officer.[115] It is perhaps no coincidence that the last half of the 1820s, years when he was most involved with the lodge, coincided with a period when he did not serve in public office. His officer positions within the lodge may have fulfilled his need to be in charge and to receive the recognition and honor he had become accustomed to as a community leader. When the lodge ceased meeting in the late 1820s, "at the commencement of the Morgan excitement,"[116] Washburn reentered the public arena, serving a number of terms as China's town clerk, beginning in 1829.

Masonry may have had other appeals for Washburn. For example, it was a way for him to establish social ties with men of various classes in town, as well as to make contacts with Masons in other places, an important consideration for a merchant. With its symbolic content relating to craft labor, Masonry also allowed "gentlemen" like Washburn to assume the identity—if only symbolically—of an artisan producer, in an era when producers were valued as the most useful members of society.[117]

In the late 1820s and early 1830s, Washburn appears to have changed careers. He seems to have sold his store (apparently rebuilt after the fire) to his son Oliver Wendell Washburn in 1828.[118] Five years later, when the elder Washburn was fifty-three, he became a newspaper publisher. This profession occupied him off and on (several years at a time) for the next decade, both in China and in Calais, Maine, where he would move in 1837.

The Orb was the four-page, weekly newspaper Washburn published in China. The first issue appeared on December 5, 1833, the last in November 1836.[119] Washburn's venture did not receive much encouragement from local townspeople.[120] Howard Owen attributes the quarto's relatively short life to the fact that "the advertising and job work of that day were very light in that purely agricultural town."[121]

The masthead of *The Orb* featured a design with a globe in the center, erroneously described by one of his detractors (an Augusta newspaper editor) as "a ball of twine." Washburn's angry response leaves no doubt about his allegiance to his country and his belief in the rights of the people:

> It is *not* "*a ball of twine*" as you "Suppose," friend Severance, but is emblematical of the Globe—On one side of which, is a figure representing a Telescope, or Spy-glass. *That* is designed to show the enemies of our *country,* and of our *Government,* that they will be watched with the strictest scrutiny, and vigilance; and on the *other* side is the figure of a Writing Apparatus; which is to show that every attempt to wrest from the *people* their *Rights* and *Liberties;* and every act of *Tyranny* and *Oppression,* in whatever *Shape,* or NAME, or from whatever source it may eminate [*sic*] will be duly *recorded* and published to the *world.*[122]

Grow describes the typical content of the various pages in *The Orb* and provides an excellent summary of some of Washburn's major endorsements. For example, he was a strong supporter of President Andrew Jackson and agreed with Jackson's arguments against the national bank; he also favored the building of railroads through China.[123] On the personal side, a Washburn editorial comment in 1834 indicates that eight years after his fire, he was still struggling to recoup his losses.[124]

J. C. Washburn is sometimes listed on the masthead of *The Orb* as "General Agent" or "Agent," sometimes as "Editor." The name of his son William V. V. Washburn (age twenty-three in 1833)[125] appears as "Printer" for volume I (1833–34); he was apparently replaced as printer by his brother George (age fifteen in 1834) for volume II and probably volume III.[126]

Japheth continued to be active in town affairs in the 1830s, based on references to his activities in the pages of *The Orb*. For example, in 1835, he was reelected town clerk[127] and was part of a group of citizens interested in a canal from China Pond to the Kennebec River at Pittson.[128] A Lyceum was organized in China on October 12, 1835, and J. C. Washburn was its elected president.[129] Washburn's involvement with the Lyceum, which held public lecture-discussions on topics of current interest, shows his continued involvement with education and cultural improvement.

The Orb provides little direct evidence linking Washburn with musical activities in China in the 1830s. One of the few sacred music references found in *The Orb* is an ad in the last issue of volume I for *The National Church Harmony* (supplement by N. D. Gould, teacher of music). The editor (Washburn) states that he has examined the book, finds it "happily adapted to the wants of our musical choirs," and recommends it.[130] The fact that he personally inspected the tunebook suggests that although he was no longer compiling tunebooks himself, he maintained an interest in those being published.

Musical societies were not unknown in China in the 1830s. Ads for meetings of a Mozart Society appear in *The Orb* in 1833 and 1835.[131] Although Washburn's name is not specifically associated with the group, he may have been a member.[132] He was often in the forefront when new organizations (such as the Masonic Lodge and the Lyceum) were founded in China. If not one of the founders of the Mozart Society, he surely would have been encouraged to join because of his musical interests.

Interest in new, "scientific" approaches to music education had apparently reached China by the mid-1830s. An upcoming public lecture on the subject of music was announced in volume II of *The Orb*. It was to take place at China Academy on Saturday evening, December 5, 1835:

> At the close of the lecture the ladies and gentlemen will be invited to form themselves into a Class for instruction in that science, upon the new and highly approved system of Pestalozi. The terms will be two dollars per evening, except the hall, fuel and light, the expense of which will be added.[133]

Washburn's role, if any, in either arranging or attending the lecture is uncertain.[134]

A few years later, Washburn, his wife, and their younger children moved to Calais, Maine. Church records imply that the move took place sometime between mid-January and late March 1837.[135] At the time, the five surviving children from Washburn's first marriage were adults (ages twenty-four to thirty-three). They apparently did not accompany their father and stepmother to Calais. Oliver Wendell Washburn (Japheth C.'s oldest son), for example, remained active in China as a shopkeeper, Mason, town clerk (1840–1850), and postmaster (1841–1850).[136] The four children from Japheth C.'s second marriage—George, Julia, Emily, and Charles—were younger (ages ten to seventeen) and apparently did move to Calais with their parents.[137]

J. C. Washburn was to spend his remaining years in Calais until his death in 1850. The town is located on the eastern extremity of Maine, adjacent to St. Stephen, New Brunswick, and is a considerable distance from China, at least 170 miles by today's highways. In 1840, its population was 2,934.[138] Why, at age fifty-seven, did Washburn leave China, where he had spent most of his adult life, to settle in Calais? Perhaps he moved so that he could start over in business in a geographical area where he was not known. In 1837, the national economy was in disarray, with a shortage of specie and a collapse of investor confidence. The effects of the Panic of 1837 in Bangor, Maine, have been described;[139] things were probably no better in China, especially for a trader such as Washburn, who probably found it difficult to collect from his debtors and thus pay his own creditors.

The agricultural frontier served as a kind of safety valve: those not successful in one area could and did try again in another locale.[140] Washburn's publication of *The Orb* had not been successful, perhaps explaining its discontinuance after volume III in November 1836. He was still interested in the newspaper business, however, and he may have seen Calais as a good location for another venture.[141]

In the 1830s, a series of newspapers of various political leanings were published in the Calais area, none of which lasted for more than a few years.[142] Washburn's first venture into newspaper publication in Calais was with the *Frontier Journal,* a renamed version of the short-lived *Down Easter* newspaper which he had purchased. The first issue appeared on January 9, 1838. Griffin describes Washburn's experience with the *Frontier Journal* as follows:

> It was Democratic in principle, and went along very smoothly until about the 21st of May, 1838, when it met with a head

> flaw which knocked the whole concern into pi [confusion], and came near annihilating the publisher. R. Whidden, Esq., having an interest in the concern, demanded a settlement,—he wanted some money. Mr. Washburn, poor man, had none to give him; whereupon Mr. Whidden seized the account books and the week's edition of the Journal, and walked out of the office with them under his arm. Thus ended the last chapter of the first volume of the *Frontier Journal*.[143]

Washburn's lack of working capital in May 1838, slightly more than a year after moving to Calais, suggests that he may have left China with little money. At any rate, he was replaced by Lucius Bradbury, Esq., who ran the paper until it ceased on April 28, 1840.

Griffin indicates that after Washburn's "sudden and unexpected termination" with the *Frontier Journal,* "he went about some other business" until the summer of 1839 when he started up publication of a newspaper called the *Eastern Democrat*. That newspaper had begun publication under other hands in 1835, but was abandoned after a split in the Maine Democratic party in the fall of 1836. Washburn hired the Democrat press and published the paper under its former name (the *Eastern Democrat*) from June 18, 1839, until June 22, 1841, the end of the term for which he hired the establishment.[144]

Knowlton does not mention Washburn's brief association with the *Eastern Democrat,* but contributes the information that the *Frontier Journal* and a third Washburn periodical, the *Christian Watchman* (which began publication in 1838) were the work of J. C. Washburn and Son. He sums up the history of the *Christian Watchman,* a Baptist paper, as follows:

> The Baptists in the vicinity not desiring a watchman over their fold, the only pious paper ever issued in the Schoodic valley, died at the tender age of one year.[145]

The firm of Washburn and Son apparently consisted of Japheth C. Washburn and son George.[146] They seem to have dissolved their partnership sometime in the last half of 1841, with George going into business with a Mr. Wharff.[147]

In October 1841, Japheth, ever the entrepreneur, wrote to his son O. W. in China and informed him of the mercantile opportunities available in Calais:

> Wish your Apo-y Store was here—a capital place for that and a Book Store. Should you become sick of China, and come to Calais early in the Spring, I will take hold with you and "estonish the Natives."[148]

His sanguine spirit—an attitude which enabled him to start over again in business after fires and failures—clearly shows through. O. W. Washburn, who had succeeded his father in the shopkeeping business, was apparently doing well in China, though, and chose to stay there.[149]

In the same letter, Japheth described his own activities as follows:

> I am doing *nothing*—shall "lay on my oars" this winter, and if the Bankrupt Act is not repealed, shall endeavor to clear myself of embarrassments, and should kind Providence permit, attempt again to do something.[150]

The letter is clear confirmation of Japheth's financial difficulties in 1841, following his three unsuccessful attempts at publishing newspapers in Calais. His situation was not unique; many other individuals were similarly affected by the economic downturn. In Bangor, for example, the depression of 1839 continued to paralyze the business community until 1843.[151] In retrospect, the late 1830s and early 1840s were not the best time to start a business.

On October 27, 1842, Washburn filed for bankruptcy and was declared bankrupt on December 13, 1842.[152] His bankruptcy file reveals that while he owned no real estate and had limited personal property, he owed over four thousand dollars to his creditors, half of whom lived in Massachusetts.[153] The effect of the Bankruptcy Act was to discharge him completely from these debts. He was allowed to keep a certain amount of household furniture and clothing. Among his itemized possessions were a Bible, valued at three dollars, and "other books," also valued at three dollars.

In spite of his optimistic plans to "do something" once cleared of his debts, he does not appear to have gone into business again; he was, after all, sixty-two years old when declared bankrupt. In the 1850 census, the occupation of Japheth C. Washburn is listed simply as "gentleman," an indicator of his standing in the community. The census also reveals that eight years after filing bankruptcy, he still did not own any real property.[154]

Although his business activities, if any, are unknown for the remaining years of his life,[155] he continued to be an active Mason in Calais until the month he died. In 1837, the year Washburn moved to Calais, the Masonic chapter in Calais—the St. Croix Lodge—was inactive, due to continuing anti-Masonic sentiment; however, Washburn signed the bylaws and officially became a member of the lodge that year.[156] When the St. Croix Lodge resumed its activities in 1844, Japheth C. Washburn held various positions. He was elected Secretary in 1844, a member of the Committee of Character in 1845, Senior Warden and Master Pro Tem in 1846, Master in 1847, and Senior Deacon Pro Tem in 1850 (just a few weeks before his death).

The family also continued to be affiliated with the Baptist church. The memberships of Japheth and Sarah and their two oldest children (George and Julia) were transferred from the Baptist Church in China to one in the Calais area (nearby Milltown) in March 1837. When some of the members formed a "spinoff" church in Calais in 1841, the Washburns were among its members.[157] This church, now the Second Baptist Church, "was composed largely of intelligent, active, and influential people, who had migrated to Calais from Massachusetts and the western part of Maine."[158]

The records of the Second Baptist Church of Calais lack the frequent mentions of Washburn which were common in the records of the China Baptist Church. According to Jackie Dudley, present clerk of the church, the records indicate that J. C. Washburn was church clerk from 1846 to 1850; however, all the records seem to have been written by an E. D. Green, who signed his own name as clerk. Church annals suggest that Japheth's wife, Sarah, was active in the church ladies' group.

Knowlton indirectly confirms Washburn's position as church clerk of the Second Baptist Church when he writes that in the year 1850, "E. D. Green was chosen Deacon; and J. C. Washburn, Esq. having died, Geo. W. Dyer was elected Clerk."[159] Knowlton also implies that Washburn was still a justice of the peace. He notes that J. C. Washburn, Esq., at the request of Rev. C. Cone and others, issued the warrant calling a meeting to organize legally the Methodist Episcopal Church of Calais and Milltown.[160]

Nothing is known of Washburn's musical activities in Calais. His last confirmed musical activities in China were a decade prior to the move to Calais. If he composed any music while in Calais, it does not seem to have been published. Calais Baptist Church records do not indicate that he took any particular role in the music at his church.

Washburn's presence in Calais, located on the Maine–New Brunswick border, may have contributed to a dissemination of Maine tunes or tunebooks into New Brunswick. The successive editions of Stephen Humbert's *Union Harmony: or British America's Sacred Vocal Musick,* compiled in St. John, New Brunswick, show not only a slight increase in the number of tunes by Maine composers, but also an increase in the number of tunes by Washburn. Although Washburn is represented by only one tune in the 1816 edition of Humbert's tunebook, four of his pieces are included in the 1840 edition, following his move to Calais in 1837.[161]

Although the *China Bicentennial History* indicates that Washburn died on August 29, 1850,[162] notice of his death appeared in the Calais *Advertiser* on August 28, 1850, indicating a slightly earlier date:

> Died: In this town on Thursday evening last [which would have been August 22], J. C. Washburn, Esq. Aged upwards of 60.[163]

He was buried in the Calais Cemetery, where his wife, Sarah, was to be buried in 1878.[164]

In China, present-day residents still associate the Washburn name with public service. On July 28, 1981, Japheth Coombs Washburn and his descendants were honored on "Remembrance Day," an annual commemoration of those who have made important contributions to China. As the Washburn Remembrance Day booklet states, the family tradition of public service begun by Japheth Coombs Washburn, elected China's first town clerk in 1818, continued "through four generations and more than 150 years, including 111 years during which the town clerk was a Washburn."[165]

In the first three decades of the nineteenth century, few citizens in the town of China (or what would become China) were as actively involved in so many areas of town life as Japheth Coombs Washburn. As town clerk, legislative representative, postmaster, justice of the peace, probate court commissioner, China Academy trustee, Mason, church member, store-owner, and newspaper publisher, he left his mark on many areas of community life.

In addition to all these activities, he was reputedly "a well known teacher and composer of music." In some ways it is amazing that he managed to find time among his other activities to compose hymn-tunes and compile tunebooks. Of course, his primary profession (merchant) may have allowed him leisure time not available to a typical farmer who worked from dawn to dusk. Like other Yankee tunesmiths, he integrated music well into a busy and versatile life.

CHAPTER IX

OTHER MAINE COMPILERS

Although Japheth Coombs Washburn and Abraham Maxim were the most prolific and arguably the most important Maine psalmodists of the period from 1800 to 1830, several other Maine residents (Edward Hartwell, Charles Robbins, Henry Little) also compiled at least one sacred music collection each. Two of the publications—*The Hallowell Collection* and Little's *Wesleyan Harmony*—were printed in two editions; Hartwell's *Chorister's Companion* and Robbins's *Columbian Harmony* were limited to one. Hartwell and Robbins were the only compilers who included some of their own tunes.

The lives of Hartwell, Robbins, Little, and publisher-compiler Ezekiel Goodale will be summarized in this chapter. In addition, some theories will be advanced about the identity of *The Hallowell Collection*'s compiler(s).

Edward Hartwell (1747–1844)

A contemporary of Supply Belcher, the principal Maine psalmodist of the eighteenth century, Edward Hartwell was a generation older than most of the later Maine composer-compilers, who were born in the 1770s and 1780s.[1] Since his tunebook was not printed until 1815, however, Hartwell (unlike Belcher) is within the scope of this study.

Born in Lunenberg, Massachusetts, to Edward and Elizabeth (Kneeland) Hartwell on August 22, 1747, he moved to Fitchburg (the town just west of Lunenberg) in 1774.[2] He served eight months as a Revolutionary War soldier, participating as a minuteman at Lexington and in the Battle of Bunker Hill.[3] He married Lydia White on December 9, 1776.[4] According to George Edwards, Hartwell lived in Concord with his wife and three children just prior to the family's move to central Maine around 1780.[5]

In Maine, the Hartwells settled on a farm on the south side of the bend in the Kennebec River above the village of Canaan. The owners of the land, the Kennebec Proprietors, lured prospective settlers to Maine by granting them a two-hundred-acre lot at no charge, on condition that they meet certain settlement requirements.[6] Like the Hartwells, many of the other early settlers in this frontier area (later to become Skowhegan) had come from Massachusetts towns northwest of Boston.[7]

After the move to Maine, the Hartwell family grew in number until there were at least ten, and possibly as many as thirteen, children.[8] In 1790, the Edward Hartwell family living in Canaan consisted of two adults and seven boys under sixteen.[9] According to Weston, the Hartwell children surviving to maturity were Edward Jr., Joseph, Thomas, Benjamin, Stephen, Samuel, and Polly.[10] Such a predominantly male family provided Hartwell with many laborers for farm chores.

Like many of his neighbors, Hartwell did not depend totally on farming to support his family. His additional income came from operating a ferry service. In 1793, he was licensed to keep a ferry over the Kennebec River from his landing to Col. John Moor's landing.[11] He continued to run the ferry until bridges across the river were completed in 1809, rendering the service unnecessary.[12]

Hartwell took his turn at filling various municipal positions in Canaan. In 1788, for example, he was chosen to be one of the town's three assessors; in 1794, he was moderator of the annual town meeting.[13] Not surprisingly for a father with so many children, Hartwell became involved with the local schools: he was a member of a six-man committee which apportioned the school funds among the various school districts in town. He also served at one time as head of the "Upper Class," one of the six school districts into which the town was divided.[14]

Nothing is known about Hartwell's own educational background, although he was said to be "a highly educated man"[15] and "a well informed man, an extensive reader for his time."[16] Whatever education he had undoubtedly dated back to his youth in Massachusetts, perhaps supplemented by reading on his own.

Judging from his musical compositions, he may also have had some instruction in music, probably in the 1760s, while growing up in Massachusetts. The harmonic tendencies in his twenty-five published sacred tunes suggest he may have received a more sophisticated musical education than most of the psalmodists, even though, like them, he probably wrote the vocal lines successively, guided by linear principles. A large number of his tunes show an understanding of tonal harmony and chord inversions. Not only does he use complete triads, even to begin a piece and at cadences, but he seems to follow "common-practice period" principles in the chord progressions formed by the voices. The quality of his tunes seems consistent with Weston's statement that Hartwell "had a better knowledge of music than any in the region around."[17]

As someone who knew comparatively more about music than most of his neighbors, Hartwell probably taught singing schools, perhaps in the late 1790s or early 1800s.[18] The theoretical introduction to *The Chorister's Companion,* the sacred music collection he published in 1815,[19] demonstrates his knowledge of the common problems encountered in teaching the rudiments of music. When discussing syncopation, for example, he notes, "This is one of the most difficult lessons for beginners."[20] Hartwell was "a good singer,"[21] certainly a helpful attribute for a singing teacher.

Neither Weston, White, nor Edwards—the principal writers on Hartwell—suggest that he taught singing school, however, although Weston indicates that Hartwell's son Samuel "taught singing school with credit."[22] One explanation may be that Edward Hartwell's teaching, if any, occurred before the memory of Weston, born in 1802. Since White and Edwards largely relied on Weston for their information, they may have been unaware of any earlier Hartwell singing schools, if not mentioned by Weston.

The earliest dates which White mentions for singing schools in Canaan are 1810 or later; Hartwell would have been in his sixties by then. Although old age did not stop him from compiling a tunebook in his late sixties, by that time he may have been bypassed in favor of younger men (such as his son) when singing school teachers were hired.[23]

His tunebook may have been compiled partly as a negative reaction to the kind of sacred music being written in his day: "the volatile and fugeing style which has characterised so much of our modern compositions."[24] He also hoped to improve the quality of performances; one object of his book was "to add some facilities to improvement in the art of singing."[25] If not able to accomplish the latter goal by teaching students in person, he could do so through his book.

His other stated purpose for publishing the book is almost identical to Washburn's in compiling *Parish Harmony* two years earlier: "to accommodate individuals, schools and singing societies, with a greater variety of approved tunes, at a more moderate expence [*sic*], than they have heretofore found."[26] Clearly, tunebooks must have been almost prohibitively expensive for many residents of frontier Maine.[27]

In spite of its relatively low selling price, *Chorister's Companion* did not sell well. According to Weston, Hartwell had published it at his own expense, "and it was not remunerative."[28] Weston adds that he does not think that any of Hartwell's compositions "ever became popular like Coronation, Complaint, Bridgewater and others, and they are now lost and forgotten."[29] Weston seems to have been correct. Although Hartwell's tunes may have been sung locally, none of them appears to have been reprinted in other tunebooks, not even those compiled in Maine.[30]

Perhaps *Chorister's Companion* was slightly ahead of the local public taste in its avoidance of fuging-tunes, to which Hartwell seems to have had a personal aversion. While only nine fuging-tunes are included, Hartwell chose "many ancient, European pieces, whose antiquity and intrinsic excellence are too well known to need eulogy."[31] The emphasis placed on simple European tunes makes his tunebook a forerunner of several later Maine collections which reflect similar reform sentiments.[32] Although reform collections had received widespread acceptance in Massachusetts by 1810, and in Hallowell, Maine, by 1817, Hartwell's potential customers in frontier Maine in 1815 may not have been ready to give up the fuging-tunes which they so enjoyed.[33] Nevertheless, his *Chorister's Companion* apparently was used locally, in what is now Skowhegan, "for many years."[34]

Weston is mistaken in believing Hartwell's tunebook to be the first "to introduce tunes not originally of a religious character."[35] Nearly all tunebooks were intended to accommodate the needs of singing schools and societies as well as churches. Not infrequently they contained tunes with secular or even Biblical texts (such as Song of Solomon) not considered appropriate for singing in church but perfectly acceptable for a singing-school exhibition or social gathering. As noted previously, even Supply Belcher's *Harmony of Maine* (1794), published two decades earlier, contains some tunes with secular texts.[36]

Perhaps more significant than Hartwell's inclusion of some nonreligious texts is his publication of many "occasional" pieces, which other Maine compilers generally avoided as being less useful. Hartwell not only includes anthems for most of the traditional occasions on which they were sung (Thanksgiving, Fast Day, funerals, and ordinations), he also prints a number of set-pieces with specific functions: a song for the Fourth of July, a Masonic ode, and an "Ode—Introductory to a Sacred Concert." Although many of his simpler psalm-tunes were quite suitable for divine worship, many of the other compositions were clearly intended for use outside of church services.[37]

As a compilation published in Hartwell's older years, the collection may represent a family album of favorites, sung together through the years.[38] The Hartwell clan was said to have been "a family of singers."[39] Son Stephen played the bass viol, probably to accompany the singing at home and possibly also at church. His younger brother Samuel, who composed a few hymn-tunes of his own,[40] had "a fine tenor voice, and taught singing school with credit."[41] It is easy to imagine the Hartwell clan, like the Abraham Maxim family, gathered together for music making around the hearth. With so many males in the family, they could easily follow Hartwell's advice that at least half the singers in a choir should sing the bass line.[42]

The Hartwells may also have sung with their neighbors. The Solomon Stewards, who lived nearby, were also a musical family: the father led the singing in the town's meetinghouse, and two of his daughters, Mary and Zilpha, were leading singers there.[43] Perhaps a common interest in music (nurtured by neighborly singing sessions) led to the romance and eventual marriage between Mary Steward and Benjamin Hartwell, son of Edward. Not surprisingly, their daughters were also musical: Emeline and Angeline Hartwell (granddaughters of Edward Hartwell) were the leading alto and soprano in the Congregational church for several years.[44]

As Edward Hartwell's children grew up and started their own families, they needed their own land. In spite of the large number of sons, equitable land distribution apparently did not present a major problem. Edward Jr. and Joseph became tanners and left the area. Thomas joined the army in 1812 and was killed while in the service.[45] Benjamin became a carpenter and joiner and bought his own lot on Skowhegan Island in 1827.[46] The two remaining sons, Stephen and Samuel, who are said to have received the family lot in Canaan,[47] probably sold it when they moved further inland to the newer settlement of St. Albans, Maine.[48]

The Hartwells probably already knew quite a few people there, since many of the residents had also come from the Skowhegan-Canaan area. Stephen Hartwell (Edward's son) seems to have been the first Hartwell to venture to St. Albans. As an early settler there in the 1820s, he built the first log house, the first sawmill, and the first frame house in the village.[49]

Stephen probably provided the encouragement which caused his parents, youngest brother Samuel, and unmarried sister Polly to settle in St. Albans,[50] probably between 1825 and 1829.[51] Psalmodist Abraham Maxim, who lived in the adjacent town of Palmyra between December 1827 and his death in 1829, may have become acquainted with the elderly Edward Hartwell. Though twenty-six years older than Maxim, Hartwell outlived him by fifteen years. Even if Hartwell did not move to St. Albans until 1829, he may have become acquainted with Maxim in 1828 or 1829, since Palmyra was only about ten miles from Bloomfield, Hartwell's former residence.

Edward Hartwell's property in St. Albans consisted of an average-sized farm with several buildings on about fifty-three acres, the whole valued at $375 in 1845.[52] It was common for farm parents to divide up the family land among their sons and then deed the house to one of the youngest ones, who would shelter and provide for the parents until their deaths. Such an arrangement, albeit informal, seems to have taken place with the Hartwells. Although the farm was not legally deeded to Samuel,[53] he is listed as the head of a household in the 1840 census, and his father (Edward) is named as a Revolutionary War pensioner ("age 93") residing with him.[54]

Lydia Hartwell (Edward's wife) died on April 1, 1837, at age eighty-two. Edward died seven years later on March 30, 1844, at age ninety-six years, seven months, and eight days. Both were buried in the South Cemetery in Bloomfield.[55] The typically brief obituary for Edward Hartwell in the *Kennebec Journal* read as follows: "Died: . . . In St. Albans, Edward Hartwell, a revolutionary soldier, aged about 97."[56]

Hartwell died intestate. In August 1845, the administrator of his estate was authorized to sell the Hartwell farm (still in Edward's name), since his personal property was not sufficient to cover his debts.[57] In spite of the sale, son Samuel continued to live in St. Albans. In 1850, he was a farmer with a wife and four children; his real estate was valued at $500.[58]

As a composer and compiler, Edward Hartwell seems to have had little impact on psalmody in Maine. Few, if any, of his original tunes were republished in other tunebooks. Still, White gives Hartwell much credit for having achieved what he did, "under the adverse conditions of that primitive and isolated existence."[59] Hartwell's *Chorister's Companion* was apparently used in the Skowhegan area for some years and was significant locally.

His tunebook may suggest which tunes were popular in central Maine between 1810 and 1820. His inclusion of a large number of Core Repertory tunes shows that these tunes were favored in frontier areas of Maine, as well as in other parts of New England. His avoidance of fuging-tunes and preference for European tunes presages the trends exemplified in later Maine reform collections.

Charles Robbins (1782–1842)

Although Charles Robbins, like Edward Hartwell, was born in Massachusetts, he came to Maine much earlier in his life: when he was only six years old. Unlike Abraham Maxim and Japheth Coombs Washburn, who moved to Maine as young adults, arriving with knowledge and expectations acquired during their youth in Massachusetts proper, Robbins was educated in Maine and probably had few memories of his birthplace.

Charles Robbins was born on February 12, 1782, in Plymouth County, Massachusetts. His hometown of Hanover is north of Maxim's and Washburn's birthplaces of Plympton and Rochester. He was the second of nine children born to Luther and Anna Robbins.[60] The family settled in the central Maine town of Greene in 1788.

Charles's father was as active in Greene town affairs as Japheth Coombs Washburn was in China. Like Washburn, Luther Robbins was a justice of the peace and served as selectman, town clerk, postmaster, and representative to the General Court of

Massachusetts. He was "proverbial for honesty and generosity."[61] His eldest son, Nathaniel, followed in his footsteps by serving in many civic leadership positions as an adult. Charles, the next son, apparently had little interest in governmental affairs, however. His only public office seems to have been collector of taxes in Greene for one year.[62]

While Nathaniel became a schoolteacher, Charles and his younger brother Reuben became cabinetmakers in Winthrop, twelve miles northeast of Greene. To learn the trade, Charles was probably apprenticed in his early teens (the mid-1790s) to a master cabinetmaker.[63] He worked at the craft only in his younger years, however.[64] After several years in Winthrop, he returned to Greene and kept a tavern there for twenty years.[65]

As a young adult, Robbins's hands may have been busy making chairs and cabinets, but his mind was probably on music. In a history of Winthrop, a paragraph devoted to the town's cabinetmakers pointedly mentions Robbins's devotion to music, rather than his skill at his craft: "Mr. Robbins devoted much time to the study of music, and acquired a respectable acquaintance with its theory."[66]

His devotion to music took tangible form in 1805, when he published a tunebook entitled *The Columbian Harmony: or Maine Collection of Church Music*. Robbins was only twenty-three at the time but had already written at least forty-seven hymn- and psalm-tunes which received their first publication in the collection. The book was divided into three parts: an introduction to the rudiments of music, psalm- and hymn-tunes by various composers, and occasional pieces for particular occasions.

In the preface, Robbins notes that he has expressed "the Rules of Music in a very plain manner," partly to aid "schools and the citizens of Maine in general, who at present have but a small opportunity of attaining musical knowledge by schools, the settlement being so new."[67] Whether Robbins himself taught any singing schools is unknown; however, he seemed to know, either as a teacher or as a former novice, which aspects of music were hardest to master: he made "some illucidations on particular Rules, which were painful to the beginner."[68] His lengthy introduction to musical rudiments is not a perfunctory summary, but a carefully thought out presentation of twelve lessons on various aspects of music theory. Following the lessons are pedagogical singing exercises providing practice in the nine most common major keys and the nine modes of time.

Still, Robbins surely did not expect that those without opportunity to attend singing school could learn to sing from his book alone. He, too, must have had some singing-school education, probably in the classroom of Supply Belcher or Abraham Maxim. In his tunebook preface, Robbins states that "the recommendations and solicitations which were given him by gentlemen who are Authors and Teachers of Music" induced him to publish the collection.[69] If not the only "Authors of Music" in Maine at the time, Belcher and Maxim were surely among the most well known ones, and both lived within a reasonable distance from Robbins.[70]

Robbins specifically mentions Belcher in his theoretical introduction when he discusses a third mood of compound time:

> One Mood of Compound Time was lately introduced by S. Belcher; it is performed the same as 6/4, only about one quarter slower, marked thus, 6/2.[71]

Since Belcher's own tunebook, *The Harmony of Maine* (1794), discusses only the traditional two moods of compound time (6/4 and 6/8), the third mood must have been taught by Belcher in his singing school.[72] As young boys, both Charles and his brother Nathaniel may have attended Belcher's singing school in Hallowell.[73]

Belcher may also have been a visitor in the Robbins home. His political activities representing the town of Farmington probably brought him into contact with the equally active Luther Robbins (Charles's father) of Greene, and he may have rested his horse at their home on his trips from Farmington to Boston to attend the General Court of Massachusetts.[74] The most conclusive evidence that Robbins had an acquaintance with Belcher is the fact that in *Columbian Harmony,* Robbins includes seven Belcher tunes, none of which were printed in Belcher's tunebook. Five of the seven appear to be first printings.[75]

Similar evidence points to a relationship between Robbins and Abraham Maxim. Robbins includes three tunes by Maxim in *Columbian Harmony:* two had been published in Maxim's *Oriental Harmony* (1802), one had not.[76] In return, Maxim printed a Robbins tune in the early editions of *Northern Harmony,* perhaps to honor one of his better students.[77]

Robbins lived even closer to Maxim than he did to Belcher.[78] Since Maxim probably did not move to Maine until 1799, however, when Robbins was seventeen, Robbins may have received his initial singing-school training from Belcher, supplemented by advice and assistance from Maxim at a later time, when Belcher lived some distance away. Stylistically, Robbins's compositions show more similarities to Belcher's tunes than to Maxim's, suggesting that Belcher may have been a more formative influence.[79]

Like many other first-time tunebook compilers, Robbins had hopes for future editions, as implied in his advertisement for *Columbian Harmony:*

> Should this book become useful, and liberal encouragement given, it is hoped more different Metres will be supplied with Music hereafter in another edition.[80]

No later editions appear to have been produced, however. In contrast, Maxim's *Northern Harmony,* published just a month after *Columbian Harmony,* went through five editions. Why the difference? Both tunebooks were dominated by American compositions and had similar proportions of tunes in the various genres.[81] *Columbian Harmony* contained even more of the popular Core Repertory tunes than *Northern Harmony,*[82] and while larger and slightly more expensive, it was not significantly so.[83]

One possibility is that Robbins, unlike Maxim, may not have been a singing-school teacher; if not, he did not have a "captive audience" of his own students to buy his tunebook. Although he expected potential buyers to include those with no opportunity to attend singing school, such schools were becoming more common in Maine by 1805. The students usually purchased a tunebook compiled or recommended by their teacher. Robbins's tunebook also faced stiff competition from the popular and better-known collections compiled outside of Maine, such as *Village Harmony* and *Bridgewater Collection.* The sixth edition of *Village Harmony,* for example, was advertised in the same ad as *Columbian Harmony;*[84] purchasers with a dollar to spare probably chose the new and improved *Village Harmony* over the unknown *Columbian Harmony.*

Robbins's sacred music collection was probably the product of youthful enthusiasm, resulting from an inborn love of music, combined with a positive singing-school experience and encouraging teachers. After 1805, though, he did not compile any other collections. If he continued to compose sacred tunes, they were not published. Those of his tunes which appear in later Maine tunebooks were all printed first in *Columbian Harmony.*[85]

His devotion to music did not diminish, though. In his mid-twenties, he simply shifted his attention to another type of music: military band music. He was not the only New England psalmodist to be interested in instrumental music. Samuel Holyoke, for example, was a clarinetist whose activities in instrumental music led him to publish *The Instrumental Assistant* (1800, 1807), two volumes containing a collection of marches and airs for instrumental ensembles, along with instructions on how to play various instruments.[86]

Although the details of Robbins's instrumental music experiences are not known, he may have played the fife in a local military band (probably associated with a militia regiment) and perhaps served as a bandmaster with the Eighth (Maine) Division of the Massachusetts Militia.[87] In 1812, he compiled a music book, called *Drum and Fife Instructor,* intended for the use of "performers [of martial music] in new settlements."[88]

In the book, he includes instructions on how to play the fife and the drum, directions for a special military flag ceremony,[89] and forty-five pages of single-line melodies: mainly marches and quick steps, gathered from American and European sources. Robbins may have written some of the tunes, all of which are unattributed. Melodies with local place names (such as WINTHROP QUICK STEP and AUGUSTA QUICK STEP) are interspersed with traditional favorites, like THE BRITISH GRENADIERS' MARCH and PRESIDENT'S MARCH. Robbins's *Drum and Fife Instructor,* published at a time when militia units were bracing for possible war with Great Britain, is significant as one of the earliest instrumental textbooks compiled in Maine.[90]

Robbins penned the prefaces to both *Columbian Harmony* (1805) and *Drum and Fife Instructor* (1812) from Winthrop, Maine.[91] He probably remained in Winthrop for a few years after 1812 because in 1815, he was a founding member of the Winthrop Society for the Promotion of Good Morals.[92] The organization, while apparently not involved with reforming church music, promoted a better observance of the Sabbath. To assist in achieving that aim, the group obtained copies of a pamphlet published by the Middlesex Convention.[93] If Robbins had compiled a later tunebook, his reform viewpoint might have been reflected in his selection of tunes. Reform collections typically emphasized plain tunes by European composers and excluded fuging-tunes, a popular genre in Robbins's earlier tunebook.[94]

Charles's affiliation with the Winthrop Society for the Promotion of Good Morals suggests that he was a man of religious faith. The members of the society acknowledged their insufficiency to effect reform and their dependence on God to produce results; they opened and closed meetings with prayer.[95] Although he probably attended church, Robbins's denominational affiliation in both Winthrop and Greene is unknown. After returning to Greene, Charles may have attended the Freewill Baptist church (organized in 1826), where his brother Luther Jr. was an early deacon.[96] Another brother, Nathaniel, and their father, Luther Sr., were officers in a Universalist church formed in Greene in the late 1820s. Since Charles's name is conspicuously absent from the petition for the latter society in 1829, however, he probably did not favor the Universalist denomination.[97]

Regardless of his affiliation, Charles does not seem to have involved himself in church affairs to the extent that his brothers and father did. He may also have eschewed a music leadership position within his church. Unlike Maine psalmodist Supply Belcher, for example, he is not described as a church choir leader, but simply as "an author and composer of several pieces of music."[98]

He must have returned to Greene to live by 1817, when he served as Greene's collector of taxes. In 1818, he is listed among "the voters and resident property holders" of Greene.[99] As mentioned earlier, he kept a tavern there for twenty years, presumably his last years.[100] It is possible that Robbins's tavern served as the meeting place for a singing school, perhaps one he taught, since singing schools were sometimes held in taverns.[101]

Not a great deal is known about Charles Robbins's immediate family. We do know that in August 1805, the month before his tunebook was published, he married Betsy Thomas, born in 1785.[102] Charles A. Robbins, born two years later (1807), was probably one of their children. By 1840, Charles A. Robbins was living in Gardiner, a busy river town about eighteen miles east of Greene.[103]

Although two of his siblings lived well into their nineties, Charles Robbins, the tunebook compiler, was not so fortunate: he died at age sixty on July 20, 1842.[104] His widow outlived him by nearly three decades.[105] Although they probably did not live in Gardiner, Charles and Betsy Robbins are buried there, perhaps because that was their son's residence.[106]

Robbins is significant as the compiler of *Columbian Harmony,* one of Maine's earliest nineteenth-century collections of sacred music. In repertory, it is similar to large, eclectic collections such as the widely popular *Village Harmony*. Alongside tunes of widespread popularity in New England are forty-seven by Robbins himself. His tunes, which frequently show sparks of originality, were known by other Maine compilers and received at least limited republication as late as 1820. The theoretical introduction to his tunebook indicates that he had a thorough understanding of those rudiments of music which pertained to psalmody.

Henry Little (1788–1878)

Henry Little was the compiler of *Wesleyan Harmony* (1820, 1821), a tunebook specifically tailored to the Methodists and their hymnbook, but also appropriate for other denominations. He was the only one of the Maine compilers who did not live in central Maine; however, his religious and political beliefs were similar to those of most inland settlers.[107] He also had connections to the central Maine area through his wife's uncle, publisher Ezekiel Goodale.

Like virtually all the other psalmodists who prepared sacred music collections in Maine, Little emigrated to Maine from another state, but from New Hampshire rather than Massachusetts.[108] Henry Little was born on August 16, 1788, in Salem, New Hampshire, to Henry Little and Elizabeth (Bailey) Little. Henry (the father) was a farmer in Salem and died there in 1807. His wife, Elizabeth, was the daughter of Rev. Abner Bailey, a Harvard graduate and minister for over fifty years in Salem.[109]

Their son Henry (the tunebook compiler) was the sixth of their eight children. Only one of Henry's five brothers became a farmer like his father. Two became tanners, one a blacksmith, and another a lawyer. Almost all his brothers and sisters settled in towns other than Salem once they reached maturity, suggesting that land and opportunities may have been limited there.

While his brothers were apprenticed to various trades or trained for a professional career, Henry may have hired on a ship's crew as a teenager or young adult, perhaps planning a career as a seaman.[110] The ports of Portsmouth, New Hampshire, and Boston, Massachusetts, were not a great distance away from his hometown of Salem, New Hampshire. The shipwreck he experienced as a young man[111] may have convinced him to seek another livelihood. He may have decided to seek adventure on the frontier rather than on the sea.[112]

His older brother Samuel had ventured northeast to Buckstown (now Bucksport), Maine, in 1805, the year he was admitted to the bar.[113] Buckstown was relatively new to settlement. The first families did not arrive there until 1764; the town was incorporated in 1792.[114] Henry Little, age twenty, settled in Buckstown three or four years after his brother, who may have written to him about the opportunities there. Samuel's contacts as a lawyer may have helped Henry obtain his positions in the Hancock County Clerk of Courts office, the Register of Deeds office, and as a deputy sheriff.

Henry Little served in the War of 1812 as a first lieutenant and commander of a local company which was called into service.[115] After the war, he was a member of the state militia and was rapidly promoted to colonel and commander of his regiment.[116] He must have achieved the rank of major by 1818: he is referred to as "Major Henry Little" in the Bucksport records of his children's births.[117]

He had married Sophia Goodale (1797–1878) of nearby Orrington, Maine, on October 29, 1816. Her father was the Hon. Ephraim Goodale, a brother of Ezekiel Goodale, the Hallowell printer. Their three children included Henry Willard Little and two girls, both named Laura Elizabeth Little (the first died as an infant).[118] Throughout his life, Henry Little was active in the fellowship of the Methodist Episcopal church, having joined the church by 1819.[119] A history of the Methodists in Bucksport names Henry Little as one of the principal members of the Methodist society there, a small group which met "at Brother William G. Chase's" for prayer meeting as early as 1824.[120]

The author of the Little family genealogy suggests that the shipwreck (and subsequent rescue) experienced by Little as a young man may have prompted his profession of religious faith soon after.[121] Although he was probably raised in a churchgoing home—his mother was a minister's daughter—he may not have become personally convinced of the reality of God until he was in a life-and-death situation and saw his prayers answered.

Little's choice of the Methodist denomination appears to be a departure from his upbringing, which was probably Congregational.[122] Methodist circuit-riding preachers visited Buckstown as early as 1793, but a Congregational church had also been organized there by the beginning of the nineteenth century. Perhaps with the background of his shipwreck experience, emotional revival meetings were more compatible with his personal faith than more restrained Congregational services. He may also have been drawn into Methodism through his wife: her parents, aunt, and uncle were all Methodists.[123]

In 1820, he compiled a collection of sacred music specifically intended for Methodist societies. His purpose in publishing *Wesleyan Harmony* was to provide sufficient tunes for every meter (especially the Particular Meters) in the Methodist Hymn Book. The tunebook was suitable for other denominations as well, since two-thirds of the tunes were in Common, Short, or Long Meters. He hoped that all Methodist societies would adopt his book, so they would have a common repertory to sing when they met together at quarterly meetings. Little had produced the collection at the request of "a number of our Ministers and other Brethren."[124]

Although nothing is known of Little's musical training or knowledge, he must have been active in the music of his denomination, probably in a leadership role, for ministers and others to have asked him to undertake the compilation. Perhaps personal experience as a song leader contributed to his "thorough conviction that a work of this kind is very much wanted in our Societies."[125] He was well aware that many of the Methodist hymns in Particular Meter were never sung because there were no suitable tunes for them; he was also aware of the difficulties encountered when Methodists from different societies tried to sing together.

Although publishers who were not musicians sometimes compiled tunebooks,[126] the nature of this tunebook suggests that Little was probably musically inclined to have attempted it. For hymns in the more unusual meters, he either had to set them to music himself or adapt existing tunes to fit them. He seems to have done none of the former: there are no tunes attributed to Little in the collection.[127] Since both he and the Methodist leaders endorsing the collection were intent on featuring tunes "from the most approved European Authors, which have long stood the test of criticism," he probably would not have identified his own tunes as such if there were any.

Although he wrote few, if any, of the tunes in the collection, he was probably the one who arranged the tunes identified as "adapted." For these six tunes, he altered the meter of existing tunes to conform to Particular Meter hymns.[128] These adaptations show him to be fairly skillful at making minor changes (a slight rhythmic change or added or subtracted slur) to end up with the right number of notes for the syllables, but he was less adept at matching the textual and musical accents.[129]

The theoretical introduction provides few clues about his own understanding of music. Perhaps because his book was chiefly intended for public worship, rather than singing school, he covered the traditional topics (note names, transposition of mi, musical terms and symbols, and modes of time) without much elaboration.[130] The one thing he omitted is a discussion of "accent, good Pronunciation, Emphasis, &c.," leaving them "to be explained by the well informed Teacher, who, it is presumed, will not omit this important duty."[131] He thus avoided having to discuss these matters, which he may have felt less competent to address. The only unusual information he provided is an odd explanation of how to pitch a tune when there is no pitch-sounding device available.[132]

Little's *Wesleyan Harmony* was published by his wife's uncle, Ezekiel Goodale, in Hallowell, Maine, and was "sold by him and the Compiler at Bucksport."[133] Little seems to have depended heavily on Goodale's recent publication, *The Hallowell Collection of Sacred Music* (1817, 1819), as a source for his own collection: two-thirds of the tunes in the first edition of *Wesleyan Harmony* are also found in *The Hallowell Collection*.[134] Although Hallowell was a considerable distance from Bucksport, Goodale may have advised or assisted Little in the preparation of the book.[135]

Little must have accurately sensed a void in the tunebook market which a book such as his could fill. Less than four months after soliciting subscriptions, the book was advertised as "just published and for sale."[136] The subscription list, published at the back of the volume, included subscribers from all the New England states except Rhode Island.[137] The rapid sale of the first edition, which was sold out or nearly so within six months, caused Little to issue a second edition in 1821.

Little seems not to have compiled any other tunebooks, perhaps because in *Wesleyan Harmony* he had accomplished what he set out to do: provide the Methodists with tunes for all their hymns. Due to the success of the first edition, he was able to publish a second edition which corrected the errors "which unavoidably appeared in the first edition"; he also was able to enlarge the book with some "choice tunes."[138]

Little continued to live in Bucksport, where he was "engaged in trade" and served as postmaster from 1816 until about 1830, when he moved to Ellsworth, Maine, a coastal town about fifteen miles southeast of Bucksport.[139] He was actively involved in the temperance movement of 1830.[140]

In 1835, after "a few years of successful business" in Ellsworth, he moved abouty twenty-five miles northwest to Bangor, Maine, where he was to spend the next thirty-eight years of his life. Bangor, favorably located at the head of the tidewaters of the Penobscot River, had grown rapidly in the early 1830s. Its population rose from 2,808 in 1830 to about 8,000 in 1834, when it was incorporated as a city.[141] Little must have been successful in weathering the dramatic downturns in Bangor's economy in the late 1830s and early 1840s; the 1850 census identifies him as a merchant owning four thousand dollars worth of real estate. He may have been in business with his son-in-law, B. F. Nourse, who was also a merchant and a part of Little's household.[142]

In 1873, when he was in his eighties, Little (and presumably his wife, Sophia) went to live with their daughter and her family in Boston. Sophia died on May 21, 1878; Henry died just five days later, on May 26, 1878, at age eighty-nine.[143]

Henry Little's *Wesleyan Harmony* apparently met the special needs of Methodist societies and, as such, filled a niche in the genre of Maine tunebooks. Its usefulness was not necessarily limited to Methodists, however, since Particular Meter tunes made up only about a third of the book.

Little differed from Washburn, Maxim, Hartwell, and Robbins in including few, if any, of his own tunes in his compilation and none that he specifically attributed to himself. The preference in the 1820s for sacred tunes by European composers may have limited his participation as a composer. In addition, composition may not have been his forte; his tune adaptations in *Wesleyan Harmony* do not reveal him to be particularly skillful at setting texts. His musical abilities may have been in the area of song leading rather than creating.

The Compiler(s) of *The Hallowell Collection*

No compiler's name is listed on the title page of *The Hallowell Collection of Sacred Music* (1817, 1819); however, several scholars have concluded that the collection was compiled by Samuel Tenney (1787–1830), a Hallowell, Maine, church choir director and singing-school teacher. One of the first to do so was Joseph Griffin in his *History of the Press of Maine* (1874).[144] Several decades later (1896), Joseph Williamson, in his monumental bibliography of books pertaining to Maine, also attributed the collection to Tenney.[145] *The Hallowell Collection* itself provides no grounds for ascribing the collection to Samuel Tenney. His name does not appear either on the title page, in the notice about the copyright deposit, or in the introductory advertisement.

In addition to Tenney, two other men are frequently credited with some role in the compilation: Hallowell gentleman John Merrick (1766–1862) and Biddeford lawyer (and later Maine's chief justice) Prentiss Mellen (1764–1840). An early source, D. R. Goodwin, writing in 1862, states that Merrick compiled the collection "in connection with Chief Justice Mellen."[146] George Edwards wrote in 1928 that *The Hallowell Collection* "was compiled by S. Tenney, assisted by two of the ablest men in the state, Chief Justice Prentiss Mellen and John Merrick, Esquire."[147] Calvin Clark, who also attributed the collection to Samuel Tenney, limited Mellen's and Merrick's participation to an "endorsement" of the work.[148]

This printed endorsement, signed by Merrick and Mellen as president and vice president, respectively, of the Handel Society of Maine, makes reference to the collection's suitability for improving musical taste.[149] Such a statement accompanying a tunebook predominantly comprised of older European tunes in a simple style earmarks the tunebook as a reform collection in the tradition of *The Salem Collection* (1805) and similar Massachusetts tunebooks of the 1805–1810 period.[150] Like *The Hallowell Collection,* these reform collections lacked an editor's name, highlighting the collective, rather than individual, nature of the selection process. Crawford suggests that the role of musicians in such compilations seems to have been purposely downplayed to emphasize religious motives in the selection of the music.[151]

In some cases, the Massachusetts reform collections were produced by a society committed to the improvement of church music. An example is *The Middlesex Collection of Church Music,* sponsored by the Middlesex Musical Society.[152] The precedence of tunebooks prepared by organizations, along with the endorsement of *The Hallowell Collection* by the officers of the Handel Society of Maine, may have led Frank Metcalf to believe that *The Hallowell Collection* was compiled by the latter society.[153] A recommendation by its officers, however, does not seem sufficient justification for attributing the book to the organization.

A more likely possibility is that Merrick and possibly Mellen may have served as musical advisors to the book's publisher, Ezekiel Goodale, a Hallowell printer who was not known to have been musical. Other publishers who were not musicians had compiled successful tunebooks. For example, Worcester publisher Isaiah Thomas, with whom Goodale may have apprenticed,[154] produced the first edition of *The Worcester Collection* (1786) with the assistance of "many gentlemen" in selecting the tunes.[155] Similarly, Henry Ranlet, a printer in Exeter, New Hampshire, relied on "several Gentlemen, who are Teachers of Musick" to put together his popular collection, *Village Harmony* (first published in 1795), which lists no compiler's name on the title page.

Likewise, in the advertisement to *The Hallowell Collection,* Goodale acknowledges the role of others:

> In the selection and arrangement of the music, and general inspection of the work, the publisher has had the assistance of several gentlemen, who have spared no pains to render it worthy of public patronage; and who were desirous of having comprised, in a moderate compass, a number of standard tunes for the use of the church and society in this place.[156]

The fact that "several gentlemen" assisted Goodale suggests that Samuel Tenney must not have been the sole compiler, although he may have had some role in the process for his name to be cited so frequently in connection with the book. At the very least, he probably used the book in a singing school he taught: ads for *The Hallowell Collection* began appearing in October 1817, only a few weeks before a "Mr. Tenny" commenced his "School for the Instruction of Sacred Vocal Music" in Hallowell.[157]

Even so, Merrick, another Hallowell citizen, is a stronger candidate for the position of musical advisor to Goodale. Largely through Merrick's efforts and guidance, the choir of Goodale's church, the Old South Church in Hallowell, became one of the most effective choirs in the country.[158] Merrick himself not only sang "with great sweetness," but "could play on any instrument" and had a "scientific" knowledge of music.[159] Born in London in 1766, he settled in Hallowell in 1798, just a few years before Goodale.

As "an English gentleman of a finished education," Merrick may have played a major role in determining that European tunes, almost exclusively, were chosen for *The Hallowell Collection.* As a person experienced in training a choir and knowledgeable about music, he may have had the background to write the theoretical introduction, portions of which are more detailed and erudite than similar sections in the typical manual compiled by less-educated singing-school masters. The writer seems to have been familiar with European art music and its theory.[160] Prentiss Mellen, Merrick's fellow officer in the Handel Society, may have contributed to the compilation as well, although his residence in Biddeford (the southern part of the state) probably made him less accessible to Goodale.[161]

An ad which Goodale ran when the second edition (enlarged and improved) was published in 1819 suggests that Goodale himself was actively involved in improving the work, either personally or in a supervisory capacity:

> The rapid sale of the first edition of the above work induces the publisher to offer a second, much improved and enlarged; and while he gratefully acknowledges the liberal patronage bestowed on his former edition, he hopes that the pains *he has taken* to improve the present will insure a continuance of public favor.[162]

My theory is that Ezekiel Goodale compiled the book with the assistance of John Merrick, Prentiss Mellen, and possibly Samuel Tenney. The Handel Society of Maine may have been indirectly involved, through the participation of two men who happened to be officers of the organization, but was probably not the driving force behind the compilation. Goodale was the one who deposited the book in the office of the Clerk of the District Court of Maine, claiming rights "as Proprietor" to obtain the copyright.[163]

While he probably did not compile the collection unaided (as he acknowledges in the advertisement to the first edition), neither did another individual, such as Samuel Tenney.

Ezekiel Goodale (1780–1828)

While Ezekiel Goodale is not specifically identified as compiler on the title page of a Maine tunebook, he at least supervised the compilation of *The Hallowell Collection,* as described in the last section, and was the only person named directly as having a role in the process. His principal significance in the field of sacred music in Maine, however, was as the publisher and seller of many of the tunebooks already discussed.

Ezekiel Goodale was born in Shrewsbury (now West Boylston),[164] Massachusetts, on September 24, 1780, to David and Dorothy or Doratha (Newton) Goodale, the fifth of their eight children. His grandparents, Edward and Sarah (Temple) Goodale, were pioneer settlers of Shrewsbury in the late 1730s.[165]

In light of Goodale's later ownership of a printing business, there is a strong possibility that as a boy, he and perhaps two of his brothers may have apprenticed under the printer Isaiah Thomas in nearby Worcester (adjacent to Shrewsbury).[166] Thomas was the leading American printer of the time and was active as a publisher in the 1790s, when Ezekiel Goodale was of apprentice age. Goodale may have learned how to set music type for tunebooks at Thomas's firm;[167] he purchased music type for his own publishing company only a few years after starting the business. Although there is no direct evidence that Goodale was an apprentice of Isaiah Thomas, he must have learned the printing trade somewhere, and Worcester's proximity to Goodale's boyhood home makes it the most likely venue for his training.[168]

After completing his apprenticeship and reaching maturity, Goodale probably wanted to start his own business. Maine may have seemed a kind of Promised Land to him: land for a business establishment was relatively cheap and available there, and there were few, if any, booksellers or printers in the newly settled areas. He would face much less competition than in an established area such as Worcester or Boston. Hallowell, located in central Maine on the Kennebec River, was an ideal location for a bookseller: books could be shipped by sea from Boston to Bath (a busy port at the mouth of the Kennebec River), and then up the river from Bath to Hallowell. Hallowell, the most thriving inland town on the Kennebec at the time, was also an important market center, second only to Portland in the amount of business done there.[169]

In October 1802,[170] Ezekiel Goodale, barely twenty-two, came to Hallowell "from New Hampshire with a brother, in a chaise."[171] Near the end of the journey, the Hallowell-Gardiner road was so rough that Ezekiel had to lead the horse, while his brother walked beside the chaise to prevent it from overturning. The brother was probably his older brother Ephraim. Although the quotation implies that they may previously have lived in New Hampshire, it seems more likely that they simply travelled through a part of the state on their trip to Maine from Massachusetts. Ephraim did not remain in Hallowell, choosing to settle a considerable distance east in Buckstown (later Orrington), Maine, on the Penobscot River. Later on, Ephraim married and had a daughter who married tunebook compiler Henry Little.[172]

Shortly after settling in Hallowell, Ezekiel Goodale opened a bookselling and bookbinding business there. His Hallowell Book Store opened on October 13, 1802, according to a local newspaper ad.[173] At the time, it was the only bookstore between Portland and Bangor.[174] His initial stock consisted of spelling books and some *New England Primers*. Later, he imported newly published books from England and also founded an excellent circulating library.[175] The latest English publications were undoubtedly well received by the English-born elite of Hallowell. Goodale's store "grew in great favor."[176]

In 1813, he added printing and publishing to his establishment "At the Sign of the Bible."[177] In February 1814, Goodale, in partnership with James Burton, Jr., as the firm of Goodale and Burton, began publishing a weekly newspaper called the *Hallowell Gazette*. The paper was Federalist in its politics, a position probably supported by the aristocratic gentlemen at the top of the social structure in Hallowell.[178] When the partnership was dissolved in 1815, Goodale published the newspaper by himself for a time.[179]

Being a newspaper publisher was not necessarily a lucrative endeavor. Periodically, Goodale would run a notice scolding his delinquent subscribers and indicating that he would accept payment not only in cash but in "butter, cheese, or rags."[180] His forbearance was especially taxed by readers who had been receiving the newspaper for several years and had not yet made a payment. By 1818, he was accepting payment "in any kind of Grain, Pork, Beef, Butter, Cheese or Cash,"[181] suggesting that Hallowell was still largely agricultural at the time.

The newspaper was an excellent medium for promoting his book store, and Hallowell Book Store ads hawked all types of books as well as a wide variety of other items, including the ever-popular patent medicines. Because he also sold musical instruments and accessories, such as fifes, German (transverse) flutes, and violin strings, his customers must have included most of Hallowell's musicians, who probably took time during their visits to browse through the latest tunebooks. Even before he started publishing sacred music collections himself, he sold those from other printers. For example, the popular *Village Harmony* could be purchased at his store as early as 1806.[182]

After Goodale's partnership with Burton was dissolved, Andrew Masters took charge of the printing office.[183] Masters, a New Hampshire native, had skills honed during a seven-year apprenticeship with C. Norris & Co. in Exeter, New Hampshire.[184] While in training there, Masters probably gained experience in setting music type; several tunebooks by Maine compilers were among the music books printed by the Exeter firm.[185]

Although Masters's probable experience with music printing may have been helpful, Goodalc had already planned to print music prior to Masters's arrival in Hallowell in 1815. A notice on the front page of the March 9, 1814, issue of the *Hallowell Gazette* notified prospective printing customers that new type had been received and that music type was on the way:

> Just received from the Foundery, a New and elegant assortment of Types.
>
> Printing in all its variety executed with elegance and dispatch, and on reasonable terms.
>
> They also inform the Public, that arrangements have been made for a handsome assortment of Music TYPES—which they will probably receive in the course of two or three months.[186]

The list of books published by the Ezekiel Goodale firms of E. Goodale or the later Goodale, Glazier, and Co. is long. Sacred music collections in addition to *The Hallowell Collection of Sacred Music* (1817, 1819) included *Wesleyan Harmony* (1820, 1821), *Temple Harmony* (1818, 1820, 1821, 1823), and *Northern Harmony* (1816, 1819).[187] All seem to have been reasonably successful, judging by the presence of multiple editions.

In 1820, Goodale formed a new bookselling and printing partnership: Goodale, Glazier, and Co. Goodale's partners were Andrew Masters and Goodale's nephew, Franklin Glazier, who had been his "faithful clerk" for some time.[188] The business continued under that name until 1824, when Goodale apparently took an early retirement, perhaps because of ill health.[189]

In the meantime, Goodale had become a family man. His first wife was Betsey Stone, daughter of Alpheus and Lucretia Stone of Oakham, Massachusetts.[190] Although they probably became acquainted in Massachusetts, they married in 1804, about a year and a half after Goodale settled in Maine.[191] Once he was established in Hallowell, he probably either went back for his future bride or sent for her to join him. The Goodales had five children, born between 1805 and 1818. Betsey died on January 27, 1822, at age forty. On June 2, 1822, Ezekiel married Mrs. Elizabeth Abbot Wingate, a widow.[192]

Both of Ezekiel's wives were members of the Old South Congregational Church, the preeminent church in Hallowell. Although Ezekiel's name does not appear among the list of members, he apparently owned a pew; the pew records show the transfer of a pew from Eliphalet Gilman, grantor, to Ezekiel Goodale, grantee (no date given).[193]

His active involvement in the church is also evident from the fact that he was chosen to be one of the directors of the church's Sabbath school in 1819, 1821, and 1822. The organization's official name, established by its constitution in 1817, was the Hallowell Sabbath School Moral and Tract Society. It was the duty of the directors to superintend the Sabbath schools, attend to and provide for the moral and religious instruction of the children, and perform any other necessary tasks.[194]

Goodale died at age forty-seven on February 22, 1828. A "prudent, economical business man,"[195] he founded a printing firm which endured, with various partners, for seven decades. His company helped to establish Hallowell as a leading center (perhaps second only to Portland) for book publishing in Maine in the nineteenth century.

If Maine had not had a music printer such as Goodale, Maine compilers could have continued to patronize other printers, such as New Hampshire's C. Norris & Co. Having Goodale's firm nearby, however, made publication that much easier for the Maine psalmodists, nearly all of whom lived in central Maine, in the vicinity of Hallowell.[196] Goodale's importance as a bookseller must also be noted. His Hallowell Book Store provided a convenient and supportive outlet for the sacred music collections produced by Maine compilers.

PART II. TUNEBOOK CONTENTS

CHAPTER X

PREFACES AND ADVERTISEMENTS

The Maine tunebooks of the period from 1800 to 1830 consist of psalm- and hymn-tunes preceded by a number of instructional pages on the rudiments of music. In addition, they all contain a prefatory page, usually entitled "preface" or "advertisement," following the title page and just before the rudiments section. On the prefatory page, the compiler typically states why he has prepared the tunebook and what types of tunes he has chosen.

One possible indirect motive for writing a book—a desire for fame and fortune—is not directly mentioned in the tunebook prefaces. Business records are not available to indicate how much money the Maine compilers received from their publications, but it was probably not great. At least one of the compilers, Edward Hartwell, personally paid for the publication of his tunebook, *Chorister's Companion* (1815), and a contemporary, Eben Weston, noted that "it was not remunerative." Maine psalmodist Japheth Coombs Washburn declared bankruptcy in 1841; however, his financial demise probably resulted from recent business failures rather than from his tunebook endeavors more than a decade earlier. The tunebooks of Washburn and Maxim must have been fairly successful to have warranted seven and five editions, respectively.

Still, judging from the introductory comments in the Maine collections, practicality, patriotism, and piety were the principal motivators for the compilers. While their remarks are similar in many respects to those of other New England psalmodists, the Maine psalmodists imply that in some ways their tunebooks were especially tailored for Maine residents.

A concern for practicality, in particular, seems to be a thread running through many of the prefaces. As recent settlers themselves, the compilers realized that many potential tunebook purchasers in their area were subsistence farmers struggling to make a living for themselves and their families. Farming was not easy in Maine with its rocky soil, harsh winters, and short growing season. Cash was not plentiful; the new settlers frequently bartered their goods and labor with one another. The depiction of the typical Down-Easter as thrifty may not be an invalid stereotype; out of necessity, the new settlers had to be frugal.

As a result, several of the Maine compilers sought to meet the need for tunebooks which cost less. In the advertisement to his *Parish Harmony* (1813), store-owner Japheth Coombs Washburn noted that the expense of the various large music books in use made it difficult for some societies to purchase them. His smaller and less expensive volume would make it possible for singing schools and societies to be "more generally furnished with Books."[1] At six dollars per dozen, *Parish Harmony* was cheaper than the very popular *Village Harmony,* for example, which sold in Maine for as much as $8.50 per dozen for some editions.[2]

A concern for expense was also expressed by Edward Hartwell, whose *Chorister's Companion* (1815) attempted to provide "a greater variety of approved tunes" at more moderate expense.[3] Similarly, Henry Little, who compiled the Methodist-oriented *Wesleyan Harmony* in 1820, hoped, among other things, "to save more than one half of the expense for Singing Books."[4] His prepublication solicitation stated that the price would be fifty cents each, bound in boards, or forty-four cents, stitched in blue paper.[5]

Several Maine psalmodists, then, specifically chose to compile books which were smaller and less expensive than others on the market. No doubt they expected that their potential customer base would be expanded if their collections were within the affordable range for more people. To produce these smaller books, the compilers probably tried to include only tunes which had a reasonable chance of being performed by Maine singers.

One genre which was cut back was the anthem. Anthems, extended settings of Biblical prose, were usually performed only on special occasions, such as Thanksgiving, Fast Days, ordinations, funerals, and at the exhibitions held at the conclusion of a singing school. Perhaps because of the greater demand for psalm- and hymn-tunes, which were sung in weekly church services, most of the early Maine tunebooks focus on such tunes and include less than a handful of anthems.[6] In the prefatory page to his *Parish Harmony,* which contains only a single anthem, Japheth Coombs Washburn explained that he had originally intended to publish several anthems in the collection, but had decided against it, believing "that Psalm Tunes might be more useful in a Book of this size, and equally acceptable to people in general."[7]

Besides tailoring their smaller collections to the needs of Maine singers, Maine compilers also took into account that singing schools were not so accessible in the newly settled areas of the District of Maine as in other areas of New England. For those who lacked the opportunity of attending singing school, the theoretical introductions (where the rudiments of music were explained) needed to be clear and comprehensive. With that in mind, Charles Robbins, in his *Columbian Harmony* (1805), purposefully laid down the Rules of Music "in a very plain manner," as he put it, acknowledging that the citizens of Maine in general "at present have but a small opportunity of attaining musical knowledge by schools, the settlement being so new."[8] His theoretical introduction (including the exercises), fills twenty-four pages, making it the longest and most detailed of any found in the Maine tunebooks.

The Maine collections also demonstrate versatility, another facet of practicality. Many of the compilers were careful to point out that their tunebooks were designed for at least two different groups: singing schools and religious societies. They often noted that no tunes had been selected which would not be suitable for singing in church. The songs might also be sung by singing societies or at family gatherings. Not only did the psalmodists choose tunes appropriate to the various occasions on which they would be sung, they also provided tunes of varying styles and difficulty to satisfy a variety of tastes and abilities.

The Maine compilers were not unique in seeking to furnish tunebooks which would be suitable for different functions, tastes, and skill levels. Such a goal was shared by most tunebook compilers throughout New England. Although some collections were intended for a single use,[9] the more common practice was to compile a multifunction work which potentially could be sold in greater numbers.

Compilers were also careful to include tunes for a variety of poetic meters, proportionate to the number of hymns and psalms written in those meters.[10] Japheth Coombs Washburn noted that the fourth edition of his *Temple Harmony* contained music "suited to every Metre contained in Dr. Watts' Psalms and Hymns and Rev. Mr. Winchell's Supplement thereto."[11] Similarly, Henry Little produced a tunebook containing tunes for all the Particular Meter hymns in the Methodist hymnbook. He had discovered that not all the Methodist hymns could be sung because there were few tunes of the appropriate meter. He hoped to remedy the situation with his *Wesleyan Harmony,* which included tunes for all the Methodist Particular Meters. Perhaps to ensure that sales were not limited to Methodists, though, his title page described the book as "Designed for the Methodist Societies, but proper for all Denominations."[12]

Besides practicality, patriotism seems to have been another motivation for compiling tunebooks in Maine. Tunes by American composers retained their popularity later in Maine than in other areas of Massachusetts. For example, in 1808, when Abraham Maxim needed to select tunes to increase the size of *Northern Harmony* for a second edition, the additional music he chose was "mostly American, from an idea that the European Music, is less agreeable to the American ear, than her own."[13] His is a remarkable statement for 1808, when American hymn-tunes were considered by many to be inferior to those by Europeans. Contemporaneous Massachusetts reform collections were emphasizing tunes by "eminent composers" (read "European composers").

While the other Maine compilers showed by their selection process that they valued American tunes, Maxim was the only one to state directly that European music was less pleasing than American music to American ears. Unfortunately, he did not explain what characteristics caused him to consider one to be more agreeable than the other. Since his statement implies that the ear had a primary role in the judgment, he does not seem to be suggesting that Americans preferred their own music solely on the basis of the composer's nationality. Instead, aural reasons were apparently particularly important.

Although the hymn-tune settings by relatively untrained American psalmodists were not significantly different from those composed by similarly trained English parish-church musicians, both differed from the harmonizations of composers trained in European, common-practice harmony. Rural Mainers may have been accustomed to American settings in which the voice parts were conceived as independent lines and were composed successively. Consequently, harmonically oriented arrangements written by European-trained composers may have sounded strange to their ears.

By 1816, though, Maxim, perhaps influenced by Washburn, appears to have tempered his opinion that American tunes were necessarily better than European ones. In the preface to the fourth edition of *Northern Harmony,* Maxim and Washburn, joint compilers, noted that they had "neither left out nor inserted a single piece of music on account of the age or country in which it was written, persuaded [that?] neither the merit nor demerit of music rests on either of those circumstances."[14] Such an unbiased approach was unusual for the time. Most other New England compilers were convinced that European tunes, particularly those of older vintage, were inherently superior to more modern, American ones.

While American tunes are less common in the later Maine tunebooks, the fact that they are included at all, well into the 1820s, suggests that American tunes retained their appeal in Maine long after they were considered unfashionable in other areas of New England. The Maine settlers, many of whom moved to the region precisely because they chafed under the authoritarian restrictiveness of Massachusetts society, were to remain independent of such shifts in taste.

A corollary to the approbation given to American tunes was an interest in fuging-tunes, largely of American origin, in Maine after they had fallen out of favor in other regions. While not an American invention, fuging-tunes had come to be associated with American psalmodists. Based on the large number of fuging-tunes included in Maxim's *Northern Harmony,* he must have considered them agreeable to the American ear. Although two of the Maine compilers—Henry Little and Edward Hartwell—expressed in their prefaces a disdain for tunes in the fuging style, other Maine compilers continued to include them.[15] As late as 1818, Washburn, compiler of *Temple Harmony,* noted that he had inserted a number of fuging pieces "to render the variety such as to give more general satisfaction."[16]

By and large, though, Maine compilers of the decade around 1820 limited the number of fuging-tunes in their collections as a result of piety and concern about the suitability of various tunes for worship. Foreshadowing the change to tunebooks with simpler, European tunes were Washburn's *Parish Harmony* and Hartwell's *Chorister's Companion,* published in 1813 and 1815, respectively. As in the Maine reform collections to come, Washburn included only music which would be suitable for use in church. The tunes are primarily "ancient" (Washburn's term), but with some of modern style and a few new pieces to make the work "acceptable to those of different tastes."[17] "Ancient music" was a phrase commonly used for tunes written many decades earlier, usually in a syllabic style without musical elaboration, and usually intended for slow, solemn performance. Hartwell's collection goes even further than Washburn's in its emphasis on plain tunes at the expense of fuging-tunes.

These transitional works were followed in 1817 by a tunebook which is clearly a reform collection: *The Hallowell Collection of Sacred Music*. Reform sentiments, similar to those expressed in Massachusetts a decade earlier, are apparent in the prefatory material. The unidentified compiler devotes the one-page preface to the role of music in worship: a role stated to be that of exciting and improving the devout affections. The advertisement on the following page notes that only music which would be of permanent use in the services of the church is included. The tunes, by authors of "well-known eminence" (i.e., European nationalities), are characterized as generally simple, dignified, and pathetic in style. The compiler continues:

> All light and flimsy airs, which debase the subject to which they are set, and can be recommended for little more than novelty, have been cautiously excluded. That kind of music, which has no tendency to exalt the mind, and excite devotional feelings, is altogether unsuitable for the temple of the Most High.[18]

Following the advertisement is an endorsement of the collection by officers of the Handel Society of Maine, who state that the collection is "well calculated to improve the musical taste of our country and aid the devotional exercises of our churches."[19]

The focus on music appropriate for worship, clearly stated in *The Hallowell Collection,* is consistent with the interests of clergymen and other community leaders in reversing the trend toward secularization in church music. Choirs, rather than congregations, were doing most of the singing in church at this time, and their desire to demonstrate their musical skill may have been stronger than their desire to enhance worship. Richard Crawford concludes that it was the secularization of psalmody more than any other factor which prompted the reform movement of 1805 and after and the return to older, time-tested pieces in a simple style.[20] Although the reform movement seems to have affected psalmody in Maine about a decade later than in Massachusetts, the circumstances precipitating it were probably similar.[21]

Summary

The advertisements to the Maine tunebooks compiled between 1800 and 1830 reveal a fundamental concern for practicality throughout the period. Particularly in the early nineteenth century, composers sought to hold down costs for new settlers by producing smaller, less expensive volumes which could serve a variety of functions and tastes. Patriotism came into play as Maine compilers continued to include American tunes, especially American fuging-tunes, even into the 1820s, well after they had been replaced by simpler European tunes in other New England collections. Compilers late in the period were guided by piety as they sought to provide time-tested music to enhance worship.

CHAPTER XI

THEORETICAL INTRODUCTIONS

In each of the tunebooks compiled in Maine between 1800 and 1830, the tunes are preceded by an instructional section on the "Rudiments of Music," a standard component of American tunebooks since the 1720s.[1] The information on musical symbols and notation served as a text for singing-school students, who studied the explanations and examples as they were expanded upon by their singing master.[2] Theoretical introductions, as they were called, were printed in most American tunebooks until the end of the nineteenth century.

The theoretical introductions published in eighteenth-century collections have been thoroughly described by Allen Britton.[3] The rudiment sections of nineteenth-century Maine tunebooks, like those in many other New England tunebooks of the time, follow the earlier models rather closely in content and sequence. The instructional material and order of presentation must have been well tailored to the singing-school setting to have been used by many different singing-school masters over the years.

While the exact wording differs among the theoretical introductions in the Maine compilations, certain core topics are discussed in nearly every one. Typically, in the space of three to twenty-four pages, the following items are addressed (usually in this order): the gamut (or scale) of music, solmization (including the transposition of mi), notes and rests, musical characters, moods (or modes) of time, keys used in music, general directions and remarks, and lessons for tuning the voice. This chapter will summarize the treatment of these topics in the ten different theoretical introductions contained in the Maine tunebooks.[4]

Comparisons will also be made with the approaches taken in several representative non-Maine tunebooks spanning the period. Like the Maine collections, *The Christian Harmony* (1805), by Vermont resident Jeremiah Ingalls, was written for a rural constituency. The *Bridgewater Collection of Sacred Musick* and *Village Harmony* were popular eclectic collections which were published in numerous editions in the first few decades of the nineteenth century. Reference will be made here to the instructional material found in the third edition (1810) of the *Bridgewater Collection* and the fourteenth edition ([1817]) of *Village Harmony.* Another non-Maine tunebook referred to is *The Boston Handel and Haydn Society Collection of Church Music* (1822), the first tunebook compiled by Lowell Mason, who ushered in a new era of sacred music.[5]

The Gamut, or Scale, of Music

As the foundational element of musical notation, the five-line staff (sometimes called "stave") is usually the first component of musical notation defined in the rudiments section. Ledger lines are introduced as a means of extending the staff. Next, the seven-letter system (A to G) for naming notes is described. To show how these letters apply to the staff, a diagram is usually provided. Each of the clefs likely to be encountered in singing books is shown on a staff, with the letter names written on the lines and spaces.[6] Either in words or through a diagram, the writer usually indicates unison equivalents among the staves, showing how a given G pitch, for example, is notated on each staff.

The number of staves delineated varies among the tunebooks, reflecting the changing practices in the course of the period. Although the counter part was notated with a C (alto) clef at the beginning of the nineteenth century, the G (treble) clef had been adopted for counter voices in the Maine tunebooks by 1816.[7] The later tunebooks sometimes describe and illustrate the earlier practice, but use only two different clefs for the collected tunes: a G (treble) clef for treble, counter and tenor, and an F (bass) clef for the bass.[8] These two clefs are also the only ones used, somewhat grudgingly, by Lowell Mason in *The Boston Handel and Haydn Society Collection of Church Music* (1822).[9]

The replacement of the alto clef by the treble clef in sacred music may be related to the more widespread use in churches of various wind and string instruments to double the vocal lines as the nineteenth century progressed. Few instrumentalists, other than violists and those who were also counter singers, were accustomed to reading the alto clef. Although well-trained church organists were capable of reading a wide variety of clefs in open score to accompany singing, those with less experience must have appreciated the publication of tunes using just treble and bass clefs. Organs were becoming more common in Maine churches by the 1820s.[10]

Solmization

Following the explanations of the staff and letter names in the theoretical introductions, the fasola syllables are presented as the "names" of the notes. All the Maine tunebooks of the period describe the use of the English, four-syllable system, practiced throughout New England, with little deviation from the traditional exposition of the topic. *The Hallowell Collection* explains the purpose of using the syllables:

> In practising musical lessons, it is thought proper to appropriate peculiar syllables to the seven intervals in the Octave; in order that the same name applied to the same interval may naturally suggest its true relation and sound.[11]

The four syllables are named faw, sol, law, and mi.[12] Mi is usually described as the leading, or governing, note because it is the only syllable which does not recur in the octave. The syllables located above mi are faw, sol, law, faw, sol, law, and then mi again. Below mi are law, sol, faw, law, sol, faw, and then mi again. Semitones are situated between mi and faw and between law and faw.

One of the elements most consistently included in the theoretical introductions is a chart showing where mi is located when there are sharps or flats in the key signature. The charts indicate that the natural place for mi is "in" (on) B, but that if there is one flat in the key signature, mi is on E, etc. Typically, the location for mi is described for all major keys through four flats and four sharps, the keys most likely to be encountered.[13]

Notes and Rests

The next topic is rhythm; the six notes, the corresponding rests, and the proportions among them are introduced. The simplest delineation merely shows each note and rest on a staff with the name of each pair indicated above or below. None of the tunebooks refers to them with the names customary in twentieth-century America (whole note, half note, etc.). Instead, the English designations "semibreve," "minim," "crotchet," "quaver," "semiquaver," and "demisemiquaver" are used to identify notes ranging from whole notes to thirty-second notes (in modern United States terminology). The relationships among the various time values are taught either by comparing the duration of a note to the next smaller one (a semibreve equals two minims, one minim equals two crotchets, etc.) or by showing the number of faster notes required to equal the slowest note.[14]

Musical Characters with Their Explanations

The next section usually gives brief explanations and illustrations of various symbols encountered in music. As might be expected, a few of the symbols are given different names in different books. The following seventeen terms are usually included, not always in this order:

1) brace
2) flat
3) sharp
4) natural
5) repeat signs (four vertical dots)
6) "figures 1, 2" (first and second endings)
7) hold sign
8) trill
9) appoggiaturas or leaning notes
10) marks of distinction (dots or vertical dashes to indicate distinct performance)
11) the figure 3 or "point of diminution" (designating three notes sung in the time of two)
12) "point" or "point of addition" or "dot" (a dot located to the right of a note, adding to it one-half of the original length)
13) slur
14) single bar
15) double bar
16) choosing notes (optional added pitches where performers may choose which to sing)
17) close (the vertical lines marking the end of a tune)

Occasionally, some terms (such as "staff" or "ledger line") usually defined elsewhere in the theoretical introduction are included instead in the musical-character section. Similarly, a few of the usual terms (such as "brace") are sometimes omitted here because they are introduced elsewhere.

"Trill" and "appoggiatura," two terms regularly defined in the later tunebooks, are excluded from discussion entirely in nearly all the Maine tunebooks published before 1815.[15] Britton notes that the great majority of eighteenth-century theoretical introductions include the trill.[16] The appoggiatura, on the other hand, was an ornament which did not receive wide acceptance in psalmody until after 1800, although it was introduced in some tunebooks prior to 1800.[17] Some New England tunebooks of the early nineteenth century, such as the first edition of the *Columbian and European Harmony: or, Bridgewater Collection of Sacred Music* (1802), include both trill and appoggiatura; others do not. As late as 1817, the fourteenth edition of *Village Harmony* defines appoggiatura, but not trill.

Graces may have received only limited mention in the early Maine tunebooks for several reasons. First of all, they were considered too difficult for beginners, as this excerpt from *Village Harmony* indicates:

> The graces and ornaments of music, such as *Holds, Trills, Appoggiatures* [*sic*], *Transitions, &c.* must be acquired by great practice and attention; the learner had better omit them, till his knowledge and judgment dictate when and where to apply them.[18]

Since theoretical introductions were written for beginners, who were not encouraged to perform graces, compilers may have considered the topic irrelevant. Another reason for their omission may be that graces were easier to demonstrate than to describe. The writer of *The Hallowell Collection*'s rudiments section, for example, suggests that the various graces of music are best learned by hearing them well performed and leaves "Notes of Transposition and the Appogiaturas [*sic*] . . . to the explanation and direction of the well informed teacher."[19]

In spite of these factors, trills and appoggiaturas are regularly mentioned in the theoretical introductions of post-1815 Maine tunebooks. As notated embellishments became more common in the latter half of the period, even beginners needed to be familiar with them.[20] Various graces are much more commonly found in tunes of the later Maine tunebooks than in the earlier ones.[21] This may be due in part to a greater number of English tunes in the later books. Various ornaments are liberally sprinkled among the tunes reprinted from the English collections of Martin Madan and Aaron Williams, in particular. The slower tempi and frequent triple meters are conducive to appoggiaturas on the first beats of measures and trills on penultimate chords.[22] Appoggiaturas and trills were less compatible with the faster, declamatory duple fuging-tunes which comprise a large part of the early Maine tunebooks.[23]

Another changing practice suggested by the definitions of musical characters concerns the number of successive pitches which are affected by a single accidental. Like most compilers of his time, Robbins states that flats and sharps placed after the beginning of a tune (i.e., not in the key signature) alter only the note to which they are affixed (a single note).[24] *The Hallowell Collection,* written twelve years later, in 1817, describes a different practice, one where accidental flats and sharps affect not only the notes they immediately precede, but also all those of the same letter name in that measure and possibly through the first note of the next measure.[25] A similar practice is described in Holyoke's *Vocal Companion* of 1807.[26]

Such a practice had not been uniformly adopted in Maine even by 1826, however, since the late editions of *Temple Harmony* (1823 and 1826), as well as Little's *Wesleyan Harmony* (1820 and 1821) teach the earlier procedure that accidental flats, sharps, and naturals affect only the notes they immediately precede. Britton implies that the practice of having accidentals affect only one note was an archaic custom already superseded in Europe in the eighteenth century.[27] Perhaps only the compiler of *The Hallowell Collection* was familiar enough with European art music to incorporate the European practice into his tunebook.

Modes of Time

Once beginners were familiar with the pitch and syllable names of the notes, the relationships of note and rest values, and such common symbols as repeat signs, they were presumably ready to be introduced to the slightly more complicated subject of the moods, or modes, of time.[28] At least nine different "time signatures" (a modern term not found in these tunebooks) were in use. Following Renaissance practice, each symbol denoted not only the quantity and type of notes contained within a measure, but also the tempo, although the tempo might be altered somewhat by other factors, such as the text or directive terms.

Categorization of the modes is quite consistent within the tunebooks. The compilers usually describe four modes of common time, three of triple time, and two of compound time. In order of increasing speed for the beat, the types of common time with their associated time signature are adagio (time signature "C"), largo ("C" with vertical line through it, like the modern "alla breve" symbol), allegro (a reverse "C," with or without a vertical line through it), and 2/4.[29] The first three contain one semibreve (whole note) per measure, the last but a minim (half note). The first two modes are beat with four beats per measure (two down, two up), the latter two with two beats per measure (one down, one up).

Those in triple time, all containing three beats and beat as two beats down and one up, use the time signatures of 3/2, 3/4, and 3/8, each indicating a faster tempo than the previous one. The two in compound time, 6/4 and 6/8, have two beats per measure, 6/8 being quicker than 6/4.

Nearly all the Maine tunebooks discuss all nine modes. The one exception is *Parish Harmony,* where Washburn's abbreviated rudiments section (only three pages long) discusses only the third and fourth modes of common time (reverse C and 2/4), and just the first modes of triple and compound time (3/2 and 6/4). While not comprehensive, his delineation includes the most frequently used meters of his day. Nearly all the tunes in *Parish Harmony,* for example, are in one of the four modes he discusses.[30]

In contrast to Washburn, who does not discuss all the possible types, Robbins includes one additional: a third mode of compound time (6/2) which he says was recently introduced by S. (i.e., Supply) Belcher, who may have been his teacher.[31] Robbins's explanation was probably necessitated by the fact that several Belcher tunes in that meter were printed in his collection.

New England tunebook compilers disagree about the relative speeds implied by the various modes of time. Similarly, the Maine compilers are not unanimous in their attributions of tempi for each. They agree that a beat is one second of time in the first modes of common, triple, and compound time and that the successive modes in these divisions are progressively faster.[32] They differ, however, on how much faster the beat is in each. For example, the fourth mode of common time is variously described as one-third or one-quarter quicker than the third mode. Still, the differences are minor and not particularly significant. The proportions were intended as general guidelines and were probably not followed slavishly.[33] Also, familiar tunes were probably sung at a tempo which had become traditional for the tune and text, rather than one in strict keeping with the mode indicated. Tempi were sometimes modified according to the "air and words" of different psalms and hymns.[34]

To assist beginners, however, Robbins (alone of the nineteenth-century Maine compilers) follows the lead of William Billings and some other Yankee psalmodists in describing how to make a pendulum, which can be used to demonstrate different beat speeds by varying the length of the cord. Robbins's measurements are very similar to those suggested by Jeremiah Ingalls of Vermont in *The Christian Harmony,* published in the same year (1805) and by the same printer (Henry Ranlet) as Robbins's *Columbian Harmony*.[35] Robbins and Ingalls may have given pendulum lengths to instruct tunebook purchasers who lived in isolated areas without access to singing schools. As singing schools became more common even in rural areas of New England during the nineteenth century, Maine compilers may have felt the citation of pendulum lengths was superfluous.

Once singers understood the various modes of time and their respective tempi, they were ready to learn to beat time with their hands. Today's beginning instrumentalists kinesthetically experience the musical pulse in much the same way when they tap their foot as they play. Some of the compilers give just the general instruction that in beating time, the hand should fall in the first part of the bar and rise in the last part in all modes of time.

Abraham Maxim notes in his earliest tunebook that beating time is better learned by example than precept;[36] however, in his last extant tunebook, the fifth edition of *Northern Harmony* (1819), he gives detailed instructions on beating time in each mode. For example, the first two modes of common time are to be beat as follows:

1st. Let the ends of the fingers fall;
2d. let the heel of the hand fall;
3d. raise the heel of the hand; and
4th. raise the ends of the fingers, which completes the bar.

He recommends that students learn to keep time by practicing the printed examples, sounding the notes while beating the bars.[37]

Keys Used in Music

All the Maine tunebook compilers explain that there are two natural, or primitive, keys in music: a major, or sharp, key (described as cheerful or designed to express the cheerful passion) and a minor, or flat, key (characterized as mournful or expressive of a pathetic passion). As in the eighteenth century, the term "key" is used in a sense similar to what we call "mode" today.[38] The books teach that the key (i.e., modern-day "mode") of a tune can be determined by looking at the last note in the bass. If the bass note is the next note above mi, the tune is in a major key; if the final note is the next note below mi, the tune is in a minor key. The two "natural" keys are C major and A minor. The use of flats or sharps at the beginning of a tune move the syllable mi, and consequently the key, to another letter, forming "artificial" keys.

Some of the later tunebooks, reflecting a "scientific" approach to music, also differentiate between major and minor on the basis of whether the third, sixth, and seventh degrees of the octave are sharp (i.e., major intervals) or flat (i.e., minor intervals). *Northern Harmony,* fifth edition (1819), lists the number of whole tones and half tones contained within sharp and flat thirds, sixths, and sevenths.[39]

The discussion in *The Hallowell Collection* (1817) goes into even more detail about "keys or scales, and their two modes, major and minor."[40] The unnamed compiler discusses the construction of successive keys (each with an additional flat or sharp in the key signature) by altering one pitch in the tetrachord, which he calls the "Fourth." Like Lowell Mason in *The Boston Handel and Haydn Society Collection* (1822), he describes alterations in the ascending and descending forms of the minor mode scale, forming what is now called the "melodic minor" scale.[41]

The compiler of *The Hallowell Collection* also goes further than most of his Maine contemporaries in labelling the tonic, subdominant, and dominant notes of the scale and in mentioning transposition and modulation and what syllables to use when a modulation has taken place. Even so, his exposition does not deal with certain topics discussed by Mason, who names all seven notes of the diatonic scale (tonic, supertonic, etc.) and who gives examples of interval inversions, a chromatic scale, and modulatory passages.[42] Nevertheless, the theoretical introduction to *The Hallowell Collection* suggests that its writer was conversant with theoretical principles and terminology associated with European art music.[43]

General Directions and Remarks

The final text section in most tunebooks contains advice on various aspects of performance. Singers are advised to sing the part most suited to their voices, to pronounce words carefully, to sing high notes softer than low notes, to sing softly in general, to pay attention to accent and dynamic markings, and to behave with decorum and propriety while singing sacred music. Some compilers felt certain matters were best explained by a teacher. For example, Henry Little writes that "Accent, good Pronunciation, Emphasis, etc. are left to be explained by the well informed Teacher, who, it is presumed, will not omit this important duty."[44]

Like other New England psalmodists, Maine compilers advocated a strong bass part. Maxim, for example, recommends that "nearly half" of the singers of a school or choir should sing bass, with the others proportionately divided among the other parts.[45] Hartwell suggests that "at least one half" of the singers should sing bass, while Robbins advises that one voice on a high part generally requires two or three on the bass.[46]

The admonitions frequently included in the "general remarks" section of the theoretical introductions suggest a sequence which may have been followed in learning to read music in the early nineteenth century.[47] Singing-school instructors probably planned activities which would facilitate mastery of the steps in the prescribed order. The introduction to *Village Harmony,* for example, implies that once students were familiar with the rudiments, they did not immediately start singing tunes. Rather, they turned to the "Lessons for Tuning the Voice," and only after they could sound the various intervals in the octave were they allowed to attempt tunes.[48]

Although such restrictions were probably justifiable in theory, it seems likely that in practice singing-school students did some singing before they had mastered all the musical fundamentals. At least one singing-school master had the students sing tunes the very first night.[49] Such a situation seems to be the basis for the criticism voiced by the compiler of *Village Harmony:*

> Many schools have begun upon tunes, when they could scarcely have given a letter upon the scale, which is another cause that there are so many half singers.[50]

As they progressed in their musical knowledge, the students were probably encouraged to try to sing larger and larger portions of a tune by note (without having it sung for them first). A common caution in the rudiments sections, however, was that tunes should not be sung in words (i.e., with the text) until they were well learned by note.[51]

Lessons for Tuning the Voice

The "Lessons for Tuning the Voice" are musical examples which usually follow the rest of the theoretical introduction and precede the tunes with text. These lessons may have been used in two ways: in the "trying" of voices by the singing master and in the training of beginners in the aural sounds of the various intervals. In "trying" the voices, the singing master had each of the students sing individually.[52] After determining the singer's range, he assigned him or her to the appropriate voice part. At the very minimum, most of the tunebooks include a one-octave scale beginning on G for that purpose. The fasola syllables are often placed below the notes to assist the neophyte in naming or calling the notes properly.

In "tuning the voice," the beginner progressed through a series of singing calisthenics. In some books, the lessons for tuning the voice include additional textless exercises in addition to the standard scale. Although usually written to be sung in unison and octaves by all the voices, the exercises may include, toward the end, some musical examples written in two or three staves with different parts for each voice. In a systematic fashion, some exercises progress through each interval in turn by a sequence of descending notes alternating with the upper note (viz., G-F-G-E-G-D-G-C, etc.). Such examples familiarized the student with the various intervals they would later encounter in tunes.

The lessons in tuning the voice are usually limited to two or three pages. Robbins's *Columbian Harmony* is exceptional in following the voice-tuning lessons with nine additional textless exercises in each of the nine most common major keys and modes of time.[53] In theory, his plan of giving students practice in all the keys and modes is a good one. In practice, however, the students may have been eager by that time to sing some real music rather than additional textless exercises.

Other Topics Sometimes Included

Robbins also discusses two other topics which are not mentioned by most of the other Maine compilers, but which, like the pendulum lengths, are included in the contemporaneous tunebook by Vermont compiler Jeremiah Ingalls. The first of these topics is syncopation. Other compilers may have felt syncopation was best explained by the instructor; such, at least, was the reason the compiler of *Village Harmony* gave for omitting an explanation of it.[54] Maine compiler Edward Hartwell, who does not define syncopation but provides a practice exercise demonstrating it, notes that syncopation is one of the most difficult lessons for beginners.[55]

Robbins also devotes a lesson in his tunebook to concords and discords.[56] Like Ingalls, he provides a chart categorizing the simple intervals and three octaves of their compound form, indicating which are concords and which are discords.[57] Other compilers may have omitted the topic because it was of little practical use in learning to sing and was of more concern to composers than to singers.

Accidentals and modulations seem to have become more frequent in the late 1810s, since the compiler of *The Hallowell Collection* (1817) includes a paragraph suggesting which syllables to use in passages where a number of accidentals occur.[58] There also seem to be more accidentals and modulations in the tunes of *The Hallowell Collection* than in those of the early-nineteenth-century Maine tunebooks, where accidentals most frequently occur to raise the leading tone in minor. Very few eighteenth-century or early-nineteenth-century theoretical introductions dealt with the solmization of accidentals, according to Britton.[59] The compiler of *The Hallowell Collection* apparently borrowed his explanation from another source, since he encloses the whole paragraph in quotation marks. A paragraph which is similar but not identical is found in the fourteenth edition of *Village Harmony,* published the same year.

Maxim's Introductions

The successive theoretical introductions written by Abraham Maxim between 1802 and 1819 show modifications which probably resulted from his experience as a singing-school teacher, coupled with stylistic changes in psalmody as the period progressed.[60]

Of the five extant Maxim editions, the rudiments sections of the second and third—the first and second editions of *Northern Harmony* (1805, 1808)—contain essentially the same text as the one in his earliest tunebook, *Oriental Harmony* (1802), with the minor substitution of "clef" for "cliff" and "me" for "mi." Three improvements are found in these tunebook introductions, however: 1) the text is divided into eight lessons (seven numbered, plus a lesson for tuning the voice); 2) more musical illustrations are included, showing the symbols as they appear in actual music; and 3) a G scale for tuning the voice is printed on tenor/treble, counter, and bass staves (no scale was included in the earlier tunebook).

Dividing the material into lessons, each covering a different topic, may have helped the students quantify how much they had learned and how much was left ("We've finished five lessons and have just two left," for example). Since many of the lessons are brief, two to three could have been covered in a single evening.

The inclusion of musical examples of various symbols, the modes of time, a sharp and a flat key, and a scale for tuning the voice (thus showing students how these elements appear in actual music) represent a considerable improvement over the early tunebook. Having taught singing school, Maxim may have recognized the need to incorporate simple exercises so students could see, sing, and beat time in different modes immediately rather than just learn about them from a verbal description.

Perhaps having seen the value of incorporating musical illustrations of the elements described, Maxim included even more of them in his last two tunebooks, the fourth and fifth editions of

Northern Harmony (1816 and 1819). These consist of written-out scales on treble and bass staves for each of the nine major keys, and simple, short examples on two staves for each of the nine modes of time. Both could be successfully performed by beginners. By writing the examples in two staves, instead of just the treble staff (as in the earlier Maxim tunebooks), he accustomed the basses to reading their own line and gave the singers an opportunity to begin singing in simple two-part harmony.

The modes-of-time examples are especially well designed, showing Maxim to be a teacher who realized the importance of presenting one new thing at a time. Since the melodic line for both treble and bass remain nearly the same in each of the examples of modes of time, the singers can focus on the note lengths and number of beats without also worrying about the pitches.[61]

The major scale examples (shown starting on C) in the last two editions of *Northern Harmony* have numbers instead of syllables written beneath the notes; the keynote in each case is numbered as "8." Maxim apparently found that beginners could understand the relationships among scale steps more easily using numbers than syllables. He had not completely abandoned syllables, however, since he advises practicing the scales in the various keys by number and then by syllable.

Trills and appoggiaturas, not mentioned in his earlier tunebooks, are included among the definitions in his last editions, suggesting that these graces had become more important between 1810 and 1820. Other changes include some minor variations in terminology, probably reflecting later nomenclature,[62] differences in the relative tempi of the various modes of time,[63] and more explicit directions on how to beat time. Perhaps reflecting the increasing interest in the science of music, he includes a mathematical tally of how many whole tones and half tones are found in certain intervals, facts having more theoretical than practical significance.

Summary

In general, the theoretical introductions to the Maine tunebooks suggest that musical instruction in Maine was little different from elsewhere in New England, especially during the first two decades of the nineteenth century. The rudiment sections in the Maine tunebooks of the period between 1815 and 1830 are not significantly different from those published earlier in the century. Compared to Boston tunebook writers of the 1820s, such as Lowell Mason, most of the later Maine compilers are slower to adopt certain European theoretical principles and terminology.

CHAPTER XII

REPERTORY

On the basis of chronology and similarity of repertory, the eighteen extant tunebooks compiled in Maine between 1800 and 1830 may be divided into five groups. In the Group I tunebooks, published between 1802 and 1808, the vast majority of tunes are by American composers, and fuging-tunes are also quite numerous.[1] The Group II tunebooks, dated 1813 to 1816, contain fewer American tunes, but pieces by Americans still predominate in quantity. The decline in the number of American tunes continues in the Group III tunebooks, printed between 1818 and 1820. European pieces are about as numerous as American ones.

The movement away from American tunes reaches its apex in the Group IV tunebooks, published between 1817 and 1821. While contemporaneous with the Group III books, they are quite different in content. Fuging-tunes and American tunes are virtually eliminated in favor of plain tunes by European composers. Fuging-tunes are also in short supply in the final group of tunebooks, the Group V collections, published between 1821 and 1826. The presence of a comparatively large number of American tunes, however, warrants assigning these tunebooks to a separate group.

Table 3 lists the abbreviations which will be used in this chapter to facilitate references to the extant editions. Table 4 summarizes several aspects of the tunebook groups.

Tune Provenance and Genre Representation

The most striking contrasts among the various groups of tunebooks relate to the provenance of the tunes (their national origin)

TABLE 3

Abbreviations for Extant Tunebook Editions (in alphabetical order by abbreviation)

Abbr./Pub. Yr.		*Tunebook*	*Compiler*
CC15	1815	The Chorister's Companion	Edward Hartwell
CH05	1805	The Columbian Harmony	Charles Robbins
HC17	1817	The Hallowell Collection	[Ezekiel Goodale]
HC19	1819	The Hallowell Collection/2	[Ezekiel Goodale]
NH05	1805	The Northern Harmony	Abraham Maxim
NH08	1808	The Northern Harmony/2	Abraham Maxim
NH16	1816	The Northern Harmony/4	Maxim & Washburn
NH19	1819	The Northern Harmony/5	Abraham Maxim
OH02	1802	The Oriental Harmony	Abraham Maxim
PH13	1813	The Parish Harmony	Japheth C. Washburn
TH18	1818	The Temple Harmony	Japheth C. Washburn
TH20	1820	The Temple Harmony/2	Japheth C. Washburn
TH21	1821	The Temple Harmony/3	Japheth C. Washburn
TH23	1823	The Temple Harmony/4	Japheth C. Washburn
TH24	1824/5	The Temple Harmony/5	Japheth C. Washburn
TH26	1826	The Temple Harmony/6	Japheth C. Washburn
WH20	1820	The Wesleyan Harmony	Henry Little
WH21	1821	The Wesleyan Harmony/2	Henry Little

NOTE: The first two letters of each abbreviation consist of the first letter of each of the two principal words in the tunebook title: "TH" for *Temple Harmony,* for example. The following two digits represent the last two digits in the publication year, all of which are nineteenth-century dates.

and the relative proportion of the various genres. Because these two aspects are often directly related, they will be discussed together.

Group I Tunebooks

Oriental Harmony is unique among the tunebooks compiled in Maine between 1800 and 1830 because it is limited to the tunes of a single composer, Maxim.[2] The other Group I tunebooks (the first two editions of Maxim's *Northern Harmony,* NH05 and NH08, and Charles Robbins's *Columbian Harmony,* CH05) contain music by a variety of composers.

At least 90 percent of the tunes in each collection are by Americans. The American emphasis in the three tunebooks published

TABLE 4

Classification of Extant Maine Tunebooks, 1800–1830

Group	*Dates*	*American Tunes*	*Fuging-Tunes*	*Books*
I	1802–1808	90–100%	26–53%	OH02, CH05, NH05, NH08
II	1813–1816	54–63%	7–39%	PH13, CC15, NH16
III	1818–1820	47–51%	17–20%	TH18, NH19, TH20
IV	1817–1821	2–7%	1–4%	HC17, HC19, WH20, WH21
V	1821–1826	19–26%	1–5%	TH21, TH23, TH24, TH26

by 1805 is not surprising. Not until about 1806 did a church music reform movement begin to have a tangible effect on the tunebooks, both reform and eclectic, being produced in urban areas of Massachusetts. By 1810, even eclectic tunebooks like *Village Harmony* contained a central core of what were referred to as "ancient tunes," largely European tunes written in a simple, nonfuging style considered more appropriate for worship.[3]

NH08, however, the one Maine tunebook published between 1806 and 1810, shows little movement in the direction being taken in urban Massachusetts. The first 151 pages are virtually the same as in NH05, and the majority of additional tunes are by Americans. In selecting tunes with which to augment NH05, Maxim chose mostly American tunes because "the European Music, is less agreeable to the American ear, than her own."[4]

As a resident of interior Maine, Maxim may have been unaware of the changes which were taking place in sacred music in Massachusetts proper. By 1808, he had lived in Maine for about a decade; his early years there were probably consumed with the struggle to make a living from teaching and farming to support his growing family. If he were aware of the changes afoot in some of the newer Massachusetts collections, he was apparently not inclined to follow suit. A former student of the patriotic William Billings, Maxim seems to have shared Billings's pride in things American; he pointedly sought American tunes when preparing the second edition of *Northern Harmony.*

The genres of the settings he added suggest that Maxim did not share the reformers' preference for plain tunes over fuging-tunes.[5] In fact, all the Group I tunebooks except OH02 contain more fuging-tunes than any other genre. On the other hand, like most Maine compilations of the period, they include only a very few set-pieces and anthems. Since extended pieces were probably performed only on special occasions, most Maine tunebook compilers chose to allocate more space to the shorter settings more likely to be performed.

Group II Tunebooks

There is a five-year gap between the last of the Group I tunebooks (1808) and the first of the Group II books (1813), since the only tunebook compiled in Maine during that time is not extant.[6] The dearth of new editions may be related to hard economic times, precipitated by the embargo which was in effect from 1807 to 1809 and the war against Great Britain which began in 1812.[7] If funds were short, singers probably "made do" with the tunebooks they had, as long as the tunes in them were still the ones being sung.[8]

By 1813, however, tunebooks like CH05 and NH08 may not have contained an adequate number of tunes considered suitable for worship if one applied the new standards resulting from the reform movement. If one excluded the fuging-tunes, there were still plenty of tunes in each of the meters; however, if one eliminated the American pieces, the few remaining European ones could scarcely have been sufficient for most purposes. Japheth Coombs Washburn's *Parish Harmony* (PH13) and Edward Hartwell's *Chorister's Companion* (CC15) were new collections which were compatible with the changing preferences in sacred music; they had the added virtue of being more moderately priced than many other books on the market.[9] The fourth edition of *Northern Harmony* (NH16), compiled jointly by Washburn and Maxim, was an updated version of Maxim's previously published tunebook.

The increased number of European tunes in the Group II collections suggests that by the period from 1813 to 1816, even rural Maine residents were showing an interest in European tunes. Nevertheless, American tunes still comprise over half the tunes in the Group II tunebooks. In that respect, they lag behind many of the popular non-Maine collections, such as the 1810 editions of the *Bridgewater Collection* and *Village Harmony,* where American pieces are limited to 8 and 46 percent of the total.[10]

In their prefaces, Washburn and Hartwell used terminology then in vogue, emphasizing that they had primarily chosen music which was "ancient." They were probably aware of the current rhetoric touting such tunes because of their time-tested quality. In keeping with their desire to meet a variety of needs, however, both also inserted tunes "of more modern style,"[11] including some entirely new pieces and a substantial number of American tunes for those who still favored them. In their joint collection, Maxim and Washburn carefully pointed out that they had not selected tunes on the basis of age or nationality.

The fact that the Maine compilers did not completely eliminate tunes deemed unacceptable by Massachusetts reformers does not appear to stem from ignorance. Japheth Washburn was a storeowner whose business and legislative career kept him cognizant of the latest trends in Boston. His unwillingness to adopt only simple, European tunes for his 1813 tunebook and for the 1816 joint collection with Maxim may have resulted from his knowledge of fellow townspeople and his conception of a tunebook which would be "acceptable to those of different tastes, and as extensively useful as possible."[12] Hartwell seems to have had similar goals in mind.

The compilers of this period differ, though, in their opinions of fuging-tunes. Fuging-tunes make up more than a third of the tunes in PH13, but less than a tenth of those in CC15. The disparity between the collections suggests that there may not have been a consensus among Mainers regarding fuging-tunes during this period. Additional evidence is the preface to Maxim's and Washburn's NH16, which notes that they consulted "some very respectable authors and practitioners of sacred music, some of whom are the friends and some the enemies of fuging music."[13] Hartwell apparently belonged to the latter camp.[14] Other Mainers may have continued to enjoy singing fuging-tunes outside of church, especially if such pieces were sung less often during worship services.[15]

The three collections also present conflicting pictures regarding the place of anthems and set-pieces in the Maine repertory. Washburn includes just one anthem and one set-piece, remarking that he thought psalm-tunes would be more useful and acceptable in a book of such small size as his.[16] Hartwell, on the other hand, prints a combined total of seventeen anthems and set-pieces, more than any other Maine tunebook published between 1800 and 1830.[17] The number of extended pieces in NH16 (eight) is halfway between. Clearly, psalmody in rural Maine, where Hartwell lived, was not limited to psalm- and hymn-tunes on Sunday, but must also have encompassed social occasions (including, but not limited to, singing-school exhibitions) where more elaborate pieces were performed.

The Group II emphasis on plain tunes contrasts with the Group I preference for fuging-tunes. Approximately half the tunes in the Group II collections are plain tunes, perhaps as a concession to those calling for simpler tunes for worship. The larger number of plain tunes is also directly related to the larger number of tunes by Europeans in these tunebooks; most of the European compositions are plain tunes.

In Maine, unlike Massachusetts proper, the inclusion of more European tunes of a simple style took place gradually, over a number of years.[18] While not reform collections in all particulars, the Group II tunebooks reflect a movement in that direction, compared to earlier (Group I) publications. American tunes are still much more prevalent in the Maine collections published from 1813 to 1816 than in most contemporaneous New England collections, however. While the reform movement may have begun to affect sacred music in Maine during this period, it does not appear to have been dominant even by 1816, judging from these tunebooks.

Group III Tunebooks

The Group III tunebooks, published between 1818 and 1820, continue the earlier trend by having even more European tunes and fewer fuging-tunes. Still, they are clearly different from the contemporaneous Maine reform tunebooks published between 1817 and 1821 (Group IV tunebooks) due to the substantial number of American tunes they contain. The contents of the three Group III tunebooks suggest that, in Maine, collections with a considerable number of American tunes were marketable as late as 1820.[19]

The three Group III tunebooks, which are strikingly similar to one another, are the fifth edition of Maxim's *Northern Harmony*

(NH19) and the first two editions of Washburn's *Temple Harmony* (TH18 and TH20).[20] They contain about an equal number of American and European tunes; contemporaneous Group IV collections, on the other hand, are completely dominated by European tunes.

Washburn explains his choices of tunes this way: "In the selection of music, the Compiler has not been wholly confined either to American or European Authors, but has taken care to select such as may be useful and pleasing."[21] His middle-of-the-road approach, also demonstrated in PH13, suggests that in 1818 there were still American tunes considered "useful and pleasing" by at least one Maine compiler, although his urban contemporaries in southern New England may have disagreed. Ever the pragmatist, concerned with satisfying as many tastes as possible, Washburn even includes a number of fuging-tunes "in order to render the variety such as to give more general satisfaction."[22]

The fact that he chooses to include almost five dozen fuging-tunes, not just a few token ones as Hartwell did in CC15, suggests that fuging-tunes were still very much a part of the repertory in Maine. Those he includes are suitable for a large number of texts since they represent a variety of meters.[23] Even if their church use was limited in some areas, they may have been popular among singers on other occasions.

More numerous than fuging-tunes, however, are plain tunes, which make up about half of the Group III collections, and tunes with extension, which represent between a quarter and a third of the whole. Continuing the trend evident in the Group II tunebooks, then, tunes without text overlap remain in the majority.

Although American tunes and European tunes are about equally numerous in the Group III tunebooks, the genres (except for tunes with extensions) are not equally represented in terms of provenance. The majority of plain tunes included (62 percent) are European while most of the fuging-tunes (91 percent) are American. The tunes with extension are equally divided between those of American and those of European origin.

The fact that most of the fuging-tunes are by American composers is not surprising. Since the fuging-tune was much more popular in America than in England in the late eighteenth century, Washburn had a larger pool of American fuging-tunes from which to draw. The predominance of plain tunes by Europeans is harder to explain since there were also many American plain tunes from which to choose. One factor may have been a preference for plain tunes in an ornamented, Methodist-style setting, in which several slurred notes were set to each syllable.[24] Although some American tunes in that style had been written, tunes in the Methodist style could more easily be found in the English collections Washburn drew upon for TH18 and TH20: the Lock Hospital Collection[25] and the collections of Aaron Williams.[26]

Group IV Tunebooks

Clearly reform collections, the four Group IV tunebooks contrast sharply with earlier publications because they contain very few American works or fuging-tunes. As we have seen, American tunes were gradually eliminated from Maine tunebooks as the nineteenth century progressed: from a high of 100% in OH02 to 47 percent in TH20. The move away from American tunes peaks in the Group IV collections, where the American tunes comprise less than 8 percent of the total.

The Group IV tunebooks consist of the two editions of *The Hallowell Collection* (HC17 and HC19) and the two editions of Henry Little's *Wesleyan Harmony* (WH20 and WH21). In his prefaces, the compiler of each collection expresses a desire to emphasize time-tested tunes by eminent European composers. Accordingly, over 82 percent of the tunes contained within each edition are European.

The quintessential European-dominated tunebook is *The Hallowell Collection*. In HC17, only 2 percent of the tunes (four tunes total) are American, and only one of these is actually attributed to an American: former Hallowell resident Supply Belcher. It was no doubt a courtesy to include a token song by Hallowell's favorite son, once dubbed "the Handell [*sic*] of Maine" by a Hallowell newspaper writer.[27]

It is likely that the increase in European tunes in published collections over the course of the nineteenth century was partly due to the national copyright statute of 1790, which covered American publications but not foreign ones. Foreign compositions could be reprinted by American publishers at will.[28] In spite of the fact that most American tunebooks after 1790 were copyrighted, however, some collections (such as the Group III tunebooks) continued to print large numbers of American tunes, suggesting that the new law must not have been the principal factor involved.[29]

A more important factor seems to have been the move to reform psalmody, which had become increasingly affected by secular concerns. Community leaders in Massachusetts proper sought to return sacred music to its rightful place as an enhancer of worship rather than merely a pleasurable activity for the singers. The reform movement there can be pinpointed as having taken place between 1806 and 1810.[30] In Maine, however, the full-scale adoption of European tunes, part of the reform platform, took place about a decade later.

In the Group IV tunebooks, plain tunes are a proportionately large part of the whole, while fuging-tunes have diminished to less than 5 percent. Set-pieces and anthems are still not a large portion of the repertory. One might expect that *The Hallowell Collection,* a tunebook endorsed by the Handel Society of Maine, would include more elaborate pieces suitable for performance by such a musical society. Since the principal aim was to provide music for church use, only music which would be of permanent use in the services of the church was selected. Apparently, the extended pieces did not qualify.

Several other aspects of *The Hallowell Collection* make it similar to earlier Massachusetts reform collections. One is that *The Hallowell Collection* does not identify its compiler, but indicates only that the publisher had the assistance of "several gentlemen," thus emphasizing the collective selection process. Also, reform-oriented sentiments are expressed by the Handel Society of Maine officers who endorse the book. They state that it is "well calculated to improve the musical taste of our country and aid the devotional exercises of our Churches."[31]

Unlike the compilers of *The Hallowell Collection,* the editor of the *Wesleyan Harmony,* Henry Little, is identified. As in *The Hallowell Collection,* however, Little includes an endorsement to confirm that the tunes selected "have long stood the test of criticism" and "are proper to be introduced into the Temple of the Most High."[32] In addition, Little states that he undertook the compilation at the request of ministers and other Methodist brethren. His efforts to minimize his role and emphasize the acceptability of his collection to community and religious leaders are consistent with the philosophies of most reform collections, which downplay the role of musicans and single compilers.[33]

Group V Tunebooks

The last four extant editions of Washburn's *Temple Harmony* (TH21, TH23, TH24, TH26) share a number of tunes with both the earlier editions of *Temple Harmony* (Group III) and the reform collections of Group IV. In other ways, however, these tunebooks of the 1820s have characteristics which set them apart from the other groups.

In comparison to the early editions of *Temple Harmony,* the percentage of American tunes has dwindled to a low of 19 percent in TH23 and TH24, down from a high of 47 percent in TH18 and TH20. The decrease in American tunes suggests that by the 1820s, European tunes had clearly won over public opinion, even in Maine. Still, compared to the Group IV tunebooks, published only a few years earlier, the number of American tunes remaining in the Group V tunebooks is significant.

Washburn omits attributions for many of the American tunes in these editions, perhaps to avoid calling attention to their provenance.[34] For example, a number of his own tunes which are identified as such in earlier editions of *Temple Harmony* are unattributed in the later editions. He also fails to provide an attribution for one of William Billings's tunes (LEBANON) and alters and changes the tune name of at least one other piece by Billings.[35] Washburn's actions may have resulted from the criticism being voiced against American tunes (for their supposed crudeness and incorrect harmony) by Lowell Mason and others in the mid-1820s.

In conjunction with the decrease in American tunes (compared to the Group III collections), the Group IV tunebooks also show a substantial decrease in fuging-tunes: from 17 percent in TH18 and TH20 to just 1 percent in TH21, TH23, and TH24. Tunes with extension also decrease: from 30 percent in TH18 and TH20 to a low of 18 percent in TH26. Plain tunes, on the other hand, no longer constitute just half of the collection, but comprise nearly three-quarters of TH26, a proportion similar to that found in WH21, a Group IV tunebook. Washburn's preference for simple tunes extends to altering some tunes of other genres to make them plain tunes.

In some ways, TH26 may represent a retrenchment. While the trend begun with TH18 and continued through TH24 was for a decreasing percentage of American tunes and fuging-tunes, TH26 shows a slight increase in American tunes, accompanied by a small decrease in European tunes, and an ever-so-slight increase in fuging-tunes. The increases and decreases are so minor that too much should not be made of them. The genre proportions of this one tunebook do not necessarily imply, for example, that the mid-1820s signalled a return to fuging-tunes and American tunes in Maine after their apparent demise by the end of the preceding decade. Throughout his compilation career, Washburn included more tunes of this type than most of his New England colleagues. Nevertheless, TH26 is noteworthy in not continuing the trends previously exhibited even in Washburn's tunebooks.

Meters Represented

While the proportion of American tunes and fuging-tunes in Maine tunebooks varies significantly from 1800 to 1830, the relative distribution of poetic meters remains fairly constant throughout the period. In nearly all the collections, Common Meter tunes are the most numerous (usually comprising about one-third of the total), followed by Long Meter, Particular Meter, and Short Meter tunes, in that order.[36] Common, Long, and Short Meter poetry consists of four-line stanzas with a set number of syllables for each line: 8.6.8.6. for Common Meter, 8.8.8.8. for Long Meter, and 6.6.8.6. for Short Meter. Particular Meter refers to other patterns. The relative frequency of the various meters probably coincides with the relative distribution of meters among the metrical psalms and hymns in common use. Many poetic texts were written in Common Meter, for example.

A few of the collections contain a disproportionate number of tunes in one meter or another. OH02, Maxim's first tunebook, shows an unusually large number of Particular Meters, especially for such a small collection: seventeen of the thirty-nine settings. These may have been texts with special appeal for Maxim as a young man. His later tunebooks greatly reduce the number of Particular Meter texts, perhaps because he found that tunes set to such texts, especially those with uncommon, irregular meters, had a much smaller chance of being performed. Washburn's PH13, on the other hand, shows an extremely small number of Particular Meter tunes and a larger-than-usual number of Common Meter tunes.[37] His book, which contains the second smallest number of tunes of all the Maine tunebooks, catered to small societies not able to afford larger collections. Accordingly, he may have decided to include greater numbers of the tunes most likely to be performed: settings for Common Meter texts.

Like Maxim's OH02, Little's WH21 is exceptional because of its large number of Particular Meter tunes (fifty-nine). The emphasis on that meter is directly related to the large number of Particular Meter texts in the Methodist Hymn Book. Little compiled WH20 and WH21 precisely because there were not enough tunes to sing with the Methodist hymns written in usual meters.[38] Since his editions provided tunes for all the meters in the Methodist Hymn Book, they contain more Particular Meter settings than do the other Maine tunebooks. A good assortment of other metrical settings is found as well, however. Like WH20 and WH21, the other Group IV tunebooks contain a large number of Particular Meter texts, perhaps related to the greater number of European settings.[39]

Other than the tunebooks mentioned, most of the Maine tunebooks, regardless of group, share the same general proportions in their metrical content. No major shifts seem to have occurred in the course of the period.

Number of Voices

Although the relative distribution of text meters is quite similar in most of the tunebooks, the tunebooks show differences in the proportion of tunes which are arranged for three, as compared to four, voices. As Table 5 reveals, these differences do not necessarily relate to publication dates. Some of the Group I tunebooks, such as CH05, are near the top of the list because many of their settings are for four voices; other early tunebooks, such as OH02, are much lower in the list.

While four-voice settings predominate in all the tunebooks, three-voice settings are included more frequently in collections published between 1815 and 1823, particularly those containing many European tunes. In fact, the three tunebooks with the largest percentage of three-voice settings are among the collections with the largest percentage of European tunes. While most American and European composers did not limit themselves to composing exclusively for three or for four voices, two-thirds of the three-voice settings in the Maine tunebooks are by Europeans. The im-

TABLE 5

Percentage of Tunes in Each Voice-Number Arrangement (arranged in order of most to least four-voice settings)

		Number of Voices				
Book	*Group*	*5*	*4*	*3*	*2*	*Comb.*
PH15	II		90%	9%	1%	
CH05	I	1%	86%	12%	1%	
TH26	V		86%	13%	1%	
TH24	V		82%	17%		1%
NH05	I		75%	25%		
NH08	I		74%	26%		
NH19	III		72%	28%		
NH16	II		70%	30%		
TH18	III		68%	31%	1%	
TH20	III		68%	31%	1%	
OH02	I		67%	33%		
CC15	II		65%	31%		4%
TH23	V		64%	33%		3%
HC17	IV		64%	35%		1%
TH21	V		62%	35%		3%
HC19	IV		58%	40%		2%
WH21	IV		55%	42%	1%	2%
WH20	IV		55%	44%		1%

plication seems to be that Europeans were more likely than Americans to write three-voice settings.[40] English composers (such as Martin Madan, for example) often wrote tunes in the treble-dominated "Methodist" style, which characteristically featured a three-voice setting with the melody in the top voice. The Methodist style does not necessarily prevail among the three-voice settings in the Maine tunebooks, however.[41]

A stronger correlation seems to exist between the four-voice settings and fuging-tunes. Fuging-tunes, at least those by Maine composers, were almost always set for four voices. The five books containing the most three-voice settings are also among the collections with the fewest fuging-tunes: less than 7 percent in each. Some of the Group I collections which are higher on the list contain a much larger percentage of fuging-tunes and, therefore, a larger percentage of four-voice settings.

This relationship is not invariable, however. Fuging-tunes make up only 5 percent of TH26, which has one of the largest percentages of four-voice settings. This may be related to personal preference on Washburn's part. His first collection tops the table because 90 percent of its tunes are set for four voices.

Tunes in Common Among the Maine Tunebooks

Group I Tunebooks

Since Maxim printed many of his own tunes in his tunebooks and since he compiled three of the four Group I tunebooks, it is not surprising that nearly half of the thirty-eight tunes printed in at least three of the collections were written by him. While many of them do not appear in Robbins's book, two of Maxim's most popular tunes, AUGUSTA and TURNER, are found in all four Group I tunebooks; both also appear in several editions of *Village Harmony,* suggesting that they were known outside of Maine.[42] Both are in the "declamatory duple" style frequently associated with American fuging-tunes, although AUGUSTA is a tune with extension.[43] PSALM FIFTIETH, a Robbins tune which had also appeared in *Village Harmony,* is printed in two of Maxim's books as well as in Robbins's. Metrical considerations may have been a factor in its selection.[44]

The non-Maxim tunes found in all the collections except OH02 (which contains only Maxim's music) may be indicative of the sacred music repertory popular in Maine around 1805.[45] More than a third of the twenty-one tunes are among the "Core Repertory of Early American Psalmody."[46] Many of the inland settlers, the potential purchasers of the Maxim and Robbins collections, were recent immigrants from other areas of New England, particularly Massachusetts. They probably continued to enjoy tunes they had learned as youngsters and which they associated with their church and home experiences. The fact that so many of the tunes shared by the Group I tunebooks are American tunes and/or fuging-tunes again suggests that these types of tunes were still fashionable in Maine around 1805, even if they were beginning to lose favor in urban areas.[47]

Group II Tunebooks

Fuging-tunes probably continued to be sung in the following decade as well, since a fuging-tune, Read's LISBON, is the only shared tune between the Group II tunebooks and the majority of the Group I collections. Even compiler Hartwell, who disliked fuging-tunes, felt the need to include such a popular tune (a Core Repertory piece) in his collection. None of the other twenty settings common to the Group II tunebooks is a fuging-tune, however.[48] While the shared tunes in the first group of tunebooks are predominantly American and primarily fuging-tunes, the majority of those in common in the second group are European plain tunes, suggesting that there may have been a change in the preferred type of music.

Significantly, two-thirds of the shared tunes are part of the Core Repertory, which is based on printings only through 1810. The presence of many of these tunes in the Maine collections printed between 1813 and 1816 shows that in Maine, and probably elsewhere, many of the tunes maintained their popular appeal beyond 1810. Those which continued to be reprinted frequently after 1810 were probably those which met the qualifying standards of reformers because they were "ancient tunes" of time-tested quality.

Group III Tunebooks

The Group III tunebooks are strikingly similar, with a large number of tunes printed in all three collections.[49] TH20 contains all the tunes in TH18, plus seven more. The only extant copy of NH19, an incomplete copy,[50] not only shares 114 of these tunes, but also prints 105 of them on the same pages.[51] The similarities are probably due to the fact that after Maxim and Washburn collaborated on a fourth edition of *Northern Harmony* in 1816, they each published a collection reprinting many of the tunes: Maxim's new edition was NH19, Washburn's was TH18.[52] A fourth of the shared tunes of which we are aware are by Maxim; nearly another fourth are Core Repertory tunes, predominantly those of European origin. A complete copy of NH19 might have additional tunes in common with TH18 and TH20.

Earlier in the chapter, we observed that European tunes became more numerous in the Maine publications after 1810. Not surprisingly, then, most of the tunes shared by all the tunebooks of Groups II and III are European.[53] Still, American tunes had not been completely displaced; a few choice American tunes (Swan's CHINA, Billings's PARIS, and Read's LISBON) are found in both groups of tunebooks.

Read's fuging-tune, LISBON, provides a link among all the collections discussed so far. The shortest fuging-tune in the Core

Repertory, LISBON had only a modest circulation in the period from 1811 to 1820.[54] Nevertheless, it was a fixture in Maine tunebooks (with the exception of the Group IV reform collections) as late as 1820. Its simplicity and easily mastered fuging section probably made it especially appealing to inexperienced singers confused by more complicated fuging-tunes.

Group IV Tunebooks

Since the compilers of *The Hallowell Collection* and *Wesleyan Harmony* used similar criteria in selecting music for their collections, they wound up selecting many of the same tunes: seventy-nine, in fact. Their plan was to choose tunes by authors of eminence, with emphasis on simple, dignified pieces; they excluded fuging-tunes or "light and flimsy airs."

About a quarter of the shared tunes are in the Core Repertory; more significantly, about half of the tunes in common are among the 101 "ancient tunes" identified by Crawford.[55] These "ancient music favorites," which met the criteria of the sacred music reformers, were commonly found in Massachusetts reform collections of 1806–1810. They were incorporated into many eclectic tunebooks by 1810; however, they did not become an important component of the Maine tunebooks until about 1817, again suggesting the later impact of the reform movement in Maine.

Groups III, IV, and V

Many of Crawford's "ancient music favorites" are among the thirty-seven tunes, all of European provenance, which form a similar core in all the Maine tunebooks published between 1817 and 1826.[56] These tunes must have been so important to the repertory that tunebook compilers felt obligated to include them, regardless of their other preferences. Washburn, who was not willing to abandon American tunes completely, selected some American pieces to be included in *Temple Harmony* along with the older European "core" tunes. The compiler of *The Hallowell Collection*, on the other hand, augmented the basic core tunes with others of the same ilk, choosing almost no music by Americans.

About a third of the Maine ancient favorites do not appear on Crawford's list of 101 ancient tunes. One explanation may be that there were regional variations affecting which European tunes were the favorites in a given area. Another possibility is that the favorite "ancient tunes" changed as time went on. Crawford's list is based on tunebooks published in 1810 or before. By 1820, other tunes of a similar style may have displaced some of the ancient tunes most popular in 1810.

While the ideal for worship was a simple tune, a variety of styles could be used. Only about a third of the Maine ancient favorites are set in the simple "common-tune style," characterized by equal-valued notes (usually half notes) with one note per syllable.[57] Although simplicity was valued, variety was also desirable. As might be expected, however, none of the tunes is in the declamatory duple style (often associated with fuging-tunes), although there is one fuging-tune (RANDALL).

The thirty-seven tunes so prevalent in the later Maine tunebooks are included much less frequently in the Maine collections published before 1817, partly because the earliest publications contained a large proportion of American tunes with little space left for European ones.[58] The European tunes that were included were often not the ones that later formed the core of ancient tunes. As the decade progressed, the core tunes became more popular and were included in increasing numbers.[59]

Tunes Most Frequently Reprinted

We have already seen that nineteen tunes, part of the Maine core of ancient favorites, were reprinted at least eleven times, since they appear in all eleven Maine extant editions published after 1816. Seven of these tunes received additional printings in several of the earlier tunebooks. As a result, they are the tunes most frequently printed in the eighteen Maine tunebooks published between 1800 and 1830. These pieces are as follows: WELLS (sixteen printings); MEAR and OLD HUNDRED (fifteen printings); COLCHESTER, IRISH, SILVER STREET, and SUTTON (fourteen printings). WELLS was printed in all the extant Maine tunebooks of the period, except Maxim's OH02 and NH05.[60]

All seven appear on the Core Repertory list; in fact, OLD HUNDRED and WELLS were ranked numbers one and two as the most reprinted tunes in America between 1698 and 1810.[61] All seven are also included in Crawford's tally of the 101 ancient music favorites, signifying that their popularity was not limited to Maine singers. To make the Core Repertory list, they had to be reprinted frequently before 1811; to make the ancient music list, they had to have numerous printings in reform and reform-influenced tunebooks after 1805. In general, they are tunes which stood the test of time and whose dignified style was appropriate even when the criteria for worship music changed after the beginning of the nineteenth century.[62] All seven are plain tunes, a genre which was never under fire. Due to their European provenance, they were not subjected to the criticism faced by many American tunes later in the period, even though they were often no more correct in compositional technique than similar American tunes.

More of the tunes are from Aaron Williams's collections than from any others, a finding consistent with the fact that more tunes in the Maine tunebooks are attributed to him (or to his collections) than to any other composer except Maxim.[63] Maxim's tunebooks are the only ones which do not include Williams's tunes.[64]

As European tunes in a simple style, the seven most frequently reprinted tunes had a place in the Maine repertory nearly from beginning to end. In contrast, the seven *American* tunes which were printed most frequently in the eighteen Maine tunebooks were not maintained in the repertory throughout the period. These tunes are as follows: Swan's CHINA, Maxim's KNOXVILLE, and Read's WINDHAM (twelve printings); Maxim's AUGUSTA and Swan's POLAND (eleven printings); Read's LISBON and Morgan's SYMPHONY (ten printings). They were usually excluded from the reform collections (Group IV). Only two (WINDHAM and LISBON) are Core Repertory tunes; only POLAND is on Crawford's list of ancient tunes. None is part of the core of thirty-seven ancient tunes reprinted most frequently in Maine. Maxim, Swan, and Read are each represented by two tunes.

As the compiler of a quarter of the extant Maine tunebook editions, Maxim had ample opportunity to publish his own tunes. Partly because of this, tunes by Maxim are more numerous in Maine tunebooks than those of any other American composer; over four hundred printings are attributable to him. For two pieces to be among the most reprinted American tunes in Maine tunebooks, however, they had to be selected by other compilers as well.[65] These tunes, clearly among his most popular ones, are even printed in *Village Harmony*.

KNOXVILLE, transcribed and discussed in Chapter XIII, is uncharacteristic of Maxim's usual writing. Part of its appeal may have been its similarity in style to the Methodist-inspired, decorated duple tunes which became so popular in the latter part of the period. KNOXVILLE continued to be printed in Maine through 1826. The other Maxim tune, AUGUSTA, was altered for post-1820 printings. The later publications omitted the second half of the tune, transforming it from a two-verse tune with extension in declamatory duple style to a one-verse plain tune. Perhaps the change was made because the declamatory duple style was less fashionable later in the period.

The two tunes by Daniel Read are both Core Repertory tunes. WINDHAM, which begins rhythmically like WELLS, the most frequently reprinted tune in Maine, was one of the few American tunes to be praised by nineteenth-century American musicians, including Lowell Mason.[66] Its stylistic similarity to the European tunes in vogue in the 1820s allowed it to slip into Maine tunebooks of that era. Consistent with the changing attitude toward fuging-tunes in the 1820s, Read's fuging-tune, LISBON, was printed in only one Maine tunebook published after 1820 (TH26).

Two tunes by Timothy Swan are also among the American tunes most often printed in the Maine collections. While Swan's tunes appeared in Maine tunebooks less frequently than those of several other American composers,[67] CHINA and POLAND were so well accepted that they even penetrated two of the reform collections.[68] Maine compiler Washburn was so fond of CHINA that he named his town after the tune and included it in every tunebook he wrote.[69] He was not alone in his high opinion of the piece; Swan himself apparently preferred it to his other works, and as one of his most enduring tunes, CHINA was published in hymnals as late as 1921.[70] As minor-mode plain tunes in slow triple meters, both CHINA and POLAND were solemn and dignified enough to be sung in church even in the 1820s.

The other American tune with many Maine printings is Justin Morgan's SYMPHONY. The piece is a setting of Isaac Watts's popular versification of Psalm 50, First Part, a Particular Meter text with six lines of ten syllables each.[71] Maine compilers may have selected SYMPHONY partly because it met the need for a tune in that meter. In addition, Morgan's setting of the last two lines is texturally interesting and unusual. The voices enter cumulatively in turn but without text overlap. Reformers later in the period could not complain that the staggered entrances obscured the words.

Summary

The repertory in the Maine tunebooks shows a definite progression in the course of two decades from predominantly American pieces and many fuging-tunes early in the period to predominantly European pieces and very few fuging-tunes later in the period. While Massachusetts sources reflect a reform movement beginning around 1805, in Maine the change took place around 1817 and was not so sudden, but reflected gradual changes in the course of the previous five years. Once the change did occur in 1817, all the tunebooks began to include a core of European tunes of simple style. While many of these tunes were also printed in the early Massachusetts reform collections of 1805–1810, some were not.

The Maine compilers reflected their individual preferences and biases by augmenting this core of ancient tunes with other tunes of various sorts. In their last extant collections, Maxim and Washburn demonstrated their independent Yankee spirit by continuing to include a comparatively large number of American tunes and fuging-tunes at a time when such tunes had been systematically eliminated from most other New England tunebooks.

CHAPTER XIII

TUNES BY THE MAINE COMPILERS

In previous chapters, the lives and tunebooks of the Maine compilers were surveyed. This chapter will examine tunes composed by Maine psalmodists Abraham Maxim, Japheth Coombs Washburn, Edward Hartwell, and Charles Robbins. Tunes by Henry Little, compiler of *Wesleyan Harmony,* are not included here because none is specifically attributed to him in the Maine tunebooks. He was probably responsible for several adaptations printed in *Wesleyan Harmony,* but he is not known to have composed any original tunes.

Although a comprehensive analysis of each composer's style remains to be done, some of their characteristic compositional practices will be discussed as we compare their approaches to the same genre or text. These four men were not the only hymn-tune composers who lived in Maine between 1800 and 1830, but they appear to have been the most prolific.[1] This chapter will be limited to a survey of their tunes.

Table 6 summarizes the output of the four Maine composer-compilers by genre (see Chapter I for genre definitions). An index of these tunes is provided in Part III.[2]

As Table 6 shows, Maxim published considerably more tunes than the others did.[3] His tunes account for about half of the total. Those by Washburn and Robbins each comprise a fifth of the Maine tunes, with Hartwell's constituting the remaining tenth.[4] The overall distribution of tunes by genre is rather similar to the proportion of tunes of each type in most of the Maine tunebooks of the period. Plain tunes and tunes with extension constitute the majority of the tunes (two-thirds in this case), with fuging-tunes accounting for slightly over one-quarter, and set-pieces and anthems trailing with less than one-twelfth of the total.

TABLE 6

Classification of Maine Tunes by Genre

	Compositions by				
Genre	*Hartwell*	*Maxim*	*Robbins*	*Washburn*	*Total*
Plain tunes	9	39	11	22	81
Tunes with ext.	8	44	20	11	83
Fuging-tunes	2	40	13	13	68
Set-pieces	6	2	1	1	10
Anthems	0	2	2	0	4
Total	25	127	47	47	246

As compilers, these men apparently thought anthems were less useful for most purposes and included only a few in their tunebooks. As composers, the same reasoning may have caused them to concentrate their creative energy on other genres of psalm- and hymn-tunes: those which would receive more frequent performance. The published tunes of Maxim and Robbins include only three set-pieces and four anthems between them. A single set-piece by Washburn is his only known extended piece. Only Hartwell wrote a proportionately large number of set-pieces, in terms of his total output.

Table 6 also displays the individuality of these composers in terms of the genres in which they most frequently wrote. For example, Hartwell wrote about the same number of set-pieces, plain tunes, and tunes with extension, but wrote noticeably few fuging-tunes, since he was "averse to the volatile and fugeing style which has characterised so much of our modern compositions."[5] Maxim wrote about an equal number of plain tunes, tunes with extension, and fuging-tunes, while Washburn wrote about twice as many plain tunes as any other type, and Robbins focused on tunes with extension.

While there is no definitive explanation for these differences, they may be related to the creativity and skill levels of the various composers. For example, Robbins, one of the few Maine composers to write in every genre, often experimented with various approaches. Instead of setting texts as he found them, he often took the creative liberty of repeating a word here, extending a phrase there, to provide added emphasis. As a result, more of his compositions are tunes with extension than any other genre. A less skilled composer (Washburn may be an example) might have preferred to rely on the structure inherent in a text, and, as a result, more of his tunes would be plain tunes.

In the remainder of this chapter, several representative Maine plain tunes, tunes with extension, and fuging-tunes will be presented. Due to the small number of set-pieces and anthems composed by the Maine psalmodists, those genres will not be examined here.[6] In general, the most frequently reprinted tunes of each composer were selected for discussion.[7] These were probably their best-known tunes, the ones singers of their day associated with them. They also exemplify the favored styles of the early nineteenth century, although metrical considerations, rather than the quality or popularity of a tune, sometimes determined which tunes were reprinted.[8] Although the selected tunes cannot show all facets of each composer's style, they will serve as a starting point from which comparisons with their other tunes can be made.

Editorial Procedures for the Musical Examples

Unless otherwise indicated, the musical examples present the pitches and rhythms as published. Obvious printing errors have been corrected and noted in an end note when the example is first mentioned by number, while momentary dissonances which were probably not printing mistakes have been left as in the original.

Although the tunes were published in open score, using treble, alto, and bass clefs, they have been transcribed onto two staves for analysis purposes. In three-voice settings, the middle (tenor) voice has been notated here on either treble or bass staves, depending on the range, but with stems opposite of those used for the treble or bass voice part.

The symbol for the third mode of common time (a reversed C) has been replaced by the modern equivalent (2/2); none of the tunes originally had a 2/2 time signature. Key signatures have been notated on each staff throughout a tune even though some of the printings include them only at the beginning of the piece.

In some passages, more than one note is provided for a given voice; these "choosing notes" allowed the singers to choose which note they wanted to sing.

Plain Tunes

A plain tune sets a single strophe (occasionally two strophes) of a psalm or hymn. Additional strophes are sung to the same music. The music is strictly dependent on the text for structure, with each textual phrase set to a single phrase of music, without verbal or musical repetition. Although plain tunes were written throughout the period, they became particularly numerous by the 1820s, prompted by reformers who touted simple, unelaborated tunes as most suitable for worship.

The plain tunes which will be discussed in this section are AUGUSTA by Washburn, FALMOUTH by Maxim, PSALM FIFTIETH by Robbins, and TRIBUNAL by Hartwell. Their titles are fairly typical. Sometimes an early-nineteenth-century psalm- or hymn-tune title, like PSALM FIFTIETH or TRIBUNAL, referred to the text most closely associated with the tune. More often, though, the title was unrelated to the text, since a tune could be sung with a variety of texts. Town names were popular choices for titles. Like many pieces by the Maine psalmodists, two of these plain tunes are named for Maine towns: AUGUSTA and FALMOUTH. These two tunes also share the same key and meter; PSALM FIFTIETH and TRIBUNAL set the same text.

Washburn's AUGUSTA and Maxim's FALMOUTH

Judging from the tunebooks in which they were printed, AUGUSTA (Example 1)[9] and FALMOUTH (Example 2) must have been favorites of their respective composers. AUGUSTA is the only Washburn plain tune to appear in every one of his extant editions. Similarly, FALMOUTH is printed in all the extant Maxim tunebooks.[10] Maxim's FALMOUTH was not published in any of Washburn's books, however, and Washburn's AUGUSTA was excluded from all of Maxim's collections except the fourth edition of *Northern Harmony,* which was jointly compiled by Maxim and Washburn.

FALMOUTH is set for four voices, while AUGUSTA is set for three. The voice parts, from top to bottom, are called treble, counter, tenor, and bass, with the counter omitted in the three-voice setting. Although both types of settings are found among the tunes by the Maine psalmodists, four-voice settings predominate.[11] As was customary in hymn-tune settings of the time, the melody, or "air," is scored for the tenor voice, while a comple-

Example 1. AUGUSTA by Japheth Coombs Washburn, from *Temple Harmony,* second edition (1820), p. 152.

Example 2. FALMOUTH by Abraham Maxim, from *Northern Harmony*, fifth edition (1819), p. 44.

mentary melody appears in the treble.[12] AUGUSTA and FALMOUTH contain several phrases in which the treble and tenor, rhythmically similar, move in parallel or contrary motion.[13] Such writing is usual in this style.

Both tunes are examples of what Richard Crawford calls "triple-time tunes."[14] They are notated in a slow triple meter (3/2) in which the half-note beat is one second in length.[15] Although the simplest and earliest type of triple-time tune was somewhat austere, alternating long and short notes to coincide with text syllables sung on the first and third beats of the measure, eighteenth-century composers often wrote more mellifluous settings, like the ones demonstrated here.[16] Instead of unadorned alternations of whole and half notes, AUGUSTA and FALMOUTH frequently feature brief melismas made up of shorter notes.[17]

Triple meters are in the minority among the tunes written by Washburn, Maxim, Robbins, and Hartwell, making up less than one-fifth of each composer's output. Excluding set-pieces and anthems, Robbins and Hartwell each wrote only one or two tunes in triple meter.[18] The Maine composers' preference for duple meters was shared by other psalmodists; triple-time tunes are generally rarer after about 1790 than before. The move toward duple meters may be related to the greater number of rhythmic and stylistic possibilities they offered.[19]

As in most of the plain tunes composed by the Maine compilers, each textual phrase of AUGUSTA and FALMOUTH is set to a different musical phrase with little, if any, resemblance between them. While Maxim uses stepwise motion throughout FALMOUTH, Washburn achieves contrast in AUGUSTA by setting the first and third phrases to melodies which include many skips (nearly all of which arpeggiate the tonic triad), while the second and fourth employ largely stepwise motion.

Due to the meters of the texts which are set, the four phrases of FALMOUTH are of equal length, while the third phrase of AUGUSTA is slightly longer than the others. FALMOUTH sets a Long Meter text, with four lines of eight syllables each (8.8.8.8.); AUGUSTA sets a Short Meter text, also four lines long, but with syllable lengths 6.6.8.6. Both texts, like the majority of psalms and hymns set by the Maine composers, are from the works of Isaac Watts, the influential eighteenth-century English hymn-writer.[20]

Although the four individual phrases of FALMOUTH differ, the last two phrases demonstrate the use of sequence, a device more commonly used by Maxim than by the other Maine composers.[21] Sequences are also frequently found in tunes by William Billings, Maxim's teacher. In a short tune with otherwise dissimilar phrases, they provide a sense of coherence.

While there are no sequences in Washburn's AUGUSTA, his setting demonstrates a simple use of another device which is often found in early American psalmody: word painting, the depiction of a text by musical means.[22] Dynamic markings indicate that the fourth phrase, "And loud repeat their song," should be sung loud, thus matching the musical expression to the text. In general, though, Washburn tends to use word painting less often than the other Maine psalmodists.

The harmonic progressions in the Maxim and Washburn settings may sound somewhat odd to the modern ear because they are not based on common-practice tonal harmony. Like Anglo-American parish-church composers of the eighteenth century, the Maine sacred music composers of the early nineteenth century seem to have been more concerned with writing smooth, predominantly linear melodies in which the simultaneous sounds formed consonant intervals, than with building chords which progress according to certain principles. The compositional procedure was additive, with a single voice written at a time and the remaining voices fitted one by one to the previously completed voice lines.[23] Except for the small minority of composers with European training, most of the New England psalmodists followed William Tans'ur's rules rather than principles of tonal harmony.[24]

Since the successive vertical sonorities were the result of the linear writing and were not conceived of as chords needing to progress in a particular order, the resulting chord sequences in some of the Maine tunes seem somewhat static. In AUGUSTA, in particular, the contrary motion of the outer voices in the second phrase produces some unusual chord successions, which would not be appropriate in a tonal setting: iii(6), I(6), ii, I, vi.[25] Nevertheless, the motion is often directed toward familiar harmonic pillars, with phrases frequently beginning and ending on tonic or dominant chords.[26]

Certain practices which are unacceptable in common-practice harmony are found in these tunes. For example, the tenor and bass form a series of parallel fifths in mm. 5–6 of Washburn's AU-

GUSTA; the parallelism is acceptable in this style, however, since Tans'ur's rules permit parallel fifths and octaves as long as they are covered by a higher part.[27] Unusual dissonances or cross-relations sometimes occur. While they may sometimes be the result of a printing error, in other cases they appear to be by-products of the linear voice leading.[28]

In this idiom, it is not uncommon for only two different pitches of a triad to be present, particularly for opening chords, where it may have been difficult to "tune" the third properly. The Maine composers seem especially prone to omit a chord tone in three-voice settings, where there are fewer voices to cover the notes of the triad. In AUGUSTA, Washburn's three-voice setting, for example, many of the triads are incomplete, with the third omitted most frequently.[29]

Two Settings of Psalm 50

Between 1770 and 1820, Isaac Watts's metrical paraphrase of Psalm 50 was set more frequently by American psalmodists than any other of his texts.[30] Two of the Maine compilers, Edward Hartwell and Charles Robbins, made plain-tune settings of the text. Both settings are in the third mode of common time (equivalent to 2/2 meter) and are in major keys, as are the majority of Psalm 50 settings by other psalmodists.[31] Robbins's is called PSALM FIFTIETH (Example 3), Hartwell's, TRIBUNAL (Example 4). Robbins's setting was one of his most popular pieces.[32] Hartwell's version, like all of his tunes, does not seem to have been reprinted.[33]

The Watts text is in Particular Meter, consisting of four lines of ten syllables each, followed by two lines of eleven syllables. As in the Maxim and Washburn plain tunes, each of the phrases in the Hartwell and Robbins settings has a different melody; however, the tenor melodies in the first and third phrases (mm. 1–4 and 9–12) of Robbins's tune are similar in contour, range, and longer pitches. All phrases are articulated by whole notes at the ends of phrases. In TRIBUNAL, the rests between most of the adjacent phrases serve to separate the tune even more clearly into six distinct units.

The text deals with the Day of Judgment and refers to the trumpet sounding, hell trembling, and heaven rejoicing. Kroeger suggests that psalmodists may have been attracted to the text by its

Example 3. PSALM FIFTIETH by Charles Robbins, from *Columbian Harmony* (1805), p. 137.

Example 4. TRIBUNAL by Edward Hartwell, from *Chorister's Companion* (1815), p. 85.

strong verbal images of universal judgment; in many of the settings—particularly fuging-tune settings—the composer responds to these images with word painting.[34]

Both of the Maine settings show several examples of word painting. Perhaps as an allusion to a trumpet fanfare, Robbins's melody is frequently triadic. In both settings, ascending tenor melodies coincide with the beginning of the last phrase ("Lift up your heads"). Robbins extends the upward motion slightly longer than Hartwell.[35] Both settings extend the duration of the word "sounds" in "The trumpet sounds": Hartwell by placing a fermata over it, Robbins by making it a whole note (the only whole note occurring in midphrase rather than at a cadence).[36] On "hell trembles" (m. 22), Hartwell inserts small notes of transition which produce a slight trembling effect in the treble and tenor voices. Perhaps the half-step dissonance formed between treble and counter in m. 19 of Robbins's setting is also intended to depict hell trembling.

Since both compositions are arranged for four voice parts, complete triads could perhaps be more easily scored than in three-voice settings. Almost all of Hartwell's triads are complete, but incomplete triads are sometimes found in Robbins's tune, where the last chord, for example, lacks a fifth. Although the use of sevenths is infrequent among the New England psalmodists, Robbins enlivens the harmony with the use of occasional dominant-seventh chords at cadences.[37] He also uses tonal-sounding cadential formulas such as ii(6), I(6–4), V, I to end the second phrase and a similar pattern for the final cadence.

Because the lines were probably composed additively, unusual dissonances and cross-relations sometimes occur in these tunes as well as in those by Washburn and Maxim. The discordances are usually momentary clashes, resulting from stepwise voice leading, although some are puzzling.[38] Several instances of parallel fifths and octaves are also found, not all of which are acceptable even by Tans'ur's rules.[39]

In these two tunes, the chords formed by simultaneous voices usually progress in a tonally acceptable manner. Hartwell's setting seems somewhat more static than Robbins's because Hartwell tends to dwell on the tonic and dominant chords for a greater length of time. Robbins achieves a greater sense of tonal sophistication and focus by using supertonic and subdominant chords to precede dominant chords.

Because they establish a tonal center (by their frequent reference to tonic and dominant chords), Hartwell and Robbins are also able to effect common-chord modulations. Such modulations turn out to be only temporary tonicizations or "quasi-modulations," however;[40] the following phrase returns abruptly to the original (tonic) key as if no key change had taken place.[41] Such a practice is common in Robbins's hymn-tunes.

Cadential resting points vary in these pieces, which contain six phrases per strophe instead of the more usual four. While phrases in most Maine tunes usually end on tonic or dominant triads, several other chords serve to conclude phrases in these two tunes. In each case, the choice of cadential triads other than tonic and dominant seems purposeful. Robbins's use of the submediant to end the fourth phrase may be a subtle form of word painting to correspond with the text "distant worlds and regions of the dead." The brief diversion to the relative minor may be intended to represent the sorrowful state of the dead as well as to move the tonal center to a "distant" area. In the Hartwell tune, the subdominant chord at the end of the fifth phrase leads to the dominant triad which begins the final phrase; the result is a linkage between the final two phrases, whose texts are related (heaven rejoices, saints lift up their heads).

Many of the American settings of Psalm 50, including William Billings's WRENTHAM, are modelled after LANDAFF, a British Psalm 50 setting frequently attributed to Edward Blancks.[42] As in LANDAFF, the phrases of both Maine tunes begin with a dactylic (long-short-short) rhythm. The phrases of Robbins's setting also have similar melodic contours to LANDAFF and WRENTHAM.[43] The similarities between Robbins's and Billings's settings of Watts's Psalm 50 suggest that Robbins may have been familiar with the latter.[44]

Although the rhythm in Hartwell's TRIBUNAL is not substantially different from that in LANDAFF, Hartwell replaces the opening dactyl of three phrases with upbeat patterns which help him to better match textual and musical accents.[45] Since LANDAFF is printed in Hartwell's tunebook (on the page before TRIBUNAL), Hartwell's setting had to be somewhat different from LANDAFF or there would be little need for it. While the first four phrases of LANDAFF use an identical rhythmic pattern, Hartwell uses one pattern for the first and third phrases, another for the second and fourth.[46] By doing so, he not only provides variety, but also organizes the six phrases into three groups of two.[47]

Tunes with Extension

Tunes with extension are slightly more elaborate settings of psalms or hymns in which the text does not completely determine the musical structure. Phrases may be extended by repeating one or more words, or entire phrases may be repeated, sometimes through the use of repeat signs. The four Maine tunes with extension to be discussed here (KNOXVILLE by Maxim, DORCHESTER by Washburn, ACCORD by Robbins, and CAPERNAUM by Hartwell) demonstrate several different types of repetition by which psalmodists extended texts.

Maxim's KNOXVILLE (Example 5), a setting of two verses of Watts's Psalm 47,[48] uses repeat signs to reiterate the words and music of the second verse. Without the repeat, KNOXVILLE would be a plain tune. Unlike many tunes, in which each phrase is different, KNOXVILLE has identical musical settings for the first and third phrases (mm. 1–5 and 8–12); in addition, the upper two voices of the fifth phrase are essentially repeated a fifth lower for the sixth phrase.[49]

Robbins's ACCORD (Example 6) also has repeat signs referring to the last part of the tune; however, within the repeated section, phrases three and four of the text are set twice, first for just two voice parts, then for all four. The setting may be prompted by the text phrase "Join in a song": two voices sing, then the other two join in.[50] In performance, then, the first two text phrases are sung once, followed by the next two phrases sung four times each.

Washburn's DORCHESTER (Example 7) shows one of the most typical forms for tunes with extension: the last of the four text phrases ("Pour out a long complaint") is repeated with a different melody, resulting in five musical phrases instead of four. As in Robbins's tune, the repetition can be related to the text ("a long complaint," requiring two phrases rather than one).

Hartwell's CAPERNAUM (Example 8), on the other hand, is a more atypical tune with extension in several ways. The Particular Meter text, taken from the Methodist Hymn Book, is itself irregular, with syllable lengths 8.7.8.7.4.4.3.[51] Another unusual feature is that the repeated phrases in Hartwell's setting are not the final

Example 5. KNOXVILLE by Abraham Maxim, from *Northern Harmony,* second edition (1808), pp. 14–15.

Example 6. ACCORD by Charles Robbins, from *Columbian Harmony* (1805), p. 31.

Example 7. DORCHESTER by Japheth Coombs Washburn, from *Temple Harmony,* second edition (1820), p. 216.

Example 8. CAPERNAUM by Edward Hartwell, from *Chorister's Companion* (1815), p. 96.

phrases, as in most Maine tunes with extension, but the short, four-syllable penultimate phrases: "He is able" and "He is willing." The tenor melody utilizes sequential or near-sequential patterns for the repetitions.[52] Hartwell may have repeated these particular phrases not only to make them of similar length to the other phrases but also to emphasize the text, which asserts Jesus' willingness and ability to save the sinner.

Besides demonstrating different ways texts were extended, these four settings illustrate four different styles of writing and show that diverse tunes exist within a given genre. Washburn's DORCHESTER, like his plain tune, AUGUSTA, is a triple-time tune, set in a slow 3/2 meter. As in AUGUSTA, the text syllables of DORCHESTER are alternately one or two beats in duration, but with slurred melismas frequently replacing whole and half notes to vary the rhythm.

KNOXVILLE, on the other hand, is written in the Methodist-inspired style which Crawford refers to as "decorated duple."[53] The popularity of this style may be part of the reason KNOXVILLE was Maxim's most frequently printed tune, published in Maine tunebooks from 1802 through 1826.[54] Like most decorated duple tunes, it is notated in a lively 2/4 meter in many of the printings,[55] is arranged for three voice parts, moves mostly in quarter and eighth notes, has a text dealing with a cheerful subject, a delicately ornamented style, and at least one repeated phrase. As in a trio sonata, the upper two voices provide the melodic interest, while the bass furnishes the harmonic foundation.[56]

Robbins's ACCORD is also in duple meter, but is an example of "declamatory duple" style. While the half note is the basic unit in this style, the declamatory quarter notes in at least one section, often the second, enliven the tune.[57] The declamatory duple style, although often found in fuging-tunes, is not limited to tunes of that type. A number of Robbins's tunes with extension qualify as declamatory duple tunes.[58] Like many fuging-tunes, they feature repeated notes in the latter part of the tune, which is then repeated. The sectional nature of most declamatory duple tunes is also found in ACCORD, where a change in texture signals the beginning of the second section at m. 5.

While the preceding three tunes exemplify triple-time, decorated duple, and declamatory duple styles, Hartwell's CAPERNAUM defies conventional labels. Although in duple meter, CA-

PERNAUM cannot be accurately described as either a decorated or declamatory duple tune. Like most decorated duple tunes, the first half of CAPERNAUM has a time signature of 2/4, but it lacks the melodic repetition, cheerful text, major key, and ornamented style typical of tunes in decorated duple style. The second half, set in the 2/2 meter common to declamatory duple tunes, lacks the insistent quarter note motion typical of that style. The difficulty one has in classifying CAPERNAUM makes it a typical Hartwell tune. Many of his tunes are characterized by diverse phrases, melodically and rhythmically, which hinder categorization into a single style.

Another of the tunes with extension, Maxim's KNOXVILLE, is somewhat unusual in terms of harmonic practice; the chords formed seem to follow tonal principles. Tonic chords are preceded by dominant chords, and dominant chords by dominant preparation chords such as ii or IV or a secondary dominant. While it is not uncommon for the Maine psalmodists to use chromatically altered chords which could function as secondary dominants, the chord which follows is frequently not the expected one. In such a case, the chromatic alteration probably results from linear rather than vertical considerations. In KNOXVILLE, however, the chromatically altered chords function as true secondary chords. A secondary dominant of the dominant is used in m. 7, and a secondary seventh of the dominant chord (vii of V) is used in m. 19. Conventional cadential formulas, such as I(6–4), V or V(7), I are found at the ends of each of the verses (mm. 14–15 and 30–31).

Even though familiar-sounding harmonic patterns exist, the triads are frequently incomplete, lacking the third or fifth. As noted previously, the use of incomplete chords seems to be more frequent in tunes set for three voices, but is not at all unusual in music of the Yankee psalmodists.

Fuging-Tunes

Although fuging-tunes did not constitute the majority of tunes written by any of the Maine compilers, they were among their most reprinted tunes and are perhaps most representative of their styles.[59] As indicated in Chapter XII, fuging-tunes continued to be printed in Maine tunebooks as late as 1820, long after they had been eliminated from other New England tunebooks.

A fuging-tune is a strophic psalm- or hymn-tune setting containing one or more sections in which the voices enter successively, producing verbal conflict. The textual overlap was one of the reasons fuging-tunes were considered by some to be unacceptable in worship services; churchgoers could not usually participate in the singing and supposedly could not understand the words being sung by the choir.

The fuging-tunes to be discussed in this section are TURNER by Maxim, NEW-PLYMOUTH by Washburn, and ELEMENT by Robbins.[60] Maxim's TURNER (Example 9), named after the Maine town where he spent most of his adult life, was printed almost as often as KNOXVILLE.[61] ELEMENT (Example 10) was the most frequently reprinted fuging-tune of Charles Robbins.[62] NEW-PLYMOUTH (Example 11),[63] one of Japheth Coombs Washburn's earliest published tunes, was reprinted more often than most of his compositions.

All three fuging-tunes use texts by Watts[64] and are written in the third mode of common time (the equivalent of 2/2), the time signature found in all of Robbins's and Washburn's fuging-tunes. Like nearly all the fuging-tunes by these three Maine composers, each of the tunes is set for four voices.[65] The effect of four overlapping voices was more dramatic than three and was apparently considered preferable.

While the other genres of tunes by the Maine composers show a variety of styles and approaches, their fuging-tunes are quite similar. The majority of their fuging-tunes, like those of other New England psalmodists, begin homophonically with all the voices declaiming the text together. In the next section, a "fugal" section, the voices enter one at a time, producing textual overlap through staggered entrances. In the final few measures, the voices usually resume the homophonic texture of the beginning. All three of the tunes under discussion exhibit the structure just described. While the section lengths and overall tune lengths vary according to the meter set, Maine fuging-tunes are typically only about sixteen or seventeen measures long, as is true of these three tunes.

Like the vast majority of their fuging-tunes, these three tunes are written in the declamatory duple style. The second (fugal) section in all three tunes features a series of quarter notes, with at least two or three repeated pitches in a row. Repeated quarter notes are a notable feature in Maxim's TURNER; they are present, though

Example 9. TURNER by Abraham Maxim, from *Northern Harmony,* second edition (1808), p. 50.

Example 10. ELEMENT by Charles Robbins, from *Columbian Harmony* (1805), p. 70.

Example 11. NEW-PLYMOUTH by Japheth Coombs Washburn, from *Northern Harmony,* second edition (1808), p. 146.

less prominent, in Washburn's NEW-PLYMOUTH. Declamatory duple tunes may differ in the amount of contrast between sections. Of the three fuging-tunes discussed here, Robbins's tune exhibits the most internal contrast.

The first two phrases of ELEMENT (mm. 1–7) are set to a smoothly flowing melody, dominated by stepwise motion, with none of the pitches in the tenor melody repeated without an intervening pitch. The melodic flow directly relates to the text ("There is a stream whose gentle flow"). Other examples of word painting, a device often used by Robbins, are the melismas on "stream" and "gentle." The second section (mm. 8–16), on the other hand, has a more angular melody, emphasizing repeated pitches and skips, rather than stepwise motion.

The sections of Maxim's TURNER display much less contrast, since repeated quarter notes appear in the tenor melody from the very beginning. Nevertheless, the textual change produced by the fugal entrances provides contrast. Perhaps to provide rhythmic impetus, the fuges[66] of all three of the tunes discussed in this section begin with an upbeat, a feature common to many fuging-tunes.

As in most fuging-tunes, the first two voices to enter in the fuges of TURNER and NEW-PLYMOUTH are the basses and tenors. Table 7, which summarizes the entrance orders used in the Maine tunes, shows that the typical practice was to begin with men's voices. Unlike Maxim and Washburn, Robbins experimented with various arrangements, including paired voices. In ELEMENT, for example, the treble and bass enter together, followed by the counter and tenor.

The type and degree of imitation between the entrances in the fugal section of a fuging-tune can vary considerably. Fuging-tunes are not "fugues" in the conventional sense and do not usually proceed with real or tonal answers. In most cases, however, the staggered entrances in a fuging-tune are similar rhythmically, if not melodically. In TURNER, as in most of Maxim's fuging-tunes, several of the entrances (bass, tenor, and treble, in this case) begin with the same melody and rhythm, usually at the unison or octave.

The typical practice in Robbins's fuging-tunes is for only two of the fuging voices to be melodically similar, although all the entrances may be rhythmically alike. ELEMENT is an example: while

TABLE 7

Fugal Entrance Order, Fuging-tunes of the Maine Compilers (number of tunes of each type)

NOTE: Voice parts separated below by a comma enter successively; those separated by a slash enter simultaneously.

	Fuging-tunes by		
Entrance Order	*Maxim*	*Robbins*	*Washburn*
Four-voice settings:			
Bass, tenor, treble, counter	24	3	7
Bass, tenor, counter, treble	14	4	4
Bass, tenor, counter/treble	1		1
Bass/treble, tenor/counter		4	1
Bass/counter, tenor, treble		1	
Tenor, bass/counter/treble		1	
Three-voice settings			
Bass, tenor, treble	1		
Bass/treble, tenor		1	
Total	40	14[67]	13

the first five beats of the tenor and bass entrances are identical, the counter and treble lines are melodically different. Robbins adds another touch of imitation in mm. 10 and 11, where the dotted-eighth/sixteenth note rhythm and descending melody in the treble is imitated an octave lower in the tenor a measure later. The uneven rhythm contrasts with the evenness of the surrounding quarter notes. The reminiscence of dotted rhythms, which were featured prominently in the first section, helps unify the piece.

Unlike Maxim's and Robbins's fuging-tunes, in which two or more voices begin with the same melody more often than not, most of Washburn's fuging-tunes have different melodies for each of the entering voices in the fugal section. Such is the case in NEW-PLYMOUTH, where the entrances differ in rhythm as well as in pitch, although the counter and bass share comparable pitch sequences and the four parts exhibit similar declamation.

American fuging-tunes are of two types. In an integrated fuging-tune, the fuging section is integral to the whole and cannot be omitted. The fuging-tune with fuging-chorus, on the other hand, features an initial homophonic section which is complete in itself, containing the complete text and ending on a tonic chord. In this type, the fuging-chorus is optional and may be omitted, if desired.

TURNER, ELEMENT, and NEW-PLYMOUTH are all integrated fuging-tunes, as are the majority of fuging-tunes by the Maine composers, as well as other American composers. In fact, all of Robbins's and Washburn's fuging-tunes are integrated fuging-tunes.[68] Maxim, on the other hand, wrote seven tunes with fuging-choruses.[69] He may have modelled them after those of his teacher, William Billings, who wrote a comparatively large number of tunes with fuging-choruses.

The harmonic practices previously observed in other tunes by these composers are evident here as well. As in his other tunes, Robbins frequently uses standard cadential formulas in ELEMENT. In the final cadence, for example, the last four chords are IV, I(6), V(7), I.[70] At internal cadences, Robbins is fond of preceding the dominant triad with its dominant, as he does here in m. 3. As in his other settings, he frequently omits the third or fifth from triads, omissions often explainable for reasons of tuning or voice leading.[71]

Maxim, too, omits chord tones in TURNER, but most frequently in the first and last chords of phrases.[72] Throughout the rest of the tune, the triads are usually complete. For the most part, the harmonic progressions, like those in a number of Maxim tunes, are perfectly acceptable from a tonal standpoint.

NEW-PLYMOUTH, on the other hand, is an example of a Washburn tune which at first seems not to be tonally oriented.[73] Although tonic chords follow dominant chords at the end of the second and fourth phrases, the other chords do not exhibit a familiar tonal direction, and unusual inversions, such as III(6–4) sometimes appear.[74]

While the frequent use of the mediant (III) and the major chord on the lowered seventh degree of the scale (VII) may at first seem odd, these triads are explainable as momentary tonicizations in the relative major key, Ab major, in which they are the tonic and dominant.[75] The fact that several phrases are organized in a similar way suggests that the successive vertical sonorities may have been planned, rather than an accidental by-product of the horizontal lines.[76]

Summary

In general, the compositional practices of the Maine psalmodists are not significantly different from those of other native psalmodists of the late eighteenth century. Like the latter, all four Maine composers frequently omit chord tones, resulting in incomplete triads, particularly at the beginning and ending of phrases. The progressions of the various New England psalmodists of the late eighteenth and early nineteenth centuries vary in the extent to which they follow tonal principles; the same can be said of the progressions of the Maine psalmodists. While Washburn's chord successions sometimes seem static, those of Maxim and Robbins, in particular, are frequently quite tonal, since they often precede dominant chords with dominant-preparation chords, such as ii and IV, and use secondary dominants conventionally. The same is true of Hartwell in some, but not all, of his writing. As in most New England psalm- and hymn-tunes of the period, modulation is not a factor in any of the Maine tunes, although quasi-modulations are quite common in Robbins's tunes.

Word painting can be found to varying degrees among psalmodists of the late eighteenth and early nineteenth centuries. William Billings used it extensively and creatively, while other composers, such as Oliver Holden and Samuel Holyoke, only rarely depicted textual images through musical means.[77] Similarly, the Maine composers differ in the amount of word painting they use; Robbins and Hartwell seem to feature it most often, Maxim somewhat less frequently, and Washburn only rarely.

In most New England sacred tunes of the time, each text phrase is set to a different melody; melodic repetition is rare, except for phrases repeated exactly due to repeat signs.[78] A similar practice is followed in almost all the Maine tunes.[79] Worst has noted in his analysis of the New England idiom that short melodic motives sometimes recur from one phrase to another or in a phraselong sequence.[80] Melodic sequences occur in a number of Maxim's tunes, but seem not to occur in pieces by the other Maine compilers.

Their tunes, particularly plain tunes and tunes with extension, exhibit the various styles described by Crawford in his *Core Repertory*.[81] Hartwell's tunes are the most difficult to categorize, stylistically, since he does not maintain a characteristic rhythmic pattern throughout many of his tunes.

The Maine composers differ from most early-nineteenth-century psalmodists in continuing to write fuging-tunes well into the second decade of the century. The popularity of fuging-tunes seems to have endured longer in Maine, as the survey of tunebooks in Chapter XII showed. Hartwell was the only one of the four to avoid the genre.

Many similarities can be found among the fuging-tunes of the other three Maine psalmodists. The overwhelming majority of Maine fuging-tunes are integrated fuging-tunes in a declamatory duple style, consist of three sections (homophonic, fugal, homophonic), and begin their fuges with bass and then tenor entrances. They share these features with the majority of New England fuging-tunes of the late eighteenth century, the period when fuging-tunes were most widely accepted. Nevertheless, many variations of the basic structure can be found among the body of New England fuging-tunes.

Like the extended pieces written throughout New England, the few set-pieces and anthems by the Maine composers are comprised of sections which contrast in various parameters. The Maine tunes primarily utilize changes in tempo, meter, and texture. Changes of mode or key are less common. Only Hartwell showed a particular interest in set-pieces and wrote enough of them to experiment with various approaches. Anthems are even more limited among the Maine composers, who apparently preferred the security of metrical texts when composing their infrequent tunes of longer length.

Like their colleagues in other parts of New England, the Maine sacred music composers set texts from a variety of sources, including the Methodist Hymn Book and Tate and Brady's "New Version." The vast majority of their texts, however, were taken from Isaac Watts. While Watts's works were popular throughout New England, especially among Congregationalists, the rural Maine psalmodists (particularly Maxim, who seems to have been a Universalist) could have chosen texts from hymnbooks written specifically for other denominations, such as the Universalists. Such does not seem to be the case, although some of the unidentified texts may prove to come from such sources.

In general, the tunes of the Maine rural psalmodists are written in the same idiom and styles as those of their predecessors of the late eighteenth century. The fact that they lived in a rural setting does not mean that they were unaware of the compositional principles followed by their contemporaries. For Maxim and Hartwell, their knowledge may have come from training they received in Massachusetts prior to their relocation to Maine. Maxim is said to have studied with William Billings;[82] Hartwell's musical training probably took place in Massachusetts, although no details are known. Robbins and Washburn probably studied with other Maine psalmodists, such as Maxim and Belcher.

While they share many common practices, the four Maine psalmodists, like their New England contemporaries, show individuality in the types of tunes they wrote most often and in the techniques they used in composing them. Their pieces deserve further study and performance.

SUMMATION OF PARTS I AND II

CHAPTER XIV

MAINE AND MASSACHUSETTS IN 1830: A GLANCE AT THE PAST, A GLIMPSE INTO THE FUTURE

The history of Maine in the first two decades of the nineteenth century cannot be separated from that of Massachusetts, her governing authority until 1820. Many of the Massachusetts emigrants who left for the frontier in the late eighteenth and early nineteenth centuries travelled northeast to Maine, due to the ease of transportation by sea. Ships frequently sailed between Maine ports and Boston, facilitating communication and influence between the two regions.

Coastal southern Maine residents, in particular, had much in common with other Massachusetts citizens; they were frequently Federalists in their politics, Congregationalists in their religion, and opponents of the move to separate Maine from Massachusetts. Due to their location, they had no trouble obtaining the latest tunebooks from Boston and from Exeter, New Hampshire, an important music printing center. These books were available in Portland bookstores as early as the 1780s and seem to have met the sacred music needs of Maine's coastal residents. After 1802, many of the same books were also stocked in Hallowell, the principal bookselling center of central Maine.

In contrast to those living in coastal Maine or Massachusetts proper, residents of the new towns surrounding Hallowell in inland Maine tended to be Democratic-Republicans, evangelicals, and supporters of separation from Massachusetts. The musical preferences and needs of the new settlers, largely subsistence farmers, differed from those of citizens living in older, southern

Maine towns. As a result, twenty-two different editions of sacred tunebooks were compiled by inland residents between 1800 and 1830. Several of the Maine collections were published in response to financial constraints. The Maine psalmodists produced tunebooks which were less expensive, partly because of their smaller size, than those imported from other parts of New England.

The Maine tunebooks differed not only in size but in repertory from other contemporaneous New England musical publications. As a result of a reform movement in Massachusetts, collections devoted to European tunes in a simple style dominated the sacred music market in Massachusetts after about 1806; even eclectic collections, such as *Village Harmony* and the *Bridgewater Collection,* began to include a core of "ancient" European tunes by 1810, but reform collections by Mainers did not appear until 1817. Even then, the reform repertory did not represent the tastes of all Maine residents. Other Maine tunebooks continued to include American tunes and fuging-tunes well into the 1820s, long after such pieces had been eliminated from most New England collections. The Maine tunebooks were about a decade behind the Massachusetts collections in incorporating a common repertory of older European tunes.

The contents of the Maine collections suggest that American tunes and fuging-tunes remained popular in the rural areas of Maine, as perhaps in other rural areas of New England, later than in the urban areas of both Maine and Massachusetts.[1] The frontier society tended to reinforce the independent, self-sufficient nature of the settlers. Those who liked fuging-tunes were not ready to give them up simply because community and religious leaders in Massachusetts believed they were not suitable for divine worship.

Just as major changes in the sacred music repertory came later in Maine than in Massachusetts, various innovations relating to singing in church were introduced in Maine churches well after they had been adopted in most Massachusetts churches. As in Massachusetts, church members in Maine at first resisted plans to abolish lining out, to allow the trained singers to sit together, and to permit instruments to accompany the singing. These developments may have been delayed slightly in Maine, compared to Massachusetts, because of the later organization of Maine singing schools.[2] Many of the church music conflicts did not arise until singers were trained and had formed choirs to lead the singing in church.

Maine singing schools, where students learned to read music, appear to have been similar to such schools throughout New England. The theoretical introductions to the Maine tunebooks, used for musical instruction, contain virtually the same information in the same order as other New England tunebooks. Singing schools, which began to be widespread in various towns in Maine after 1800, were still an important institution in the 1850s, both in inland areas and on the coast.[3]

In the formation of musical societies, Maine was not far behind Massachusetts. In fact, the Handel Society of Maine, organized in 1814, preceded the Boston Handel and Haydn Society, founded in 1815.[4] Portland boasted one of the first Beethoven societies in the country in the early 1820s. Other societies were established in the later 1820s, and by mid-century, societies were flourishing throughout much of the state.[5] The popularity of amateur musical societies in the early part of the century may have been partly due to the lack of competing cultural entertainments in the smaller towns. This was more the case in smaller towns than in the larger Maine towns, such as Hallowell and Portland, where concerts and musical theater presentations featuring Boston musicians were not uncommon even in the early decades of the nineteenth century.

In 1822, when musical societies were just beginning to be formed in various parts of Maine, Boston's most illustrious musical society sponsored the publication of a tunebook which would have a profound impact on sacred music in America: *The Boston Handel and Haydn Society Collection of Church Music*. The collection, which went through twenty-two editions, was a great financial success for its compiler, Lowell Mason, as well as its sponsor, the Boston Handel and Haydn Society. Advertised in Maine in the 1820s, *The Boston Handel and Haydn Society Collection* seems to have displaced the Maine tunebooks in the Portland area as early as the mid-1820s (see Chapter V).

The success of this and later compilations encouraged Lowell Mason in his crusade for "scientific music." In practical terms, "scientific music" referred to music which utilized complete triads and was faithful to European common-practice harmonic principles. In Mason's collections, most of the compositions other than his own were adaptations of works by such acknowledged European master composers as Handel, Haydn, Mozart, and Beethoven.

Tunes written by American psalmodists of the late eighteenth and early nineteenth centuries were not considered worthy of inclusion because of their supposedly crude melodies and incorrect harmonies. By the 1830s, compositions by American psalmodists such as Billings and his successors which did manage to be published often appeared in arrangements with "corrected" harmony.

Not everyone was pleased with the modifications (or mutilations, depending on the point of view) which were made to favorite old tunes.[6] Opponents formed themselves into societies to sing the music of the American composers in their original versions. One such group, founded in the 1830s, was the Billings and Holden Society of Boston, named in honor of American psalmodists William Billings and Oliver Holden. Since singers favoring American music over European music organized into Billings and Holden societies in a number of locales, the place name was often included in the official name. A Bangor (Maine) Billings and Holden Society was formed in 1846.[7]

In so-called retrospective collections, compiled both by societies and by individuals, tunes from the eighteenth and early nineteenth centuries were reprinted in their original arrangements. The older tunes published in these collections were featured at "Old Folks Concerts," a popular entertainment well into the 1870s. Old Folks Concerts, originated by Robert Kemp ("Father Kemp"), featured performers dressed in eighteenth-century costumes. The programs included newer patriotic and popular tunes in addition to the older hymn-tunes.[8]

One of the first retrospective collections to appear was the *Stoughton Collection of Church Music,* sponsored by the Stoughton Musical Society of Stoughton, Massachusetts. While the compilers made some corrections to the settings, they did not significantly alter "the best old tunes."[9] Two tunes by Maxim are included among those in the fourth edition (see Table 8), implying that even after his death, his tunes were known outside Maine.[10]

Maine residents were not far behind in producing publications providing the original arrangements of older tunes. *Songs of Sion, or Maine Collection of Sacred Music* (1830) was compiled in inland Charleston, and like the earlier Maine collections, was printed in Hallowell.[11] Prepared in response to musical publications in which "frequent alterations . . . are made in old and ap-

TABLE 8

Maine Tunes in Selected Retrospective Collections, 1831–1855

Title	*Stought. Coll./4*[12]	*Cumb. Coll.*[13]	*Anc. Har/2*[14]	*Anc. Har/3*[15]	*Anc. Har/6*[16]
Date:	1831	1839	1848	1850	1855
I. Tunes by Belcher					
ARCHDALE (TWX)[17]			70	70	72
BELCHER (PT)[18]		170			
HYMN 98TH (TWX)			160	160	
HYMN 116TH (TWX)			186	186	188
TOPSHAM (FT)			120		
II. Tunes by Maxim					
ALBANY (PT)		16			
ANSON (PT)		22			
BATH (FT)			168	168	170
BUCKFIELD (FT)			39	39	41
COLUMBIA (TWX)		65			
FLUVANNA (FT)			102		174
HALLOWELL (FT)	138	248	93	93	95
HANOVER (TWX)		236			
HARTFORD (FT)			130	130	132
HATFIELD (PT)		83			
LAPLATA (TWX)		63			
MINOT (PT)		122			
MONMOUTH (FT)		240			
NEW DURHAM (TWX)	141	117			
NO. YARMOUTH (FT)			98		
PORTLAND (FT)		210	42	42	44
ROSLIN CASTLE (SP)[19]		94			
SANDWICH (FT)		202			
SPRING (FT)		148			
SUMNER (TWX)		21	101	101	103
TURNER (FT)		183	121	121	123
WESTFORD (PT)		259			
WINTHROP (FT)		90			
WISCASSET (PT)		153			
III. Tunes by Robbins					
ELEMENT (FT)			32	32	
UNION-NEW (TWX)			145	145	147
ZENITH (PT)			129		

NOTE: Below the publication dates are the numbers of the pages on which the tunes appear. Genre abbreviations (FT, fuging-tune; PT, plain tune; SP, set-piece; TWX, tune with extension) are provided next to the tune titles.

proved pieces of Church Music," *Songs of Sion* printed "the ancient pieces . . . in their original form, or nearly so."[20]

In spite of this stated philosophy, the compilers differed from the editors of most retrospective collections in selecting very few older tunes by Americans, although some of the many unattributed tunes may be American.[21] None of the Maine composers discussed previously is represented, perhaps because of the emphasis on "simple and easy compositions of approved excellence," i.e., European tunes.[22] Fuging-tunes are as scarce as in the earlier Maine reform tunebooks, such as *The Hallowell Collection* (1817, 1819) and *Wesleyan Harmony* (1820, 1821).[23] Because of its contents, *Songs of Sion* should be considered a later tunebook in the reform tradition rather than the first Maine retrospective collection.

Among Maine's next two sacred music collections, both published in Portland in 1839, are a true retrospective collection (the *Cumberland Collection of Sacred Music*)[24] and one in the "scientific" tradition of Lowell Mason (the *Portland Sacred Music Society's Collection of Church Music*).[25] They epitomize the two divergent schools of sacred music in the decades following 1830 and suggest that both had their adherents in Maine.

The *Cumberland Collection of Sacred Music* by Benjamin Sweetser, Jr., presents "a selection of old music as it was forty years ago."[26] At least one Maine musical society, the Bangor Billings and Holden Society, would soon be formed (1846) to sing music of that type. There were probably many other Maine singers who enjoyed singing the tunes as they remembered them from their youth and who provided a market for collections such as *Songs of Sion* and the *Cumberland Collection.*

In contrast to the compilers of *Songs of Sion,* who chose to include only a very few fuging-tunes, Sweetser inserted "much old plain and fugueing music, of a highly pleasing character . . . (which has been excluded from modern popular publications)."[27] William Billings is well represented with fifty-one tunes, Abraham Maxim with nineteen (see Table 8 for the Maxim tunes). The reprinting of Maxim pieces in the *Cumberland Collection* allowed Mainers of another generation to become acquainted with his music. One of the Maxim pieces, ALBANY, may have been provided to Sweetser by Maxim himself, since Sweetser indicates that the tune is original; ALBANY is not printed in any of the extant Maine tunebooks from 1830 or before, and is stylistically unlike many of his earlier tunes in its periodic phrase structure and faster tempo (3/4).[28]

Contrasting with the *Cumberland Collection* and representing the opposing trend toward "scientific" music is the *Portland Music Society's Collection of Church Music,* published the same year (1839). The Portland Sacred Music Society, apparently modelled after societies such as the Boston Handel and Haydn Society, was formed in 1836 "to aid in creating a more general taste of music with the public, and likewise, in cultivating a correct style of performing Church Music."[29] Unlike many other Maine musical societies, whose programs featured excerpts from various oratorios, the Portland Sacred Music Society frequently presented complete oratorios and holds the distinction of being the first organization to present an entire standard oratorio at a public performance in Maine.[30]

The collection sponsored by the society includes shorter psalm- and hymn-tunes in addition to anthems. David Paine, uncle of composer John Knowles Paine and organist for the society, compiled the collection and composed or arranged many of the original new tunes which comprise more than three-fourths of the tunebook. Like *The Boston Handel and Haydn Society Collection,* the Portland collection contains many adaptations of works by European "classical" composers, including Mozart, Haydn, Spohr, Rossini, Beethoven, and Handel. As in other "modern" collections of the time, the music includes small notes in the lower two staffs to facilitate keyboard accompaniment; the introduction to music uses the Pestalozzian system, one of the most widely taught music-education methods of the day.[31]

American tunes are not completely avoided, since a number of the tunes are by musicians active in Portland at the time;[32] however, no tunes are attributed to any of the early-nineteenth-century Maine composers who have been the focus of this study. Tunes by Maxim and Washburn may have been excluded because their harmonies did not match up to the "scientific" standards of the 1830s. In addition, their tunes were not of the right vintage: they were not old enough to have passed the test of time, and not new enough to have been written in an acceptable modern style. The early Maine composers also lacked the prestige of the European masters.

While "a number of the most favorite old tunes" are included in unaltered form, few of them are American.[33] Swan's CHINA is one of the few older tunes by an American composer. The popularity of CHINA in Maine had apparently not diminished since the earlier period, 1800–1830, when it tied for first place as the most frequently reprinted American tune in the Maine tunebooks (see Chapter XII).

The Portland publication of the two 1839 collections suggests that Portland had come of age in cultural matters and was no longer willing to be dependent on Boston for musical leadership, as had been the case earlier in the century. Politically, Maine had been independent of Massachusetts for nearly two decades; culturally, Maine's largest city now had a sufficient number of well-trained musicians to present high-quality local performances in churches and concert halls.[34] The compilers of the two sacred music collections published in Portland may have felt they knew better than Boston compilers the types of music preferred by their fellow citizens.

In the next decade, several other Maine collections were published, including at least one important retrospective collection.[35] *Ancient Harmony Revived* (1847 and later editions) provides a link to the earlier Maine tunebooks through its place of publication (Hallowell) and the large number of Maine tunes reprinted (see Table 8).[36] Older tunes in their original form are predominant in *Ancient Harmony Revived,* as the title suggests.

The publication of several retrospective collections in Maine appears to reflect the continuing Maine partiality for fuging-tunes and American tunes which was evident in the 1820s. In Massachusetts, the retrospective collections marked a renewal of interest in American tunes for use as entertainment pieces by social singing groups; meanwhile, "scientific" music was still sung in churches. In Maine, the popularity of fuging-tunes may have continued unabated, with the retrospective collections merely providing new publications of the favorite older tunes.

The preface to *Ancient Harmony Revived* provides insight into the motivation for the collection. Although Old Folks Concerts may have emphasized entertainment,[37] neither entertainment nor nostalgia was the principal reason for this publication. Instead, the older tunes, along with modern pieces, were selected for their effectiveness in arousing devotional feelings, something tunes of a "scientific" nature were less able to achieve.[38] The compilers sensed the need and the public demand for the following:

> a collection of those approved Psalm and Hymn tunes, ancient and modern, which are calculated to call into action the devout affections of the soul, and purify and exalt the spirituality of social and public worship.[39]

Like earlier reformers of sacred music, these compilers were seeking to stem the tide of secularization in church music, a frequent problem throughout the history of sacred music.[40]

The older tunes printed in *Ancient Harmony Revived* include a sizable number by Maxim as well as a few by Robbins and Belcher. The title page includes Belcher and Maxim in its list of "old and approved authors," on equal footing with such major figures as Billings, Edson, Holden, Holyoke, Read, and Swan.[41] Although a collection published in Maine might be expected to have an elevated opinion of the Maine psalmodists, retrospective collections published outside the state also often included tunes by Maxim, if not by the other Maine composers, suggesting the esteem in which his tunes were held.[42]

Later reprintings of the Maine tunes were not limited to Massachusetts. In the 1830s and 1840s, some of them became known in the Canadian province of New Brunswick, another of Maine's neighbors, through the publication of *Union Harmony,* compiled in Saint John, New Brunswick, by Stephen Humbert.[43] *Union Harmony,* the first English-language music book originating in what would later become Canada, resembles American tunebooks in its shape and contents.[44] Although the first edition (1801) is not extant, the second edition (1816) is similar to the Maine tunebooks of 1813–1815 in the large number of fuging-tunes included and the predominance of American tunes.[45] Four of the five Maine tunes selected for the second edition are fuging-tunes, and more than half of the total reprintings in all the editions are of that genre (see Table 9). Since New Brunswick residents seem to have enjoyed fuging-tunes, Maine collections provided them with relatively new ones with which to augment their repertory.

In the preface to *Union Harmony,* Humbert, a Methodist, defended the use of fuging-tunes in worship, fully aware that some

TABLE 9

Maine Tunes in Humbert's *Union Harmony*

Composer	*Title*	*Genre*	*UH16*[46]	*UH31*[47]	*UH40*[48]
Date:			1816	1831	1840
Maxim	AUGUSTA	PT	308		
Maxim	BOHEMIA	PT			134
Maxim	BUCKFIELD	FT		40	
Maxim	COLUMBIA	TWX		54	
Maxim	HALLOWELL	FT		50	140
Maxim	HANOVER	TWX			132
Maxim	HATFIELD	PT			164
Maxim	MACHIAS	FT	309		
Maxim	MONMOUTH	FT		43	
Maxim	ORANGEBURGH	TWX		55	
Maxim	PARADISE	TWX		42	
Maxim	POLAND	FT	228		
Maxim	PORTLAND	FT		47	63
Maxim	SANDWICH	FT			62
Maxim	SUMNER	TWX		39	
Maxim	TURNER	FT	312		126
Maxim	WOODSTOCK	FT		45	131
Robbins	ELEMENT	FT		46	
Washburn, A.[49]	WAYNE	FT			142
Washburn, J.	DORCHESTER	TWX			167
Washburn, J.	LOCH LOMOND[50]	FT	316		
Washburn, J.	WARD	TWX			65
Washburn, J.	WARREN	PT			132
Washburn, J.	WHITEFIELD	FT			133
Total Number of Tunes by:					
Maxim			4	9	8
Robbins			0	1	0
Washburn, A.			0	0	1
Washburn, J. C.			1	0	4
Total Maine Tunes			5	10	13

NOTE: Below the publication dates are the numbers of the pages on which the tunes appear. Genre abbreviations (FT, fuging-tune; PT, plain tune; TWX, tune with extension) are provided next to the tune titles.

compilers considered them unacceptable for that purpose.[51] Although fuging-tunes were not allowed in Methodist services in the United States, such was not the case in British North America. In fact, Blum suggests that the longevity of the fuging-tune in the latter region was largely due to the interest of Methodists in the genre.[52]

As Table 9 shows, the number of Maine tunes doubles in the third and fourth editions (1831, 1840) of Humbert's collection. Improved trade relations between the United States and Great Britain may have contributed to a greater knowledge of Maine tunebooks and tunes in British North America by 1831, compared to 1816, the date of the previous edition. Earlier in the century, trade restrictions resulting from the U.S. Embargo Act (1807–1809) and the U.S. war with Great Britain (1812–1815) sometimes made it difficult for New Brunswick residents to obtain goods from Maine and vice versa. These circumstances may help explain the lack of advertisements for the New Brunswick collection in Maine[53] and for the Maine collections in Humbert's town of Saint John, New Brunswick.[54] While smuggling seems to have been commonplace,[55] tunebooks were probably not in enough demand to warrant illegal importation.[56]

Even when the international trade was legal, one wonders how much commerce took place between the two regions. Although ships could sail relatively quickly and easily between Maine and New Brunswick, they exported the same types of items (primarily timber and fish), which would seem to limit the desirability of direct trade between them. By midcentury, though, ships regularly sailed from Maine ports to Saint John as part of a northern triangular trade route which took timber from Saint John to Liverpool and brought salt back from Liverpool to Maine for use in shipbuilding and the fishing industry.[57] On the shortest leg, from the salt entrepôts in Maine to the timber ports in New Brunswick, the ships travelled light; ships which did take cargo usually carried coal, although flour, corn, and "sundries" were sometimes transported. The northern triangle was firmly established by 1850, but it is unclear how much earlier ships might have followed the route.

Improved trade relations between Maine and New Brunswick may not have been the only factor involved in Humbert's inclusion of a greater number of tunes by Maine psalmodist Japheth Coombs Washburn in the fourth edition of *Union Harmony* (1840). Washburn's move in the mid-1830s from China in inland

Maine to Calais in extreme eastern Maine (near the New Brunswick border) may also have contributed. By the time Humbert compiled the last two editions of *Union Harmony* (1831, 1840), he had apparently obtained a copy of either the Maxim-Washburn fourth edition of *Northern Harmony* (1816) or the first or second edition of Washburn's *Temple Harmony* (1818, 1820), judging from the Maine tunes he includes.[58] After Humbert's collection introduced the Maine tunes into British North America, several later Canadian collections, dating from 1835 to 1887, reprinted Maxim, Robbins, and Washburn tunes which had made their Canadian debut in *Union Harmony*.[59]

Humbert's apparent familiarity with several Maine collections is matched by Washburn's knowledge of Humbert's collection. Since *Union Harmony* does not appear to have been widely distributed in Maine, if at all, Washburn may have become familiar with the collection through his trips to Boston; he includes several tunes attributed to "Humbert's Collection" in *Temple Harmony,* although none written by Humbert himself (see Chapter VIII). In general, though, the sacred music repertory and practices of New Brunswick seem to have had little impact on sacred music in Maine, especially compared to the contributions of Massachusetts.

In addition to the influences previously noted, Maine was beholden to Massachusetts for most of her earliest psalmodists except for Henry Little, who was born in New Hampshire. Composers Supply Belcher, Abraham Maxim, Japheth Coombs Washburn, Edward Hartwell, and Charles Robbins, and publisher Ezekiel Goodale were all born in Massachusetts, but later moved to Maine. Belcher and Maxim probably received most of their musical training from Boston psalmodist William Billings.

While the Maine psalmodists who were born in Massachusetts proper emigrated to Maine for the greater opportunities offered there, the trend was reversed in the years after 1830. Several of Maine's most musically talented natives left Maine for Massachusetts (and beyond) because of the greater opportunities for training in larger urban centers, such as Boston. Among them were some who became extremely successful in the field of sacred music, either as composers, educators, or both. William B. Bradbury, Luther Whiting Mason, Luther Orlando Emerson, and John Knowles Paine were all Maine natives who earned national reputations in their fields in the last half of the nineteenth century.

William Bradbury (1816–1868) was born in York, Maine, but moved with his family to Boston when he was fourteen. He studied at the Boston Academy of Music and later taught music to children in New York. A leading exponent of the scientific music movement, along with Lowell Mason, he wrote some sixty music books between 1841 and 1867. Some of his hymn-tunes which are still sung today include "Just as I Am," "Sweet Hour of Prayer," "He Leadeth Me," and "Jesus Loves Me."[60]

Luther Whiting Mason (1818–1896), born in Turner, Maine, is best known as a music educator. He received his teaching certificate after attending the school of Lowell Mason, George Root, and William Bradbury in Boston. Mason developed a school music system and travelled and taught extensively in this country and all over the world, including in Japan and Europe.[61]

Luther Emerson (1820–1915) was born in Parsonfield, Maine, but studied music in Boston once he came of age. A teacher, lecturer, and music festival conductor, he became most famous as a composer of church and school music. His thirty-five or so music books, published for the use of schools, churches, societies, and homes, sold in excess of a million copies.[62]

John Knowles Paine (1839–1906) was born in Portland, Maine, but lived most of his life in the Boston area after studying several years in Germany. He became the first full professor of music at an American university (Harvard in 1875) and was one of the few internationally recognized American composers of art music in the late nineteenth century. His oratorio, *St. Peter,* was the first oratorio by an American composer to be performed in this country; it was premiered in his native city of Portland.[63]

Recognizing the fact that these talented men left Maine is not to say that opportunities for music making were scarce in Maine by the mid–nineteenth century, only that professional training and contacts were more efficacious in cities larger than those in Maine. While Mainers of the early nineteenth century attended singing school and utilized their new skills in church choirs, Mainers of the mid-nineteenth century had abundant opportunities for amateur singing, not only in singing schools and churches,[64] but also in the many musical societies formed throughout the state.[65] In addition to the numerous countywide associations, a statewide chorus, the Maine State Musical Association, was organized in 1843 and continued successfully for more than fifteen years.[66]

The various musical societies performed different types of music, represented by the two divergent Portland publications of 1839. Mainers preferring music in the classical, European tradition could join such organizations as the Portland Sacred Music Society (or similar ones formed elsewhere in the state) to sing works in a "correct," scientific style. Those favoring the older, American tunes could join such groups as the Bangor Billings and Holden Society or simply gather together informally with others to sing tunes from retrospective collections such as Sweetser's. In the decades after 1830, as in the period from 1800 to 1830, Maine residents had available to them tunebooks which had been prepared by fellow Mainers with their preferences in mind.

In the early part of the century, Maine may be likened to a teenager. Self-willed and assertive in nature, she had different tastes in music than her parent (Massachusetts). While balking at parental authority and wanting her freedom, she was still dependent for some of her needs. By midcentury, Maine was a full-fledged adult. Not only was she politically autonomous, she had made great strides musically. Having taken charge of her life, she was confident of her ability to succeed on her own. As Maine grew and developed, one thing remained constant. She continued to enjoy "divine song," both for worship and entertainment.

PART III. CATALOG OF MUSIC

A. INDEX OF TUNES BY MAINE COMPILERS IN MAINE TUNEBOOKS, 1794–1830

This section provides a page-number index of the tunes composed by Maine compilers Supply Belcher, Abraham Maxim, Japheth Coombs Washburn, Charles Robbins, and Edward Hartwell and printed in the extant Maine collections, 1794 to 1830.[1] The period covered has been extended back to 1794 to assist those interested in Belcher's tunebook, *The Harmony of Maine* (1794), abbreviated here as "HM1794." The other collection titles are abbreviated using the symbols shown in Table 3, page 178. The two editions of *Wesleyan Harmony* do not contain any tunes by the five Maine compilers and are not listed here. Although some pieces by the Maine psalmodists were reprinted in tunebooks compiled outside the state, only Maine printings will be enumerated.[2]

The tunes are listed alphabetically within genres, which appear in the following order: plain tunes, tunes with extension, fuging-tunes, set-pieces, and anthems. Tunes of Belcher, Maxim, and Robbins are listed twice to encompass all the Maine publications in which they appeared. Sections listing the same tunes are identified with the same Roman numeral followed by A or B. For example, Maxim's plain tunes are listed twice: in section VI-A to show the printings in Maxim's tunebooks and in section VI-B for those in Washburn's collections. All the Maine printings of Robbins's and Hartwell's tunes are shown on a single page.

While Robbins and Hartwell clearly identify their own tunes as such in their tunebooks, Maxim and Washburn do not always do so, making it difficult to know whether they composed the unattributed tunes in their compilations. The first two editions of Maxim's *Northern Harmony,* for example, contain fifty-seven tunes lacking composer attributions but labelled as "Original," a term usually meaning "never before published." Some can be assigned to Maxim from attributions in later Maxim or Washburn editions. Others are more problematical because no attribution has been located in any source.

Since Maxim and Washburn are careful to provide a composer's name along with "Original" for other first printings in their tunebooks, the implication is that those lacking a composer's name were written by the book's compiler. Accordingly, I have assigned such tunes (i.e., those marked "Original" but otherwise unattributed) to the tunebook's compiler, barring evidence to the contrary.[3] Handwritten notations by John Maxim, Abraham's younger brother, in an extant copy of a Maxim tunebook support the theory that Maxim wrote the "Original" tunes not printed with a composer's name. That John was wrong about at least one tune does not necessarily discredit all his attributions.[4]

While unattributed tunes marked "Original" in Maxim or Washburn tunebooks are assumed to have been written by the book's compiler, no such assumptions have been made about unattributed tunes not marked "Original." Only those attributed to one of the Maine compilers in another source have been included in the following index. As a result, it is likely that some tunes by Maxim and Washburn have not been identified as such.[5] Washburn's practice of omitting attributions to himself in his post-1820 editions may also contribute to an incomplete index.[6] Due to the problem of unattributed tunes in their tunebooks and the fact that some of their editions exist only in incomplete copies or are not extant at all, the indexes of Maxim and Washburn tunes should be considered tentative and not necessarily comprehensive.

To show whether a given printing has an attribution or not, page numbers are underlined when the printing is attributed to the listed composer. Page numbers not underlined lack an attribution. Brackets around tune titles indicate pieces for which no attribution (other than "Original") has been found in any source. A tilde (˜) to the right of a page number denotes a printing marked as "Original."[7]

Other symbols can be found in the left margin, preceding certain tunes. A plus sign (+) points out tunes which are discussed in Chapter XIII; a complete musical transcription of the tune can also be found there. The number, or pound, sign (#) indicates the most frequently printed compositions of each composer. Known printings outside Maine have been taken into account in determining which tunes were published most often. Asterisks (*) denote tunes which I consider to be particularly interesting or worthy of further study or performance. These judgments are purely subjective opinions, however, and do not imply that the other tunes are uninteresting or insignificant. They are provided simply as a possible starting point for scholars, performers, and composers. All three margin symbols are provided for only the first listing of each composer's tunes.

Some tune names appear in more than one category because they were published in more than one form. For example, since Maxim's NOBLEBOROUGH is printed both as a fuging-tune and as a plain tune (omitting the fuging-chorus), it is listed in both categories. Where two different tunes with the same title appear to be by one composer, they are differentiated by "(1)" or "(2)" after the title, with (1) assigned to the one which was printed first. For example, Maxim's EXETER (1) was printed in OH02, while his EXETER (2) was first published in NH08.[8]

Besides being a useful tool for locating specific tunes, the index reveals the extent to which the compilers printed tunes of their fellow Mainers. For example, while Washburn published many Maxim tunes in his collections, a much smaller number of Washburn pieces were included in Maxim's tunebooks, partly, of course, because Washburn wrote fewer tunes. Hartwell's tunes were not printed in any of the other collections, and he selected only a few tunes by his Maine colleagues, suggesting perhaps that he was more isolated from the other three than they were from one another.

The genres of the tunes reprinted are consistent with trends noted previously. For example, some of Maxim's plain tunes are published in many of Washburn's late collections, while Maxim's fuging-tunes are more often limited to Washburn's early collections or, like NOBLEBOROUGH, transformed into plain tunes for later printings. The index suggests which tunes maintained popular appeal throughout the period, as well as the genres favored at different times.

Summary of Symbols

+ A tune discussed in Chapter XIII, where a complete musical transcription can be found (see Table of Musical Examples on p. vi for page number).

- # One of the composer's most frequently reprinted tunes.
- * A tune I consider to be particularly interesting or worthy of further study and performance.

[Tune Title]: No attribution found in any of the printings available to me.

Page number (underlined): A printing which is attributed to the listed composer on this page.

Page number (not underlined): A printing which is unattributed in this publication.

˜ (following a page number): A printing marked "Original" in this source.

For tunebook abbreviations (OH02, etc.), see Table 3. (Additional abbreviation: "HM1794" is Belcher's *Harmony of Maine,* 1794.)

NOTE: The fourth edition of *Northern Harmony* (NH16), listed under Maxim's name in the index headings, was a joint compilation by Maxim and Japheth Coombs Washburn.

	Compiler:	Belcher	Robbins	Maxim	
	Title	*HM1794*	*CH05*	*NH16*	*NH19*
	I-A. Belcher Plain Tunes				
*	Alpha	17			
	Bath	94			
	Chester	32			
	Creation	20			
*	Cumberland	102			
*	Fiftieth Psalm Tune	37			
	Gethsemane	58			
	Handsel	57			
	Hymn Hundred & Seventieth		91		
	Lamentation	80			
	Potency	67			
	Reedfield	90			
	Reflection	42			
	Sovereignty	81			
	St. Andrews	65			
	St. John's	95			
	St. Luke's	60			
*	Sublimity	79			
	Sunday	93			
	The Lilly	36			
*	Turner	91			
	Victory	62			
*	Waterloo				
	York	102			

	Compiler:	Belcher	Robbins	Maxim	
	Title	*HM1794*	*CH05*	*NH16*	*NH19*
	II-A. Belcher Tunes with Extension				
#*	Canton				
	Captivity	101			
	Content	42			
	Emancipation	74			
	Friendship	47			
	Funeral Hymn	61			
#	Hymn Hundred & Sixteenth		92		
#	Hymn Ninety-eighth		93		
	Hymn Thirty-fifth		94		
	Jewry				
	Omega	103			
	Unity	73			
	III-A. Belcher Fuging-Tunes				
	Admiration	45			
	Advent (1)	21			
	Advent (2)		32		
	Appearance	27			
	Bliss	75			
*	Carol	38			
#	Conversion	41		155	75

	Compiler:	Belcher	Robbins	Maxim	
	Title	*HM1794*	*CH05*	*NH05*	*NH08*
*	The Dawn	25			
	Ecstacy	66			
*	Farmington	92			
#	Hallowell	20		82	82
	Harmony	19			
	Heroism	35			
#*	Jubilant	39		80	80
	Lincoln	40			
	Majesty	18			
	New Sharon	82			
*	Ocean	83			
	Pittston[9]				
*	Plenitude	72			
	Protection	44			
#*	Rapture	48		142	142
	St. David's New	23			172
	St. Mark's	59			
	St. Paul's	24			
#*	Topsham		158		
*	Transition	29			
	Union	51			
	Winthrop	49			
IV-A. Belcher Set-Pieces					
*	Invitation	30			
*	The Power of Musick	84			

Compiler:	Belcher	Robbins	Maxim	
Title	*HM1794*	*CH05*	*NH05*	*NH08*
IV-A. Belcher Set-Pieces (cont'd)				
The Request	33			
Spring	63			
* Transmigration	96			
V-A. Belcher Anthems				
* An Anthem for Easter	68			
* An Anthem of Praise	52			
#* Ordination Anthem		199		
* Funeral Anthem	76			

Compiler:	[Goodale?]		J. C. Washburn		
Title	*HC17*	*HC19*	*PH13*	*TH18*	*TH20*
I-B. Belcher Plain Tunes					
Waterloo		207			
II-B. Belcher Tunes with Extension					
Canton	178	173		222	222
Jewry		206			
III-B. Belcher Fuging-Tunes					
Conversion			100	75	75
IV/V-B. Belcher Set-Pieces and Anthems (None)					

	Compiler:	Abraham Maxim					Robbins	Hartwell
	Title	*OH02*	*NH05*	*NH08*	*NH16*	*NH19*	*CH05*	*CC15*
	VI-A. Maxim Plain Tunes							
	Anson			153~		77		
	[Arundle] or [Arundel]			195~	159			
	Augusta (1)							
	Augusta (2)							
#	[Bath (2)]							
	or [Bengal]				39~	83		
#*	Bohemia			188~	215			
	[Boston]				141~			
	[Cambridge]				67~			
*	Castine			189~	160			
*	[Columbus]				11~	11		
	Delectation	10				120		
	[Fairfax]		97~	97				
+#*	Falmouth	17	57	57	83	44		
	Farmington							
*	Friendship							
*	Gardiner				104	54		
	Georgetown	37			77	12		
	Greene	9				119		
#*	Hatfield				200			
	Jay	21						
	Kingston					77		
	Machias							
	Magnificence	26						
	[Messiah]		150~	150				

	Compiler:	Abraham Maxim					Robbins	Hartwell
	Title	*OH02*	*NH05*	*NH08*	*NH16*	*NH19*	*CH05*	*CC15*
	VI-A. Maxim Plain Tunes (cont'd)							
#*	Minot	<u>14</u>			<u>163</u>			
	[Mount Vernon (1)]				230˜			
	Mount-Vernon (2)							
	[Newbury-port]		147˜	147				
	New-Castle							
	New-Durham							
	[New-London]		86˜	86		35		
	New-York				<u>56˜</u>			
	Nobleborough (2)							
	[Norway]		132˜	132				
	Philadelphia							
	[Providence]				126˜			
*	[Richland]		135˜	135	222	100		
	Roxbury				<u>67˜</u>			
	Sidney (2)							
	Sovereignty				<u>150</u>	<u>79</u>		
*	[Stratham]		76˜	76	118			
	[Switzerland]		64˜	64	168	118		
#	Vassalborough	<u>23</u>	<u>31</u>	<u>31</u>	<u>46</u>			
	Westford				57˜			
	[Winslow]		53˜	53	77	13		
	Wiscasset				<u>39˜</u>	<u>18</u>		
	VII-A. Maxim Tunes with Extension							
	Adoration	<u>34</u>						
#	Augusta (1)	<u>45</u>	<u>22</u>	<u>22</u>	<u>34</u>	<u>21</u>	<u>37</u>	<u>27</u>

	Compiler:	Abraham Maxim					Robbins	Hartwell
	Title	*OH02*	*NH05*	*NH08*	*NH16*	*NH19*	*CH05*	*CC15*
	[Beatitude]		98˜	98				
*	Bedford	22						
#	Bridgeton			183˜	189			
	Burton	13						
	Chelsea			171˜	172			
#	Columbia	43	20	20	24			
	Counsel	33						
	Dresden	19						
	[Ecstacy]		68˜	68	96			
	Exeter (1)	12						
	Exeter (2)			29˜	43	20		
	Fair-Haven	36						
*	Farmington		126˜	126	183			
	[Firmament]			157˜		14		
	Granville	23				43		
*	Hanover				63˜			
*	Harlem			182˜	191			
*	Hatfield			178˜				
+#*	Knoxville	41	14	14	14	22		26
*	La Plata[10]		72˜	72	100	45		
	Morning Hymn			179˜	213	104		
	New-Castle	35			94			
#	New-Durham		73˜	73	116			
	Nobleborough (1)	39						
#	Orangeburgh		128˜	128	146			
	[Oxford]			156˜				
#	Paradise		63˜	63	165	68		
	[Peru]		74˜	74	117			

	Compiler:	Abraham Maxim					Robbins	Hartwell
	Title	*OH02*	*NH05*	*NH08*	*NH16*	*NH19*	*CH05*	*CC15*
VII-A. Maxim Tunes with Extension (cont'd)								
	Phenomenon	38						
	[Piety]		123~	123				
*	[Pittsburgh]		119~	119				
	[Portland (2)]				121~			
	Portsmouth			167~	188	53		
	Prodigy[11]		87~	87				
	Psalm 50	30						
	Quincy	32						
	Renovation	40						
	[Request]			162~				
	Salem		83~	83		67		
#*	Sumner		49	49	69	29	154	
	Supplication	24						
	Wayne	15	56	56	80			
VIII-A. Maxim Fuging-Tunes								
	America					50		
*	[Asia]		124~	124				
#	Bath (1)	46	23	23	37	38		
	[Behest]		121~	121				
#*	Buckfield	31	15	15	17	33		
	Cumberland		88~	88	135	71		
	[Danville]					48~		
	[Dixfield]		134~	134				
#	Fluvanna		67~	67	95			
	[Franklin]				231~	125		

	Compiler:	Abraham Maxim					Robbins	Hartwell
	Title	*OH02*	*NH05*	*NH08*	*NH16*	*NH19*	*CH05*	*CC15*
	Freeport					81		
#*	Hallowell	18	58	58	84			
	Harpswell				158~			
#	Hartford	29	18	18	104			
	[Leeds]			153~				
#*	Machias	20	60	60	88			
#	Monmouth				144	69		
*	Nobleborough (2)				35~	82		
	North-Hampton				53			
*	[North-Yarmouth]		85~	85	130	116		
	[Northborough]		113~	113				
*	[Paris]			185~		113		
	Pittston	28						
#	Poland			163				
#*	Portland (1)	25	16	16	102	112		
	[Psalm Fiftieth]			160~				
	Randolph	16	39	39	55			
	[Readfield]			197~				
	Salutation	44						
#	Sandwich		66~	66	76	87		
	[Sidney (1)]			158~				
*	Spring				38~			
	Trinity[12]		62~	62				
*	[Troy]		59~	59	87			
+#*	Turner	11	50	50	70	28	160	
	[Waterville]			152~				
	[Winthrop]		65~	65	75			
	[Woodford]		110~	110				

Compiler:	Abraham Maxim					Robbins	Hartwell
Title	*OH02*	*NH05*	*NH08*	*NH16*	*NH19*	*CH05*	*CC15*
VIII-A. Maxim Fuging-Tunes (cont'd)							
Woodstock				176˜	74		
[Woolwich]				162˜			
IX-A. Maxim Set-Pieces							
[Contrast]			186˜				
[The Golden Air]		70˜	70	98			
X-A. Maxim Anthems							
Anthem, Thanksgiving	52	115	115				
Anthem of Praise	47	92	92				

Compiler:	Japheth Coombs Washburn						
Title	*PH13*	*TH18*	*TH20*	*TH21*	*TH23*	*TH24*	*TH26*
VI-B. Maxim Plain Tunes							
Anson		77	77				
[Arundle] or [Arundel]							
Augusta (1)				34	34		
Augusta (2)					151		
[Bath (2)] or [Bengal]		83	83	71	71	63	
Bohemia		185	185			41	73
[Boston]							
[Cambridge]							
Castine		210	210				
[Columbus]							
Delectation							

Compiler:	Japheth Coombs Washburn						
Title	*PH13*	*TH18*	*TH20*	*TH21*	*TH23*	*TH24*	*TH26*
[Fairfax]							
Falmouth							
Farmington							78
Friendship					156	78	86
Gardiner		54	54				
Georgetown							
Greene							
Hatfield		214	214	96	96	89	100
Jay							
Kingston		77	77				
Machias						107	
Magnificence							
[Messiah]							
Minot		206	206	80	80		36
[Mount Vernon (1)]							
Mount-Vernon (2)					155	106	117
[Newbury-port]							
New-Castle							79
New-Durham						41	76
[New-London]							
New-York		231	231				
Nobleborough (2)							25
[Norway]							
Philadelphia					154		
[Providence]							
[Richland]		100	100				
Roxbury							
Sidney (2)					153	26	52

Compiler:	Japheth Coombs Washburn						
Title	*PH13*	*TH18*	*TH20*	*TH21*	*TH23*	*TH24*	*TH26*
VI-B. Maxim Plain Tunes							
Sovereignty		79	79				
[Stratham]						162	15
[Switzerland]							
Vassalborough		165	165	51	51		
Westford		190	190				
[Winslow]							
Wiscasset		18	18				
VII-B. Maxim Tunes with Extension							
Adoration							
Augusta (1)		21	21				
[Beatitude]							
Bedford							
Bridgeton		263	263	101	101	103	
Burton							
Chelsea		153	153				
Columbia		257	257				
Counsel							
Dresden							
[Ecstacy]							
Exeter (1)							
Exeter (2)		20	20				
Fair-Haven							
Farmington		159	159				
[Firmament]							
Granville							

Compiler:	Japheth Coombs Washburn						
Title	*PH13*	*TH18*	*TH20*	*TH21*	*TH23*	*TH24*	*TH26*
Hanover		172	172				
Harlem		212	212				
Hatfield							
Knoxville		22	22	38	38	37	66
La Plata							
Morning Hymn		104	104				
New-Castle		158	158				
New-Durham		163	163	45	45		
Nobleborough (1)							
Orangeburgh		208	208				102
[Oxford]							
Paradise		68	68				
[Peru]							
Phenomenon							
[Piety]							
[Pittsburgh]							
[Portland (2)]							
Portsmouth		53	53				
Prodigy							
Psalm 50							
Quincy							
Renovation							
[Request]							
Salem		67	67				
Sumner		29	29				
Supplication							
Wayne							

Compiler:	Japheth Coombs Washburn						
Title	*PH13*	*TH18*	*TH20*	*TH21*	*TH23*	*TH24*	*TH26*
VIII-B. Maxim Fuging-Tunes							
America		50	50				
[Asia]							
Bath (1)							
[Behest]							
Buckfield							
Cumberland		71	71				
[Danville]							
[Dixfield]							
Fluvanna		167	167				77
[Franklin]							
Freeport		81	81				
Hallowell		160	160				
Harpswell		213	213				
Hartford		211	211				98
[Leeds]							
Machias	110	240	240				119
Monmouth		69	69				
Nobleborough (2)		82	82				
North-Hampton	83˜	242	242				
[North-Yarmouth]							
[Northborough]							
[Paris]							
Pittston							
Poland		216	216				
Portland (1)		112	112				

Compiler:	Japheth Coombs Washburn						
Title	*PH13*	*TH18*	*TH20*	*TH21*	*TH23*	*TH24*	*TH26*
[Psalm Fiftieth]							
Randolph							
[Readfield]							
Salutation							
Sandwich		87	87				
[Sidney (1)]							
Spring		282	282				
Trinity							
[Troy]							
Turner	106	28	28				
[Waterville]							
[Winthrop]							
[Woodford]							
Woodstock		74	74				
[Woolwich]							
IX-B. Maxim Set-Pieces							
[Contrast]							
[The Golden Air]							
X-B. Maxim Anthems							
Anthem, Thanksgiving							
Anthem of Praise							

Compiler:	Abraham Maxim				Robbins	Hartwell
Title:	*NH05*	*NH08*	*NH16*	*NH19*	*CH05*	*CC15*
XI-A. Washburn Plain Tunes						
+# Augusta			25			
Baldwin			81			

	Compiler:	Abraham Maxim				Robbins	Hartwell
	Title:	*NH05*	*NH08*	*NH16*	*NH19*	*CH05*	*CC15*
XI-A. Washburn Plain Tunes							
#	Brunswick			33˜	24		
	Bucksport				24		
	Chaplin						
	Concord			76˜			
	Fairfield			72˜			
	Fountain			26˜			
*	Freedom						
	Friendship			63˜			
#	Hallowell			28			
	Houghton						
	Lord's Day						
	[Monroe]						
	North-Yarmouth			155			
*	Passion		184˜	190			
	Pilgrim			81˜			
#	Readfield			124˜			
	Thanksgiving						
#*	Warren			31˜			
*	[Westbrook]						
*	Whitefield (2) or Wakefield						
XII-A. Washburn Tunes with Extension							
	Bloomfield			42	23		
	Bloomville						
	China						

Compiler:		Abraham Maxim				Robbins	Hartwell
Title:		*NH05*	*NH08*	*NH16*	*NH19*	*CH05*	*CC15*
+#*	Dorchester			154˜			
	Fayette			89˜			
	New-Milford	84˜	84				
	New-Plymouth						
	Sydney or Sidney			101˜			
	[Vinal Haven]						
	Ward			178˜			
	Waterville (2)						
*	Winthrop			65˜			
XIII-A. Washburn Fuging-Tunes							
	Bristol						
	Broad						
	Fairfax						
	Garland			126˜			
	Harlem			106˜			
	Joy						
	Litchfield						
+#*	New-Plymouth	146˜	146	216			
	Orland						
	[Palermo]						
*	Waterford		165˜				
	Waterville (1)						
	Whitefield (1)			170˜			
XIV-A. Washburn Set-Pieces							
*	Vassalborough			226˜			
XV-A. Washburn Anthems (None)							

Compiler:	Japheth Coombs Washburn						
Title	*PH13*	*TH18*	*TH20*	*TH21*	*TH23*	*TH24*	*TH26*
XI-B. Washburn Plain Tunes							
Augusta	114~	152	152	88	88	76	85
Baldwin	48	124	124				
Brunswick		24	24	14	14		
Bucksport		24	24				
Chaplin		252~	252~				
Concord		39	39	35	35		
Fairfield		144	144				
Fountain		259	259			114	132
Freedom	130~						
Friendship		225	225			128	
Hallowell	117~	150	150	90	90		
Houghton		145~	145~				
Lord's Day		48	48				
[Monroe]		11~	11~				
North-Yarmouth		152	152				
Passion		261	261				
Pilgrim		258	258				
Readfield		189	189	85	85	73	34
Thanksgiving		193~	193~				
Warren		173	173	50	50	47	72
[Westbrook]	133~						40
Whitefield (2) or Wakefield		186	186	51	51	48	
XII-B. Washburn Tunes with Extension							
Bloomfield		23	23				

Compiler:	Japheth Coombs Washburn						
Title	*PH13*	*TH18*	*TH20*	*TH21*	*TH23*	*TH24*	*TH26*
Bloomville		113	113				
China		151~	151~				
Dorchester		216	216	95	95	88	96
Fayette		180	180				
New-Milford							
New-Plymouth						72	
Sydney or Sidney		170	170				
[Vinal Haven]		179~	179~				
Ward		191	191				
Waterville (2)		193~	193~				
Winthrop		130	130				
XIII-B. Washburn Fuging-Tunes							
Bristol	86~						
Broad	58						
Fairfax	66~	143	143				
Garland							
Harlem		120	120				
Joy		119	119				
Litchfield		225	225				
New-Plymouth	96	207	207		172		
Orland	101						
[Palermo]		199~	199~				
Waterford							
Waterville (1)	118~						
Whitefield (1)		154	154				
XIV-B. Washburn Set-Pieces							
Vassalborough							
XV-B. Washburn Anthems (None)							

	Compiler:	Maxim				Robbins	Washburn		
	Title	*NH05*	*NH08*	*NH16*	*NH19*	*CH05*	*PH13*	*TH18*	*TH20*
	XVI. Robbins Plain Tunes								
	Alpha					29			
	Dissolution					69			
	Fair-Haven					74			
*	Midsummer					118			
	Omega . . . A Doxology					207			
+#*	Psalm Fiftieth	137	137			137			
	Quincey					142			
	Winthrop					167			
*	Xerxes					169			
*	Yarmouth-New					170			
#	Zenith					170			
	XVII. Robbins Tunes with Extension								
	Abingdon					30			
+	Accord					31			
	Aspiration					36			
	Braintree					46			
	Condolence					53			
*	Consonance					55			
	Contemplation					56			
	Deliverance					62			
	Dependence					67			
	Easter-Sunday					71			
	Greene					80			

	Compiler:	Maxim				Robbins	Washburn		
	Title	*NH05*	*NH08*	*NH16*	*NH19*	*CH05*	*PH13*	*TH18*	*TH20*
	Hallowell					84			
	Hanover					87			
	Harmony					88			
	Ocean-New					126			
	Participation					130			
	Prospect					136			
	Request					144			
*	Trenton					159			
#	Union-New					161			
XVIII. Robbins Fuging-Tunes									
#*	Albany			225		34	72	157	157
	Castine					49			
#	Delight					61	26		
+#*	Element			123	111	70	84	111	111
	Freeport					75			
#	Innocence					94	88		
	Kentucky					99			
	Lord's-Day					107			
	Marshfield					114			
	Resolution					145			
	Scituate					148			
	Supplication					155			
	Weymouth					166			
XIX. Robbins Set-Piece									
	Independent Anniversary . . . An Ode					193			
XX. Robbins Anthems									
	Anthem . . . For a Day of Public Thanksgiving					179			
	Anthem . . . Psalm 47					186			

	Compiler:	Hartwell
	Title	*CC15*
	XXI. Hartwell Plain Tunes	
	Ashford	18
	Judah	65
	Nativity	101
	Norridgwock	24
	Orrington	29
	Shiloh	88
+	Tribunal	85
	Tyre	166
	Union	81
	XXII. Hartwell Tunes with Extension	
	Adoration	17
	Anson	91
	Bloomfield	43
+	Capernaum	96
	Emmaus	99
	Meditation	36
*	Petition	39
	Wedlock	94

Compiler:	Hartwell
Title	*CC15*
XXIII. Hartwell Fuging-Tunes	
Compliance	106
Cornville	30
XXIV. Hartwell Set-Pieces	
* Chorazin	155
* Creation	119
* Independence	148
Salutation	102
* Self-Consecration	104G259.ps
* Skowhegan	122
XXV. Hartwell Anthems (None)	

B. SURVIVING COPIES OF MAINE TUNEBOOKS, 1794–1830

This section provides locations of the extant Maine tunebooks to assist those interested in examining them. Although the focus of this book is on the period from 1800 to 1830, I have expanded the scope here to include two additional tunebooks—Belcher's *Harmony of Maine* (1794) and *Songs of Sion* (1830)—as well as the text-only hymnal compiled by Maine psalmodist Abraham Maxim, *The Gospel Hymn-Book* (1818). These publications are referred to as HM, SS, and GH, respectively; the other collections are abbreviated as listed in Table 3, p. 178. References in this section refer only to original editions and do not include holdings of the 1972 Da Capo Press reprint edition of *The Harmony of Maine*.

The information was obtained from mail surveys, various printed sources (including Metcalf's *American Psalmody;*[13] the new bibliography by Britton, Lowens, and Crawford;[14] and the National Union Catalog), and firsthand research.[15] I have appreciated the cooperation of the numerous librarians who have answered my inquiries. Copies I have personally seen are marked with an asterisk (*).

The locations are indexed two ways. To show which collections are owned by each library, the appropriate tunebook abbreviations are notated at the end of entries in "Collections Surveyed." The next enumeration, "Locations of Maine Tunebooks," shows where a given tunebook can be found; the sigla are based on the National Union Catalog/Library of Congress system. The three-part symbol consists of letters identifying the state, city, and specific library (if needed).

In the hopes of finding a previously unknown edition or other rare treasure, I have thoroughly scoured libraries and historical societies in Maine, particularly the towns where the Maine psalmodists lived. Although many of them did not own any original copies of the Maine tunebooks, the libraries have been listed here to acknowledge that their resources have been checked.[16]

Collections Surveyed

CLU	University Research Library, University of California, Los Angeles, California. (HM)
CSmH	Henry E. Huntington Library, San Marino, California. (CC15, HM)
CoBU	University of Colorado (including the American Music Research Center), Boulder, Colorado. (*WH21)
CtMW	Wesleyan University Library, Middletown, Connecticut. (None)
CtY	Yale University Library, New Haven, Connecticut. (CC15, HC17 [2 copies], HM, WH20)
CtYT	Yale Divinity Library, New Haven, Connecticut. (None)
DLC	Library of Congress, Washington, D.C. (CC15, CH05, HC17, HM, NH08, NH19, OH02, WH21)
GEU	Pitts Theological Library, Emory University, Atlanta, Georgia. (HC17)
ICN	Newberry Library, Chicago, Illinois. (HC17, HC19, HM, NH16)
ICU	Joseph Regenstein Library, University of Chicago, Chicago, Illinois. (HC19)
IaU	Rita Benton Music Library, University of Iowa, Iowa City, Iowa. (TH20)
MB	Boston Public Library, Boston, Massachusetts. (CC15, HC17, HM)
MBC	Congregational Library, Boston, Massachusetts. (HC19, WH20)
MBNec	New England Conservatory of Music Library, Boston, Massachusetts. (None)
MBU-T	Theological Library, Boston University, Boston, Massachusetts. (CC15, WH20, WH21)
MH	Houghton Library, Harvard University, Cambridge, Massachusetts. (CC15, HC17, HM)
MHT	Andover-Harvard Theological Seminary Library, Cambridge, Massachusetts. (GH)
MHi	Massachusetts Historical Society, Boston, Massachusetts. (HC17, HC19, HM, NH08, TH [edition uncertain], WH21)
MSaE	Essex Institute, Salem, Massachusetts. (HC17, HM, NH16, TH21, WH21)
MWA	American Antiquarian Society, Worcester, Massachusetts. (*CC15, *GH, *HC17, *HC19, *HM, *NH08, *WH20)
MeAFw	Fort Western Museum, Augusta, Maine. (None)
Me	Maine State Library and Museum, Augusta, Maine. (*GH, *HC17, *HC19)
MeBHi	Bangor Historical Society, Bangor, Maine. (None)

MeBP	Bangor Public Library, Bangor, Maine. (*CC15, *HM, *HC19)
MeBT	Moulton Library, Bangor Theological Seminary, Bangor, Maine. (None)
MeBhB	Bagaduce Music Lending Library, Blue Hill, Maine. (None)
MeBrB	Hawthorne-Longfellow Library, Bowdoin College, Brunswick, Maine. (*HM, *WH20)
MeBuHi	Bucksport Historical Society, Bucksport, Maine. (None)
MeChB	Brown Memorial Library, China, Maine. (None)
MeChC	Personal collection, Margaret Clifford, China, Maine. (*PH, *TH24, *TH26, *TH, the last-named being a composite of several editions)
MeChHi	China Historical Society, China, Maine. (None)
MeClP	Calais Free Library, Calais, Maine. (None)
MeCsW	Wilson Museum/Castine Scientific Society, Castine, Maine. (None)
MeFP	Farmington Public Library, Farmington, Maine. (HM)
MeFU	Mantor Library, University of Maine at Farmington, Farmington, Maine. (None)
MeFkU	University of Maine at Fort Kent Library, Fort Kent, Maine. (None)
MeGU	Gorham Campus Library, University of Southern Maine, Gorham, Maine. (None)
MeHH	Hubbard Free Library, Hallowell, Maine. (*HC17, *HC19, *HM, *WH20, *WH21, *TH26, *SS)
MeHi	Maine Historical Society, Portland, Maine. (*GH, *NH08, *TH18, *TH23, *WH21)
MeLB	Ladd Library, Bates College, Lewiston, Maine. (None)
MeLN	Norlands Living History Center, Livermore Falls, Maine. (None)
MeMU	Merrill Library, University of Maine at Machias, Machias, Maine. (None)
MeOU	Raymond Fogler Library, University of Maine, Orono, Maine. (None)
MePP	Portland Public Library, Portland, Maine. (None)
MePT	Tate House, Portland, Maine. (None)
MePTh	General Theological Center Library, Portland, Maine. (None)
MePU	Portland Campus Library, University of Southern Maine, Portland, Maine. (None)
MePV	Victoria Mansion, Portland, Maine. (None)
MePaH	Hamlin Memorial Library, Paris, Maine. (None)
MePiU	University of Maine at Presque Isle Library, Presque Isle, Maine. (None)
MeSaD	Dyer Library/York Institute Museum, Saco, Maine. (None)
MeSkH	History House, Skowhegan, Maine. (None)
MeSkP	Skowhegan Public Library, Skowhegan, Maine. (None)
MeTHi	Turner Historical Society, Turner, Maine. (None)
MeWC	Colby College Library, Waterville, Maine. (None)
MeWR	Redington Museum/Waterville Historical Society, Waterville, Maine. (None)

MeWiHi	Winthrop Historical Society, Winthrop, Maine. (None)
MeYHi	Old York Historical Society, York, Maine. (None)
MiU-C	William L. Clements Library, University of Michigan, Ann Arbor, Michigan. (CC15, HM, WH20)
MnHi	Minnesota Historical Society, St. Paul, Minnesota. (HM)
NBu	Buffalo and Erie County Public Library, Buffalo, New York. (CC15, HC17, WH20)
NHi	New-York Historical Society, New York, New York. (None)
NN	New York Public Library, New York, New York. (HC17, HM, NH05, TH26 [film])
NNUT	Union Theological Seminary Library, New York, New York. (HM, WH21)
NRU-Mus	Sibley Music Library, Eastman School of Music, University of Rochester, Rochester, New York. (HM, WH20)
NcD	Duke University Library, Durham, North Carolina. (WH21)
NcWsM	The Moravian Music Foundation, Winston-Salem, North Carolina. (CC15, HC19, HM, TH26, WH21)
NhC	New Hampshire State Library, Concord, New Hampshire. (None)
NhEHi	Exeter Historical Society, Exeter, New Hampshire. (None)
NhEP	Exeter Public Library, Exeter, New Hampshire. (None)
NhEPe	Phillips Exeter Academy Library, Exeter, New Hampshire. (*NH08)
NhHD	Dartmouth College Library, Hanover, New Hampshire. (CH05)
NhHi	New Hampshire Historical Society, Concord, New Hampshire. (CC15)
NhU	University of New Hampshire Library, Durham, New Hampshire. (CC15)
NjP	Princeton University Library, Princeton, New Jersey. (NH05)
NjPT	Princeton Theological Seminary Library, Princeton, New Jersey. (GH, HM, NH05, WH20)
OCl	Cleveland Public Library, Cleveland, Ohio. (WH21)
PMA	Pelletier Library, Allegheny College, Meadville, Pennsylvania. (HC17)
PPiPT	Clifford E. Barbour Library, Pittsburgh Theological Seminary, Pittsburgh, Pennsylvania. (HC17, HM, WH20, WH21)
RHi	Rhode Island Historical Society, Providence, Rhode Island. (None)
RPB	John Hay Library, Brown University, Providence, Rhode Island. (CC15, CH05, HC17, HC19, HM, NH05, PH, SS, TH21, WH20)
WaU	University of Washington Library, Seattle, Washington. (HM)

Locations of Maine Tunebooks

NOTE: Following each bibliographic citation is the Evans or Shaw/Shoemaker number assigned to the publication. (The pre-1800 tunebook has an Evans number; all the rest, as post-1800 works, have Shaw/Shoemaker numbers.) These numbering systems are used for the Readex Microprint Series of Early American Imprints Before 1820. Pre-1820 American publications were filmed for this series, which is available at many larger libraries. The microprint cards (somewhat similar to microfiches) can be viewed on a microprint reader.

Belcher, Supply. *The Harmony of Maine*. Boston: Isaiah Thomas & Ebenezer T. Andrews, 1794. [E26636]

CLU, CSmH, CtY, DLC, ICN, MB, MH, MHi, MSaE, *MWA, *MeBP, *MeBrB, MeFP, *MeHH, MiU-C, MnHi, NN, NNUT, NRU-Mus, NcWsM, NjPT, PPiPT, RPB, WaU.

The Hallowell Collection of Sacred Music. Hallowell, ME: printed and published by E. Goodale, 1817. [S40978]

CtY, DLC, GEU, ICN, MB, MH, MHi, MSaE, *MWA, *Me, *MeHH, NBu, NN, PMA, PPiPT, RPB.

The Hallowell Collection of Sacred Music, second edition. Hallowell, ME: printed and published by E. Goodale, 1819. [S48138]

ICN, ICU, MBC, MHi, *MWA, *Me, *MeBP, *MeHH, NcWsM, RPB.

Hartwell, Edward. *The Chorister's Companion*. Exeter, NH: C. Norris & Co. for the author, 1815. [S34877]

CSmH, CtY, DLC, MB, MBU-T, MH, *MWA, *MeBP, MiU-C, NBu, NcWsM, NhHi, NhU, RPB.

[Hinkley, Smith, and Christopher T. Norcross]. *Songs of Sion, or Maine Collection of Sacred Music*. Charleston, ME: Hinkley & Norcross, 1830. [1830–1839 series, 3547]

*MeHH, RPB.

Little, Henry. *The Wesleyan Harmony*. Hallowell, ME: E. Goodale, 1820. [1820–1829 series, 1974]

CtY, MBC, MBU-T, *MWA, *MeBrB, *MeHH, MiU-C, NBu, NRU-Mus, NjPT, PPiPT, RPB.

———. *The Wesleyan Harmony,* second edition. Hallowell, ME: Goodale, Glazier & Co., 1821. [1820–1829 series, 5833]

*CoBU, DLC, MBU-T, MHi, MSaE, *MeHH, *MeHi, NNUT, NcD, NcWsM, OCl, PPiPT.

Maxim, Abraham. *The Northern Harmony*. Exeter, NH: Henry Ranlet, for the compiler, 1805. [S8882]

NN, NjP, NjPT, RPB.

———. *The Northern Harmony,* second edition. Exeter, NH: Norris & Sawyer, 1808. [S15568/15569]

DLC, MHi, *MWA, *MeHi, *NhEPe.

———. *The Northern Harmony,* fifth edition. Hallowell, ME: E. Goodale, 1819. [S48653]

DLC (incomplete copy; ends on p. 142).

———. *The Oriental Harmony*. Exeter, NH: Henry Ranlet, 1802. [S2643]
DLC.

[Maxim, Abraham]. *The Gospel Hymn-Book*. N.p.: n.p., 1818. [S44186]
MHT, *MWA, *Me, *MeHi, NjPT.

Maxim, Abraham, and Japheth C. Washburn. *The Northern Harmony*, fourth edition. Hallowell, ME: E. Goodale, 1816. [S38205]
ICN (incomplete copy) MSaE (incomplete copy; ends on p. 56).

Robbins, Charles. *The Columbian Harmony; or Maine Collection of Church Music*. Exeter, NH: printed at the music-press of Henry Ranlet, for the author, 1805. [Not in S/S]
DLC, NHi, NhHD, RPB.

Washburn, Japheth Coombs. *The Parish Harmony, or Fairfax Collection of Sacred Musick*. Exeter, NH: C. Norris & Co. for the author, 1813. [S30447]
*MeChC, RPB.

———. *The Temple Harmony*. Hallowell, ME: E. Goodale & J. C. Washburn, Esq., 1818. [S46698]
*MeHi.

———. *The Temple Harmony*, second edition. Hallowell, ME: Goodale, Glazier & Co., 1820. [Not in 1820–1829 series]
IaU.

———. *The Temple Harmony*, third edition. Hallowell, ME: Goodale, Glazier & Co., 1821. [1820–1829 series, 7589]
MSaE, RPB.

———. *The Temple Harmony*, fourth edition. Hallowell, ME: Goodale, Glazier & Co., 1823. [1820–1829 series, 14832]
*MeHi.

———. *The Temple Harmony*, fifth edition [?]. [Hallowell, ME]: [Goodale, Glazier & Co.], [1824 or 1825]. [Not in 1820–1829 series]
*MeChC.

———. *The Temple Harmony*, sixth edition. Hallowell, ME: Glazier & Co., 1826. [Not in 1820–1829 series]
*MeChC, *MeHH, NN (film only), NcWsM.

———. *The Temple Harmony*, edition uncertain.
MHi (imperfect copy lacking title page).

———. *The Temple Harmony*, composite (pages from several editions).
*MeChC.

END PAPERS

END NOTES BY CHAPTER

Notes for Chapter I

1. A number of towns had been established in southern coastal Maine in the seventeenth and eighteenth centuries.
2. A psalm is a metrical version, usually a rhymed paraphrase, of one of the 150 psalms in the Bible; a hymn is a man-made devotional text which does not directly paraphrase the Scriptures.
3. "Psalmody" is a term referring to the sacred music (both psalms and hymns) sung in Protestant churches in England and America from the seventeenth century to the early nineteenth century. Richard Crawford, "Psalmody," in *The New Grove Dictionary of American Music,* 4 vols., ed. H. Wiley Hitchcock and Stanley Sadie (London: Macmillan Press, 1986), III, p. 635. A "psalmodist" was one who composed sacred music of this type or compiled psalmody collections (or both).
4. Until Maine statehood was achieved in 1820, the official name of the region was the District of Maine. To simplify references, however, I will frequently use "Maine" to refer to the District of Maine as well as the State of Maine.
5. Although there were Quakers (or "Friends") in Maine, they did not allow any music at their meetings, so there is none to discuss.
6. The period from the end of the American Revolution (1783) to Maine's statehood (1820) is the focus of an important series of papers from the "Maine at Statehood" project, published as *Maine in the Early Republic: From Revolution to Statehood,* ed. Charles E. Clark, James S. Leamon, and Karen Bowden (Hanover, NH: University Press of New England, 1988; hereafter cited as *Maine in the Early Republic*). A similar period (expanded to include two earlier decades) is covered in Alan Taylor, *Liberty Men and the Great Proprietors . . . 1760–1820* (Chapel Hill: University of North Carolina Press, 1990).
7. Earl McLain Owen, Jr., "The Life and Music of Supply Belcher (1751–1836), 'Handel of Maine' " (D.M.A. document, Southern Baptist Theological Seminary, 1969); Frieda B. Reynolds, "The Music of Supply Belcher" (M.M. thesis, Chicago Musical College, Roosevelt University, 1968).

8. [Smith Hinkley and Christopher T. Norcross], *Songs of Sion, or Maine Collection of Sacred Music* (Charleston, ME: Hinkley & Norcross, 1830).
9. Not until 1839 would other sacred music collections be published in Maine, and by then, both the place of publication and focus would be completely different. The two 1839 publications, both published in Portland, are Benjamin Sweetser, Jr., *Cumberland Collection of Church Music* (Portland: William Hyde, 1839), and David Paine, *Portland Sacred Music Society's Collection of Church Music* (Portland: William Hyde; Colman & Chisholm, 1839). See Chapter XIV for an introduction to some of the Maine collections published in 1830 and after.
10. David P. McKay and Richard Crawford, *William Billings of Boston: Eighteenth-Century Composer* (Princeton: Princeton University Press, 1975).
11. David Wilferd McCormick, "Oliver Holden, Composer and Anthologist" (S.M.D. dissertation, Union Theological Seminary in the City of New York, 1963).
12. David G. Klocko, "Jeremiah Ingalls's 'The Christian Harmony: or, Songster's Companion' (1805)," 3 vols. (Ph.D. dissertation, University of Michigan, 1978).
13. David W. Steel, "Stephen Jenks (1772–1856): American Composer and Tunebook Compiler" (Ph.D. dissertation, University of Michigan, 1982).
14. Richard Crawford, *Andrew Law, American Psalmodist* (Evanston, IL: Northwestern University Press, 1968).
15. Betty Bandel, *Sing the Lord's Song in a Strange Land: The Life of Justin Morgan* (Rutherford, NJ: Fairleigh Dickinson University Press, 1981).
16. Vinson C. Bushnell, "Daniel Read of New Haven (1757–1836): The Man and His Musical Activities" (Ph.D. dissertation, Harvard University, 1978).
17. Nym Cooke, "American Psalmodists in Contact and Collaboration, 1770–1820," 2 vols. (Ph.D. dissertation, University of Michigan, 1990).
18. Karl Kroeger, "The Worcester Collection of Sacred Harmony and Sacred Music in America, 1786–1803" (Ph.D. dissertation, Brown University, 1976).
19. Ralph T. Daniel, *The Anthem in New England Before 1800* (Evanston, IL: Northwestern University Press, 1966).
20. Nicholas Temperley and Charles G. Manns, *Fuging Tunes in the Eighteenth Century* (Detroit: Information Coordinators, 1983).
21. Allen P. Britton, "Theoretical Introductions in American Tunebooks to 1800" (Ph.D. dissertation, University of Michigan, 1949).

22. Alan Buechner, "Yankee Singing Schools and the Golden Age of Choral Music in New England, 1760–1800" (D.Ed. dissertation, Harvard University, 1960).
23. Richard Crawford, ed., *The Core Repertory of Early American Psalmody* (Madison: A-R Editions, 1984). This edition forms volumes XI and XII of A-R's Recent Researches in American Music series. To facilitate modern performance, multiple stanzas of texts are printed for all except through-composed pieces.
24. *The Complete Works of William Billings,* 4 vols., ed. Karl Kroeger (Boston: American Musicological Society and Colonial Society of Massachusetts, 1981–1990), IV.
25. Allen Britton, Irving Lowens, and Richard Crawford, *American Sacred Music Imprints, 1698–1810: A Bibliography* (Worcester: American Antiquarian Society, 1990).
26. George Thornton Edwards, *Music and Musicians of Maine* (Portland: Southworth Press, 1928). He discusses the history of music in Maine from 1604 to 1928.
27. Ronald Fred Cole, "Music in Portland, Maine, from Colonial Times Through the Nineteenth Century" (Ph.D. dissertation, Indiana University, 1975).
28. Donald A. Sears, "Music in Early Portland," *Maine Historical Society Quarterly,* Vol. XVI/3 (Winter 1977), pp. 131–160.
29. With Congregational parishes not established in the newer areas, many of the settlers became followers of itinerant preachers of the Baptist, Methodist, and Universalist faiths.
30. Although Belcher lived until 1836, the majority of his compositions were published before 1800 in his only tunebook, *The Harmony of Maine* (1794). A few additional compositions were published later in other tunebooks.

    James Lyon, whose sacred music collection, *Urania,* was published in 1761, moved to Maine in 1772, and in a sense, may be considered an eighteenth-century Maine psalmodist. Although he did not publish any tunebooks while living in Maine, a few of his tunes were published in the tunebooks of others. See Chapter VI for information on his musical career in Maine.
31. See note 7 above for complete citations.
32. References to him can be found in Gilbert Chase, *America's Music from the Pilgrims to the Present,* revised third edition (Urbana: University of Illinois Press, 1987), pp. 113, 120; H. Wiley Hitchcock, *Music in the United States: A Historical Introduction,* third edition (Englewood Cliffs, NJ: Prentice Hall, 1988), pp. 15, 19, 39; and Charles Hamm, *Music in the New World* (New York: W. W. Norton and Company, 1983), pp. 153, 154.

33. Besides having an unusual name, he was a tavern-keeper before his move to Maine, where he was dubbed "the Handel of Maine" by a Hallowell newspaper writer in 1796. See Chapter VI for more information on Belcher.
34. Frank J. Metcalf, *American Writers and Compilers of Sacred Music* (New York: Abingdon Press, [1925]; repr. Russell & Russell, 1967), pp. 161–163.
35. Simeon Pease Cheney, *The American Singing Book* (Boston: White, Smith & Co., 1879; repr. New York: Da Capo Press, 1980), pp. 183–184.
36. Britton, Lowens, and Crawford, pp. 155, 454–455, 525. Previously, the principal biographical reference to Robbins in the musicological literature was Richard J. Wolfe, *Secular Music in America, 1801–1825: A Bibliography,* 3 vols. (New York: New York Public Library, 1964), II, p. 746.
37. China's town history, while containing many references to Washburn, says little about him as a musician and composer. Mary M. Grow, *China, Maine: Bicentennial History, including 1984 Revisions* (Weeks Mills, ME: Marion T. Van Strien, [1984?]). A history of Skowhegan contains information on Edward Hartwell, including his musical endeavors. Louise Helen Coburn, *Skowhegan on the Kennebec,* 2 vols. (Skowhegan, ME: Independent-Reporter Press, 1941). The best source of information on Henry Little is George Thomas Little, *The Descendants of George Little, Who Came to Newbury, Massachusetts, in 1640* (Auburn, ME: published by the author, 1882), pp. 215–216.
38. Supply Belcher, *The Harmony of Maine* (Boston: Isaiah Thomas & Ebenezer T. Andrews, 1794; repr. New York: Da Capo Press, 1972).
39. See, for example, S15568, Abraham Maxim's *Northern Harmony,* second edition (1808); S30447, Japheth Coombs Washburn's *Parish Harmony* ([1813]); and S40978, *The Hallowell Collection of Sacred Music* (1817).
40. Robbins's *Columbian Harmony* (1805), for example, was not filmed for the Readex series.
41. For example, the only known first edition of Washburn's *Temple Harmony* is at the Maine Historical Society in Portland and is not currently available on microfilm.
42. For each tune, the data consists of tune title, book code, page number, composer attribution, nationality, lyricist, text source, tune incipit, text incipit, number of voice parts, key, and genre.
43. Richard Crawford, "Set-piece," in *The New Grove Dictionary of American Music,* 4 vols., ed. H. Wiley Hitchcock and Stanley Sadie (London: Macmillan Press, 1986), IV, p. 197.

Notes for Chapter II

1. The area now known as the State of Maine was granted to Massachusetts in 1691 by a charter of William and Mary of England. The area was designated the "District of Maine of Massachusetts" in 1778. After a long struggle for separation, which began in 1785, Maine finally gained independence from Massachusetts in 1820 and was established as a separate state.
2. Maine's population was 56,321 in 1784 and 298,335 in 1820. Moses Greenleaf, *A Survey of the State of Maine, in Reference to Its Geographical Features, Statistics and Political Economy* (Portland: Shirley & Hyde, 1829), p. 134.
3. The definition of mid-Maine as the territory between the Androscoggin and Penobscot rivers comes from Alan Taylor, *Liberty Men and Great Proprietors: The Revolutionary Settlement on the Maine Frontier, 1760–1820* (Chapel Hill: University of North Carolina Press, 1990), p. 1.
4. *Ibid.*, pp. 14–15.
5. The state of Massachusetts also offered to sell prospective settlers 150 acres of land on Maine's rivers and navigable waters at a dollar an acre or to give them 100 acres elsewhere, if they would clear 16 in four years. William Williamson, *The History of the State of Maine,* 2 vols. (Hallowell, ME: Glazier, Masters & Co., 1832), II, pp. 591, 507.
6. Taylor, pp. 9, 61.
7. *Ibid.*, p. 63.
8. *Ibid.*, pp. 62–63. His analysis of the pre-migration tax valuations of their fathers reveals that the average settler came from a family well under the threshold of rural prosperity.
9. Henry Little came from southern New Hampshire.
10. See Chapters VII to IX for more biographical information on the compilers.
11. Taylor, pp. 66–73.
12. Stephen A. Marini, *Radical Sects of Revolutionary New England* (Cambridge, MA: Harvard University Press, 1982), p. 29.
13. Farmers frequently shared and exchanged skills and goods with their neighbors. Marcie Cohen, "The Journals of Joshua Whitman, 1809–1811: An Analysis of Pre-Industrial Community in Rural Maine" (M.A. thesis, College of William and Mary in Virginia, 1985), pp. 33, 41. See also Thomas C. Hubka, "Farm Family Mutuality: The Mid-Nineteenth-Century Maine Farm Neighborhood," in *The Farm* (Annual Proceedings, Dublin Seminar for New England Folklife, 1986), pp. 13–23.
14. Marini, *Radical Sects,* p. 31.

15. For example, Massachusetts citizens, who lived in a society dominated by a political and religious elite, were required to pay taxes to support the legally established religion of Congregationalism, regardless of their personal beliefs.
16. Reginald Horsman, *The Frontier in the Formative Years, 1783–1815* (New York: Holt, Rinehart & Winston, 1970), p. 21.
17. Marini observes that by 1820, evangelical sects and the Jeffersonian Democratic-Republican party were dominant in rural, inland Maine, while the Congregational religion and Federalist politics continued to be supported in the older coastal settlements. He notes that "Maine's religion and politics developed simultaneously geographically and sociologically between 1780 and 1820." Stephen A. Marini, "Religious Revolution in the District of Maine, 1780–1820," in *Maine in the Early Republic,* pp. 118–119.

    The Federalist party, which favored a strong central government, was dominant in Massachusetts, while the Anti-Federalist or Democratic-Republican party, was dominant in Maine after 1805. The Democrats were united in their belief that the Federalist monopoly of politics, religion, and education in Massachusetts deprived Republicans, Baptists, Methodists, and farmers of opportunities for success. Ronald F. Banks, *Maine Becomes a State: The Movement to Separate Maine from Massachusetts, 1785–1820* (Middletown, CT: Wesleyan University Press, 1970), pp. 42, 49.
18. Taylor, p. 33.
19. The conflicts between settlers and the proprietors are the subject of Taylor's book.
20. See Table 3, "Religious Bodies in the District of Maine, 1780–1820," in Marini, "Religious Revolution," p. 120. Some of the Presbyterian churches became Congregational; others gradually died out. While individual Episcopalians had been among the earliest settlers of Maine, there were few Episcopal churches in Maine. Two of the Catholic organizations were located among Maine's Native American tribes (the Penobscots and the Passamaquoddies), who had been visited at an early date by French missionaries, resulting in some Catholic conversions. Jonathan Greenleaf, *Sketches of the Ecclesiastical History of the State of Maine* (Portsmouth, NH: Harrison Gray, 1821), pp. 223, 233, 264.
21. Taylor, pp. 131–132. In 1790, for example, only twelve of the sixty mid-Maine communities had organized a Congregational church.
22. The "New Lights," converted through the preaching of men such as George Whitefield and Jonathan Edwards, believed in the sinfulness of man, one's need for salvation by God through Christ, and the necessity of a conscious "new birth" through the Holy

Spirit. The Awakening's opponents, called "Old Lights," saw no need for a conversion experience, believing that a reasoned understanding of the Bible was sufficient for true religion. Unlike the Old Lights, the New Lights insisted that assurance of one's salvation was both possible and necessary. C. C. Goen, *Revivalism and Separatism in New England, 1740–1800* (New Haven: Yale University Press, 1962), p. 44.

23. Their primary objections to the Standing Order centered around two issues: 1) the continued reception and retention of unconverted members by the churches, and 2) an ecclesiastical platform which relinquished church control to a clerical class and enforced support through civil power. *Ibid.*, p. 36.
24. Marini, "Religious Revolution," pp. 122–123. Rev. Samuel Deane of the First Parish in Portland (Falmouth until 1786), for example, was a moderate Old Light who was also able to satisfy the New Lights in his congregation.
25. *Ibid.*, pp. 129–130.
26. Marini, *Radical Sects,* p. 65. A convert of George Whitefield, Randel was called to preach "a combination of the Arminian theology of human free will, the general atonement of Christ, and a 'day of grace' granted to all souls for their free choice of salvation or damnation, with consensus as the polity for Christ's church, and the 'open communion' of all true Christians." Marini, "Religious Revolution," p. 131.
27. Marini, *Radical Sects,* p. 6.
28. Arminians maintain the possibility of salvation for all and oppose the absolute predestinarianism of strict Calvinism. "Arminian" in *Webster's Seventh New Collegiate Dictionary* (Springfield, MA: G. & C. Merriam Company, 1965), p. 48.
29. The Universalists believed in universal salvation, a reconciliation of alienated humans to God through the atonement of Christ.
30. Marini, "Religious Revolution," p. 134.
31. Banks, pp. 141, 149. The Toleration Act aimed at abolishing the compulsory ministerial tax. Previously, a dissenter's tax could be directed to a minister of his choice only if the dissenting group was incorporated by the General Court and had its own resident minister. The Toleration Act removed these obstacles.
32. Marini, "Religious Revolution," p. 134. York was the original Maine county; Cumberland and Lincoln counties were established in 1760 from parts of York County.
33. Marini, *Radical Sects,* p. 5; Goen, p. 107.
34. Although there is no proof that Maxim was a Universalist, the evidence seems to point that way. See Chapter VII for more information.

35. Watts "Christianized" and modernized the psalms by freely composing versions (not translations or paraphrases) similar to what the psalmist King David might have written had he been a Christian contemporary of Watts. He also wrote other spiritual songs ("hymns"), reflecting New Testament Scriptural thought. Louis F. Benson, *The English Hymn: Its Development and Use in Worship* (New York: George H. Doran Co., 1915; repr. Richmond, VA: John Knox Press, 1962), pp. 110–113.
36. The definitive Freewill Baptist hymnal was John Buzzell's *Psalms, Hymns, and Spiritual Songs* (1823). The Universalists, who considered evangelical hymnody, especially the lyrics of Watts, to be too pervasively Calvinistic for Universalist congregations, prepared an original hymnal, *Hymns Composed by Different Authors,* published in 1808. Marini, *Radical Sects,* pp. 159, 162. The first hymnal of American Universalism was James Relly's *Christian Hymns, Poems and Spiritual Songs,* first printed in London and reprinted in Burlington, New Jersey, in 1776. Benson, pp. 327, 421.
37. Banks, p. 7.
38. Richard M. Candee, "'The Appearance of Enterprise and Improvement': Architecture and the Coastal Elite of Maine," in *Agreeable Situations: Society, Commerce, and Art in Southern Maine, 1780–1830* (Kennebunk, ME: Brick Store Museum, 1987; hereafter cited as *Agreeable Situations*), p. 67.
39. According to Allis, lumbering was the most widely practiced occupation of Maine settlers living east of Portland in 1790. Frederick Allis, Jr., "The Maine Frontier," in *A History of Maine: A Collection of Readings on the History of Maine, 1600–1970,* ed. Ronald F. Banks (Dubuque, IA: Kendall/Hunt Publishing Company, 1969), p. 127.
40. Banks, p. 7.
41. Tunebooks compiled in Maine during the first few years of the nineteenth century were Maxim's *Oriental Harmony* (1802) and *Northern Harmony* (1805) and Robbins's *Columbian Harmony* (1805). While Maxim had moved to Maine in the 1790s as a young adult, Robbins, who came to Maine with his family in 1788 when he was only six, was too young throughout most of the 1790s to compile a tunebook.
42. While the embargo law was enacted to compel England and France to stop interfering with American commerce, the cessation of trade caused more difficulties in the United States than in the other countries. Louis Clinton Hatch, *Maine: A History,* 5 vols. (New York: American Historical Society, 1919), I, p. 71.
43. Banks, p. 57.

44. *Ibid.,* pp. 59–60. The apparent indifference of Massachusetts toward Maine's problems during the war fueled the desire of many Mainers to be free of Massachusetts rule.
45. The war ended in December 1814, but word did not reach Massachusetts until February 15, 1815. Banks, p. 66.
46. The three were a second and third edition of Abraham Maxim's *Northern Harmony* (1808 and 1810) and the first edition of Japheth Coombs Washburn's *Parish Harmony* (1813).
47. Washburn notes in the advertisement at the front of the book that the expense of large music books "is such, as to render it difficult for some societies in the country to purchase them." Japheth Coombs Washburn, *The Parish Harmony, or Fairfax Collection of Sacred Musick* (Exeter, NH: C. Norris & Co. for the author, 1813), p. [3].
48. Formerly, a profitable triangular trade route had been established in which ships delivered lumber and dried fish from Maine to the West Indies, returning to American ports with sugar, molasses, and rum from the islands. Some of the West Indies goods were then carried to Europe, where they were exchanged for manufactured goods needed in America.
49. Joyce Butler, "Rising Like a Phoenix: Commerce in Southern Maine, 1775–1830," in *Agreeable Situations,* p. 30.
50. Taylor, pp. 238–239.
51. These works were Edward Hartwell's *Chorister's Companion* (1815), two more editions of Maxim's *Northern Harmony* (1816 and 1819), two editions of *The Hallowell Collection* (1817 and 1819), two editions of Henry Little's *Wesleyan Harmony* (1820 and 1821), and seven editions of Washburn's *Temple Harmony* (1818 to 1827).
52. The reform movement, discussed at more length in Chapter III, had affected church music in Massachusetts by 1810, but seems to have reached Maine nearly a decade later.
53. Although the separation movement began in 1785, a consensus was not reached until several decades later. Some Mainers only gradually became convinced to vote for separation.
54. The act required coasting vessels sailing along the Atlantic coast to enter and clear at all states other than those contiguous to their own. As a part of Massachusetts, Maine ships could sail, nonstop, as far south as New Jersey since New Hampshire, Rhode Island, Connecticut, and New York were all contiguous to Massachusetts. Once Maine became a separate state, shippers would have to stop at Massachusetts and all of the above except New Hampshire, since only the latter would be contiguous. Banks, pp. 35, 127, 128–129.

55. Fuging-tunes and tunes by Americans continued to be included in Maine tunebooks of the 1820s although they had been largely displaced in many other New England collections by that time.
56. Taylor (p. 148) has noted that evangelicals and agrarians shared a spirit of anti-authoritarian localism, while orthodox Congregationalists and the wealthy land proprietors shared a desire for a hierarchical, stable society.

Notes for Chapter III

1. Elijah Fisher of Livermore, for example, frequently reports in his diary in the late 1810s and early 1820s that meeting was at "the East S-H" or "E-S-H" (presumably East School-house). Not until April 1822 does he note, "We began to frame our Meeting-house." Elijah Fisher, manuscript diary, 1796–1837, Box 1/3 of the Elijah Fisher Papers (Manuscript Collection 55, Maine Historical Society, Portland). In Skowhegan, church services were held in inhabitants' homes until the first meetinghouse in town was built in 1788, per Edwards (p. 33). Other examples are numerous.
2. Praying, reading a sermon, and singing were the activities engaged in by the eighteenth-century believers in New Gloucester, Maine, when they had no preacher. Isaac Parsons, "Some Account of New Gloucester," in *Collections of the Maine Historical Society,* first series, 10 vols. (Portland: Maine Historical Society, 1847), II, p. 158.
3. Ada Douglas Littlefield, *An Old River Town* (New York: Calkins & Company, 1907), p. 208.
4. Belcher, p. [3].
5. Hon. Ammi R. Mitchell, *An Address on Sacred Music . . .* (Portland: Hyde, Lord & Co., 1812), p. 7.
6. Daniel Dana, A.M., *An Address on Sacred Musick . . .* (Exeter, NH: Charles Norris & Co., 1813), pp. 8–10.
7. During the intermission, worshippers left the building not only to eat lunch, but also to try to get warm, a matter of practical importance in the days of unheated churches.
8. Calvin Montague Clark, *History of the Congregational Churches in Maine,* 2 vols. (Portland: Congregational Christian Conference of Maine, [c. 1935]), II, pp. 189–195. While Clark's description is of a typical eighteenth-century service, his later chapter on changes between 1783 and 1826 does not suggest that the sequence changed.
9. Gilman, on the other hand, suggests that services in New England country churches customarily began with singing rather than with praying, which took place between the first and second songs. The

fictional (c. 1805) New Hampshire village choir he describes was called upon to sing a total of five times per Sabbath, probably three times in the morning and twice in the afternoon. [Samuel Gilman], *Memoirs of a New England Village Choir, with Occasional Reflections* (Boston: S. G. Goodrich, 1829; repr. New York: Da Capo Press, 1984), pp. 4–5, 13, 84, 95–96.

10. The forenoon and afternoon pastoral discourses were sometimes presented by two different preachers, according to the diary notations of Martha Ballard, a Hallowell midwife, who often noted on Sunday that she had attended worship all day. See "The Diary of Mrs. Martha Moore Ballard (1785 to 1812)," in Charles E. Nash, *The History of Augusta* (Augusta: Charles E. Nash & Son, 1904), pp. 229–464.
11. The musical portions were restricted to sung psalms and hymns; they did not usually encompass all-instrumental pieces. Once instruments were allowed into churches, they supported the singing but were rarely used independently of the voices.
12. These services are discussed later in this chapter.
13. G. T. Ridlon, Sr., *Saco Valley Settlements and Families* (Portland: G. T. Ridlon, Sr., 1895), pp. 246–268. The general meeting described was a Tuesday-through-Sunday event which gathered delegates from all the churches of the same denomination in the area for mutual support and encouragement. Some sessions were business meetings, others were worship services. Like Gilman in his *Memoirs of a Village Choir,* Ridlon depicts fictionalized events, based on his personal experiences.
14. (Spelling as in the original source.) Instead of learned clergy, the speakers consisted of various elders, deacons, and brethren who were moved by the spirit to sermonize or pray. Ridlon, p. 253.
15. Cochran, whose sect combined aspects of the worship and doctrines of the Freewill Baptists, Shakers, and Universalists, promoted spiritual wifery (wife swapping), a practice which led to his later conviction for adultery and "open gross lewdness and lascivious behavior." Joyce Butler provides perspective on the life and beliefs of Cochran in an excellent article, "Cochranism Delineated: A Twentieth-Century Study," in *Maine in the Early Republic,* pp. 146–164.
16. Daniel Remich, *History of Kennebunk from Its Earliest Settlement to 1890* (n.p.: n.p., 1911), p. 271. Some of those attending fell into a trance during the service; when they became conscious again, they told about the visions they had seen, while other "worshippers" shouted, groaned, jumped, and clapped their hands.
17. Ephraim Stinchfield Papers, 1777–1830 (Manuscript Collection 44, Maine Historical Society, Portland), box 1/1, letter written by

Ephraim Stinchfield, April 1819. Quoted by permission of the Maine Historical Society.

18. Butler, "Cochranism Delineated," pp. 148, 156.
19. Joel M. Marshall, "The Cochrane Craze," *Biddeford Daily Journal,* January 10, 1894.
20. *Ibid.*
21. Coburn, I, pp. 364–365. Based on the texts provided, the songs may be somewhat longer than the typical camp-meeting hymn.
22. Camp meetings, first held in Kentucky in 1800, were organized primarily to provide sacramental services to frontier residents without access to churches. The large gatherings, which lasted for several days, were usually held in a wooded clearing. People travelled from miles around to attend and pitched tents to live in while there. The camp meetings were frequently ecumenical, featuring preachers from several denominations, such as Methodists, Baptists, and Presbyterians. Many were converted at the marathon sessions of preaching and singing. The frontier camp meetings spread to other areas, including the Northeast, where they were often held in a church or other auditorium and were somewhat less flamboyant. Ellen Jane Lorenz, *Glory, Hallelujah! The Story of the Campmeeting Spiritual* (Nashville, TN: Abingdon, 1980), pp. 14–15, 32, 33.
23. Coburn, p. 365.
24. "Pennyroyal Hymns," a generic term rather than the title of a specific volume, is an obsolete phrase once used interchangeably with "gospel song" and "spiritual song" to refer to a tune sung with "unction and vivacity." Mitford M. Mathews, ed., *A Dictionary of Americanisms on Historical Principles,* 2 vols. (Chicago: University of Chicago Press, 1951), II, p. 1223.
25. Coburn, p. 365.
26. *Ibid.*; Lorenz, pp. 49, 57.
27. Except when contained in a quotation from another source, tune titles will be indicated in this book by the use of capital letters (without quotation marks).
28. Coburn, p. 365; Lorenz, pp. 42–43, 61–62.
29. Coburn, p. 365.
30. Lorenz, p. 55.
31. Rev. Stephen Allen and Rev. W. H. Pilsbury, *History of Methodism in Maine* (Augusta: Press of Charles E. Nash, 1887), p. 10.
32. For example, a funeral anthem is mentioned in connection with the public funeral services at the meetinghouse in Augusta for the murdered Purrinton family: the services were "solemn and pertinent—commenced by a Funeral Anthem." *Gazette of Maine/Hancock Advertiser* (Buckstown, ME), II/3 (July 17, 1806), p. 2.
33. William Bentley, *Diary,* 4 vols. (Salem, MA: Essex Institute, 1907; repr. Gloucester, MA: Peter Smith, 1962), II, p. 290.

34. See "The Introduction of Musical Instruments," later in this chapter.
35. Washburn notes in the preface that he had originally planned to include several anthems, but decided that "Psalm Tunes might be more useful in a Book of this size, and equally acceptable to people in general" and consequently included but one anthem. Washburn, *Parish Harmony,* p. [3].
36. Abraham Maxim, *The Oriental Harmony* (Exeter, NH: Henry Ranlet, 1802). Abraham Maxim, *The Northern Harmony* (Exeter, NH: Henry Ranlet, for the compiler, 1805).
37. Japheth Coombs Washburn, *The Temple Harmony,* sixth edition (Hallowell, ME: Glazier & Co., 1826).
38. Washburn suggests the "special occasion" aspect of anthems in the Advertisement to the third edition of *The Temple Harmony* (Hallowell, ME: Goodale, Glazier & Co., 1821), when he writes (p. [3]) as follows: "The design has been to furnish Societies at a moderate expense, with a Book of convenient size containing a selection of standard pieces suitable for Temple worship, and several Anthems and other pieces for particular occasions."
39. *Order of Exercises at the Ordination of Rev. Darvin [i.e., Darwin] Adams, Camden, Maine* ([Belfast, ME]: n.p., [1828], Broadside Collection, American Antiquarian Society.
40. *Order of Exercises at the Ordination of the Rev. George Shepard* ([Hallowell, ME]: n.p., [1828]), Collections of the Hubbard Free Library, Hallowell, ME.
41. For example, the 1827 service dedicating the Bethlehem Church in Augusta began with "Music" (title unspecified) and included a six-stanza dedication hymn as well as "Music" immediately preceding the dedication sermon and again before the benediction. *Order of Exercise at the Dedication of the Bethlehem Church, in Augusta, October 18, 1827* ([Augusta]: n.p., [1827]), Broadside Collection, American Antiquarian Society.
42. For example, OLD HUNDRED was the tune for the hymns sung at these special services: the dedication of the Unitarian Church in Hallowell (1824), the Fourth of July celebration in Hallowell (1827), and the ordination of Rev. Shepard in Hallowell (1828). *Hallowell Gazette,* XI/38 (September 22, 1824), p. 3; XIV/28 (July 11, 1827); *Order of Exercises at the Ordination of the Rev. George Shepard.*

    OLD HUNDRED was the most frequently printed tune in American tunebooks between 1698 and 1810. *Core Repertory,* p. lxxvii. It continued to be a stalwart in the repertory after 1810 as well, especially among those of reform sentiments.
43. *Hallowell Gazette,* IX/26 (June 26, 1822), p. 3.
44. The same singers, reinforced by members of other choirs, presented two such exhibitions of sacred music in September and October of

1822 under the name of the "Augusta Oratorio." The anthem "Strike the Cymbal," sung at the Masonic ceremony, was also included on the oratorio program. See Chapter IV for more information.

45. *Herald of Liberty* (Augusta), I/22 (July 10, 1810), p. 3.
46. Mitchell, pp. 14–15.
47. As cited in Edwards, p. 34. The *Bridgewater Collection* was a leading eclectic tunebook, published in Boston in twenty-seven editions between 1802 and 1839. See Chapter V for more information on the collection.
48. Rev. Paul Coffin, "Memoir and Journals (1760–1800)," in *Collections of the Maine Historical Society,* first series, 10 vols. (Portland: Published for the society, 1856), IV, p. 312.
49. A description of services at the east meetinghouse in Brunswick, Maine, notes that Deacon Snow "sat under or in front of the pulpit, and 'lined out' the hymn, so that every man present might have an opportunity to sing. This was the common practice." George Augustus Wheeler, M.D., and Henry Warren Wheeler, *History of Brunswick, Topsham, and Harpswell, Maine* (Boston: Alfred Mudge & Son, Printers, 1878), p. 213.
50. Henry Wilder Foote, *Three Centuries of American Hymnody* (Cambridge, MA: Harvard University Press, 1940), pp. 379–380.
51. Buechner, pp. 267–271. The First Parish Church in Falmouth was one exception in forming a choir by 1765.
52. See Chapter IV for more information on Maine singing schools.
53. Lining out ceased at about the same time, or shortly after, the members voted in 1756 to purchase 380 copies of Tate and Brady's Psalm Book with the tunes annexed. By 1765, if not before, sixteen of the trained singers had banded together to form a choir. Clark, p. 191.
54. Buechner, p. 273.
55. Wheeler, p. 370.
56. As late as 1823, lack of books presented a problem in East Winthrop. The music for the dedication of the newly erected meetinghouse was to include several special pieces in addition to the hymns. Since the number of copies available was not sufficient, the church had additional copies printed and bound in pamphlet form. It is not clear whether only the words or both words and music were printed. W. Harrison Parlin, *Reminiscences of East Winthrop* (East Winthrop, ME: Banner Publishing Company, 1891), p. 27.
57. Washburn, *Parish Harmony,* p. [3].
58. Wheeler, p. 363.
59. Georgia Drew Merrill, ed., *History of Androscoggin County, Maine* (Boston: W. A. Fergusson & Co., 1891), p. 531. The church was built in 1794.

60. The original church was built in 1796 but destroyed by fire in 1878. Emma Huntington Nason, *Old Hallowell on the Kennebec* (Augusta: Burleigh & Flynt, 1909), pp. 193, 200.
61. Annie F. Page, *Historical Sketch of the South Congregationalist Church (Old South Church) of Hallowell* (Hallowell, ME: Register Press, 1900), p. 12.
62. Letter written by J. T. Little to his cousin, J. L. Stevens, in 1896 (Collections of the Castine Scientific Society, Castine, ME). Quoted by permission of the Castine Scientific Society. The meetinghouse, built in the 1790s, was the church of the First Congregational Society (now Unitarian).
63. Nathaniel D. Gould, *Church Music in America* (Boston: A. N. Johnson, 1853; repr. New York: AMS Press, 1972), pp. 109–110.
64. *Notes taken from the Records of the First Parish, York, Maine* (Typescript in the Old York Historical Society, York, ME), entry for March 19, 1799.
65. *Ibid.,* entry for March 18, 1800.
66. Hugh D. McLellan, *History of Gorham, Maine,* compiled and edited by Katharine B. Lewis (Portland: Smith & Sale, 1903), pp. 215–216.
67. A Common Meter text consists of four-line stanzas in which the first and third lines of each stanza have eight syllables; the second and fourth, six.
68. Page, p. 16.
69. D. R. Goodwin, *Memoir of John Merrick, Esq., Prepared for the Maine Historical Society* (n.p.: Henry B. Ashmond, 1862), p. 25. One of the prominent members of the choir was Jacob Abbot, Esq., a fine singer who had moved to Hallowell in 1800. Previously he had been one of the founders of the Concord Musical Society and chorister at the Old North Meeting-house. Nason, p. 122.
70. Parlin, p. 27.
71. Gilman, p. 25.
72. As we have noted previously, however, the fact that relatively few anthems (or set-pieces) are included in the early Maine tunebooks suggests that anthems may not have been performed so frequently in rural Maine as in other parts of New England in the early nineteenth century. The situation seems to have changed somewhat by the 1820s, probably due to the greater number of trained singers by then.
73. It is unclear how often tunebooks were used in church, even by choir members. Gould (pp. 113–114), speaking of some unspecified period in the past, claims that all the tunes were memorized before being sung in church and that perhaps only the chorister had a singing-book or note-book in his hand. He contrasts that time with the 1850s, when the singers' gallery was flooded with books.

74. Gilman, pp. 40–41.
75. *Ibid.*, p. 41.
76. While the Methodist congregations in Maine were undoubtedly much smaller than the convention-size group described by Gilman, the singing practices of their services may have been similar.
77. Buechner, p. 278.
78. As late as 1800, there were perhaps fewer than twenty church organs in all of New England. Foote, p. 85.
79. The positions, pro and con, are set forth in some detail in a Vermont pamphlet of 1807: Samuel Manning, *Two Dialogues, in which are stated, first, Arguments for and against the use of musical instruments in the public worship of God* . . . (Windsor, VT: printed by Alden Spooner for the author, 1807).
80. Parlin, p. 23.
81. Clark, p. 194.
82. Gilman (p. 17), referring to the violoncello, adds "or, as we term it in New England, the bass-viol." Gould (p. 170) indicates that the bass viol was "here and there" introduced into churches around the beginning, and sometimes long before, the nineteenth century.
83. Thirty-five dollars was raised "for purchasing a bass viol for the use of the parish and building a box therefor." North, p. 324.
84. Clark, p. 345, quoting from *History of York Co. Conference,* p. 58.
85. J. T. Little letter. While Little does not indicate when the bass viol was introduced or when the cupboard was built, it was at least prior to 1830, since Little was describing the church structure as it existed before the 1831–1832 remodeling.
86. Buechner (pp. 179–180) notes that a viol was played for the first time in Roxbury, Massachusetts, in 1788; he also cites the diary of William Bentley of Salem, who notes the introduction of the clarinet and violin into the church music in 1792, and the bass viol and German flute in 1795.
87. Wheeler, p. 214.
88. Nathan Webb, *Reminiscences of Portland* (n.p.: n.p., c. 1875), final page, unnumbered. Willis seems to be referring to the same situation when he discusses the 1829 church split which led to the erection of the "Christian Chapel" on Portland's Temple Street in 1830. Those who seceded not only opposed instrumental music in church but also wanted to exclude unconverted persons from participating in the singing. William Willis, *The History of Portland, from 1632 to 1864* (Portland: Bailey & Noyes, 1865; repr. Somersworth, NH: N. H. Publishing Co. and Maine Historical Society, 1972), pp. 692–693.
89. Wheeler, pp. 388–389.
90. Samuel Emerson, A.M., *An Oration on Music Pronounced at Portland, May 28, 1800* (Portland: E. A. Jenks, 1800), p. 16.

91. Mitchell, pp. 8–10. Mitchell was a deacon of the Congregational church, a beloved physician, and the most prominent citizen of North Yarmouth. William Hutchinson Rowe, *Ancient North Yarmouth and Yarmouth, Maine, 1636–1936: A History* (Yarmouth, ME: Southworth-Anthoensen Press, 1937), p. 336.
92. Gould, pp. 172–174.
93. Quote of Rev. Elijah Kellogg, cited in Edwards, p. 35. The cornet is an instrument not mentioned by Gould. Although Kellogg does not provide a date for the introduction of the cornet and clarinet, he implies that they were used to augment the bass viol prior to 1798, when the church acquired an organ. Unless the cornet used was a posthorn-type, valveless cornet, however, he must be referring to a later date; valved cornets were not made until the 1820s.
94. Cole, p. 17.
95. Edwards, p. 22.
96. The First Parish Church of Portland installed its first organ in 1822, the First Baptist Church in 1833, and the Chestnut Street Methodist Church in 1836. Cole, pp. 20–21.
97. Remich, p. 312. After 1820, the church became known as the First Congregational Parish in Kennebunk.
98. McLellan, p. 174.
99. Wheeler, p. 372.
100. William Henry Kilby, *Eastport and Passamaquoddy* (Eastport, ME: Edward E. Shead & Company, 1888), p. 348.
101. North, p. 443.
102. Quoted from an article by "Dr. Benjamin Vaughn" [actually Vaughan] in Page, pp. 19–21. The original article appeared in the *Hallowell Gazette* in 1823.
103. Organs did not totally replace other instruments in all cases. The organ at Wells First Church, for example, was accompanied by a bass viol and bassoon "on one or two interesting occasions." Edward E. Bourne, *The History of Wells and Kennebunk* (Portland: B. Thurston & Company, 1875), p. 626.
104. Wheeler, pp. 372–373.
105. Edwards, pp. 12–13. Foote (pp. 74–75) notes that the frequently made statement that early-eighteenth-century churches were limited to ten tunes, with few singing more than five, was probably not entirely accurate.
106. Charles Robbins, *The Columbian Harmony; or Maine Collection of Church Music* (Exeter, NH: printed at the music-press of Henry Ranlet, for the author, 1805), p. iv.
107. Parlin, pp. 23–24.
108. Representative versions of the tunes are printed in *The Core Repertory of Early American Psalmody,* ed. Richard Crawford (Madison:

A-R Editions, 1984). Although Crawford (p. xi) does not claim that these tunes were necessarily *the* 101 "most popular" sacred tunes at any given time in the period, they constitute a central, representative core of tunes which were undoubtedly sung again and again.

"Broad is the road" was a text frequently associated with American composer Daniel Read's tune WINDHAM, a Core Repertory piece.

109. Fuging-tunes and plain tunes, as well as the other genres of American psalmody (tunes with extension, set-pieces, and anthems), are introduced and defined in Chapter I. See Chapter XII for a more detailed discussion of the changing repertory in Maine tunebooks.
110. The origins and results of the reform movement are thoroughly discussed in Richard Crawford's essay, " 'Ancient Music' and the Europeanizing of American Psalmody, 1800–1810," in *A Celebration of American Music: Words and Music in Honor of H. Wiley Hitchcock,* ed. Richard Crawford, R. Allen Lott, and Carol J. Oja (Ann Arbor: University of Michigan Press, 1990), pp. 225–255.
111. *The Middlesex Collection of Church Music: or, Ancient Psalmody Revived* (Boston: Manning & Loring, 1807; second edition, 1808). The collection was sponsored by the Middlesex Musical Society of Massachusetts.
112. Mitchell, p. 8. Oliver Bray also made derogatory remarks about fuging-tunes in his address before the Hans Gram Musical Society of Fryeburg, Maine, in 1811; see Chapter IV.
113. *The Hallowell Collection of Sacred Music* (Hallowell, ME: printed and published by E. Goodale, 1817), p. [iii]. Although the compilers do not clarify what they mean by "light and flimsy airs," they seem to be referring to tunes whose style and faster tempo encouraged a lighthearted, rather than solemn, approach by the singers. Fuging-tunes were undoubtedly among the "light and flimsy airs"; with their staggered entrances and declamatory quarter notes, they were thinner in texture and more lively than solid, syllabic plain tunes (such as OLD HUNDRED, for example) which were homophonic throughout and featured half notes sung at a dignified, slow tempo.
114. Gilman, pp. 78, 80.
115. *Ibid.*, pp. 75–97.
116. *Ibid.*, pp. 95–96.
117. *Ibid.*, pp. 78–84.
118. James A. Keene, *Music and Education in Vermont, 1700–1900* (Macomb, IL: Glenbridge Publishing, 1987), p. 21. To have introduced Lowell Mason–style harmonizations, Mr. Duren must have arrived in Woodstock after 1821 or been exposed to the "newer" style after his arrival, since Lowell Mason's first collection was not

published until 1822 and he did not become widely known until about 1826. See Carol Ann Pemberton, *Lowell Mason: His Life and Work* (Ann Arbor: UMI Research Press, 1985).

Notes for Chapter IV

1. Irving Lowens, "Daniel Read's World: The Letters of an Early American Composer," in *Music and Musicians in Early America* (New York: W. W. Norton & Co., 1964), p. 177.
2. Maxim, *Northern Harmony,* p. [1].
3. Although singing often did improve as the result of singing schools, congregational singing in some churches became less frequent as the trained singers took over. See Chapter III.
4. William Willis, *Journals of the Rev. Thomas Smith, and the Rev. Samuel Deane* (Portland: Joseph S. Bailey, 1849), pp. 256, 358. Deane's diary entry was "Mr. Gage, the singer, came and began"; Smith's journal entry was "We are all in a blaze about singing; all flocking at 5, 10 and 4 o'clock to the meeting-house, to a Master hired, (viz. Mr. Gage)." Gage was from Essex County, Massachusetts.
5. Cole (p. 31) provides a list of the instructors, locations, and advertisement dates of these schools.
6. William Allen often travelled six or seven miles on moonlit winter nights to attend singing school taught by Supply Belcher. William Allen, *History of Industry, Maine,* second edition (Skowhegan, ME: Smith & Emery, Printers, 1869), p. 26.
7. Belcher, p. [1].
8. The entry for December 16, 1798, reads: "Sunday. Cyrus conducted Sally to Mr. Kitridge's to singing school. They returned, 9 h. 35 m." "The Diary of Mrs. Martha Moore Ballard," p. 378.
9. The entry for October 21, 1797, Pittston, includes the following: "The hearers gave good attention [to his preaching]. I believe they were satisfied. Had good singing. In the evening Major Coburn, Mr. Smith, singing-master, his son-in-law, his daughters and their cousin Sally Coburn, sang some excellent tunes." Coffin, p. 354.
10. Edwards, p. 28.
11. Cole, p. 31. Of course, it may be that newspapers became a more popular means of publicizing singing schools after 1800, not necessarily that more schools were held than before. Cole points out that the December 1799 advertisement announces the commencement of a "new school," implying that there had been prior schools.
12. *Hallowell Gazette,* XI/8 (February 25, 1824), p. 3; XI/12 (March 24, 1824), p. 3.

13. The note on the University of Iowa's copy is as follows: "This book was carried to Singing School in 1820 by a seventeen year old girl, whose name [Dorcas Goodwin] is written in the back." Town and genealogical records confirm the 1803 birth of Dorcas Goodwin, the first of fifteen children of Simeon Goodwin, a farmer in Litchfield, Maine, a town about ten miles southwest of Hallowell, where the book was published. Unfortunately, no information is available about the location or instructor of her singing school. John Hayes Goodwin, *Daniel Goodwin of Ancient Kittery, Maine, and His Descendents* (n.p.: n.p., 1985), p. 98; *History of Litchfield and an Account of Its Centennial Celebration, 1895* (Augusta: Kennebec Journal Print, 1897), pp. 133–134. Some of Dorcas's twentieth-century descendants lived in Iowa City, thus explaining the book's migration to Iowa.
14. See Chapter VII for more information on Maxim and his tunebooks.
15. Hamilton C. Macdougall, *Early New England Psalmody: An Historical Appreciation, 1620–1820* (Brattleboro, VT: Stephen Daye Press, 1940; repr. New York: Da Capo Press, 1969), p. 101. On the other hand, other tunebooks (such as William Billings's *Singing Master's Assistant*) went through several editions without change.
16. See Chapter V for a discussion of the tunebooks available in Maine.
17. *The Middlesex Collection of Church Music: or, Ancient Psalmody Revived* (Boston: Manning & Loring, 1807).
18. *Portland Gazette,* August 31, 1812, as cited in Cole, p. 33.
19. *The Village Harmony, or Youth's Assistant to Sacred Musick* (Exeter, NH: Henry Ranlet, 1795 and later). The final edition was the seventeenth edition, published in 1821.
20. Bartholomew Brown, A.M., and others, *Columbian and European Harmony: or, Bridgewater Collection of Sacred Musick* (Boston: Isaiah Thomas & Ebenezer Andrews, 1802). Later editions, many of which were entitled *Templi Carmina. Songs of the Temple, or, Bridgewater Collection of Sacred Music,* continued through 1839.
21. Buechner, pp. 187, 195.
22. As late as 1863, subscription papers were circulated in Cape Neddock (now Cape Neddick, part of York), Maine, to support a singing school in that town. Sums subscribed for schools held in 1850, 1856, 1857, and 1863 ranged from fifty cents to two dollars. *Subscription Lists for Cape Neddock Singing Schools, 1850–1863* (Manuscript Collection 422, Old York Historical Society, York, ME).
23. In some cases, a singing master would simply arrive in a town, unbidden, and advertise his services. For information about itinerant

singing masters, see Nym Cooke, "Itinerant Singing Masters in the Eighteenth Century," in *Itinerancy in New England and New York* (Annual Proceedings, Dublin Seminar for New England Folklife, 1984), pp. 16–36.

24. Although schoolhouses seem to have been a frequent location for Maine singing schools, Gould (p. 82) says that, in general, a common schoolhouse was considered "too dull and lonely a place" for singing schools. According to him, a hall in a public house or tavern was considered more desirable for the purpose, especially since the tavern's barroom would then be conveniently close for "recess" and postschool entertainment. A veteran singing master, Gould was notoriously cynical, but probably realistic, in his old age.
25. For example, the school attended by William Sewall in Hallowell lasted for about two and a half months (from January 14 to March 28, 1817) and met on Tuesday and Friday evenings, regardless of the weather. *Diary of William Sewall (1797–1846), 1817 to 1846,* ed. C. E. Goodell (Springfield, IL: Hartman Printing Co., 1930), pp. [7]-12.
26. *Diary of William Sewall,* p. 12.
27. *Hallowell Gazette,* V/49 (December 9, 1818), p. 3.
28. *Ibid.,* IV/45 (November 5, 1817), p. 3; V/4 (January 27, 1818), p. 3; V/48 (December 2, 1818), p. 1.
29. *Ibid.,* V/49 (December 9, 1818), p. 3.
30. *Ibid.,* VI/52 (December 29, 1819), p. 3.
31. Gould, p. 79.
32. Although he does not indicate the age of the other students, William Sewall, who attended singing school in Hallowell in 1817, was nearly twenty at the beginning of the sessions. He may have been slightly older than many of the other students. *Diary of William Sewall,* p. [7].

    While the New England singing school was basically a youth organization, adults were not completely excluded, judging from the "adult" singing schools listed by Gould (pp. 238–240) as having been taught by him.
33. Parlin, p. 91.
34. Chapter XI provides more detailed information on each of the components of the theoretical introductions.
35. Since only four different syllable names (fa, sol, law or la, and mi) were used, each of the syllables except mi occurred twice in the compass of an octave. Determining the location of mi in a given key was essential to knowing what to call each of the pitches surrounding it. The notes of the scale above mi were fa, sol, la, fa, sol, la, and then mi again. Below mi were la, sol, fa, la, sol, fa, followed by mi. The intervals mi to fa and la to fa were half steps; other ad-

jacent syllables represented whole steps. Most tunebooks had a chart showing the location of mi for various key signatures. For example, mi was on B when there were no sharps or flats in the signature, on E when there was one flat, etc.

36. Nine modes of time, indicated by symbols similar to modern time signatures, were commonly used. Each mode was associated with a particular tempo and contained a specified quantity and type of notes in each measure.
37. Buechner, pp. 134–139.
38. Boys with changing voices were frequently assigned to the counter, which usually had a limited range.
39. Robbins's *Columbian Harmony,* for example, has twelve lessons.
40. Gould, p. 96.
41. *Portland Gazette,* December 2, 1799, as cited in Cole, pp. 30–31. Not all schools were so restrictive about later enrollments. At the school attended by William Sewall in Hallowell, about thirty regular scholars were attending by the fourth meeting, with more expected "soon." Those joining the class later may have received instruction at a prior singing school. *Diary of William Sewall,* p. 8.
42. Buechner, pp. 237–241.
43. *Ibid.,* p. 242. Since William Sewall's account of the final session of the singing school he attended indicates only that "a considerable number called to see the performance," an oration may not have been part of the program. *Diary of William Sewall,* p. 12.
44. Edward Hartwell, *The Chorister's Companion* (Exeter, NH: C. Norris & Co. for the author, 1815). All three were written by American composer Oliver Holden.
45. Three months may have been sufficient for some students if they continued to practice their skills after the sessions concluded.
46. Buechner, p. 139.
47. For more about the Billings connection to Belcher and Maxim, see Chapter VI, note 19, and Chapter VII.
48. Gould, p. 103.
49. Buechner, p. 266.
50. Sewall's account is supported by Annie Page (p. 16), who notes that Samuel Tenney was the choir leader at the Old South Congregational Church in Hallowell, "before the days of the organ" (acquired in 1823). He found the keynote with the aid of a large bass viol, then gave the starting pitches to the choir with his "clear, musical voice."
51. Buechner, pp. 285–286.
52. Fisher diary, entries for February 5, 1819, and March 11 and 12, 1820.
53. Elijah Fisher's children attending singing school were "E," "G," "Sally," and "Priscila," presumably referring to children Elijah

(born 1793), Grinfil (born 1795), Salome (born 1806), and Priscilla (born 1801). Elijah's children's names and their birth years are given in Ira Thompson Monroe, *History of the Town of Livermore* . . . (Lewiston, ME: Lewiston Journal Printshop [1928]), p. 113.

54. William Sewall of Hallowell also seems to have attended more than one singing school at a time. One apparently met Tuesdays and Fridays, another on Mondays.
55. Fisher diary, entry for March 12, 1820. Although singing-school teacher Abraham Maxim lived at the time in nearby Turner (which bounded Livermore on the south), potentially close enough to have taught in Livermore, his responsibilities in Turner may have kept him too busy to seek further teaching opportunities in neighboring towns.
56. For example, Massachusetts psalmodist William Billings was a tanner by trade, Daniel Read was a comb maker, and Timothy Swan was a hatter.
57. *Notes, Historical, Descriptive, and Personal, of Livermore in Androscoggin (formerly in Oxford) County, Maine* (Portland: Bailey & Noyes, 1874), p. 164; Monroe, p. 167.
58. Cole, p. 34.
59. Edwards, p. 40; Cole, p. 34.
60. See, for example, his ads in the *Hallowell Gazette,* I/1 (February 23, 1814), p. 3; I/35 (October 19, 1814), p. 3.; IV/46 (November 12, 1817), p. 3; and V/1 (December 31, 1817), p. 3.
61. Buechner, p. 151.
62. *Hallowell Gazette,* XI/1 (January 6, 1824), p. 3; (Hallowell) *American Advocate and General Advertiser,* XV/1 (January 10, 1824), p. 1.
63. For more information on church choirs, see Chapter III.
64. Sewall may very well have attended the meetings of more than one singing society, since the meetings took place every night of the week except Saturday (different evenings in different weeks) and in various locations, including the room over the clerk's office, the county house, the Register office, and Lincoln Academy in Bloomfield (when he was a student there). The singing society which elected Mr. Tenney chorister on April 1, 1817, may have been a church choir; however, other singing societies attended by Sewall may not have been. He does not refer to "singing society" when discussing his assistance in the church singing. *Diary of William Sewall,* pp. 12, 13, 16, 22, 24, 30.
65. Sewall attended singing society meetings in April, June, August, September, November, and December 1817, following the completion of singing school in March 1817.
66. For a thorough discussion of musical societies in Massachusetts, see Donald A. Nitz, "Community Musical Societies in Massachu-

setts to 1840" (D.M.A. dissertation, Boston University, 1964). Maine musical societies are included in Nitz's Appendix C, "List of Musical Societies in New England Outside Massachusetts," but are not discussed in the text.

67. Musical Society in Falmouth, *Constitution, September 1, 1807* (Manuscript Collection S-627, Misc. Box 24/4, Maine Historical Society, Portland). Quoted by permission of the Maine Historical Society.
68. Articles 2 and 3 of the Constitution, Musical Society of Falmouth.
69. The "List of Subscribers to the Musical Society in Falmouth" consists of seventeen male names.
70. A newspaper ad for an August 27, 1811, anniversary of a "Beneficient [*sic*] Musical Society of Falmouth" probably refers to the same group. The upcoming anniversary was announced in an ad in the *Eastern Argus* of August 15, 1811, according to Cole, p. 90.
71. Mitchell, pp. 17–18. Other than the newspaper advertisement previously cited, the principal evidence for the existence of this society is the printed copy of Mitchell's address.
72. *Ibid.,* p. 8.
73. *The Salem Collection of Classical Sacred Musick* (Salem, MA: Joshua Cushing, 1805).
74. For a discussion of the reform movement, particularly its Massachusetts roots, see Crawford, "'Ancient Music,'" pp. 225–255. For a discussion of its expansion into Maine, see Chapter III above.
75. Dana, p. 23n.
76. Edwards, p. 23.
77. Oliver Bray, *An Oration on Music* (Portland: Arthur Shirley, 1812), pp. 17–18. Bray, who was an honorary member of the Hans Gram Musical Society, performed on the bass viol at the First Parish Church in Portland and was the caretaker of various other instruments. Cole, p. 18.
78. As examples of this jargon, he cites "Montgomery, Deanfield, and many other tunes in the *Village Harmony*." Bray, p. 18. As an eclectic tunebook, *Village Harmony* still contained American tunes and fuging-tunes in 1812, although the number had decreased from previous editions.
79. *Ibid.,* p. 18.
80. *Ibid.*
81. The last three pages of the oration (pp. 21–24) are devoted to a biographical note on Hans Gram (1754–1804), a Copenhagen-born musician who moved to Massachusetts, c. 1785, and married a Windham, Maine, woman. Organist of the Brattle Street Church in Boston, Gram was also a composer of sacred and secular music. He arranged the settings for the third edition of *The Worcester Collection* (1791) and is assumed to have written the detailed theoret-

ical introduction for *The Massachusetts Compiler of Theoretical Principles* (1795), "considered a milestone in the European reform movement in American music." Maribel Meisel, "Gram, Hans," in *The New Grove Dictionary of American Music,* 4 vols., ed. H. Wiley Hitchcock and Stanley Sadie (London: Macmillan Press, 1986), II, p. 275; Kroeger, "Worcester Collection," p. 177.

82. *Hallowell Collection,* p. [iii]; *The Hallowell Collection of Sacred Music,* second edition (Hallowell, ME: printed and published by E. Goodale, 1819), p. [3]. For a discussion of the Handel Society's role, if any, in the compilation of the collection, see Chapter IX.
83. *Portland Gazette,* February 7, 1814, as cited in Edwards, p. 38. What little is known about the Handel Society of Maine comes from newspaper notices which have been summarized by Edwards (pp. 38–41) and Cole (pp. 90–92).
84. The "Handellian Musical Society" of Amherst, New Hampshire, was incorporated in 1805; a Handel Society was established at Dartmouth College in 1807. Louis Pichierri, *Music in New Hampshire* (New York: Columbia University Press, 1960), pp. 167, 169, 214.
85. Cole, pp. 91–92.
86. Although the text of the endorsement in the second edition is the same as in the first, the later edition's list of Handel Society officers includes "John Abbot, V. President." *Hallowell Collection*/2, p. [3].
87. Edwards's statement (p. 38) that the Handel Society must have intended to have each county in the state represented by a vice president is rather puzzling. The four counties represented by the vice presidents—York, Cumberland, Lincoln, and Kennebec—were only half of the counties existing in Maine by 1814, when the Handel Society was formed. The other Maine counties at the time were Hancock and Washington (both established in 1789), Oxford (established in 1805), and Somerset (established in 1809). There were no vice presidents elected from these counties.
88. Cole, p. 92.
89. Edwards, p. 41.
90. Ira Berry, *Sketch of the History of the Beethoven Musical Society, of Portland, Maine, 1819–1825* (Portland: Stephen Berry, Printer, 1888).
91. Edwards, pp. 42–58.
92. Cole, pp. 92–97.
93. Sears, pp. 142–147.
94. Nitz, pp. 220, 226.
95. Berry, pp. 5, 8. *The Old Colony Collection* was sponsored by the Old Colony Musical Society (of Plymouth County, Massachu-

setts), not the Boston Handel and Haydn Society, as Berry implies. The *Handel and Haydn Society Collection of Sacred Music,* vol. I (1821), should not be confused with Lowell Mason's slightly later collection with a similar title: *The Boston Handel and Haydn Society Collection of Church Music* (1822). The former was a large edition containing European vocal concert music; the latter, an oblong tunebook comprised of psalm-tunes and a few anthems. See Nitz, pp. 232–233.

96. Cole, p. 95.
97. Edwards, p. 51. According to Cole (p. 95), *The Intercession* by English composer Mathew Peter King was probably the first work of its type to be heard in its entirety in Portland (on November 9, 1821).
98. Sears, p. 145.
99. Edwards, p. 59.
100. *Hallowell Gazette,* IX/38 (September 18, 1822), p. 3; IX/39 (September 25, 1822), p. 3; IX/41 (October 9, 1822), p. 3.
101. The first, second, third, sixth, and ninth selections in Part I and the final piece in Part II are from *Messiah;* the recitative and air in Part II are from *The Creation.*
102. The pieces by Chappel, Mason, Pucitta, and Avison are printed in the first volume of the *Old Colony Collection of Anthems,* second edition (Boston: James Loring, [1818]); those by Bray and Whittaker, plus "Hark! the Vesper Hymn" and two of the Handel choruses sung in Part II are in the second volume.
103. "Communication. To the Musical Amateurs of Hallowell, Augusta, and Gardiner," *Hallowell Gazette,* IX/52 (December 25, 1822), p. 3 (reprinted from the Boston *Euterpeiad*).
104. *Hallowell Gazette,* IX/6 (February 6, 1822), p. 3; IX/30 (July 24, 1822); IX/39 (September 25, 1822), p. 3. Kennebec and Somerset are the names of two counties in central Maine. Kennebec County includes the communities of Augusta, Hallowell, and China; Somerset County includes Skowhegan and Palmyra. Meetings of the society were held in the middle of the day (noon or one p.m.) at Marshall's tavern in Vassalboro, the Baptist Meeting-House in Vassalboro, and Kimball's Hall in Waterville.
105. Changes in the repertory are discussed in more detail in Chapter XII.
106. Edwards, pp. 59, 61, 62.
107. (Hallowell) *American Advocate and General Advertiser,* XV/1 (January 10, 1824), p. 1.
108. "Old Folks" concerts presented favorite tunes from the late eighteenth and early nineteenth centuries; the retrospective collections printed the tunes in their original form, not in the "corrected" ver-

sions which appeared in the 1820s and 1830s. See Chapter XIV for more information on these later trends.

Notes for Chapter V

1. Worshippers who owned copies probably brought them to church with them. Since sacred music was sung on a variety of occasions (not just in church), an individual had good reason to own his or her own tunebook. Smaller evangelical churches, in particular, may not have had the funds to purchase books for all the members; however, the fact that books are advertised at prices "per dozen" and sometimes even "per hundred" suggests that some groups were able to buy them in bulk.
2. Newspapers scanned were as follows: (Augusta) *Herald of Liberty,* vols. I–IV (1810–1815); (Augusta) *Kennebec Journal,* vol. I (1825), scattered issues only; (Buckstown, later Bucksport) *Gazette of Maine/Hancock Advertiser,* vols. I–IV (1805–1809); (China) *The Orb,* vols. II–III (1833–1836); *Eastport Sentinel and Passamaquoddy Advertiser,* vols. I–II (1819–1820); (Gardiner) *Christian Intelligencer and Eastern Chronicle,* vols. IX–X (1829–1830); (Hallowell) *American Advocate and General Advertiser,* vols. XIV–XV (1823–1824); (Hallowell) *The Tocsin,* 1796–1797; *Hallowell Gazette,* vols. I–XIV (1814–1827); *Portland Gazette,* vols. V–VIII, XXV–new series, vol. II (1802–1806, 1822–1824); (Portland) *Eastern Argus,* XXIV–XXV (1829–1830). Not every issue of every year was examined, due primarily to missing issues. I was not able to utilize the reportedly excellent collection of newspapers at the Maine Historical Society because they were being microfilmed in 1990 and were not available for use during my research trips.

   For my information on tunebooks advertised in Portland, I have relied heavily on Appendix 2 (pp. 197–199) of Cole's dissertation on the music of Portland. Cole, who indicates (p. vii) that he "examined thoroughly" all Portland newspapers published between 1785 and 1820 and "systematically scanned" the (Portland) *Eastern Argus* from 1803 to 1899, provides the titles and years advertised of all tunebooks appearing in Portland newspaper ads between 1785 and 1820 (and beyond, in some cases).
3. Frederick Gardiner Fassett, Jr., *A History of Newspapers in the District of Maine, 1785–1820* (Orono, ME: University Press, 1932), p. [185].
4. Portland, located approximately a hundred miles northeast of Boston, has one of the largest and best-protected deepwater ports

on the East Coast, providing easy access by sea to Boston as well as other American and foreign ports. In 1820, Portland's population of 8,581 was more than double that of any other Maine town. In 1832, with a population of 13,000, Portland was incorporated as a city. Cole, pp. 1, 7; Gerald E. Morris, ed., *Maine Bicentennial Atlas: An Historical Survey* (Portland: Maine Historical Society, 1976), p. 12.

5. Nearly sixty miles northeast of Portland, Hallowell served as the business center for a wide area. Its location on the Kennebec River made it "practically a seaport town," with many commercial and maritime interests, including shipbuilding. In 1820–1821, Hallowell boasted 2,919 residents, 71 stores (including 3 bookstores), and 2 printing establishments which published the town's two weekly newspapers in addition to many books. Nason, pp. 67–69; *Maine Bicentennial Atlas,* p. 12.
6. Such an inference must be tempered somewhat in cases where the bookseller was also the publisher. Such was the case with Ezekiel Goodale of Hallowell, who published many of the Maine tunebooks and also sold them in his Hallowell bookstore.
7. Title pages of the fifth through tenth editions, published between 1800 and 1810, indicate that each of the editions was sold in one or more of the Portland bookstores. Similarly, the title pages indicate that they were sold in Hallowell at Ezekiel Goodale's bookstore, beginning with the seventh edition (1806). Britton, Lowens, and Crawford, pp. 596–601.
8. Although the first ten and last four editions of *Village Harmony* were published in Exeter, New Hampshire, the eleventh through the thirteenth were printed in Newburyport, and the fourteenth in Boston. Britton, Lowens, and Crawford, pp. 592–602.
9. He was the publisher of Abraham Maxim's *Oriental Harmony* (1802) and *Northern Harmony* (1805), and Charles Robbins's *Columbian Harmony* (1805).
10. Britton, Lowens, and Crawford, p. 7. For a definition of the Core Repertory, see Chapter III, p. 43 and note 108, above.
11. Crawford, "'Ancient Music,'" pp. 244–245.
12. The work was compiled by Bartholomew Brown and others. Beginning with the fourth edition (1816), the work was entitled *Templi Carmina. Songs of the Temple, or, Bridgewater Collection of Sacred Music*. Britton, Lowens, and Crawford, pp. 200, 203.
13. Crawford, "'Ancient Music,'" p. 244.
14. Meanwhile, the 1821 seventeenth edition of *Village Harmony* still contains nineteen American tunes, comprising 6 percent of the whole.
15. By 1820, European tunes were clearly dominating even the tune-

books compiled in Maine. For more information, see Chapter XII on the comparative repertory of Maine tunebooks.

16. *Hallowell Gazette,* VI/46 (November 17, 1819), p. 3; *Portland Gazette,* I/8 (October 28, 1823), p. 3.
17. Cole, pp. 197–199. Although both John Norman and Asahel Benham published tunebooks called *Federal Harmony* in several editions in the early 1790s, the one advertised in Portland in 1792 and 1795 was probably Norman's since it was printed in Boston and his *Massachusetts Harmony* was also advertised in Portland. Tunebooks from Connecticut, where Benham's *Federal Harmony* was published, were less common in Maine than those from Massachusetts.

    The Billings and Holyoke collections were probably Billings's *Continental Harmony* (1794) and Holyoke's *Harmonia Americana* (1791), judging from the advertisement date of 1795. Since many of the new Maine settlers emigrated from Massachusetts, some of them may have attended singing schools taught by Billings or Holyoke.
18. Cole, p. 198.
19. No copies of the first edition are known to be extant.
20. I did not find any ads for *Union Harmony* in the Hallowell or Portland newspapers, and Cole apparently did not find it among the Portland newspapers he surveyed; however, Maine compiler Washburn was apparently familiar with *Union Harmony* because he gives the attribution "Humbert's Collection" to several of the tunes in his *Temple Harmony* (1818). See Chapter XIV for further information on Humbert's *Union Harmony.*
21. Karl Kroeger provided the information on the Maine subscribers from his data base of tunebook subscribers.
22. The subscription paper for a Holyoke publication which was later called *The Occasional Companion* and which was published 1806–1809 had subscription agents in Kennebunk, Portland, Hallowell, Wiscasset, and Bangor. Wiscasset is a coastal town in mid-Maine. Britton, Lowens, and Crawford, p. 329.
23. Cole, pp. 197–199.
24. There are 50 American compositions, 87 non-American, and 1 unidentified. Britton, Lowens, and Crawford, p. 239.
25. Cole, pp. 31–34.
26. Britton, Lowens, and Crawford, p. 237.
27. The date of this work is uncertain; it does not appear to be listed in Britton, Lowens, and Crawford.
28. *Gazette of Maine/Hancock Advertiser* (Buckstown, ME), I/13 (October 17, 1805), p. 3.
29. These works were Abraham Maxim's *Oriental Harmony* (1802),

his *Northern Harmony* (1805), and Charles Robbins's *Columbian Harmony* (1805).

30. *Oriental Harmony* was sold in Portland in December 1802, *Northern Harmony* and *Columbian Harmony* in September and October 1805. *Jenks' Portland Gazette/Maine Advertiser,* V/242 (December 13, 1802), p. 3; *Portland Gazette, and Maine Advertiser,* VIII/20 (September 2, 1805), p. 3; VIII/25 (October 7, 1805), p. 3.
31. The first three tunebooks named were selling for ten dollars per dozen or one dollar, single. Law's was eight dollars per dozen or 75 cents, single. *Portland Gazette, and Maine Advertiser,* VIII/20 (September 2, 1805), p. 3.
32. The store opened in 1802.
33. The title pages of the three Maine tunebooks (Maxim's *Oriental Harmony* and *Northern Harmony* and Robbins's *Columbian Harmony*) do not indicate where they were sold.
34. Goodale is listed as a seller of *Village Harmony* on the title pages of the editions published between 1806 and 1810. Britton, Lowens, and Crawford, pp. 598–601. He is not specifically named on the title pages of later editions, which sometimes print the words "and by all the principal Booksellers in the United States" in place of an exhaustive list. Hallowell-area booksellers named as vendors of these editions, however, include Parker Sheldon of Gardiner (for the fifteenth edition, 1818) and Wm. F. Laine of Hallowell (for the sixteenth and seventeenth editions, 1819, 1821).
35. The other collections were *The Lock Hospital Collection* (an English publication), *The Newburyport Collection,* and the ever-popular *Bridgewater Collection.* The ad is printed on the back of the Ammi Mitchell address on sacred music which was published by Hyde, Lord & Co. *The Salem Collection of Classical Sacred Music,* first published in 1805, was advertised in Portland as early as 1806, according to Cole, p. 199.
36. See Chapter IV for information on the content of Mitchell's sacred music address (whose printed form includes the Hyde, Lord ad on the back cover).
37. *Hallowell Gazette,* I/8 (April 13, 1814), p. 3.
38. Goodale's firm was later known as Goodale, Glazier, and Co. After he left the firm in January 1824, it was called Glazier and Co., then Glazier, Masters and Co., etc. See Chapter IX for more information on Goodale.
39. For example, a Goodale ad which ran for several months in 1816 advertises *Songs of the Temple, or Bridgewater Collection of Sacred Music* and Samuel Worcester's *Christian Psalmody in Four Parts* (containing tunes in Part 4) along with a Goodale publication, the fourth edition of Maxim's *Northern Harmony.* An ad in

1819 advertises the sixteenth edition of *Village Harmony* along with three Maine tunebooks published by Goodale (*The Hallowell Collection, Temple Harmony,* and a fifth edition of *Northern Harmony*). *Hallowell Gazette,* III/52 (December 25, 1816), p. 3; VI/48 (December 1, 1819), p. 3.

40. Among the church's records housed at the Hubbard Free Library in Hallowell is a small slip of paper dated January 7, 1819: a handwritten invoice to "First Parish in Hallowell" from Ezekiel Goodale, apparently requesting payment for a dozen hymnbooks (title unspecified) for five dollars and a dozen copies of *Village Harmony* for ten dollars. According to a notation on the invoice, payment was received February 6, 1819. The invoice is filed in a folder entitled "Old South Congregational Church Parish Accounts, 1820–24 [*sic*]."
41. Ezekiel Goodale, the publisher of *The Hallowell Collection,* attended the Congregational church and seems to have had the assistance of John Merrick, who at one time was a choir leader at the church, in selecting the music. See Chapter IX for more information on the compilation of this collection.
42. A second edition of *The Hallowell Collection,* advertised as "just published" in February 1819, would not yet have been available in January 1819. *Hallowell Gazette,* VI/6 (February 10, 1819), p. 3.
43. *Eastport Sentinel and Passamaquoddy Advertiser,* II/53 (August 28, 1819), p. 4. It is noteworthy that the Hallowell singing books were slightly less expensive than *Village Harmony,* perhaps to help them compete against the better-known collection. The fact that they contained fewer pages probably also contributed to the lower price.
44. *Hallowell Gazette,* IX/40 (October 2, 1822), p. 3; XI/37 (September 15, 1824), p. 3.
45. *Ibid.,* IX/40 (October 2, 1822), p. 3.
46. *Ibid.,* XI/45 (November 10, 1824), p. 3.
47. *Ibid.,* IX/45 (November 10, 1824), p. 3; XII/2 (January 12, 1825), p. 4.
48. *Ibid.,* XIII/14 (April 5, 1826), p. 4.
49. *Portland Gazette,* I/11 (November 11, 1823), p. 3. The *Bridgewater Collection* is the only music book listed in this ad for "School Books."
50. There are no subscribers from the following counties: Oxford, Androscoggin (where Turner was located), Washington (extreme eastern Maine), and York County (the southern tip of Maine).
51. Sixty copies (about one-tenth of the total subscribed copies) were for residents of Boston, with another forty-nine (including six to one of Little's brothers) for those living in northeastern Massa-

chusetts towns. The advance sales in New Hampshire, Vermont, and Connecticut accounted for only about six percent, including a few in Little's hometown of Salem, New Hampshire. No subscribers were listed for Rhode Island.

52. *Hallowell Gazette,* XIV/39 (September 26, 1827), p. 3. *The Christian Intelligencer and Eastern Chronicle* (Gardiner, ME), new series IV/45 (November 5, 1830), p. 3.
53. The *Handel and Haydn Collection* (if referring to *The Boston Handel and Haydn Society Collection of Church Music*) was sponsored by the Boston Handel and Haydn Society and was first published in 1822; other editions followed. The first of many collections compiled by Lowell Mason, it represented a new chapter in American hymnody, in which the emphasis was on a "scientific" musical ideal rooted in such European composers as Handel, Haydn, Mozart, and Beethoven. H. Wiley Hitchcock, "Introduction" to *The Boston Handel and Haydn Society Collection of Church Music* (Boston: Richardson & Lord, 1822; repr. New York: Da Capo Press, 1973). For information on a different collection with a similar name, see Chapter IV, note 95.
54. The *Stoughton Collection of Church Music,* while also sponsored by a musical society (the Stoughton Musical Society), was not limited to tunes in the new, approved "scientific" style, but included older tunes of the type which had either been excluded from recent publications or modified beyond recognition. The 1831 edition includes several tunes by Maine composer Abraham Maxim: HALLOWELL and NEW DURHAM.
55. *Portland Gazette,* XXV/41 (January 21, 1823), p. 1. Also listed in this ad for Isaac Adams's bookstore are the *Handel and Haydn Society Collection* and *Village Harmony.*
56. Cole, pp. 197–199.
57. *Eastern Argus* (Portland, ME), XXV/1399 (December 1, 1829), p. 3.
58. See Chapter IV for more information on this musical society.
59. Berry, p. 8. Some members also had copies of the *Messiah* and *The Creation* oratorios.

Notes for Chapter VI

1. Oscar G. T. Sonneck, *Francis Hopkinson and James Lyon* (Washington, DC: McQueen, 1905; repr. New York: Da Capo Press, 1967). Richard Crawford's extensive Preface to the Da Capo reprint edition of *Urania* is intended as an emendation of Sonneck's essay, which Crawford characterizes as "factually reliable," although written many years earlier. Crawford, Preface to reprint

of James Lyon's *Urania* (Philadelphia: n.p., 1761; repr. New York: Da Capo Press, 1974), p. xvii n. 1.

2. See Map 1 for the location of Machias and other Maine towns referred to in Chapters VI to IX.
3. Sonneck, pp. 124, 132–133; Crawford, Preface, *Urania,* p. iii.
4. Sonneck, p. 133.
5. Richard Crawford, "Lyon, James," in *The New Grove Dictionary of American Music,* 4 vols., ed. H. Wiley Hitchcock and Stanley Sadie (London: Macmillan Press, 1986), III, p. 132. The genres of psalmody, including fuging-tunes and anthems, are defined in Chapter I.
6. Sonneck, p. 185.
7. Crawford, Preface, *Urania,* pp. xix-xx n. 18. Of the six "new" tunes, the four tunes which are probably by Lyon are PSALM 8, PSALM 95, THE LORD DESCENDED, and WATTS'S. The anthem LET THE SHRILL TRUMPET'S is probably not by Lyon; PSALM 23 is definitely not by Lyon, having been composed by Francis Hopkinson.
8. The diary entry includes these words: "He [Lyon] is about publishing a new Book of Tunes which are to be chiefly of his own Composition." Cited in Sonneck, p. 186.
9. Sonneck, pp. 187–192. Sonneck cites the printing of PSALM 19TH in Andrew Law's *Rudiments of Music,* fourth edition (1792), rather than the earlier publication in Bayley's *New Royal Harmony.*
10. The Maine tunebooks which contain the largest number of tunes in common with *Urania* are those dating from 1815 or later: *Chorister's Companion* (1815), *The Hallowell Collection* (1817, 1819), *Wesleyan Harmony* (1820), and *Temple Harmony* (1818–1826). These tunebooks contain more of the older European tunes than the earlier Maine tunebooks, so it is not surprising that they contain some of the same tunes as *Urania,* whose tunes are all European, except for six. The settings of some of these tunes in the Maine books are quite similar to those in *Urania;* in other cases, there are differences, such as number of voice parts, key, and harmonization.
11. George W. Drisko, *Narrative of the Town of Machias* (Machias, ME: Press of the Republican, 1904), p. 196.
12. *Ibid.*
13. Francis Gould Butler, *History of Farmington, Franklin County, Maine: 1776–1885* (Farmington, ME: Knowlton, McLeary, & Co., 1885; repr. Somersworth, NH: New England History Press, 1983), p. 378.
14. This organization should not be confused with the "Old Stoughton Musical Society," which was formed in 1786 (after Belcher had left for Maine). Metcalf, *American Writers,* p. 83.
15. Butler, pp. 378–379.

16. *Ibid.,* pp. 331, 335, 378–380.
17. *The Tocsin* (Hallowell, ME), May 10, 1796, p. 3. An original edition of this issue is owned by the Hubbard Free Library, Hallowell, ME.
18. As discussed in Chapter I, Belcher's life and music have been the topic of a master's thesis by Reynolds and a doctoral dissertation by Owen (see Chapter I, note 7, for complete citations). Three Belcher tunes contained in Charles Robbins's *Columbian Harmony* (ADVENT, HYMN HUNDRED and SEVENTIETH, and HYMN THIRTY-FIFTH) were apparently unknown to Reynolds and Owen.

    Concerning Belcher's life, my research turned up only some rather insignificant new tidbits of information, not directly related to his musical activities. Several entries in "The Diary of Mrs. Martha Moore Ballard," a Hallowell midwife, refer to Belcher and his wife. See the entries for May 30 and June 1, 1787, and for February 23, 1790. Several ads in the *Hallowell Gazette* name Supply Belcher of Farmington as the administrator of the estate of a deceased or as one of the commissioners appointed to examine claims against an estate. See, for example, vol. III/31 (July 31, 1816), p. 3; IV/34 (August 20, 1817), p. 3; and VI/29 (July 21, 1819), p. 4.
19. Supply Belcher's name is not among the list of students who attended William Billings's singing school in Stoughton in January 1774. However, Owen (p. 9) believes "in all probability" that Belcher was a student of Billings; Reynolds (p. 8) concludes that "it is more than likely that Supply knew Billings and his music, and had the opportunity to attend" his classes. Stylistically, Belcher's music is closer to Billings's than to most other psalmodists, such as Oliver Holden or Daniel Read.
20. Crawford, " 'Ancient Music,' " pp. 242–245.
21. Belcher, p. [3].
22. Anthems were not performed in church during regular services but were limited to special occasions, such as Thanksgiving, Fast Day, etc. See Chapter III for more information.
23. Of the six tunes Belcher lists as "Anthems, &c." in the index (ANTHEM OF PRAISE, ANTHEM FOR EASTER, FUNERAL ANTHEM, THE POWER OF MUSICK, TRANSMIGRATION, and OMEGA), I have classified the first three as anthems and the next two as set-pieces. I consider OMEGA to be a tune with extension. In addition, three other tunes, which are included in the general index of psalm- and hymn-tunes, appear to be set-pieces: INVITATION, SPRING, and THE REQUEST.
24. The first music book published by Ranlet was the first edition of *Village Harmony* in 1795. Nancy Merrill, "Henry Ranlet: Exeter Printer, 1762–1807," *Historical New Hampshire,* XXXVII/4 (Winter 1982), p. 256. Exeter was closer and perhaps more conve-

nient than Boston for the later Maine psalmodists, who patronized the Exeter firms of Ranlet, then Norris & Co., and finally Norris & Sawyer. Once printer Ezekiel Goodale in Hallowell, Maine, acquired music type (c. 1814), most of the Maine tunebooks were published by his firm or its successors.

25. The first and second editions were published by Isaiah Thomas (partner in the later firm of Thomas and Andrews); all subsequent editions were printed by Thomas and Andrews. Kroeger, "Worcester Collection," p. 63.
26. *Ibid.*, p. 465.
27. See Chapter XI for a discussion of the theoretical introductions contained in the Maine tunebooks, 1800–1830. Charles Robbins, who may have been a Belcher student, is the only one of the Maine psalmodists who, like Belcher, discusses the various intervals in terms of concords and discords and provides pendulum lengths for the various moods of time.
28. Oscar G. T. Sonneck, *A Bibliography of Early Secular American Music (Eighteenth Century)*, revised and enlarged by William Trent Upton (1945; repr. New York: Da Capo Press, 1964), p. 180. I tend to agree, however, with Britton (p. 505), who considers seven of those songs (all except THE POWER OF MUSIC) to be hymns, although not songs of praise.
29. Henry Little, *The Wesleyan Harmony* (Hallowell, ME: E. Goodale, 1820), p. [3].
30. Hartwell, p. [3].
31. Charles Evans, *American Bibliography, 1638–1820* (Chicago: Columbia Press, 1903–1955), entry no. 31791, p. 140.
32. Kroeger, "Worcester Collection," pp. 612, 621, 627. Interestingly, one of Belcher's tunes, APPEARANCE, was printed in the second edition of *The Worcester Collection* (1788) in advance of publication in *The Harmony of Maine* (1794).
33. See Chapter IX for more information about the possible relationship between the two.
34. In the first edition of *The Hallowell Collection* (1817), Belcher's CANTON is one of only four American tunes, two of which are unattributed. In the second edition (1819), three of the eight American pieces are by Belcher; no other American composer is represented by more than one.
35. *Hallowell Collection,* p. [iii].
36. "Particular Meter" refers to texts with patterns other than the more usual four-line stanzas of Common Meter (8.6.8.6.), Long Meter (8.8.8.8.), and Short Meter (6.6.8.6.).
37. These retrospective collections, as well as other trends in Maine sacred music of the 1830s and 1840s, are discussed in Chapter XIV.

38. None of these tunes had appeared in *The Harmony of Maine,* either, although three of the four were among those in Robbins's *Columbian Harmony*. The remaining tune, ARCHDALE, may be misattributed to Belcher since it is usually attributed to Andrew Law.
39. The tunes are ARCHDALE (again, probably misattributed) and HYMN HUNDRED AND SIXTEENTH. Old Stoughton Musical Society, *The Stoughton Musical Society's Centennial Collection of Sacred Music* (Boston: O. Ditson, 1878; repr. New York: Da Capo Press, 1980), pp. 45, 164.

Notes for Chapter VII

1. According to Edwards (p. 30), a record found in an old pocketbook once belonging to Maxim states that he was born on that date in Plympton, County of Plymouth. Since his birth is recorded in Carver, rather than Plympton, he must have been born in the part of Plympton which was established as "Carver" in 1790. *Vital Records of Carver, Massachusetts, to the Year 1850* (Boston: New England Historic Genealogical Society, 1911), pp. [3], 47.
2. The census of 1776 lists Plympton's population as 1,707. *Vital Records of Plympton, Massachusetts, to the Year 1850* (Boston: New England Historic Genealogical Society, 1923), p. 3.
3. Records and histories of the Plympton-Carver area include various surnames which appear to be variant spellings of Maxim, such as "Maxam," "Muxam," "Muxom," and "Muxsom," as well as "Muxham."
4. Wareham was a coastal town bounding Carver (and the original Plympton) on the south and west. John Muxham was born on February 7, 1745, Martha (Norris) Muxham on December 3, 1750. *Vital Records of Carver,* pp. 47, 48.
5. *Vital Records of Plympton,* p. 353. *Records of the First Church of Wareham, Mass., 1739–1891,* transcribed and indexed by Leonard H. Smith, Jr. (Clearwater, FL: n.p., 1974), pp. 10, 74. The latter reference lists the marriage of a "John Muxom Jnr." to Martha Norris. He was probably designated "Jnr." to differentiate him from the John Muxom of Wareham whose wife's name was Silence.
6. The children of John and Martha Muxhum included Silvanus (b. 1769), Abraham (b. 1773), Andrew (b. 1778), William (b. 1781), Martha (b. 1784), Mary (b. 1786), Sophronia (b. 1792), and John (b. 1795). *Vital Records of Carver,* pp. 47–48.
7. They were buried in the Union Cemetery in South Carver. According to gravestone records, Martha (Norris) Maxim died on March 13, 1813, John Maxim in 1827. *Vital Records of Carver,* p. 161.
8. Cheney, p. 184. Cheney (1818–1890) was a Vermont farmer,

singing-school teacher, and choir leader. For the biographical notices included in his tunebook, he frequently sought information from relatives or acquaintances of the musicians; nevertheless, the data must be used with care since some of the anecdotes are "of doubtful veracity." Karl Kroeger, Introduction to the Da Capo edition, pp. viii-xi. In the case of Maxim, Cheney's sources seem fairly reliable: a letter from John Maxim (Abraham's youngest brother) and one written by Abraham Maxim himself in 1815. The letters do not appear to be extant.

9. According to Cheney (p. 184), "Turner, Buckfield and other good tunes he composed in Carver." If so, the tunes were probably named or renamed later for publication in Maxim's *Oriental Harmony*: Turner was the name of the town Maxim moved to in Maine; Buckfield was a town near Turner.
10. *Ibid.* Because Cheney shows this as a quote, it must have been an excerpt from John Maxim's letter about his brother. John was born in 1795, when Abraham would have been twenty-two years old. Since he could not have had any direct knowledge of Abraham's youth, he must have been repeating what he had been told.
11. "Here and There," *Boston Transcript,* no. 19,422 (February 8, 1894), p. 6. Flora Barry was a Boston contralto of the late nineteenth century.
12. McKay and Crawford, pp. 24–25.
13. As far as we know, his published compositions consist only of choral sacred music.
14. Although no specific information suggests that his family was poor, several studies have concluded that the Maine frontier tended to attract the poor rather than the prosperous. Young people from more financially able families tended to move to such frontier areas as Vermont or western New York. Since Maine could be reached inexpensively by sea, those without the resources for a long inland trip often headed for Maine. See Taylor, p. 63.
15. These genres are defined in Chapter I. See Chapter XIII for a tally of his tunes by genre and for musical transcriptions and discussion of three representative tunes: FALMOUTH, KNOXVILLE, and TURNER. See Part III for an index of his tunes.
16. The anthems, ANTHEM FOR THANKSGIVING and ANTHEM OF PRAISE, appear in *Oriental Harmony* and the first two editions of *Northern Harmony*. The set-pieces are THE GOLDEN AIR (unattributed in the first two editions of *Northern Harmony*) and CONTRAST (indicated simply as "Original" in the second edition of *Northern Harmony*).
17. Tans'ur's rules for composition were printed in several British tunebooks of the period, such as Tans'ur's *Royal Melody Compleat*

(1755), and guided many country psalmodists as they composed successive vocal lines which, while consonant with one another, were conceived horizontally rather than vertically. More information about these principles may be found in Chapter XIII.

18. Cheney (p. 184) indicates that Maxim was able to entertain others "at music parties" by doing several things simultaneously: "singing, playing the bass viol, doing a sum in the rule of three, and telling what the company was talking about."
19. Even in nearby Wareham, the bass viol was not always considered acceptable for public worship. Although it was approved for worship in Wareham in 1794, a town meeting order in 1796 banned it from the meetinghouse. Daisy Washburn Lovell, *Glimpses of Early Wareham* (Wareham, MA: Wareham Historical Society, 1970), p. 55.
20. Cheney (p. 184) indicates that he moved to Turner "after he became of age"; Metcalf (p. 161) states that the move took place "before 1800." Since Maxim was not even eighteen until 1791, the move must have taken place sometime in the 1790s.

    He may have resided in Buckfield, a town adjacent to Turner, before settling in Turner. An Abraham "Moxam" of Buckfield purchased half of a hundred-acre lot in Buckfield from Thomas Lincoln for $158 in May 1799; Abraham "Maxim" sold the same lot back to Lincoln less than a year later for $28 less than he paid for it. Cumberland County Register of Deeds, vol. 31, pp. 165–166; vol. 32, p. 261. The deeds refer to land only and do not mention a dwelling. After buying the land, Maxim may have decided to settle in Turner and to sell the Buckfield property; however, extant deeds provide no information about any Turner purchases he may have made. See Oxford County Register of Deeds, vol. 25, pp. 203–204, though, for the sale of some land in Turner by a group of men (including Abraham Maxim) to Jabez Merrill (Maxim's father-in-law) in 1806.
21. His older brother Silvanus (born in 1769) may also have emigrated to Maine. The *Maine Direct Tax Census of 1798,* vol. II, p. 284, lists a "Sylvanus" Maxim of Hebron (a town adjacent to Turner) as owning 46 acres, valued at $184, but no dwelling, suggesting he was a recent settler. His name does not appear in the Maine census listings for 1800–1850, however. A Sylvanus Maxham was counted as a head of household in Plymouth County, Massachusetts, in 1800. They may be two completely different men, or Maxim may have found Maine not to his liking and returned to Massachusetts.
22. Coffin, p. 304.
23. Timothy Howe, *History of the Town of Turner from the First Grant*

in 1765 to the Close of 1843 (manuscript written in 1843; typescript by Samuel D. Rumery in 1927; housed at the Maine Historical Society), pp. 47, 71.

24. Based on the age-group delineations, Abraham appears to be a member of the John Muxham household of Carver, Massachusetts, in 1790, but the family is not listed in the 1800 Massachusetts census. No Maxims or Muxhams are listed as heads of families in Maine, either, in 1790 and 1800. The two "Maxhams" (Ephraim and Nathan) who appear in the 1800 Maine census as heads of families in Kennebec County (not the county in which Turner was located) do not seem to be related to Abraham Maxim. As a single male (twenty-seven years old) in 1800, Abraham Maxim would probably have been living with and counted with some other family, possibly even his future in-laws. He appears as a head of family for the first time in the 1810 Maine census. By then, he had been married for nine years and had four children. *Heads of Families at the First Census of the United States Taken in the Year 1790, Massachusetts* (Washington, DC: Government Printing Office, 1908), p. 168; *Heads of Families at the First Census of the United States Taken in the Year 1790, Maine* (Washington, DC: Government Printing Office, 1908); Ronald Vern Jackson, ed., *Massachusetts 1800 Census Index* (Bountiful, UT: Accelerated Indexing Systems, 1981); Ronald Vern Jackson, Gary Ronald Teeples, and David Schaefermeyer, eds., *Maine 1800 Census Index* (Bountiful, UT: Accelerated Indexing Systems, 1977); *Population Schedules of the Third Census of the United States, 1810: Maine* (microcopy no. 252, roll 12), p. 409.
25. *Vital Records of Turner, Maine, 1787–1839* (microfilm reel 478, Maine State Archives), book 1, no. 1, p. 293. The marriage date matches the one cited by Edwards (p. 30) from the old pocketbook once belonging to Maxim: "May 1st 1781, Anna Merrill was born. 1801, Sept. 11. They [Anna and Abraham] joined their hands in wedlock's bands." Anna's birth is listed in the Turner *Vital Records* as May 1, 1780, rather than 1781.
26. *Vital Records of Turner,* book 1, no. 1, p. 351. Rev. W. R. French, *A History of Turner, Maine, from Its Settlement to 1886* (Portland: Hoyt, Fogg & Donham, 1887; repr. Bowie, MD: Heritage Books, 1986), p. 57; Howe, p. 176.
27. "Here and There," *Boston Transcript,* no. 19, 422 (February 8, 1894), p. 6.
28. *Ibid.*
29. At least two tunes specifically named by Cheney as having been composed in Carver—TURNER and BUCKFIELD—are included in *Oriental Harmony.* Also printed is HALLOWELL, the tune supposedly inspired by his unhappy love affair.

30. Maxim, *Oriental Harmony,* p. [i].
31. Cheney (p. 184) incorrectly states that *Northern Harmony* was published in 1803, rather than 1805.
32. Sixteen of the fifty-one tunes which appear to be by Maxim had been printed in Maxim's first tunebook, and one (SUMNER) had an earlier printing in Charles Robbins's *Columbian Harmony,* published just a month before *Northern Harmony.* Thirty-six tunes are unattributed but starred in the index as "Original," a term frequently used in tunebooks to designate previously unpublished tunes. All but two (INVOCATION and LILY) appear to be by Maxim, who frequently labelled his own tunes simply as "Original" in their first printing. Since there are no stylistic reasons that these thirty-four unattributed tunes could not be by Maxim and since some are attributed to him in later Maine collections, I am assuming that they are his. See Part III for a list of the Maxim tunes and for more information on his attribution practices.
33. Of the twenty-two additional tunes which appear to be by Maxim in the second edition of *Northern Harmony,* one (POLAND) is specifically attributed to Maxim, while the other twenty-one are unattributed but marked as "Original." See Part III for a list of the Maxim tunes in this edition.
34. Abraham Maxim, *The Northern Harmony,* second edition (Exeter, NH: Norris & Sawyer, 1808), p. [2].
35. See Chapter III for more information about the reform movement.
36. Their names and birthdates are as follows: [Sop]horona Norris Maxim, born March 19, 1806; Clementina Noris [*sic*] Maxim, born December 18, 1807; Charles Merrill Maxim, born July 20, 1809; Laurens Sawyer Maxim, born August 25, 1809; Sullivan Adams Maxim, born September 15, 1811; William Harrison Maxim, born December 17, 1813 (died February 23, 1814); Moses Franklin Maxim, born April 1, 1815; John Batten Maxim, born May 31, 1818 (died October 10, 1818); Nancy Ann Maxim, born September 9, 1819; Clarissa Snow Maxim, born July 21, 1822. *Vital Records of Turner,* book 1, no. 1, pp. 339, 344, 352, 361, 366; vol. II, book 1, pp. 8, 13, 23.

    Timothy Howe (pp. 109, 117) provides the cause of death of the two Maxim sons who died in infancy: William due to fits, John from the measles.

    There seems to be an error in the year of birth of either Charles or Laurens; they are recorded as having been born a month apart. The error probably occurred in copying, since the Turner birth records are listed alphabetically by first name, rather than chronologically. The birth date given for Laurens is consistent with his gravestone, which indicates that he died on November 2, 1888, aet

79 yrs. 3 months. Maine Old Cemetery Association, *Cemetery Inscription Project* (Augusta: Maine Old Cemetery Association, 1982), part V, series I, p. 1009.

Several of the names have obvious family significance. The first two children have Abraham's mother's maiden name (Norris) as a middle name. The third child has his own mother's maiden name (Merrill) as a middle name. One of the girls (Sophorona, whom one source refers to as "Sophronia") appears to have been named for Abraham's sister Sophronia.

37. Cheney, p. 184.
38. *Ibid.* Turner employed a teacher as early as 1790 and raised funds to build a schoolhouse in 1793. A few of the early teachers are specified by name in Merrill, p. 832, but Maxim is not among them.
39. Coburn, II, p. 541.
40. Mark J. Sammons, "'Without a Word of Explanation': District Schools of Early Nineteenth-Century New England," *Families and Children* (Annual Proceedings, Dublin Seminar for New England Folklife, 1985), p. 78.
41. Cheney, p. 184.
42. Sammons, p. 85.
43. Letter from Zadoc Long to Isaac Ellis, September 7, 1827, in *From the Journal of Zadoc Long, 1800–73,* ed. Peirce Long (Caldwell, ID: Caxton Printers, 1943), pp. 81–82.
44. French, p. 127.
45. His mother was baptized in the First (Congregational) Church of Wareham as an infant, and his parents were married there. Although his family lived in Plympton-Carver, rather than Wareham, there is nothing to suggest a change in their religious affiliation.
46. French, pp. 126–127. The Calvinist Congregationalists, who predominated in New England society, believed in the preordained salvation of only a few, the Elect. Universalists, on the other hand, believed in universal salvation for the whole human race through God's grace as revealed by Jesus Christ. The first Universalist church in the United States was founded in Gloucester, Massachusetts, in 1779 by Rev. John Murray of England, who had been converted to Universalist teaching by James Relly, another former Methodist. See Sydney E. Ahlstrom, *A Religious History of the American People* (New Haven: Yale University Press, 1972), p. 482.
47. Jabez Merrill's support for the Universalist Society is somewhat surprising in light of his father's long-standing commitment to the established church (his position as deacon in the New Gloucester church, etc.).

48. See Chapter II for more information on the decline of Congregationalism and increased interest in evangelistic denominations in Maine at this time.
49. Coffin, pp. 304–305.
50. For reasons which are unclear, the act was later rescinded by the Maine legislature, and the original members of the society and their descendants officially became members of the First Parish; however, their doctrinal positions were not altered. French, pp. 135–136; Howe, p. 196.
51. French, pp. 136–137, 139.
52. Of course, several earlier Universalist hymnbooks had been published in Boston and could probably have been obtained in Hallowell.
53. [Abraham Maxim], *The Gospel Hymn-Book* (n.p., 1818), p. [ii].
54. *Ibid.,* pp. iii–iv.
55. Joseph Williamson, *A Bibliography of the State of Maine from the Earliest Period to 1891,* 2 vols. (Portland: Thurston Print, 1896; repr. Somersworth, NH: Maine State Library and the New England History Press, 1985), II, p. 107.
56. Washburn's aunt Lydia (Washburn) married Samuel Norris (born in Plymouth, Massachusetts) in 1749. After living in Wareham, Massachusetts, the Norrises moved to Wayne, Maine, in 1784–1785. Abraham Maxim's mother was the former Martha Norris of Wareham. Although I have not been able to determine a relationship between Martha and Samuel Norris, it is possible that they were related (perhaps as uncle and niece). If so, Japheth Washburn and Abraham Maxim would be distantly related. Even if there was no blood kinship between them, they and many of their relatives lived close enough to one another to suppose that they had mutual acquaintances and possibly direct contact even before their separate moves to Maine.
57. The incomplete copy of *Northern Harmony,* fourth edition, at the Essex Institute in Salem, Massachusetts, has a title page, preface, the rudiments section, and music through page 56. The copy at the Newberry Library in Chicago lacks a title page and most of the pages prior to page 11 (where the tunes begin), but includes pages 11 through 242, except for pages 131 to 134, which are missing. A complete copy would contain 256 pages (see next note).
58. The second edition contained 205 pages, the third edition apparently about 210. According to Williamson (II, p. 107), the fourth edition had 256 pages. Although a prepublication newspaper ad for that edition announced that it would contain "280 pages, which is about 70 more than either of the former editions," the fourth edition's preface (p. [2]) states that the authors added "about fifty

pages" to the previous edition. *Hallowell Gazette,* III/34 (August 21, 1816), p. 3.

Compared to second edition copies, the most complete copy of the fourth edition features a net gain of sixteen American tunes, ninety European tunes, and twelve of undetermined nationality.

59. Seventeen of the twenty-two added Washburn tunes are marked "Original," implying that their first printing was in the fourth edition, while eighteen of the twenty-six additional Maxim tunes are so marked.
60. Cooke, in "American Psalmodists" (I, pp. 62–63), suggests that financial considerations were often a motive for other co-compilerships. Washburn's role in the production of *Northern Harmony*/4 may have been similar to Abraham Wood's in the publication of *Columbian Harmony,* a compilation by Wood and Joseph Stone in 1793. Wood was a successful tradesman who was able to contribute capital toward the book's printing and enhance sales in his area.
61. By 1816, he had served two terms as the representative from Fairfax: 1812–13 and 1813–14.
62. Of course, even without Washburn's help, *Northern Harmony*/2 was sold, according to its title page, in Exeter, Portsmouth, Portland, and Boston bookstores.
63. Without a complete copy of the fifth edition, we cannot determine what the corrections or additions were. The Library of Congress copy, the only one known to be extant, ends on page 142. A complete copy would have 280 pages. See Chapter XII, note 50.
64. Judging from the most complete extant copy of *Northern Harmony,* fourth edition, he eliminated at least forty-nine American tunes, eleven European ones, and ten of unknown nationality for the first edition of his *Temple Harmony.* Not surprisingly, he replaced some of the tunes with his own; Washburn is represented by thirty-seven tunes, thirteen more than in the extant joint edition with Maxim. The fact that twenty-six Maxim tunes were among those cut does not necessarily mean Washburn had a low opinion of Maxim's works. In spite of the eliminations, *Temple Harmony* still contained forty-eight Maxim tunes, more than by any other composer.
65. See Chapter XII, note 51, for more information on the similarities between the first two editions of Washburn's *Temple Harmony* (1818 and 1820) and the fifth edition of Maxim's *Northern Harmony* (1819).
66. Buckfield is the town adjacent to Turner on the west; Woodstock is approximately thirteen miles northwest of Turner. The tune was first printed in *Northern Harmony,* fourth edition (1816). The wed-

ding date was April 19, 1818, according to *Town of Buckfield Vital Records, Marriages and Intentions, 1804–58* (reel 90, Maine State Archives).

67. William Berry Lapham, *History of Woodstock, Maine* (Portland: Stephen Berry, Printer, 1882; repr. Somersworth, NH: New England History Press, 1983), p. 132.
68. Cheney, p. 184.
69. Turner's population more than doubled just in the twenty years between 1800 and 1820, as these census figures from Howe (pp. 47, 71, 98, and 120) show:
    1790: 356
    1800: 704
    1810: 1,128
    1820: 1,726
70. *Palmyra 175th Anniversary, 1807–1982* ([Palmyra, ME: Town of Palmyra], 1982), p. 38.
71. Lawrence (Laurens?), Sullivan, and Moses are named in *The East Somerset County Register of 1911–1912* (Auburn, ME: compiled and published by Chatto & Turner, [1912]), p. 156, as among those who made their home in Palmyra. This publication contains a directory of residents of the eleven towns (including Palmyra) which are located in the eastern half of Somerset County, as well as a brief historical account of each town.

    Abraham's eldest son, Charles Merrill Maxim, age eighteen in 1827, is not mentioned in this account of Palmyra settlers. He appears, however, to have made the move to Palmyra, based on census records which indicate that separate households were headed by Sullivan A. Maxim, Charles M. Maxim, Lawrence S. Maxim, and Anna Maxim in Palmyra in 1840. Abraham Maxim had died in 1829.
72. The name of Maxim's daughter is spelled several ways in the various town records and histories: [Sop]horona, Sophrona, Sophronia, and Sophronie. She and Snow Keene had five children, born 1824–1840: Norris, Moses, Saraphina, Marva, and Rose, according to *The East Somerset County Register, 1911–12,* p. 102, and *Vital Records of Palmyra, Maine, 1800–1867* (microfilm reel 335, Maine State Archives), p. 60. *The East Somerset County Register* appears to be in error about her birth year: Turner town records list her birth as 1806, rather than 1802.
73. Occasionally, a resident is designated as "farmer and ______," some other occupation, such as teacher, school agent, machinist, or carpenter. *Atlas of Somerset County, Maine* (Houlton, ME: George N. Colby & Co., 1883), p. 74.
74. The writer refers to Maxim as Lawrence Maxim's father, rather than as Abraham Maxim per se. *The East Somerset County Register, 1911–12,* p. 156.

75. The "Ell" refers to the southwestern corner of Palmyra, which was "L-shaped," due to the annexation of a rectangular piece of Palmyra by the adjacent town of Pittsfield.
76. *Palmyra 175th Anniversary,* p. 19.
77. In September 1839, Sullivan "was set apart to the work of an evangelist, and the next year received the pastoral charge of the church" (apparently the Baptist church in Palmyra). He was pastor for only a short time, leaving to "labor in other fields," but returned as pastor in 1843. Rev. Joshua Millet, *A History of the Baptists in Maine* . . . (Portland: Charles Day & Co., 1845), p. 390.

    "Rev. S. A. Maxim" died on June 4, 1849 (when he was only thirty-seven), according to his gravestone. Maine Old Cemetery Association, *Cemetery Inscription Project,* part V, series I, p. 1010.
78. Cheney, p. 184.
79. I am indebted to Nym Cooke for this information.
80. Maxim's death date is contained in the paragraphs written by Latham inside the copy of *Northern Harmony.* I have been unable to confirm this date in any other sources. The Palmyra vital records appear to have been lost or destroyed for the period in question. No mention of Maxim was found in the obituary notices of several Maine newspapers (the Hallowell *American Advocate,* the Portland *Eastern Argus,* the Augusta *Kennebec Journal,* and the Gardiner *Christian Intelligencer and Eastern Chronicle*) for 1829 and early 1830.

    I also was not able to determine where he was buried, either in the Maine State Library's surname index (on microfilm) or in the bound volumes listing cemeteries by geographical location. The surname index includes a large number of Maxims, including his wife and some of his children, but not Abraham Maxim. A check for Maxim's name in each of the Palmyra and Turner cemeteries listed in the bound volumes was also unsuccessful. A "Mrs. Ann Maxim" (apparently Anna, his wife) and two of his sons (Laurens S. and Sullivan A.) are buried in Palmyra's Pooler Cemetery, but he apparently is not.

    Latham's inscription in the Massachusetts Historical Society's copy of *Northern Harmony* states that Abraham's wife "died in Maine April 28, 1876, ae 96 lacking 2 dys [days]." There is little reason to doubt Latham, particularly since his inscription was dated November 20, 1877, just nineteen months after she allegedly died. In addition, the information has internal consistency: since Anna was born on May 1, 1780, the age he gives for her on the stated death date would be only one day off. The Palmyra gravestone of Mrs. "Ann" Maxim lists her death date as April 29, 1876, and her age at death as 96 years. Maine Old Cemetery Association, *Cemetery Inscription Project,* part V, series I, pp. 1009–1010.

81. Maxim's last tunebook contains a smaller percentage of American tunes and fuging-tunes than his early ones. A still later book, if prepared, may have continued further in that direction, especially since the reform movement does not appear to have affected central Maine until the 1820s, judging from the musical societies formed in that decade. See Chapters III and IV for more information.
82. *The East Somerset County Register, 1911–12,* p. 156.
83. Lapham, p. 132.
84. "Here and There," *Boston Transcript,* p. 6.
85. *Ibid.*
86. See Chapter XIV for more information about the continued reprinting of Maxim tunes after his death.
87. Edwards, p. 30.
88. There are several as yet unidentified hymn-tune composers who are represented by tunes in *Northern Harmony:* Bonney, for example. Like Washburn, some of them may have been Maxim's students. See Cooke, "American Psalmodists," I, pp. 91–92 n. 64, and pp. 118–119, for information on Maxim's "network" (probable Maine residents who received first printings in his books). See Chapter IX for possible relationships between Maxim and Maine psalmodists Charles Robbins and Edward Hartwell.

Notes for Chapter VIII

1. Japheth Washburn's middle name, if any, is not known. Perhaps to avoid confusion with his father, the son, Japheth Coombs Washburn, almost always used his middle name or initial.
2. Breton P. Washburne, *The Washburn Family in America* (n.p.: n.p., 1983), n.p. (see descendants A2C9, A-J). Japheth's mother's name is given as Phebe in Henry D. Kingsbury and Simeon L. Deyo, eds., *Illustrated History of Kennebec County, Maine* (New York: H. W. Blake & Co., 1892), p. 1170.
3. Grow, II, p. 114.
4. *Ibid.;* 1984 corrections, n.p. The marriage intentions (but not the marriage) of "Japheth Washbon of Plimtown" and "Prescilla Combs" appear in the vital records of Priscilla's hometown, Rochester, on September 24, 1768. *Vital Records of Rochester, Massachusetts, to the Year 1860,* 2 vols. (Boston: New England Historic Genealogical Society, 1914), II, p. 311.
5. Rochester had a population of 2,449 at the time of the 1776 Provincial Census. *Ibid.,* p. [3].

   The Washburns may also have lived in Middleborough, Massachusetts, at one time. In the *Vital Records of China: Deaths* (reel

117, Maine State Archives), n.p., Japheth C.'s father (Japheth) is referred to as "Japheth Washburn, formerly of Middleborough, MS." Middleborough is adjacent to the other towns associated with Washburn: it is west of Plympton and Carver and north of Rochester. His name does not appear in a Middleborough town history, suggesting that his residence there may have been brief.

6. As quoted in William Root Bliss, *Colonial Times on Buzzard's Bay* (Boston: Houghton, Mifflin & Company, 1888), p. 76.
7. Grow, II, p. 114. The source of this information is not stated.
   Japheth Washburn is probably the man referred to as "Japhath" and "Japhet" Washburn in *Massachusetts Soldiers and Sailors of the Revolutionary War,* 17 vols. (Boston: Wright & Potter Printing Co., 1896–1908), XVI, p. 666. He was a private, serving in the companies of Capts. Jabez Cottle, Barnabas Doty, and Jonah Washburn, May 6–7, 1778, September 5–11, 1778, and August 1–9, 1780, respectively.
8. Grow, II, p. 114.
9. *Ibid.* The *Wayne Vital Records, 1773–1900* (reel 524, Maine State Archives) lists the birth dates of Japheth and Priscilla Washburn's children, although they were not born in Wayne. This listing gives the birth date of "Cloe" as June 20, 1777, rather than June 28, 1777.
10. Grow, II, pp. 114–115. The information was provided to the editor by Margaret Clifford, his great-great-granddaughter. Although the published vital records of Rochester, Massachusetts, do not list him among births in the town, the manuscript town records of China, Maine, where he served as town clerk, state the above as his date and place of birth. The records appear to have been written by him personally. *Vital Records of China: Births* (reel 117, Maine State Archives), n.p.
11. Bliss, p. 141. Rochester's population decreased by nearly a hundred between 1790 and 1800: 2,644 to 2,546. *Vital Records of Rochester,* I, p. [3].
12. Wayne's population rose from 500 in 1800, to 819 in 1810, and 1,051 in 1820. George W. Walton, *History of the Town of Wayne, Kennebec County, Maine, from Its Settlement to 1898* (Augusta: Maine Farmer Publishing Company, 1898), pp. 218, 220.
13. Washburne, n.p. Lydia Washburn Norris is descendant A2C9B, born in 1728 and married in 1749. See also Walton, pp. 18–19.
14. The house was valued at $60; the total value assigned to land and house was $240. "Zal. Washburn" (probably Japheth's eldest brother, Zalmuna, age twenty-six in 1798) owned thirty acres (no dwelling) valued at $120. *Maine Direct Tax Census of 1798,* reel 1, vol. 2, p. 16.
15. Ronald Vern Jackson, Gary Ronald Teeples, and David Schaefermeyer, eds., *Maine 1800 Census Index* (Bountiful, UT: Acceler-

ated Indexing Systems, 1976), p. 99. Family members are not listed by name but are enumerated by age groupings. The two older sons, Zalmuna and Abisha, ages twenty-eight and twenty-five in 1800, seem not to be included in the "Japhet" Washburn household; Zalmuna (and possibly Abisha, too) had a family of his own. The youngest Washburn child, Priscilla, supposedly age fourteen, seems to be included in the "female, age 16–26" category.

16. Grow, II, p. 114. Abisha is listed as a head of family in Wayne in the 1810 census and was elected as one of Wayne's highway surveyors and tithingmen in 1811. Walton, p. 219. *Records of the Town of Wayne* (reel 524, Maine State Archives), book 2, p. 111.
17. He paid $30 to Jonathan Howe for a quarter and a half-quarter of an acre of land on March 25, 1802, and an additional $20 for what appears to be an adjoining eight square rods of land on July 23, 1802. Kennebec County Register of Deeds, vol. 4, pp. 111, 440. The high expense for such a small tract suggests it may have been a prime location or a developed lot. That Washburn would have purchased such a small plot suggests that he did not intend to farm for a living; farmers frequently purchased fifty- or one-hundred-acre lots.
18. Betsy was born on March 13, 1782, in Epping, New Hampshire. Grow, II, p. 115. The marriage intentions of "Japheth C. Washburn of Wayne and Mrs. Betsy Lowney of Monmouth" were registered in Wayne on April 5, 1802. Monmouth is just south of Wayne. Walton, p. 122.
19. The July 23, 1802, land purchase from Jonathan Howe refers to "said Washburn's house frame." Kennebec County Register of Deeds, vol. 4, p. 440. The fact that a legal meeting of the voting inhabitants of Wayne was held "at the dwelling-house of Japheth C. Washburn" on November 1, 1802, implies that the house must have been largely finished by then. *Records of the Town of Wayne,* book 2, p. 33.
20. *Vital Records of China: Births,* n.p. The first births listed in these records are those of Washburn, his wife, and his first six children; the entries appear to have been written by Japheth himself. Abra's birth is listed, probably incorrectly, as February 13, 1803, in Grow, II, p. 115, and, probably correctly, as February 14, 1803, on p. 11.
21. A trader, in the legal sense, is "one who makes it his business to buy merchandise, or goods and chattels, and to sell the same for the purpose of making a profit." John Bouvier, *Bouvier's Law Dictionary,* 2 vols., revised by Francis Rawle (Boston: Boston Book Co., 1897), II, p. 1131.

    For his land transactions in Wayne, see Kennebec County Register of Deeds, vol. 4, pp. 111, 440; vol. 6, pp. 367, 368, 473; vol. 8, p. 196.

22. Richard P. Horwitz, *Anthropology Toward History: Culture and Work in a Nineteenth-Century Maine Town* (Middletown, CT: Wesleyan University Press, 1978), p. 107.
23. His father is referred to as a yeoman on land deeds from 1804–1815. Kennebec County Register of Deeds, vol. 8, p. 216; vol. 9, p. 138; vol. 18, p. 576; and vol. 22, p. 333. His brothers Zalmuna and Abisha are among those engaged in agriculture in their towns in the *Population Schedules of the Fourth Census of the United States, 1820* (Washington, DC: National Archives, 1959), microcopy no. 33, roll 35 (Kennebec County, ME), vol. 3, pp. 679, 681.
24. See Chapter VII for more information on their possible relationship. Quite a number of Maxims lived in Wayne in the early 1800s, according to the *Wayne Vital Records,* including a Jacob Maxim, born in Wareham, Massachusetts, who was married to the former Sally Washburn of "Plimton." Their relationship, if any, to Abraham Maxim or Japheth Washburn is uncertain.

    Although Maxim is said by Metcalf to have arrived in Maine "before 1800," his Maine land deeds are dated 1799 and 1800, suggesting that he probably did not begin teaching singing school until at least 1800, following his settlement in Maine.

    Since Farmington, where Supply Belcher lived, was some twenty-two miles from Wayne (a day's ride on horseback), it seems unlikely that Washburn attended Belcher's singing school. If he had, he probably would have included more than just one Belcher tune in his tunebooks.
25. The tune WAYNE appears in *Parish Harmony* (1813), the first two editions of *Temple Harmony* (1818 and 1820), and the Maxim-Washburn fourth edition of *Northern Harmony* (1816). Although the attribution "A. Washburn" could possibly refer to Japheth's daughter Abra, she would have been only nine years old when the tune was published. If she were writing tunes at such a young age, she would probably have written others which her father would have published. WAYNE is, however, the only tune attributed to A. Washburn. The naming of the tune also points to the authorship of Abisha, who continued to live in Wayne for some years after Japheth and his family had moved to Fairfax.
26. He was reelected as constable in April 1803 but was replaced in April 1804. He was also elected to the school committee in April 1803 and was the moderator of the town meeting on July 11, 1803. *Records of the Town of Wayne,* book 2, pp. 3, 10, 26, 39, 42, 44, 49, 57.
27. The last mention of Washburn in the Wayne town meeting records was in July 1803, when he served as moderator of the meeting. He was reelected constable in April 1803; if he served out his full term

(and there are no indications that he was replaced in midterm), he was in Wayne through March 1804. *Records of the Town of Wayne,* book 2, pp. 42, 49.

By August 1804, when he sold part of a lot in Wayne, Washburn was living in Fairfax. He sold his other Wayne properties in February 1803 and July 1805. Kennebec County Register of Deeds, vol. 4, p. 440; vol. 6, p. 473, vol. 8, p. 196.

28. The name of the town in which Washburn lived changed several times in the 1810s. His land in Fairfax, adjacent to the town of Harlem, was annexed to Harlem in 1816. Two years later, Washburn's property became a part of China, a town formed from parts of Harlem, Fairfax, and Winslow. Grow, I, pp. 5, 26–27.
29. *Ibid.,* II, p. 115.
30. By 1804, Japheth C.'s brother Zalmuna had moved to Albion, a town adjacent to Fairfax on the north; his fourth through seventh children were born there between 1804 and 1811. Brother Abisha moved to Fairfax by 1820. Japheth C.'s parents (Japheth and Priscilla) emigrated to Fairfax in late 1804 or early 1805 and apparently resided there until their deaths in 1828 and 1830. Grow, II, p. 114. Jackson, Teeples, and Schaefermeyer, eds., *Maine 1820 Census Index,* p. 110. Kennebec County Register of Deeds, vol. 8, p. 216; vol. 9, p. 138.
31. Subsequently he built a residence and store on the first site. Kingsbury and Deyo, pp. 1145, 1170.

    Grow, who supplements Kingsbury's information with Burrill's *Masonic History,* states (I, p. 18), that when the frame house and store which Washburn built burned in 1806, he built another store across the street. Her description is of a home and store, then a store across the street; Kingsbury's is of a store, then a store across the street, and finally a home and store on the first site. It is difficult to reconcile the two accounts.
32. Kingsbury and Deyo, p. 1146. It is unclear how, if at all, this fire relates to the other Washburn fires described by Grow and by Kingsbury and Deyo.
33. In a January 14, 1850, letter to A. H. Abbott, he described the location of his properties: "The Town of China is composed of the Town of Harlem and a few lots from Albion and Winslow. Before the Incorporation of China [1818] at one period, my Dwelling House was in Winslow—across the road, directly opposite, stood my store in Albion, and 40 rods south, stood my Potash, in Harlem." Japheth C. Washburn, letter to A. H. Abbott, Esq., January 14, 1850 (personal collection, Margaret Clifford).
34. Taylor, p. 155.
35. Horwitz, p. 109. Washburn's uniqueness in China is clear from the

1820 census: while 179 residents were engaged in agriculture and 13 in manufactures, only 2 (Washburn and another individual) were engaged in commerce. *Population Schedules of the 1820 Census.*

36. By 1816, for example, he had apparently accumulated substantial capital: he and his neighbor, John Brackett, paid the large sum of $5,000 to the town of Harlem as surety for highway repair on their properties in case the Harlem town highway taxes were insufficient. *Records of the Town of Harlem, Maine,* Highway Section, n.p.
37. *Hallowell Gazette,* XI/24 (June 16, 1824), p. 3. "W.I. Goods" are goods from the West Indies: rum, molasses, etc.
38. *Parish Harmony* was advertised as "for sale by E. Goodale, and by J. C. Washburn, Esq. the author, at Fairfax." *Temple Harmony,* too, was sold by various bookstores "and by the Author in China." *Hallowell Gazette,* I/40 (November 23, 1814), p. 3; V/43 (October 28, 1818), p. 3.
39. Kennebec County Register of Deeds. These deeds include various types of documents: quitclaim and warranty deeds, mortgages, and levies. In eight cases, he acquired properties to satisfy judgments he had received against delinquent debtors, probably customers of his store.
40. Washburn's commission as justice of the peace was renewed in 1810, suggesting an initial appointment of 1803 although his name does not appear in the 1803 Kennebec County index. Commonwealth of Massachusetts, *Record of Civil Commissions, 1806–1816* (manuscript records at the Massachusetts Archives), p. 210. Richard C. Kaplan, Reference Archivist, Massachusetts Archives, personal letter, December 4, 1990.
41. Fees, some as little as ten cents, were established by law for various services performed by justices of the peace. Edward S. Morris, *Maine Civil Officer: A Complete Guide for Justices of the Peace . . .,* revised and corrected by Hon. Ether Shepley (Portland: Bailey & Noyes, 1861), p. 46.
42. Unlike today, when "Esquire" normally applies principally to lawyers, in the nineteenth century Esquire was a courtesy title given to public officials of various levels. The usage comes from English law, where Esquire is a title of dignity above gentleman and below knight and is also a title of office given to sheriffs, sergeants, barristers-at-law, justices of the peace, and others. Henry Campbell Black, *Black's Law Dictionary,* fifth edition (St. Paul, MN: West Publishing Co., 1979), p. 489. On his land deeds, Washburn's occupation was frequently listed simply as "esquire."
43. An early notice listing Washburn as a Commissioner was dated February 7, 1810, and was published in the second issue of the

Herald of Liberty (Augusta, ME), I/2 (February 20, 1810), p. 4. Another example is a legal notice in the *Hallowell Gazette,* III/23 (June 5, 1816), p. 3, which announced that J. C. Washburn and Josiah Ward, Commissioners, would receive claims of creditors to the estate of the deceased Elihu Hanson of Harlem "at the dwelling-house of J. C. Washburn in said Harlem on the last Monday's of July and October next at two o'clock P.M." His "dwelling-house" was also the venue for claims to be presented for two estates in April 1820; he was listed as one of the two Commissioners who would examine the claims. *Hallowell Gazette,* VII/14 (April 5, 1820), p. 1; VII/16 (April 19, 1820), p. 3.

44. See, for example, the notice in the *Hallowell Gazette,* VI/29 (July 21, 1819), p. 4.
45. Justice of the Peace commission of Henry Sewall of Augusta, February 14, 1806, in Abbie Sewall Manley, *Collected Manuscripts Connected with the Sewall Family of Augusta* (copies in the Maine State Library).
46. From the postal legislation of 1792 and 1794, according to Arthur Hecht, "Postal History of the District of Maine in 1795," in Sterling T. Dow, *Maine Postal History and Postmarks* (Lawrence, MA: Quarterman Publications, 1976), p. 193.
47. Kingsbury and Deyo, p. 1146. Dow, pp. 203, 207. Grow (I, p. 43) notes that until the mid–twentieth century, it was customary to locate the post office in whatever building was most convenient for the postmaster.
48. Grow, I, p. 21. Abra's age is not consistent with the date of "sometime before 1810": Abra would not have been ten until 1813.
49. Arthur Hecht and Paul Hannemann, "The Post Offices of the District of Maine," in Dow, p. 199.
50. *Gazette of Maine* (Buckstown), IV/28 (January 14, 1809), p. 4. See Chapter II for more information about the embargo.
51. *Gazette of Maine,* IV/28 (January 14, 1809), p. 4.
52. Card file of Maine legislative representatives, Law Library, State House, Augusta. Although the card file does not list 1819–20 as a term served by Washburn, the minutes of the May 3, 1819, China town meeting indicate that Japheth C. Washburn was chosen the town's representative to the General Court to be convened in Boston on the last Wednesday of May 1819. *Vital Records of China.* He is also listed as China's representative in a May 12, 1819, article in the *Hallowell Gazette* and in *The Massachusetts Register and United States Calendar for the year of our Lord 1820* (Boston: James Loring; West, Richardson & Lord, n.d.), p. 29 (for the 1819–20 political year).
53. Washburn letter to Abbott, January 14, 1850.

54. William B. Bailey, *A Heritage and a Trust: China Baptist Church, 1801–1964* (typescript, May 1964, Brown Memorial Library, China), p. 2. Bailey does not indicate his source for that information.

CHINA, a popular sacred tune by Timothy Swan, is included in Washburn's first tunebook, *Parish Harmony* (1813). The British composer Cuzens also composed a tune he named CHINA, which is included in Plate 2 of the *China Bicentennial History.* This plate prints the CHINA tunes by both Swan and Cuzens with the caption: "Two versions of the hymn for which China was named." Actually, of course, they are not two versions of a single hymn, but two distinctly different tunes which happen to have the same name. Since Swan's was by far the more popular and was the only CHINA included in *Parish Harmony,* his must have been the one for which Washburn named the town, even though Washburn's later tunebook, *Temple Harmony* (1818–1826), prints both Swan's and Cuzen's CHINAS, perhaps out of homage to China.

Another Maine town named for a hymn-tune was Bangor, whose incorporation with that name was procured in 1790 by Rev. Seth Noble, "an excellent singer." The minor-key tune BANGOR was a favorite of his. *The Centennial Celebration of the Settlement of Bangor, September 30, 1869* (Bangor: Benjamin A. Burr, Printer, 1870), pp. 42–43.

55. The pay was two dollars per day for each day's attendance during the sessions plus two dollars for every ten miles travelled from the representative's home to Boston. *Resolves of the General Court of the Commonwealth of Massachusetts . . . [1812–1814, 1817–1819]* (Boston: Russell, Cutler & Co., 1812–1814, 1817–1819). Since Harlem was officially considered to be 190 miles from Boston, according to the 1818 *Massachusetts Register,* p. 28, Washburn's travel pay during his 1817–18 term was thirty-eight dollars per trip to Boston.

56. The Massachusetts General Court was in session for the following periods during the years when Washburn was a representative:

1812–13:	May 26–June 27, 1812
	October 14–24, 1812
	January 27–February 27, 1813
1813–14:	May 26–June 16, 1813
	January 12–February 28, 1814
1817–18:	May 28–June 18, 1817
	January 14–February 24, 1818
1818–19:	May 27–June 13, 1818
	January 13–February 20, 1819
1819–20:	May 26–June 19, 1819
	January 12–February 5, 1820

Resolves of the General Court . . . [1812–1814, 1817–1819], title pages; *Resolves of the General Court of the Commonwealth of Massachusetts . . . [1819–1824]* (Boston: True & Greene, 1824), title pages.

57. In the late 1810s, for example, he may have attended choral performances by the Boston Handel and Haydn Society, accompanied by the Philharmonic Society (a Boston orchestra), or instrumental programs of the Philharmonic Society. Both organizations often featured guest soloists. The concerts of the Handel and Haydn Society, founded in 1815, sometimes included complete oratorios but often consisted of selected sacred music, chiefly from the works of Handel and Haydn. At least three of their concerts (June 2, 1818; June 22, 1819; February 3, 1820) were held during or shortly after Washburn's legislative terms. H. Earle Johnson, *Musical Interludes in Boston, 1795–1830* (New York: Columbia University Press, 1943; repr. New York: AMS Press, 1967), pp. 94–97, 108–109, 130–132, 147–148; Charles C. Perkins and John S. Dwight, *History of the Handel and Haydn Society,* 2 vols. (Boston: A. Mudge, 1883–1913; repr. New York: Da Capo Press, 1977), I, pp. i–ii (appendix).
58. Sources for the information on Holden are McCormick; and Richard Crawford, "Holden, Oliver," *The New Grove Dictionary of American Music,* 4 vols., ed. H. Wiley Hitchcock and Stanley Sadie (London: Macmillan Press, 1986), II, pp. 408–409.
59. If they did not meet until the beginning of their first joint legislative term in late May 1818, it may have been too late for Holden to have had any influence on the first edition of Washburn's *Temple Harmony,* deposited for copyright on June 15, 1818, and printed in October 1818.

The early editions of Washburn's *Temple Harmony* do include more Holden tunes than the previously published *Parish Harmony* (1813). This fact is, however, probably more related to the larger size of *Temple Harmony* and the continued suitability and popularity of Holden's tunes in the late 1810s (when reform tendencies were having an impact in Maine) than to any personal relationship between the men.

Holden tunes in *Parish Harmony* (1813) are CONCORD, LORD'S DAY, and PERSIA. Those in *Temple Harmony,* first and second editions (1818 and 1820), are LORD'S DAY, OMEGA, PARADISE, PROVIDENCE, REFUGE, SALEM, and TEMPLE. The only tune attributed to Holden in the third and fourth editions (1821 and 1823) is PARADISE; in the fifth and sixth editions (1824/25? and 1826), LORD'S DAY. Another Holden tune, A DIRGE, ON THE DEATH OF A YOUNG LADY, appears without attribution in the first through fourth editions of *Temple Harmony*. His AUSPICIOUS MORN is unattributed in the fifth and sixth editions.

60. Stewart Mitchell, "Mitchell, Nahum," in *Dictionary of American Biography*, 22 vols., ed. Dumas Malone (New York: Charles Scribner's Sons, 1928–1958), XIII, pp. 58–59. Washburn's collections do not include any tunes attributed to Mitchell, who was also a composer.
61. No date of publication is printed on the title page, but Washburn deposited the book to receive copyright protection on September 15, 1813. *The Parish Harmony, or Fairfax Collection of Sacred Musick* was printed by C. Norris & Co. in Exeter, New Hampshire, "for the author."
62. *Hallowell Gazette*, I/40 (November 23, 1814), p. 3; II/52 (December 25, 1816), p. 3; III/34 (August 21, 1816), p. 3.
63. *Ibid.*, II/7 (February 15, 1815), p. 3; IV/48 (November 26, 1817), p. 3. No copies of the second and third editions are known to be extant. Although it contains no publication date, the copy at Brown University (reproduced for the American Antiquarian Society/Readex Microprint Series) is probably a first edition, since the title page does not contain any statements to the contrary.
64. See Chapter VII for more information on their collaboration.
65. Two in the first edition of Maxim's *Northern Harmony* (1805), those plus two more in the second edition of *Northern Harmony* (1808), and ten in *Parish Harmony* (1813).
66. The second edition, which represents a slight enlargement over the first edition, contains exactly the same Washburn tunes as the first edition. It is possible, however, that some of the unattributed tunes in the third through six editions (1821–1826) of *Temple Harmony* may be by Washburn. The third edition, for example, does not contain any tunes attributed to Washburn, but some are clearly his because they bear his name in other printings. Some of the other pieces, unattributed in all sources, may also be his. He may not have identified them as his own to avoid calling attention to their American origin. Most of the pieces in question received first printings in the third edition (1821), indicating that his compositional activity probably did not extend much beyond 1820. If he did continue to compose, the growing preference for European tunes may have hindered him from including them in his tunebooks.
67. Only six of the thirty-four Washburn tunes first printed in Maine tunebooks after 1815 are fuging-tunes. See Chapter XII for a discussion of the changing trends in Maine psalmody in the course of the period 1800–1830.
68. This church, later to become the First Baptist Church of China, was organized in Freetown Plantation on May 23, 1801. Freetown

Plantation was later incorporated as the town of Fairfax, and in 1818 became part of the new town of China. Bailey, p. 2.

69. Becoming baptized and joining a church are not necessarily simultaneous actions. Baptism (symbolizing commitment and obedience to Christ) is usually a requirement for membership in a Baptist church, but one can be baptized without having to join the church. Joining the church signifies one's desire to be an active participant within a certain body of believers. Washburn was apparently ready to take that step only several years after his baptism.
70. Believers were baptized in water "on profession of faith in Jesus Christ and obedience to him," according to the doctrines outlined in 1787 by the Bowdoinham Baptist Association (a regional alliance which Washburn's church joined in 1802). Henry S. Burrage, *History of the Baptists in Maine* (Portland: Marks Printing House, 1904), pp. 87–89; Grow, I, p. 24.
71. New converts are notoriously "on fire" for the Lord; the passing of time sometimes cools one's ardor and commitment.
72. Washburn notes in the preface to *Parish Harmony* that it consists almost exclusively of "Psalm Tunes" (said to be "more useful in a Book of this size"), with the addition of just one anthem (an anthem for Thanksgiving).
73. Contained within Bailey, pp. 6–7. Although Willis was not born until 1846, some of the other information he related occurred prior to his birth. The references to congregational versus choir singing are not inconsistent with practices elsewhere in New England in the early nineteenth century. See Chapter III.
74. He may have been the choir leader in the decade from 1815 to 1825, before the series of dismissals and reinstatements of his membership (to be discussed shortly) began.
75. The one-line newspaper announcement of their marriage (which took place in Vassalboro) refers to her as "Miss Sally Blish of Vassaboro." *Hallowell Gazette,* V/38 (September 23, 1818), p. 3.
76. The children and their birth dates are as follows: George Washburn, June 29, 1819; Julia C. Washburn, September 16, 1820; Emily B. Washburn, May 9, 1822; and Charles Francis Washburn, June 6, 1826. Grow, II, p. 115. These dates agree with the record of Washburn births in *China Family Records, 1800–1891* (reel 118, Maine State Archives), p. 100, except for George, whose birth date is listed in the town records as January (rather than June) 29, 1819.
77. *Records of the Town of China,* n.p.
78. Kingsbury and Deyo, p. 1143. His second tenure as town clerk actually seems to have extended from 1829 into part of 1837. The *Vital Records of China* indicates that he was chosen town clerk in

July 1829 (perhaps to complete a term) as well as in March of 1830 and 1831. His attestations of marriage intentions as town clerk extend through March 1837; a new town clerk began his service in April 1837.

79. Kingsbury and Deyo, p. 1143. He was on the three-man school committee and on various committees involved with the annexations which ultimately produced the town of China. *Records of the Town of China,* n.p.

80. Washburn had introduced the legislative bill to charter China Academy in 1818. The school's stated purpose was to promote piety and virtue and to educate youth in languages and liberal arts and sciences. Nelson Bailey suggests that during the 1820s, it may have served as a preparatory school for Colby College. Grow, I, pp. 141–142.

81. Horwitz (pp. 112–118) suggests that teachers did not share the status of other "professional men" (doctors, lawyers, and ministers) and discusses the inconsistencies of views toward teachers in Winthrop, Maine, 1820–1850.

82. He served at least those years, based on China Academy's newspaper notices, issued in the name of "J. C. Washburn, Sec'y." The trustees meetings were sometimes held at China Academy; other times, they were held at Washburn's home or hall. Examples of the latter are found in the *Hallowell Gazette,* VI/33 (August 18, 1819), p. 1, and XIV/43 (October 24, 1827), p. 3.

83. Grow, I, pp. 141–142.

84. Washburn letter to Abbott, January 14, 1850.

85. China Academy (ME), *Catalogue of the Officers and Students of China Academy, November, 1822* (Hallowell, ME: Goodale, Glazier & Co., Printers, [1822], Broadside Collection, American Antiquarian Society). The Washburn household must have been a large one in November 1822, with perhaps seven children from his two marriages still at home, along with the two adults (Japheth and Sarah), and three female boarders.

86. One example of his apparent unwillingness to serve: he was chosen one of three auditors of town accounts in March 1823, but was excused from the position at a meeting three weeks later. Minor town positions he held during the 1820s included occasional moderator at a town meeting (June 1823, September 1825), member of miscellaneous committees (1821, 1825, 1826), one of three auditors of town accounts (1825, 1827). He came in a distant third in the voting for state legislative representative in 1826 and 1828. In July 1829, for the first time in nearly a decade, he was elected town clerk. *Records of the Town of China.*

The uniting of the town of Harlem with China in 1822 may also have been a factor in Washburn's "fall from power." An immediate result of the unification was an almost complete turnover of town offices in favor of Harlem residents. Grow, I, p. 48.

87. The second edition was published in 1820, the third in 1821, the fourth in 1823, the fifth probably in 1824 or 1825, the sixth in 1826, the seventh in 1827. The seventh edition is not known to be extant. A tunebook which may be a fifth edition is in the personal collection of Margaret Clifford of China, a descendant of Washburn; although it lacks a title page, it has many similarities with the fourth and sixth editions.
88. The first edition of *Temple Harmony* was advertised in the *Hallowell Gazette* as "just published" in October 1818. The second, fourth, and sixth editions were similarly promoted as "just published" in November of 1820, 1823, and 1826, respectively. In each case, the new books were available for use in singing schools which began in December, whether the schools were taught by Washburn or not.
89. Singing schools often began in November or December and extended through January or February.
90. See Chapter IV, note 13, for more information about this copy.
91. Thomas Burrill, *History of Central Lodge, No. 45, China, Maine* [December 27, 1823, to September 15, 1875] (unpublished manuscript, personal collection, Margaret Clifford), p. 3. Both a manuscript and typescript version of Burrill's *History of Central Lodge* exist, with the typescript in the possession of Mr. and Mrs. William Foster. Page numbers are to the manuscript version, unless otherwise indicated.
92. The early town meeting records of China are filled with his handwriting and signature as town clerk; in addition, as justice of the peace, he performed many marriages, based on the frequency of his name in the record of marriages. Transitory activities, such as singing schools, are not recorded in the town annals, making them more difficult to trace.
93. *American Advocate* (Hallowell, ME), XVIII/1 (January 6, 1827), p. 3. Washburn had taken on Benson as his partner in the mercantile business in June 1824; the new firm was called Washburn & Benson and transacted business "at the Store recently occupied by J. C. Washburn." On September 30, 1826, Washburn and Benson dissolved the co-partnership; however, a final settlement between the two had apparently not been completed by the end of the year, since properties jointly owned with Benson were still in the store.
94. *Hallowell Gazette,* XIII/52 (December 27, 1826), p. 3.
95. *American Advocate* (Hallowell, ME), XVII/52 (December 30, 1826), p. 3.

96. *Ibid.,* XVIII/1 (January 6, 1827), p. 3. The fire undoubtedly convinced Washburn of the value of fire insurance; he later entered into the business himself. In an October 3, 1835, notice in the China newspaper, *The Orb,* II/44, p. 3, Washburn, as secretary of the China Mutual Fire Insurance Company, announced a meeting for the annual election of officers.
97. *American Advocate,* XVIII/1 (January 6, 1827), p. 3.
98. *Ibid.* He was then forty-six years old with nine surviving children, ranging in age from six months to twenty-three years.
99. *Ibid.*
100. *Hallowell Gazette,* XIII/47 (November 22, 1826), p. 3.
101. This edition is not known to be extant.
102. Although the circular letter is unsigned, Washburn must have been its author, judging from item 10 in the minutes of the September 21, 1815, meeting: "Voted to accept the Circular Letter prepared by brother Japheth C. Washburn . . ." *Minutes of the Lincoln Association, Holden at St. George, Sept. 20 and 21, 1815* (Hallowell, ME: N. Cheever, 1815), p. 5.

    The card catalog entry for this pamphlet at the American Antiquarian Society indicates that the Circular Letter is by *Rev.* Japheth C. Washburn (italics added), but there seems to be nothing in the minutes (or in other information about Washburn) that would indicate he was a minister. The names of the "Elders and Messengers" listed for each church were printed in small capital letters if they were "ordained ministers" and italics if they were "licensed preachers." Washburn's name was not printed in either capital letters or italics.
103. *Records of the First Baptist Church in China, 1801–March, 1852* (typescript copy in the possession of Mrs. William Foster, Church Clerk), pp. 3–5.
104. *Ibid.,* pp. 15, 24–26.
105. He, his wife, and his parents were dismissed from the "watch and care" of the church on February 26, 1826. Notwithstanding this vote, a committee was empowered on November 25, 1826, to inquire about the difficulty between Brother Joseph Brackett and Japheth C. Washburn. On May 3, 1827, the church, after hearing a committee report, withdrew fellowship from Washburn, who had apparently already voluntarily withdrawn from the church. He was restored to membership on August 23, 1828, excluded on March 13, 1829, then restored again on August 17, 1831, following a confession and reconciliation with his brother Zalmuna. On March 17, 1832, the church voted to send a committee to inform him that "the church believes he has been in the habit of using intoxicating liquors to excess by times ever since he was restored to

the church." He was excluded from the watch care of the church on November 28, 1832, but restored to church fellowship on July 28, 1833. *Ibid.*, pp. 28, 31, 33–34, 36–37, 39, 43–45, 49, 54–56, 63.

106. *Ibid.*, pp. 51, 53.
107. In one case, the disagreements came only a few months after the fire had destroyed his store and livelihood. Is it any wonder that he spoke less tactfully then than he might have at another time?
108. One of his daughters recalled that he visited the Masonic Lodge in Hallowell and may have become a Mason there, perhaps around 1816. Burrill, p. 2. According to Wallace Gage, Grand Historian of the Grand Lodge of Maine, however, Washburn must have already become a Mason prior to this visit, which is noted on his Grand Lodge record card. Glendon Newcombe, the secretary of the Kennebec Lodge, searched the lodge records from 1796 to 1850 and did not find Washburn's name. (Personal letter, September 6, 1990.) The Grand Lodge of Massachusetts has no record of Japheth Washburn's membership in a Massachusetts lodge. (Personal letter, November 1, 1990.)
109. Grow, I, p. 179n, based on Burrill (typescript), p. 29.
110. The lodge history indicates that he was chosen Senior Warden at the June 29, 1825, meeting; a July 6, 1825, newspaper account of the installation lists J. C. Washburn as Treasurer. Burrill, p. 14. *Hallowell Gazette,* XII/27 (July 6, 1825), p. 3, reprinting an article from the *Augusta Journal*.
111. Burrill, p. 9. Wallace M. Gage, Grand Historian, Grand Lodge of Maine, in a personal letter dated October 6, 1990, indicates Washburn also served as Junior Deacon in 1829.

    Traditionally, Masonic officers "come up through the ranks," progressing through a series of officer positions (the first three appointed by the new Master; the latter three elected by the lodge): Steward, Junior Deacon, Senior Deacon, Junior Warden, Senior Warden, and finally Master. Perhaps because of his prior Masonic experience, Washburn skipped several lower positions in the China Lodge, beginning as Senior Warden and advancing to Master the following year. The positions of Secretary, Treasurer, and Tyler were not in the line of succession, but were frequently held for years by the same person. Lynn Dumenil, *Freemasonry and American Culture, 1880–1930* (Princeton, NJ: Princeton University Press, 1984), p. 14.
112. *Hallowell Gazette,* XIII/30 (July 26, 1826), p. 3. Although this quotation may indicate that there were instrumental performers in China in 1826, the term "band" did not always refer to instrumentalists. Newspaper accounts in the 1820s referred to "the band of singers" from Rev. Mr. Tappan's church, for example.

113. Possibly Thidden? (handwriting difficult to read). The typescript version of Burrill's lodge history interprets the name as Kidder.
114. Burrill, pp. 15–16. This may be the hymn entitled THE THREE FRIENDS, which Washburn included in the sixth edition of *Temple Harmony* (1826). The text begins, "When shall we three meet again" and consists of six phrases of seven syllables each (the meter labelled "7's"); the similar opening phrase quoted in the Lodge minutes ("When shall we three meet like then") also has seven syllables. The tune is unattributed in *Temple Harmony.* It is not found in the fourth edition (1823), but does appear in the tunebook which I believe to be a fifth edition of *Temple Harmony.*
115. Dumenil (p. 14) suggests that fraternal orders give average men ways of achieving distinction and that officeholding is a major way of attaining prestige within Masonry.
116. A nationwide anti-Masonic movement swept the country following the 1826 kidnapping, disappearance, and presumed murder of William Morgan of Batavia, New York. A former Mason, Morgan had announced the forthcoming publication of a book revealing the secrets of Masonry. The incident itself, plus possible complicity or coverups by local authorities and the press, confirmed fears that Masonry set itself above the Church and the State. Mary Ann Clawson, *Constructing Brotherhood: Class, Gender, and Fraternalism* (Princeton, NJ: Princeton University Press, 1989), pp. 115–118.

    Nearly all the Maine Masonic lodges suspended meetings until the 1840s, when anti-Masonic sentiment had died down. The charter of Central Lodge was not renewed until 1849. Hatch, I, p. 285; Kingsbury and Deyo, p. 1157.
117. Clawson, pp. 14, 55.
118. Kennebec County Register of Deeds, vol. 62, p. 476. This warranty deed, dated June 11, 1828, for payment of $200, gave Oliver W. Washburn the right of redeeming three acres of land in China, including the land on which J. C. Washburn lived, as well as the buildings on it; also J. C.'s store and the land it was on.
119. Grow, I, p. 175.
120. In *The Orb,* II/52 (November 28, 1835), p. 2, Washburn suggests the somewhat discouraging circumstances under which the paper had begun, two years previously: "Some looked upon the undertaking as altogether visionary, and hopeless. But *few* spake encouraging, and *fewer still* was the number of those who generously afforded pecuniary aid in its establishment. To the generous *few* who did step forward with a helping hand in time of need, we tender our greatful [*sic*] acknowledgements."
121. Howard Owen, "The Newspaper Press," in Kingsbury and Deyo, p. 253. He incorrectly states that the publication was discontinued at the end of the second year, rather than the third.

Confirming the agricultural nature of the town is one of Washburn's requests for subscriber payment: "Such of our subscribers as wish, can pay in corn, grain, or wood." *The Orb,* II/52 (November 28, 1835), p. 2.

122. *The Orb,* II/1 (December 6, 1834), p. 2.
123. Grow, I, pp. 175–176.
124. Following the report of a fire in Calais, Maine, which had destroyed the office of the *St. Croix Courier* and everything in it, Washburn adds: "The editor of the Orb most heartily sympathizes with his friend Bates [editor of the *St. Croix Courier*] in the loss of his property, by that devouring element *Fire*! by which *he also,* has been twice reduced to poverty and distress, which still presses heavily upon him." Washburn expressed his hope that the public would be generous in lending a helping hand. *The Orb,* II/4 (December 27, 1834), p. 2.
125. His full name was William Vinal Vaughan Washburn.
126. The twenty issues of vol. III in the Brown Memorial Library in China do not include a printer's name on the masthead.

    It is unknown where the younger Washburns learned the craft of printing; however, several printing firms operated in the neighboring towns of Augusta and Hallowell. Their father's associations with the Hallowell printing establishment of Ezekiel Goodale may have facilitated one or more of his sons apprenticing in Hallowell (about eighteen miles from China), although Ezekiel Goodale himself retired from the printing business in 1824 and died in 1829. His former partners (and their new partners) continued the business under various names into the late nineteenth century.

    Although one would not expect the son of a relatively affluent businessman like Washburn to be apprenticed and learn a trade, Washburn's dire financial straits, resulting from the fire, undoubtedly altered his sons' future possibilities. Printing was one of the more respectable trades.
127. *The Orb,* II/17 (March 28, 1835), p. 2.
128. *Ibid.,* II/30 (June 27, 1835), p. 3; II/31 (July 4, 1835), p. 2. He called to order a meeting of the group and was on the committee to prepare a resolution expressing the sense of the meeting.
129. *Ibid.,* II/46 (October 17, 1835), p. 3.
130. *Ibid.,* I/52 (November 29, 1834), p. 4.
131. *Ibid.,* I/1 (December 5, 1833), p. 3; II/11 (February 14, 1835), p. 2.
132. None of the members' names appears in the ads.
133. *The Orb* (China, ME), II/52 (November 28, 1835), p. 3.
134. Even though new methods for teaching music were being introduced by Lowell Mason and his followers in the 1820s and 1830s, the theoretical introductions to Washburn's tunebooks were not

completely outdated in comparison. The newer tunebooks contained much of the same information contained in Washburn's rudiments section, with the addition of such items as names for the notes of the diatonic scale, a discussion of intervals, and an example of the chromatic scale. See, for example, "Introduction to the Art of Singing" in Lowell Mason, *The Choir: or Union Collection of Church Music,* second edition (Boston: Carter, Hendee & Co., 1833).

135. The minutes of the China Baptist Church meeting held on January 17, 1837, were attested to by "J. C. Washburn, clerk pro tem." At the church meeting held March 25, 1837, several of the Washburns were dismissed from the China Church to the church in Calais. Those dismissed ("as members in good standing") were J. C. Washburn and his wife, Brother George Washburn (their seventeen-year-old son) and Sister Julia Washburn (their sixteen-year-old daughter). *Records of the First Baptist Church in China,* pp. 87, 90.

136. Grow, I, pp. 279, 283; II, p. 115.

137. A letter from Washburn to O. W. Washburn on October 25, 1841 (personal collection, Margaret Clifford), seems to confirm that his four youngest children (those born to Sarah) made the move to Calais. Family members who appear to be with him include George, Julia (who was not in good health), Frank (a nickname for Charles Francis), and Mr. Taylor (probably Edward Taylor, who married Emily Washburn, Japheth's daughter). Frank was going to go to school in the coming winter to "try to 'git some larnin' so that he can do business in a store or elsewhere." The 1850 census lists Emily and Charles as still living with their parents in Calais; George was a head of household there.

138. Rev. I. C. Knowlton, *Annals of Calais, Maine, and St. Stephen, New Brunswick* (Calais, ME: J. A. Sears, 1875), p. 187.

139. John Christopher Arndt, "The Solid Men of Bangor: Economic, Business and Political Growth on Maine's Urban Frontier, 1769–1845" (Ph.D. dissertation, Florida State University, 1987), pp. 177–180.

140. *Ibid.,* pp. 263–264.

141. He had at least one friend there: former editor Bates of the defunct *St. Croix Courier* newspaper. Washburn speaks of Bates as his friend in the account of the fire which destroyed the *Courier*'s office. *The Orb,* II/4 (December 27, 1834), p. 2. Washburn may also have been acquainted with lodge brothers in Calais.

142. Knowlton, p. 130.

143. Joseph Griffin, *History of the Press of Maine (with 1874 Supplement)* (Brunswick, ME: Press of J. Griffin . . . Charles H. Fuller, Printer, 1874), p. 151.

144. *Ibid.,* p. 152.
145. Knowlton, p. 132.
146. A successful suit brought by Washburn and Son against Aroostook County for a delinquent payment names the plaintiffs as "Japhet [*sic*] C. Washburn and George Washburn, both of Calais in our County of Washington, Printers and late Copartners doing business under the firm and style of J. C. Washburn and Son." District Court Records, District Court for the Eastern District, Washington County in Machias (Maine), vol. 4 (February Term, 1842), Docket 526 (Washburn & al. *vs.* County of Aroostook), pp. 176–177.
147. Washburn letter to O. W. Washburn, October 25, 1841. The last issue of the newspapers published by J. C. Washburn and Son was in June 1841.
148. *Ibid.*
149. Kingsbury and Deyo, p. 1145.
150. Washburn letter to O. W. Washburn, October 25, 1841. The Bankruptcy Act, which was passed on August 19, 1841, was repealed on March 3, 1843. *The Public Statutes at Large of the United States of America, from the Organization of the Government in 1789, to March 3, 1845* (Boston: Charles C. Little & James Brown, 1846), V, p. 440.
151. Arndt, p. 220.
152. Bankruptcy petition no. 2363, filed by "Japhet" C. Washburn on October 27, 1842, United States District Court, Maine District.
153. It is impossible to determine from Schedule A (which lists his creditors, along with their place of residence and amount owed) when and for what reason the debts were incurred, since the debts are described simply as "account or notes." The Boston creditors may have been vendors whose products or services he used in his unsuccessful newspaper ventures in Calais. The amount owed to creditors in China ($631 to three creditors) was not substantial, suggesting that he probably did not leave China owing significant sums to townspeople. Only $75 was owed to creditors residing in Calais. His largest single creditor was James Blish of Hallowell, to whom he owed $1,200. Blish, who was referred to as a yeoman from Vassalboro when Washburn bought two hundred acres of land from him in 1815 (Kennebec County Register of Deeds, vol. 23, p. 564), may have been an in-law: Japheth's wife was the former Sarah Blish of Vassalboro. The total amount owed to creditors (Schedule A) was $4,246; the value of his property, including furniture and clothing (Schedule B) was $216. Bankruptcy petition no. 2363, Japhet C. Washburn, United States District Court, Maine District.
154. The 1850 census, unlike previous ones, gives the names of each individual in the household. Japheth's household included wife Sarah, age fifty-one; daughter Emily B., age twenty-six; son Charles F., age

twenty-four, occupation listed as trader; grandson Charles E. Taylor, age seven (Emily's son); and a Mary McFarland, age twenty-one. Son George, age thirty, occupation "trader," was listed in Calais with his own household, consisting of a wife, one-month-old daughter, and two other persons. Unlike his father, who did not own any real estate, George owned real estate valued at $1,500. *Population Schedules of the Seventh Census of the United States, 1850* (Washington, DC: National Archives, 1963), microcopy no. 432, roll 273 (Maine), pp. 125, 138.

155. His last extant letter, written on January 14, 1850, to Abbott in China, deals with the history of China and does not contain any personal references.
156. The St. Croix Lodge was organized in December 1824, soon after the China Lodge: Central Lodge in China was Maine Lodge No. 45; St. Croix Lodge in Calais was Lodge No. 46. Like the China chapter, the St. Croix Lodge ceased holding meetings in 1829. Knowlton, pp. 98–100. Information about Washburn's activities in the St. Croix Lodge was provided by Glendon Ayer, a member of St. Croix Lodge, in a personal letter dated August 18, 1990. Mr. Ayer kindly examined the handwritten records of the lodge for me.
157. The Baptist Church in Milltown was the parent church of the Calais Village Baptist Church, organized in 1841 by fifty of the Milltown members who wanted a place of worship nearer home. In 1851, its name was changed to the present Second Baptist Church. Knowlton, p. 187.
158. *Ibid.*
159. *Ibid.*, p. 189.
160. *Ibid.*, p. 72. A function of his position as justice of the peace, his action does not indicate that he had any affiliation with the Methodist church.
161. There are five tunes by Maine composers in the second edition (1816), ten in the third edition (1831), and thirteen in the fourth edition (1840). The first edition (1801) is not extant. See Chapter XIV for a discussion of factors other than Washburn's geographical proximity which may have contributed to the greater number of Maine tunes in the later Humbert editions.
162. Grow, II, p. 115.
163. *Calais Advertiser*, IX/39 (August 28, 1850), p. 2.
164. Washburn was buried in Block 64, Lot 2, Tyler Lane section. City of Calais Cemetery Records, Family name F. A. Pike, Washburn. I am grateful to Karen Herrick of the Calais Free Library for locating Washburn's obituary and cemetery records. She also served as a liaison to representatives of the Second Baptist Church in China and the St. Croix Masonic Lodge.

Although Washburn's name is inscribed on the Washburn family stone (a vertical monument) in the Village Cemetery in China, Maine, he is not buried there, according to his descendant, Margaret Clifford. Japheth's first wife, Betsy, is buried there, however, as are his parents and his son Oliver Wendell Washburn.

Official confirmation of his death date is not available: a Calais fire in the early twentieth century destroyed most of the records prior to that date, according to a letter from the Calais City Clerk's Office, September 13, 1990. The Calais vital records on microfilm at the Maine State Archives do not contain any death records from February 1849 to 1854. *Vital Records of Calais, 1840–1905* (reel 96, Maine State Archives).

165. China Historical Society, *Japheth Coombs Washburn and His Descendants: Four Generations of Service to the Town of China* [Remembrance Day booklet] (Typescript, 1981), pp. 1, 3–5. Japheth's son Oliver Wendell Washburn was town clerk from 1840 through 1850, grandson Willis Wendell Washburn from 1872 through 1877 and again from 1888 until his death in 1942 (a total of sixty years!), and great-granddaughter Mary Washburn from 1942 through 1970.

Notes for Chapter IX

1. See Chapter VI for more information on Belcher.
2. Coburn, II, p. 994.
3. In 1775, he held positions as a corporal in Capt. Ebenezer Bridges's company, Col. John Whitcomb's regiment of minutemen (which marched to Cambridge), and as a sergeant in Capt. John Fuller's company, Col. Asa Whitcomb's regiment. *Massachusetts Soldiers,* VII, p. 392.
4. She was born on March 5, 1755, in Leominster, Massachusetts. Coburn, II, p. 994.
5. Edwards, p. 32.
6. Each settler had to build on his lot a house at least twenty feet square with seven foot stud, to clear five acres of land for tillage within three years of the grant, and to live on the premises himself (or by substitute). The grantee also had to help build the public house of worship and do some work on the public roads. Hartwell, who was officially granted Lot 23 on December 18, 1792 (although he supposedly settled there in 1780), sold fifty of his acres to another former Fitchburg resident on April 10, 1787. Coburn, II, pp. 648–649, 664. Lincoln County Register of Deeds, book 21, pp. 187–188.
7. Coburn, I, p. 192.

8. According to Coburn (II, p. 994), the Hartwells had thirteen children (nine of them boys), with nine of them born in Maine. Eben Weston claims, however, that the Hartwells had only ten children and that three of the ten died before adulthood. Eben Weston, *The Early Settlers of Canaan* (written for the *Somerset Reporter,* 1890–1892; typewritten copy by Kathleen A. Martin, Skowhegan Free Public Library, Skowhegan, ME), pp. 75–76. Edwards, p. 32.

   Much of the information which is known about Edward Hartwell and his family comes from the Eben Weston Papers, which consist of biographical sketches of "Early Settlers of Canaan," originally written for the *Somerset Reporter* by area resident Weston, born in 1802. Because Weston was related to Mrs. Edward Hartwell and had personal knowledge of the family, his sketch of the Hartwells is assumed to be fairly reliable. Edward Hartwell's wife, Lydia, was Weston's aunt: her father, John White, was his grandfather.
9. *Heads of Families, 1790: Maine,* p. 36. Females are also enumerated in the census, but apparently the only Hartwell female in the household at the time was Lydia Hartwell, Edward's wife. Coburn states that nine of the thirteen children were boys; Weston, that six of the seven children living to adulthood were boys.
10. Weston, p. 76.
11. He was allowed to charge the following fares: 2 pence for a man, 7 pence for a man and horse, and a shilling for a yoke of oxen.
12. Coburn, I, pp. 103, 413, 416.
13. *Ibid.,* pp. 237, 272.
14. Being head of the class entailed convening the residents of the district to decide how the money appropriated for the district's schools should be spent and who should be hired to teach. The heads of the six classes in town were also the members of a school committee which made periodic visits to the schools. Lillian Clayton Smith, "The Schools of Old Canaan," in Coburn, II, pp. 512–515.
15. Elise Fellows White, "Music," in Coburn, I, pp. 325, 327.
16. Weston, p. 77.
17. *Ibid.* See Chapter XIII for musical transcriptions and discussion of two representative tunes (TRIBUNAL and CAPERNAUM) and Part III for an index of his tunes.
18. During the 1780s, Hartwell's first decade of settlement, the initial demands of frontier life probably superseded thoughts of such diversions as singing schools.
19. The advertisement on p. [3] of *Chorister's Companion* is signed "Bloomfield, November, 1815"; however, Hartwell probably had not moved. In 1814, the town of Bloomfield was established from part of Canaan, probably including the area where Hartwell lived. Coburn, I, p. 44.

20. Hartwell, p. 9.
21. Weston, p. 77.
22. *Ibid.*, p. 76.
23. The disparaging remark that he makes in his tunebook (p. 12) about unqualified singing-school teachers may reflect a twinge of jealousy: he writes with the critical pen of an older man eying the young whippersnappers who have displaced him: "If teachers are employed (as is too often the case) who themselves need instruction in the first principles of music, it rather helps to degrade than promote this noble science. For every day while pupils are practising under the tuition of an inaccurate leader, they are rendering more distant the prospect of attaining to accuracy themselves." On the other hand, the fact that he published a tunebook in 1815 may argue for his own continued involvement in singing schools as late as 1815.
24. Hartwell, p. [3].
25. *Ibid.*
26. *Ibid.*
27. An ad for *Chorister's Companion* in the *Hallowell Gazette,* III/2 (January 10, 1816), p. 3, announced that the newly published book was for sale in Hallowell at 75 cents single, $7.50 per dozen. Its price was halfway between that of *Parish Harmony,* which sold for 50 cents, and many of the larger collections, which were a dollar per copy.
28. Weston, p. 77. The title page indicates that the book was printed in Exeter, New Hampshire, by C. Norris & Co. "for the author."
29. *Ibid.* The tunes he named are sacred pieces by American composers Oliver Holden, Parmeter, and Lewis Edson, respectively. CORONATION and BRIDGEWATER were so popular that they are part of the Core Repertory of early American psalmody, the 101 sacred pieces printed most frequently in American tunebooks between 1698 and 1810.
30. Surprisingly, two Hartwell tunes (PETITION and UNION) are contained within a manuscript collection: [W. Crouch?], *The North-Western Harmony and Musician's Companion,* 2 vols. (Manuscript Collection at Brown University), I, pp. 100, 102. Another tune, HARLINGTON, which is unattributed in Hartwell's collection, is also included in *North-Western Harmony,* where it is attributed to "E. Hartwells Col." The compiler may have been familiar with other Maine tunebooks, since six pieces by Maxim and one by Washburn are among the tunes copied. Karl Kroeger brought the above information to my attention.
31. Hartwell, p. [3].
32. *The Hallowell Collection of Sacred Music* (1817, 1819) and Henry Little's *Wesleyan Harmony* (1820, 1821).

33. See Chapter III for more information on the reform movement and Chapter XII for a comparison of the repertory in Hartwell's collection with that of other Maine tunebooks.
34. White, "Music," in Coburn, I, p. 327.
35. Weston, p. 77.
36. See Chapter VI for more information on Belcher's secular tunes.
37. The singing-school function of the tunebook was touted in an ad which said the book was "recommended with confidence to Singing Schools and Societies as peculiarly adapted to their use." *Hallowell Gazette,* III/48 (November 27, 1816), p. 3.
38. A quarter of the tunes in Hartwell's collection (a total of 34 tunes) are part of the Core Repertory.
39. Weston, p. 76.
40. White, "Music," in Coburn, I, p. 326, identifies Samuel as the "S. Hartwell" who wrote the tunes SOUTHWICK and MORNING STAR (actually MORNING SONG), "the last two pieces" in Edward Hartwell's tunebook. White may have been looking at an incomplete copy, since there are three pieces following these. Presumably, Samuel also wrote JEHOVAH REIGNS, the other tune attributed to S. Hartwell. Besides Samuel's natural musical endowments, he may have reaped the benefits of being the youngest son: his father may have had more undivided time to teach him what he knew of music.
41. Weston, p. 76. White ("Music," in Coburn, I, p. 327) tentatively sets the date of his singing school as about 1810 or later. Although Samuel was only eighteen in 1810, it is possible that he may have taught at that age. By 1815, he had written at least the three tunes which were published in his father's tunebook.
42. Hartwell, p. 12.
43. Steward "led the singing in the old meeting-house, and afterward in the Baptist Church for several years." White, "Music," in Coburn, I, p. 324.
44. Weston, p. 76. Weston refers to the girls and their voice parts in the order used here, implying that Emeline was the alto and Angeline the soprano, although he does not specifically say so.
45. *Ibid.* Coburn (I, p. 592) may be referring to the same person when she states that one of the Hartwell boys (she says it was Edward) was a soldier in the War of 1812 and died from his wounds in 1814.
46. Coburn, II, pp. 743, 745.
47. *Ibid.,* p. 664.
48. Settlers did not begin arriving in St. Albans until about 1800.
49. *East Somerset County Register,* p. 221. Gladys M. Bigelow and Ruth M. Knowles, *History of St. Albans, Maine* (n.p.: Gladys M. Bigelow & Ruth M. Knowles, 1982), p. 6. Ruth McGowan

Knowles, *Warren's Four Towns: St. Albans, Hartland, Palmyra, Corinna* (n.p.: Ruth McGowan Knowles, 1988), pp. 8, 9.

Knowles's date of 1822 for the building of the sawmill seems inconsistent with the dates Bigelow and Knowles give for the log house (1823) and frame house (1829). Why would the sawmill be built before the log house? *The East Somerset County Register* does not give specific dates, but implies a more logical sequence of construction: first the log house, then a sawmill, with a frame house the next year.

50. Weston (p. 76) is probably mistaken in stating that the four Hartwells (Edward, Lydia, Samuel, and Polly) moved to Palmyra, Maine, a town approximately ten miles northeast of Canaan and directly south of St. Albans. Census records place Edward and Stephen in St. Albans by 1830 and specifically name Stephen, Samuel, and Edward as residents of St. Albans in 1840 (other family members are identified only by quantity within age groups, not by name). Since Palmyra is adjacent to St. Albans, one explanation for Weston's apparent error is that the Hartwells may have resided near the Palmyra line.
51. Samuel was still living in Bloomfield as late as 1825, when he was elected a Bloomfield selectman. Coburn, I, p. 272. Census data identify Edward Hartwell as a head of household in Bloomfield in 1820, but in St. Albans in 1830. Assuming that the elderly Edward and Lydia (ages seventy-seven and seventy in 1825) travelled to St. Albans with their son Samuel (who seems to have been living with them in 1820 and 1830), the move must have been after 1825, but before 1830.
52. Probate Court Records, Somerset County, Maine, 1845, vol. 18, p. 34.
53. After Edward Hartwell's death, the report of his estate described his real estate as "the farm lately occupied by the said Edward Hartwell and now occupied by Capt. Samuel Hartwell situated in St. Albans." Probate Court Records, Somerset County, Maine, 1845, vol. 18, p. 34.
54. *Population Schedules of the Sixth Census of the United States, 1840* (Washington, DC: National Archives, 1967), microcopy no. 704, roll 151, p. 238. Coburn (II, p. 995) also states that Edward and Lydia Hartwell "passed their last years" with Samuel in St. Albans.
55. Weston, p. 77. Coburn, II, p. 995.
56. *Kennebec Journal* (Augusta), XX/19 (May 3, 1844), p. 3.
57. Probate Court records pertaining to Edward Hartwell are in Somerset County, Maine, as follows: vol. 16, pp. 509–510; vol. 17, pp. 108–109; vol. 18, pp. 34–35; vol. 19, pp. 31, 194.

58. *Population Schedules of the 1850 Census,* microcopy no. 432, roll 268, p. 138. Samuel Hartwell was fifty-eight in 1850; his wife, Mary, was twenty-five. Their children ranged in age from eleven months to five years.
59. White, "Music," in Coburn, I, p. 327.
60. His siblings were Nathaniel, Luther Jr., Reuben, Martin, Calvin, Nancy, Betsey, and Lydia. Merrill, pp. 515–516.

    Although the *Vital Records of Greene, Maine, 1784–1859* (microfilm reel 204, Maine State Archives), p. 24, list the names and birth dates of Luther and Anna Robbins's children, the four older children were probably not born in Maine, but in Hanover, where the family lived prior to 1788. Robbins's birthplace is given as Hanover, Massachusetts, in Britton, Lowens, and Crawford, p. 525. Their source, Walter Lindley Mower's *Sesquicentennial History of the Town of Greene* (Auburn, ME: n.p., 1938), pp. 250–251, while not specifically stating that Charles was born in Hanover, implies it.
61. Merrill, p. 515.
62. Mower, p. 134.
63. Charles Robbins may have apprenticed under Joseph Metcalf in Winthrop. The following statement, from David Thurston, *A Brief History of Winthrop, from 1764 to October 1855* (Portland: Brown Thurston, 1855), pp. 86–87, is ambiguous as to whether both Robbins and a Capt. Benjamin—or just Capt. Benjamin—were apprentices with Deacon Metcalf: "Dea. Joseph Metcalf was the first Cabinet and Chair maker. Mr. Charles Robbins and Capt. Samuel Benjamin, who served an apprenticeship with Deac. Metcalf, pursued their trade at the village."
64. Merrill (p. 515) says Charles was a cabinetmaker "in early life."
65. Mower, p. 252. If Mower is correct about the length of time he was a tavern-keeper, he must have returned to Greene at least by the early 1820s, since he died in 1842. Although Mower writes that Robbins "acquired the Dr. Ammi R. Cutter property in 1835 and kept tavern twenty years," the two actions must not have been directly related, since Robbins lived for only seven years (not twenty) after 1835.
66. In contrast, Capt. Benjamin is described as "a skilled workman." Thurston, p. 87.
67. Robbins, *Columbian Harmony,* p. [iii].
68. *Ibid.*
69. *Ibid.*
70. Maxim's "recommendations and solicitations" to Robbins may have included assistance in arranging for Robbins's tunebook to be published by Henry Ranlet in Exeter, New Hampshire. Ranlet had printed Maxim's earlier tunebook in 1802.

71. Robbins, *Columbian Harmony,* p. 10.
72. Two Belcher tunes in Robbins's tunebook are in 6/2 meter: HYMN HUNDRED AND SIXTEENTH and HYMN THIRTY-FIFTH. None of Robbins's tunes is in this meter.
73. One of the tunes in Robbins's tunebook, PENOBSCOT, is attributed to "N. Robbins," probably Charles's brother, Nathaniel, born in 1779.

    Belcher lived in Hallowell only until 1791, when Nathaniel was twelve and Charles was nine. Hallowell is about eighteen miles from Greene and only about six miles from Winthrop (but Charles probably had not begun his apprenticeship in Winthrop by 1791). Once Belcher moved to Farmington in 1791, he lived further away from Robbins: Farmington is about thirty-three miles from Greene and about twenty-five miles from Winthrop.
74. Greene is almost directly south of Farmington. Although Supply Belcher and Luther Robbins were both legislative representatives, they never served together: Belcher's terms began in 1798, 1801, and 1809; Robbins's in 1807, 1811, and 1814. Both men were justices of the peace, and each was elected town clerk and selectman of his respective town in various years. Butler, pp. 329, 331, 335; Mower, pp. 130–131, 137.
75. See Part III for the tune names.
76. The latter tune, SUMNER, is also printed in Maxim's *Northern Harmony,* which was published about a month after *Columbian Harmony* by the same printer: Henry Ranlet of Exeter, New Hampshire. Ads for *Columbian Harmony* first appear in the *Portland Gazette and Maine Advertiser* in early September, those for *Northern Harmony* in early October 1805. *Portland Gazette,* VIII/20 (September 2, 1805), p. 3; VIII/25 (October 7, 1805), p. 3.
77. Maxim also included first printings of two tunes by Japheth Coombs Washburn, probably also a student of his.

    PSALM FIFTIETH is the Robbins tune included in *Northern Harmony,* first and second editions (1805 and 1808). Its first printing was in Robbins's *Columbian Harmony* (1805), which came off the presses a month ahead of *Northern Harmony.* Since the manuscript of *Northern Harmony* was probably delivered to the printer prior to *Columbian Harmony*'s publication, however, Maxim must have obtained the tune directly from Robbins, rather than from Robbins's published tunebook. Although Henry Ranlet, publisher of both tunebooks, may have been printing the books at nearly the same time, the same plate was not used for the two printings of PSALM FIFTIETH: the tune takes up three staves in *Columbian Harmony,* only two in *Northern Harmony.*

    Another of Robbins's tunes, ELEMENT, is included in the fourth and fifth editions of *Northern Harmony* (1816 and 1819).

78. Turner, where Maxim lived, is adjacent to Greene and only about thirteen miles from Winthrop.
79. A stylistic survey of the various composers' tunes is the topic of Chapter XIII. Included are musical transcriptions and discussion of three of Robbins's tunes: PSALM FIFTIETH, ACCORD, and ELEMENT. Suffice it to say here that Robbins's tunes, like Belcher's, display more rhythmic vitality and variety than is usually found in Maxim's tunes and show a greater use of word painting.
80. Robbins, *Columbian Harmony,* p. [ii].
81. Neither tunebook contained many set-pieces or anthems. *Northern Harmony* had slightly more fuging-tunes.
82. *Columbian Harmony* includes thirty Core Repertory tunes, *Northern Harmony* only thirteen. Britton, Lowens, and Crawford, pp. 455, 526.
83. Single copies of *Northern Harmony* sold for seventy-five cents, *Columbian Harmony* for a dollar. The latter was the standard price for such popular tunebooks as *Village Harmony* and the *Bridgewater Collection. Portland Gazette,* VIII/20 (September 2, 1805), p. 3; VIII/34 (December 9, 1805), p. 3.
84. *Portland Gazette,* VIII/20 (September 2, 1805), p. 3.
85. See Part III for a listing of Robbins's tunes which were reprinted in Maine tunebooks of the period.

    According to Britton, Lowens, and Crawford (pp. 598–601), the only other tunebooks (prior to 1811) which contained tunes attributed to Robbins were the seventh through tenth editions of *Village Harmony* (1806, 1807, 1808, [1810]), which contained one Robbins tune (PSALM FIFTIETH) in each edition. No Robbins tunes appear in the later editions of *Village Harmony.*
86. Richard Crawford, "Holyoke, Samuel," in *The New Grove Dictionary of American Music,* 4 vols., ed. H. Wiley Hitchcock and Stanley Sadie (London: Macmillan Press, 1986), II, p. 414.
87. Wolfe (II, pp. 746–747) appears to draw the conclusion that he was a bandmaster from the contents of his *Drum and Fife Instructor.*

    Although experienced in military music, Robbins acknowledged assistance in writing the instructions for the drum. Since he did not say the same for the fife instructions, he must have known how to play the fife, thus my suggestion that he may have been a fife player in the band. The preface to his *Drum and Fife Instructor* stated: "But having been in personal practice in a part of Martial Music, for a number of years; and having applied to Mr. Branscome, of Hallowell, and some others of merit for instructions for the Drum—he flatters himself that the work will meet with some patronage from a candid public." Later on, he thanked those who had supplied him with music or instructions.

88. Charles Robbins, *Drum and Fife Instructor* (Exeter, NH: C. Norris & Co., 1812).
89. The ceremony was for receiving the Regimental Standards in the Eighth Division [of the Massachusetts Militia]. The Eighth Division included residents of such central Maine towns as Augusta, Hallowell, and Vassalboro. Robbins noted that the ceremony could be amended or excluded for other divisions of the militia with slightly different rites.
90. As the number of amateur instrumentalists grew in Maine during the early nineteenth century, various instrumental tutors and collections of instrumental music were produced, including Alvan Robinson, Jr.'s *Massachusetts Collection of Martial Musick* (1818) and Ezekiel Goodale's *Instrumental Director* (1819), both published by Goodale in Hallowell, Maine. Robbins's book was specifically written for military band musicians.
91. The title page of the latter indicated that the book would be sold by various bookstores in New England "and by the Author, at Winthrop." Robbins, *Drum and Fife Instructor,* p. [i].
92. According to its constitution, "The object of this society shall be to promote good morals and discountenance vice universally, particularly to discourage profaneness, idleness, gross breaches of the Sabbath, and intemperance." Thurston, pp. 144–145, 243.

    As will be discussed shortly, there were two Charles Robbinses living in Winthrop in 1820; however, the Charles Robbins who belonged to the society is probably the musician and former cabinetmaker. Deacon Joseph Metcalf, a cabinetmaker who may have been Charles's master, was also a member of the society. It seems likely that as a friend or father figure to his former apprentice, he encouraged Robbins's participation in the organization.
93. Thurston, p. 145. There may have been a connection between the Middlesex Convention and the Middlesex Musical Society, sponsor of an early reform tunebook, *The Middlesex Collection* (1807). At the very least, both organizations reflected reform sentiments in the Middlesex, Massachusetts, area. *The Middlesex Collection* eschewed fuging-tunes in favor of simpler plain tunes, considered more suitable for worship.
94. One of the earliest Maine reform tunebooks was *The Hallowell Collection of Sacred Music* (1817, 1819). The reform movement in sacred music is discussed in Chapter III.
95. Thurston, p. 244.
96. Mower, p. 60.
97. Merrill, pp. 516, 531–532.
98. *Ibid.,* p. 515.
99. *Ibid.,* p. 504. The only problem with this chronology is that the 1820

census lists two Charles Robbinses as heads of households in Winthrop, and no Charles Robbins in Greene. One of the Charles Robbinses had a family of four and was employed in agriculture; the other had a family of six and was employed in commerce. Based on an 1820 ad in the *Hallowell Gazette,* the latter apparently had a store.

Since the musical Charles Robbins, who died in 1842, kept a tavern in Greene for twenty years, he must have lived there by the early 1820s and is probably not one of the Charles Robbinses in Winthrop in 1820. It does not seem reasonable that he moved to Greene in 1816–17, returned to Winthrop by 1820, and then settled in Greene again within a year or two; it is more likely that he returned to Greene permanently by 1817 and was simply not counted in the census there in 1820.

Jackson, Teeples, and Schaefermeyer, *Maine 1820 Census Index,* p. 88. *Population Schedules of the 1820 Census,* microcopy no. 33, roll 35, p. 640.

100. One wonders if Supply Belcher offered him any advice on the tavern business. Belcher had been a tavern-keeper in Stoughton, Massachusetts, before moving to Maine.
101. For example, an 1812 singing school held in Portland met at "Folsom's Tavern." Cole, p. 31. See Chapter IV for more information on singing schools.
102. Their marriage intentions in August 1805 (no day given) are listed in Mower, p. 139.
103. Ronald Vern Jackson and Gary Ronald Teeples, eds., *Maine 1840 Census Index* (Bountiful, UT: Accelerated Indexing Systems, 1978), p. 157.
104. Mower, p. 250.
105. She died on March 19, 1871, age eighty-five. Henry Sewall Webster, *Vital Records of Gardiner, Maine, to the Year 1892. Part II, Marriages and Deaths* (Boston: Stanhope Press, 1915), p. 638.
106. Henry Sewall Webster, *Vital Records of Gardiner, Maine, to the Year 1892. Part I, Births* (Gardiner, ME: Reporter-Journal Press, 1914), p. 153; Webster, *Vital Records of Gardiner. Part II,* p. 638. Charles, Betsey (*sic*), and Charles A. are all buried in the Oak Grove Cemetery in Gardiner. The 1840 census record for the household of Charles A. Robbins of Gardiner does not list anyone of his parents' ages; however, after Charles died in 1842, Betsy may have gone to Gardiner to live with her son and his family.
107. Like many inland residents, Little supported the separation of Maine from Massachusetts and belonged to an evangelical denomination (Methodist). See Chapter II for a discussion of the typical ideological differences between inland and coastal residents.
108. A rather complete account of Little's life can be found in George

Thomas Little, *The Descendants of George Little, who came to Newbury, Massachusetts, in 1640* (Auburn, ME: Published by the author, 1882), pp. 215–216.

109. G. Little, pp. 83, 39n.
110. This supposition is based on the statement that "while a young man he suffered shipwreck on the island of Bermuda." *Ibid.,* p. 216. His employment as a seaman's apprentice could explain how he happened to be on a ship near Bermuda. Many New England ships sailed south to the British West Indies, as well as to southern United States ports, for trade purposes.
111. *Ibid.*
112. George Little says only that the shipwreck occurred while Henry was "a young man." I assume it took place before he moved to Maine, but it may not have.
113. Samuel lived in Bucksport until his death in 1846. He was a prominent citizen and represented the town at the state constitutional convention in 1819. G. Little, p. 214.
114. Henry Little, "An Account of Bucksport in 1827," *Bangor Historical Magazine,* VI/1–3 (July–September 1890), pp. 42–45.
115. He served as a lieutenant and captain in Lt. Col. Cobb's or McCobb's Regiment of the Massachusetts Militia. Virgil D. White, transcriber, *Index to War of 1812 Pension Files* (Waynesboro, TN: National Historical Publishing Co., 1989), II, p. 1187.
116. G. Little, pp. 215–216.
117. Three letters and a petition signed by Henry Little are among the William King Papers (Manuscript Collection 165, Maine Historical Society). Dated April 17, 1819 (Box 16/12), July 17, 1820 (Box 18/6), September 13 and 25, 1820 (Box 18/9), they indicate that Little supported the separation of Maine from Massachusetts, served as Bucksport's representative at a county convention which nominated a candidate for sheriff, and favored the court-martial of a fellow officer, Col. Hawse, for neglect of duty and conduct not befitting an officer and a gentleman. Glenn Skillin alerted me to these letters.
118. The son was born in 1818 and lost at sea in 1842 while performing hazardous duty; the first daughter died four months after birth in 1819; the second daughter was born in 1821. G. Little, pp. 215–216. D. Hoffman, *Bucksport Vital Records, Vol. I* ([Bangor]: Cay-Bel Publishing Co., [1980?]), p. 83.
119. J. W. Porter, "A Register of the Names of the Members of the Methodist Episcopal Church, in Orrington Circuit, A.D. 1819," *Bangor Historical Magazine,* I/2 (August 1885), p. 26. The records indicate those admitted to the church between 1796 and 1819.
120. Rev. W. H. Pilsbury, *History of Methodism in East Maine,* Book II (Augusta: Press of Charles E. Nash, 1887), pp. 92–93.

121. G. Little, p. 216.
122. His grandfather, Rev. Abner Bailey, was educated at Harvard. Harvard-educated ministers in the eighteenth century were typically Congregational, rather than Methodist.
123. Inexplicably, Henry's wife's name does not appear on the list of members of the local Methodist Episcopal Church, as of 1819. Her relatives on the list include Ephraim and Prudence Goodale (her parents) and Melinda [Goodale] and Simeon Fowler, Jr. (her aunt and uncle). Porter, pp. 23, 24, 26.

    Without knowing when Little and his wife became Methodists, it is impossible to suggest whether he may have met her through their common Methodist activities or whether he became a Methodist after becoming acquainted with her and her family.
124. Little, *Wesleyan Harmony,* p. [3].
125. *Ibid.*
126. These publishers included Henry Ranlet (*Village Harmony*), Isaiah Thomas (*The Worcester Collection*), and Ezekiel Goodale (*The Hallowell Collection of Sacred Music*). They acknowledged the assistance of unnamed musical advisors. See also the following section of this chapter.
127. While as many as six of the eleven unattributed tunes in the first edition might possibly be by Little, their tune names do not particularly suggest Maine origin. Of these tunes (ALBANY, ALLEGANY, BRIGHAM, NEWCASTLE, WESLEY, and an ISLE OF WIGHT which is a different tune than the Core Repertory tune of the same name), only Newcastle is the name of a Maine town. The tunes are in a simple style; their texts are generally not in Particular Meters. Only WESLEY is in an unusual meter (11.12.11.12.), suggesting (along with its name) that it was specifically written to fit a Methodist hymn.
128. The adapted tunes are DIRGE, CLARKE'S, FEVERSHAM, SUSSEX, VENTO'S PLYMOUTH, and BUCKSPORT (an adaptation of Jesser's SWITHINS).
129. In VENTO'S PLYMOUTH, for example, the phrase "in glory" is set so "in" and "-ry" (which should be unaccented syllables) are on the first beats of measures in 3/4 time. The tune is not included in the second edition. In Handel's DIRGE, the two syllables of "mercy" are separated by a quarter rest, producing an unmusical effect.
130. His rudiments section is only five pages long, compared to twenty-four pages for the one in Robbins's *Columbian Harmony,* for example. The church function is indicated on the title page, which states that the book is "a compilation of choice tunes for public worship."
131. Little, *Wesleyan Harmony,* p. 7.
132. "Every Choirester [*sic*] should have a *Pitchpipe,* or something by which he can pitch the tune correctly; this is of the greatest impor-

tance; and when there is none at hand, the pitch of a tune may be taken very nearly from the *lower line* in the *Bass*. Sound on the lower line and count up until you are in unison with the *Key Note,* from which the pitch of each part is to be taken." *Ibid.,* p. 8. It is unclear how one without perfect pitch or a pitch-sounding device would know where to sound the lower line of the bass.

133. *Ibid.,* p. [i].

134. See the following section in this chapter for information on the authorship of *The Hallowell Collection.*

More than half of the other tunes in *Wesleyan Harmony* (those not derived from *The Hallowell Collection)* are in Particular Meters; Little probably had to find these elsewhere than in *The Hallowell Collection.* Even if *The Hallowell Collection* was not used by Little as a source, *Wesleyan Harmony* would naturally include many of the same tunes since the compilers of both collections sought to include time-tested tunes by Europeans and exclude "trifling airs" and fuging-tunes.

135. Hallowell is about seventy miles from Bucksport by land. Both are river towns, however, and travel between them would be fairly easy by water (sailing down the Kennebec or Penobscot rivers, along the Maine coast, and then up the other river).

136. *Hallowell Gazette,* VII/7 (February 16, 1820), p. 3; VII/24 (June 14, 1820), p. 3.

137. Little, *Wesleyan Harmony,* pp. [131]-[134]. The geographical distribution of the subscribers is discussed in Chapter V.

138. Henry Little, *Wesleyan Harmony,* second edition (Hallowell, ME: Goodale, Glazier & Co., 1821), p. [3].

139. He became postmaster on July 13, 1816, according to records in the National Archives. He was replaced on January 15, 1830, although he apparently still lived in Bucksport in June 1830, since that was his residence for the 1830 census. Alice F. Buck, *Bucksport . . . Past and Present* (n.p.: n.p., 1951), p. 21; *Population Schedules of the Fifth Census of the United States, 1830* (Washington, DC: National Archives, 1946), microcopy no. 19, roll 47, p. 186.

Indexes of the Hancock County Registry of Deeds list a large number of real estate transactions involving Henry Little as grantor or grantee in the 1820s and 1830s, suggesting that, like Japheth Coombs Washburn, he may have been involved in land speculating.

140. G. Little, p. 216. Census reports for 1820 and 1830 also confirm Little's residence in Bucksport, county of Hancock. He is not named in the 1810 census, probably because only heads of households were listed by name; as an unmarried male of twenty-two in 1810, he was probably living at his brother Samuel's house and was counted with that household.

141. Edward Mitchell Blanding, compiler, *The City of Bangor* (Bangor: Bangor Board of Trade, 1899), p. 21.
142. The Henry Little household in 1850 consisted of Henry, his wife, their daughter, her husband (B. F. Nourse), the Nourses' four young children, and an Irish girl (perhaps a nanny). *Population Schedules of the 1850 Census,* microcopy no. 432, roll 264, p. 117.
143. G. Little, p. 216.
144. Griffin, p. 229.
145. J. Williamson, II, p. 508.
146. D. Goodwin, p. 25.
147. Edwards, p. 31.
148. Clark, II, pp. 347–348. He perpetuates Edwards's incorrect date of 1824 for the second edition of *The Hallowell Collection,* which was actually published in 1819.
149. The endorsement is quoted in Chapter IV, where the Handel Society of Maine is discussed.
150. See Chapter III for more information on the reform movement.
151. Crawford, " 'Ancient Music,' " p. 240.
152. *The Middlesex Collection of Church Music: or, Ancient Psalmody Revived* (Boston: Manning & Loring, 1807).
153. Metcalf, *American Writers,* p. 185.
154. See the following section on Goodale in this chapter.
155. Kroeger, "Worcester Collection," p. 66.
156. *Hallowell Collection,* p. [iii].
157. The tunebook is advertised in the *Hallowell Gazette,* IV/43 (October 22, 1817), p. 3. The singing school was to begin "this evening," according to an ad in the *Hallowell Gazette,* IV/45 (November 5, 1817), p. 3. The latter ad does not mention the name of the tunebook to be used.
158. D. Goodwin, p. 25.
159. *Ibid.,* pp. 4, 7, 25. William Allen, "Now and Then," in *Collections of the Maine Historical Society,* first series, 10 vols., VII (1876), p. 282.
160. The dictionary of musical terms includes such terms as "recitative," "rondeau," "siciliano," and "thorough bass." There is also a detailed discussion of scale construction, dealing with overlapping tetrachords and the relationship of keys adjacent to each other in the circle of fifths (although those terms are not used). The writer relates the "degrees" of the scale to a "tonic" and says other principal sounds are the dominant and subdominant. He or she also brings up a topic seldom mentioned in most tunebooks: which fa-sola syllables to use when accidentals result from a modulation.
161. As noted earlier, D. Goodwin (p. 25) stated that Merrick compiled the tunebook "in connection with" Mellen.
162. *Hallowell Gazette,* VI/6 (February 10, 1819), p. 3. Italics added.

163. *Hallowell Collection,* p. [iv].
164. The family homestead, located in Shrewsbury at the time, would now be within the boundaries of West Boylston (incorporated in 1808), if it were still standing. Although Metcalf (p. 185) states that Goodale was born in West Boylston, it would be more accurate to say that he was born in what is now West Boylston, since "West Boylston" did not exist in 1780.
165. Andrew H. Ward, *History of the Town of Shrewsbury, Massachusetts, from Its Settlement in 1717 to 1829* (Boston: Samuel G. Drake, 1847), p. 294; Leon A. Goodale, *Notes on the Lives of Edward and Sarah Temple Goodale, Pioneer Settlers of Shrewsbury, Massachusetts, 1738–1786* ([Worcester]: mimeographed, [1948]; located at the American Antiquarian Society), pp. 1–2; *Vital Records of Shrewsbury, Mass., to the End of the Year 1849* (Worcester: Franklin P. Rice, 1904), p. 41.
166. His brothers Ephraim and Enoch learned the bookbinding trade, if not at Thomas's firm, probably somewhere in the Worcester area. Later on, Ephraim was a bookbinder and farmer in Orrington, Maine; Enoch was a bookbinder, bookseller, and chemist in South Berwick and then Saco, Maine. Russell Cox, *History of Orrington, Maine,* genealogy by David L. Swett (n.p.: Cay-Bel Publishing Co., 1988), pp. 258–259. Glenn Skillin, "Goodale, Enoch," in *Bibliography of Printing in Maine Through 1820* (unpublished), biographical appendix.
167. Learning to set music type "apparently required no special musical ability and could be learned after only a short period of training," according to Karl Kroeger, in "Isaiah Thomas as a Music Publisher," *Proceedings of the American Antiquarian Society,* vol. 86, part 2 (1976), p. 329.
168. None of the sources consulted mentions Goodale's activities from birth to age twenty-two, when he came to Maine. The absence of Goodale's name among the few apprentices specifically named (for being paid overtime in 1796) in the miscellaneous business records of Thomas at the American Antiquarian Society does not entirely rule out the possibility that he may have worked for Thomas. Isaiah Thomas Papers (Special Collection at the American Antiquarian Society, Worcester, MA), Box 8 (1792–1806 Uncatalogued Business Records), Folder 1.

    Griffin apparently did not believe Goodale was trained as a printer: he writes (p. 229) that "Mr. Goodale was not a practical printer."
169. Allen, p. 283. Goodale's use of connections in Bath is suggested by a letter he wrote on February 25, 1807, to Charles Metcalf, a Bath bookseller. Goodale asks Metcalf to send his box of books

from onboard a certain vessel and to inquire about whether there is anything else for him on any other vessels from Boston. William King Papers, 1760–1834 (Manuscript Collection 165, Maine Historical Society), Box 6/10. I appreciate Glenn Skillin's calling this letter to my attention.

170. Metcalf's date of 1822 for Goodale's removal to Hallowell (p. 185) is obviously a misprint.
171. "Business Men of 50 Years Ago," *Hallowell Register,* VII/49 (January 3, 1885).
172. Ephraim's arrival in Orrington is variously dated as 1803, April 1806, and "after 1806." Listed as a head of household in Buckstown in the 1810 census, he appears under Orrington in the 1820 census because he lived in the part of Buckstown which was annexed to Orrington, according to his son-in-law, Henry Little, in "An Account of Bucksport in 1827," p. 43. See also Mitchell, Daggett, Walton, and Lawton, compilers, *The Town Register, 1907: Bucksport, Orland, Orrington, Verona* (Brunswick, ME: H. E. Mitchell Co., 1907), p. 188; H. B. Wright and E. D. Harvey, *The Settlement and Story of Oakham, Massachusetts,* 2 vols. (n.p.: n.p., 1947), II, pp. 728–729; Cox, p. 259.

    Melinda Goodale Fowler, the youngest sister of Ephraim and Ezekiel Goodale, also settled in Orrington, Maine, based on the 1810 baptismal record of her son. Cox, p. 164.
173. *Edes Kennebec Gazette* (Augusta), October 21, 1802, according to the American Antiquarian Society "authority card" for the Ezekiel Goodale printer file card. Griffin (p. 229) suggests that Goodale may have begun selling and binding books as early as 1800 and that he began printing and publishing as early as 1810. The actual commencement dates seem to have been a few years later in both cases.
174. "Business Men."
175. Nason, pp. 235, 243.
176. "Hallowell in the Olden Time, No. 4," *Hallowell Gazette,* December 12, 1863 (clipping pasted in *Memories of Hallowell Scrapbook,* Scrapbook no. 43, Hubbard Free Library, Hallowell, ME, p. 8).
177. Metcalf, p. 185; Nason, p. 243; "Business Men."
178. The Federalist political party, which favored a strong central government, had strong support in Massachusetts, while the opposing party, the Democratic-Republican party, was dominant in Maine after 1805. Many persons of high social standing, such as merchants, lawyers, Congregational ministers, and conservative persons generally, were Federalists; the bulk of the farmers as well as those who were poor or discontented were Republicans. Griffin, p. 88; Fassett, pp. 181–182; Hatch, I, pp. 68, 70.
179. Clarence S. Brigham, *History and Bibliography of American*

Newspapers, 1690–1820 (Worcester: American Antiquarian Society, 1947), I, p. 203.

180. *Hallowell Gazette,* II/34 (August 23, 1815), p. 3.
181. *Ibid.,* V/1 (January 7, 1818), p. 3.
182. Title pages of the seventh, eighth, and tenth editions of *Village Harmony* (1806, 1807, [1810]) indicate that the books were "sold also by" Ezekiel Goodale, Hallowell. Britton, Lowens, and Crawford, pp. 598, 599, 601.
183. Griffin, p. 229.
184. Born in 1793 in Newmarket, New Hampshire, Masters began his apprenticeship at age thirteen (c. 1806). Charles Norris had been the partner of Exeter printer Henry Ranlet, until the latter's death in 1807. Griffin, p. 229; Nason; p. 247; Glenn Skillin, "Masters, Andrew," in *Bibliography of Printing in Maine Through 1820,* appendix; N. Merrill, p. 254.
185. Washburn's *Parish Harmony* (1813) and Hartwell's *Chorister's Companion* (1815) were printed by C. Norris & Co.
186. *Hallowell Gazette,* I/3 (March 9, 1814), p. 1. A later ad for *The Hallowell Collection,* published by Goodale in 1817, indicates that it was "printed on a fine paper and new type," probably referring to the music type he had purchased several years earlier.
187. His publications also included hymnbooks (sacred texts without music), such as *Songs of Zion* (second edition, 1818; third edition, 1819) by local resident Moses Springer, Jr.; secular music books such as Alvan Robinson, Jr.'s *Massachusetts Collection of Martial Music* (1818); numerous sermons and addresses; a quarterly periodical entitled *The Christian Monitor;* and a District of Maine map. One of his earliest publications (1811), printed by Peter Edes in Augusta, was a collection of song texts entitled *The Musical Repertory. A Selection of the Most Approved Ancient and Modern Songs in Four Parts.*
188. Glazier was the son of Ezekiel's sister, Dorothy, and her husband, John Glazier. Griffin, p. 229; "Business Men"; Printer File Card for Franklin Glazier, American Antiquarian Society, Worcester, MA.
189. Goodale's death four years later at age forty-seven suggests that he may have left the business for health reasons. Subsequent forms of his firm, which continued into the late nineteenth century, included "Glazier and Co." "Glazier, Masters and Co.," "Masters, Smith and Co." and "Masters and Livermore." Printer File Cards for Ezekiel Goodale and Franklin Glazier, American Antiquarian Society, Worcester, MA; "Business Men"; Griffin, p. 229.
190. Oakham is in Worcester County, west of Worcester, West Boylston, and Shrewsbury.

191. It is not clear where they were married. Their marriage intentions were recorded in Oakham on January 13, 1804, according to J. Gardner Bartlett, *Gregory Stone Genealogy* (Boston: published for the Stone Family Association, 1918), p. 308. An 1804 marriage (along with a bracketed intention date of March 3), however, is listed for them in the Hallowell vital records. Mabel Goodwin Hall, ed., *Vital Records of Hallowell, Maine, to the Year 1892,* 6 vols. (Auburn, ME: Merrill & Webber Co., 1924–1929), III, p. 65. Still another source (Wright and Harvey, II, p. 729) gives their marriage date as May 3, 1804, without stating where it occurred.
192. W. B. Lapham, "Hallowell Records," in *Collections and Proceedings of the Maine Historical Society,* second series (Portland: n.p., 1895), VI, pp. 95–96; Hall, III, p. 65; V, p. 216; L. Goodale, p. [70].
193. *Pew Records of the South Parish Church, Hallowell, 1794–1838* (Churches, Book 163, Hubbard Free Library, Hallowell, ME); *Manual of the [South] Congregational Church, Hallowell, Maine, 1790–1873* (Hallowell, ME: Masters & Livermore, 1873). Goodale's ownership of a pew does not necessarily imply he was a member. As an institution supported by the taxpayers of Hallowell, the Hallowell church was probably required to allow any of the town's citizens to buy a pew, regardless of whether they were members of the church. Perhaps his wife's membership also gave him the right to buy a pew.
194. *Old South Congregational Church Sabbath School, 1820–1825* (manuscript at the Hubbard Free Library, Hallowell, ME), pp. 4, 7, 9, and unnumbered page; Page, pp. 30–32.
195. "Hallowell in the Olden Time, No. 4."
196. The exception to the rule was Henry Little, who lived in Bucksport in eastern Maine. His familial tie to Goodale, through his wife, offset the geographical distance between Bucksport and Hallowell.

Notes for Chapter X

1. Washburn, *Parish Harmony,* p. [3].
2. The sixteenth edition of *Village Harmony* (1819), containing 350 pages, sold for $8.50 per dozen in 1822, according to an advertisement in *Hallowell Gazette,* IX/40 (October 2, 1822), p. 3. The considerably smaller *Parish Harmony,* which was less than half the size of the *Village Harmony* edition, was advertised at 50 cents a copy and $6 per dozen in *Hallowell Gazette,* I/40 (November 23, 1814), p. 3, and II/7 (February 15, 1815), p. 3.
3. Hartwell, p. [3].
4. Little, *Wesleyan Harmony,* p. [3].

5. *Hallowell Gazette,* VII/7 (February 16, 1820), p. 3. Once published, the price was slightly higher (62½ cents, single), but still on the low side for tunebooks. The selling price was even less a few years later (1822 and 1824) when *Wesleyan Harmony* was advertised at $3.50 per dozen, a cost of less than 30 cents a copy. *Hallowell Gazette,* VII/24 (June 14, 1820), p. 3; IX/40 (October 2, 1822), p. 3; XI/37 (September 15, 1824), p. 3.
6. See Chapter III for a discussion on the use of anthems in special services.
7. Washburn, *Parish Harmony,* p. [3].
8. Robbins, *Columbian Harmony,* p. [iii].
9. The publications of both William Billings and Andrew Law included books intended for a particular purpose and directed toward a specific clientele. For example, Billings's *Music in Miniature* (1779) was a tune supplement containing plain tunes for congregational singing. His *Psalm-Singer's Amusement* (1781), like Law's *Collection of Hymn Tunes* (1783), was intended not for beginners, but specifically for accomplished singers. McKay and Crawford, p. 110; Crawford, *Andrew Law,* p. 35.
10. This idea is suggested by Richard Crawford in an essay entitled "William Billings (1746–1800) and American Psalmody: A Study of Musical Dissemination," in *The American Musical Landscape* (Berkeley: University of California Press, 1993), pp. 146–147. He notes that the nineteen Billings tunes selected from *The Singing Master's Assistant* to be reprinted in Simeon Jocelin's *Chorister's Companion* (1782) represent a balanced cross-section of meters and styles of declamation found in eighteenth-century Anglo-American psalmody. He proposes that Jocelin chose the tunes (which cover all but one meter in the hymnbook) because they met his need for tunes of various meters.
11. Japheth Coombs Washburn, *The Temple Harmony,* fourth edition (Hallowell, ME: Goodale, Glazier & Co., 1823), p. [3].
12. Little, *Wesleyan Harmony,* pp. [3], [1]. The tunebook's usefulness to other denominations rested in the fact that a substantial number of tunes were in the usual Common, Short, and Long Meters in which most hymns and psalms were written.
13. Maxim, *Northern Harmony*/2, p. [2].
14. Abraham Maxim and Japheth C. Washburn, *The Northern Harmony,* fourth edition (Hallowell, ME: E. Goodale, 1816), p. [2]. Because the contents of the preface were transcribed from an oral reading over the telephone, the spelling or punctuation may vary slightly from the original. The bracketed word has been supplied; the page is torn where it would have been printed.
15. See Chapter XII for a comparison of the tunebooks, according to percentage of fuging-tunes selected.

16. Japheth Coombs Washburn, *The Temple Harmony* (Hallowell, ME: E. Goodale and J. C. Washburn, Esq., 1818), p. [2].
17. Washburn, *Parish Harmony,* p. 3.
18. *Hallowell Collection,* p. iii.
19. *Ibid.*
20. Crawford, "'Ancient Music,'" pp. 232–233.
21. See the section entitled "The Church Music Repertory" in Chapter III for more information on the reform movement.

Notes for Chapter XI

1. The practice of prefacing sacred tunebooks with musical instruction had begun in England in the late seventeenth century and continued into the eighteenth century. In 1721, the first American books to combine a discussion of music fundamentals with a collection of psalm- and hymn-tunes were published. They were the work of Rev. John Tufts and Rev. Thomas Walter, leaders in the movement to improve congregational singing.
2. See Chapter IV for more information on singing schools.
3. Allen P. Britton, "Theoretical Introductions in American Tunebooks to 1800" (Ph.D. dissertation, University of Michigan, 1949).
4. Several of the extant tunebooks contain essentially the same theoretical introduction as an earlier edition of the same work. The ten different theoretical introductions may be grouped as follows: 1) *Oriental Harmony* (1802), 2) the first and second editions of *Northern Harmony* (1805, 1808), 3) the fourth and fifth editions of *Northern Harmony* (1816, 1819), 4) *Columbian Harmony* (1805), 5) *Parish Harmony* (1813), 6) *Chorister's Companion* (1815), 7) the two editions of *The Hallowell Collection* (1817, 1819), 8) the first and second editions of *Temple Harmony* (1818, 1820), 9) the third, fourth and sixth editions of *Temple Harmony* (1821, 1823, 1826), and 10) the two editions of *Wesleyan Harmony* (1820, 1821).
5. Complete citations are as follows: Jeremiah Ingalls, *The Christian Harmony; or Songster's Companion* (Exeter, NH: Henry Ranlet, for the compiler, 1805; repr. New York: Da Capo Press, 1981); Bartholomew Brown, A.M., and others, *Bridgewater Collection of Sacred Musick,* third edition (Boston: Thomas & Andrews; J. West & Co., 1810); *The Village Harmony: or New-England Repository of Sacred Musick,* fourteenth edition (Boston: West & Richardson, [1817]); [Lowell Mason], *The Boston Handel and Haydn Society Collection of Church Music* (Boston: Richardson & Lord, 1822; repr. New York: Da Capo Press, 1973). Mason, to whom reference is made in the preface of the last work, is generally considered to be its compiler, although his name does not appear on the title page.

6. Some of the tunebooks (including *Oriental Harmony, Northern Harmony*/5, and *Chorister's Companion*) use the older term "cliff" instead of "clef." According to Britton (pp. 174–175), the terms were not synonymous. "Cliff" was "a generic term for any sign which serves to assign a definite pitch to a definite degree of the staff."
7. The music in the extant Maine tunebooks from 1813 and before uses a C clef for the counter part; the tunebooks from 1816 and after employ a G clef and notate the part an octave above pitch. Hartwell's *Chorister's Companion* (1815) shows a transitional practice. Hartwell (p. [4]) notes that the C clef ("cliff") is commonly used for the counter, but that the G clef is sometimes used. Examples of both can be found in the tunes of his collection.
8. Little (*Wesleyan Harmony,* p. [4]), for example, indicates that while the C clef was formerly used for the counter, "modern Musicians" use only the G clef for that part.
9. Mason (pp. ix–x) describes the proper clef usage as consisting of a C clef on the third line for the highest men's voices (i.e., the counters or altos) and a C clef on the fourth line for the middle voices of men (the tenors), with the treble clef used for female voices. In this collection, however, he uses the treble clef for all three upper voices, explaining on p. xi: "In many late publications, the C Clef has been omitted, and the F and G Clefs only have been used; the latter being appropriated (though improperly) to the Tenor and Alto as well as to the Treble. This use of the G Clef has been necessarily adopted in the present work."
10. Although a few churches in southern Maine had organs by 1810, the first organs did not appear in central Maine churches until the early 1820s. When available, they were used to guide and reinforce the vocalists. See Chapter III.
11. *Hallowell Collection,* p. 2.
12. Like Ingalls's *Christian Harmony* (1805) and *Village Harmony*/14 ([1817]), most of the Maine books (all except *Columbian Harmony, Parish Harmony,* and *The Hallowell Collection*) use the spelling "faw" and "law," instead of the "fa" and "la" used in the *Bridgewater Collection*/3 (1810), *The Boston Handel and Haydn Society Collection* (1822), and other tunebooks. The Maine compilers probably used the spelling they had learned, but may also have added the ending letter "w" to suggest the correct pronunciation. Mi is spelled "me" in *Northern Harmony,* first and second editions, and in *Parish Harmony.* Britton (p. 195), in his discussion of solmization in eighteenth-century tunebooks, notes that the spellings "faw" and "law" were most frequently found in tunebooks issued toward the end of the century (and presumably beyond), "especially in those works which feature music in the American idiom."

13. Hartwell's *Chorister's Companion* is the only Maine tunebook to extend the chart to five sharps and flats. None of the tunes has a key signature exceeding four sharps or flats, though.
14. In *Columbian Harmony* (p. 7), Charles Robbins gives an example of six measures, each filled with a different type and number of notes, depending on their time value: a measure containing one semibreve, another with thirty-two demisemiquavers, etc.
15. The trill is first discussed in the 1813 *Parish Harmony* and becomes a standard item in all the Maine tunebooks from 1817 and later; the appoggiatura is defined in the 1805 *Columbian Harmony*, but not again until the 1815 *Chorister's Companion.*
16. Britton, p. 277.
17. Karl Kroeger, "Performance Practice in Early American Psalmody," in *The Complete Works of William Billings,* 4 vols. (Boston: American Musicological Society and Colonial Society of Massachusetts, 1990), IV, p. lvii.
18. *Village Harmony*/14, p. 9.
19. *Hallowell Collection,* p. 3.
20. The scarcity of notated graces in the earlier music does not imply that they were never performed. The practice of embellishing tunes with various ornaments dates back to the "Old Way of Singing" of the late seventeenth and early eighteenth centuries. Britton (p. 279) suggests that eighteenth-century performers supplied graces according to their taste, whether written in the music or not. Certain ornaments, such as notes of transition, were rarely notated but commonly performed. In *Columbian Harmony* (p. 18), Robbins gives an example of an unembellished phrase and suggests how it should be performed with notes of transition added.
21. Only three tunes in *Oriental Harmony* (1802), for example, include appoggiaturas or trills. On the other hand, such embellishments are quite common in *The Hallowell Collection* (1817).
22. Kroeger ("Performance Practice," p. lx) associates the appoggiatura with the so-called Methodist tunes in fast duple, rather than triple, meters.
23. Only exceptionally do fuging-tunes in the Maine tunebooks include appoggiaturas or trills. Declamatory duple tunes, as defined by Crawford in *Core Repertory* (pp. xiv–xvi), are discussed in Chapter XIII in connection with representative fuging-tunes by the Maine composers.
24. Robbins, *Columbian Harmony,* p. 8.
25. "If one Measure ends, and the next begins with the same Note, the accidental Character which alters the first note, is understood to affect the second." *Hallowell Collection,* p. 2.
26. In Holyoke's instructions, however, the accidentals do not extend to the first note in the next measure: "When accidental Flats,

Sharps, or Naturals appear in any bar, they influence the letter in that bar only. If there be a necessity for using them in a succeeding bar, they are again inserted." Samuel Holyoke, *Vocal Companion* (Exeter, NH: Norris & Sawyer, 1807), p. 8.

27. Britton, p. 265.
28. "Moods of time," apparently the earlier term, is found in the Maine tunebooks published in 1808 or before. "Modes of time" is used in *Parish Harmony* (1813) and tunebooks from 1816 and later.
29. The beat is equal to a second in both the first and third modes of common time; however, in the third mode, the minim (half note) rather than the crotchet (quarter note) has the value of one beat.
30. Only four tunes in *Parish Harmony* fall outside his explanation: three in the second mode of triple time (3/4) and one in the second mode of compound time (6/8). Fully 89 percent of the tunes in Maxim's *Northern Harmony*/2 (1808) and 75 percent of those in Hartwell's *Chorister's Companion* (1815) are in modes of time covered by Washburn's abbreviated description.
31. See Chapter IX for more information on the possible relationship between Robbins and Belcher.
32. Most also say that the beat is equal to one second in the third mood of common time.
33. Only rarely would most singers be required to set the tempo of a tune; usually they would simply follow the one established by their singing master or chorister.
34. *The Cumberland Melodist; or, A Choice Selection of Plain Tunes* (Philadelphia: William M'Culloch for John M'Carrell [Shippensburg, PA], 1804), p. 12.
35. For the first and third modes of common time and the first mode of both triple and compound time, Robbins, like most other compilers who give pendulum lengths, says the length should be $39\frac{2}{10}$ inches. Ingalls suggests the unusual lengths of $37\frac{2}{10}$ inches for the first and third modes of common time and the first mode of triple time and 40 inches for the first mode of compound time. For the third mode of triple time (3/8), the lengths are stated as $5\frac{1}{21}$ (probably a misprint of $5\frac{1}{2}$) inches by Robbins, $5\frac{1}{2}$ by Ingalls. Both Robbins and Ingalls list a length of $12\frac{4}{10}$ inches for the fourth mode of common time, indicating a slower tempo than the one advised by William Billings, who, in *The Singing Master's Assistant*, names $9\frac{8}{10}$ inches as the pendulum length for that mode. Robbins may have decided to include the pendulum lengths because they are included in the theoretical introduction of *The Harmony of Maine* by Supply Belcher, who may have been his teacher.
36. Maxim, *Oriental Harmony*, p. vii.
37. Abraham Maxim, *The Northern Harmony*, fifth edition (Hallowell, ME: E. Goodale, 1819), pp. 8, 10.

38. Britton, p. 217.
39. Maxim, *Northern Harmony*/5, p. 9.
40. *Hallowell Collection,* pp. 4–6.
41. According to Britton (p. 231), the minor scale with raised intervals in the ascending form was not taught in eighteenth-century theoretical introductions.
42. Mason (p. xxii) does note, however, that his comments on these topics "perhaps rather more properly belong to musical science than to the mere art of learning to sing." For that reason, there was no particular need to include them in tunebooks.
43. The dictionary of musical terms on p. [iv] of *The Hallowell Collection* includes terms such as "recitative" ("kind of musical recitation between speaking and singing") and "thorough bass" ("the instrumental Bass, with figures for the Organ"). Although none of the tunes in the collection has a figured bass (those in Mason's collection do), the compiler was apparently familiar with the concept.
44. Little, *Wesleyan Harmony,* p. 7.
45. Maxim, *Oriental Harmony,* p. viii.
46. Hartwell, p. 12; Robbins, *Columbian Harmony,* p. 16.
47. These four steps are listed in the discussion of singing schools in Chapter IV.
48. *Village Harmony*/14, p. 9.
49. See Moses Cheney's account of his first night at singing school (in 1788) in Chapter IV. Buechner, who quotes extensively from Cheney's account, wrestles with the question of how successful singing masters were at teaching their students to read music. He concludes that "most singing masters were forced to make a compromise between their own interest in teaching the rudiments and their scholars' interest in learning tunes 'by word.' " As a result, students often became musically literate only after attending a number of singing schools over a period of years. Buechner, pp. 250–253.
50. *Village Harmony*/14, p. 9.
51. *Ibid.*
52. The eyewitness account of Moses Cheney, a New Hampshire singing-school student in 1788, includes a description of this process. Buechner, pp. 134–139.
53. The exercises are in C major and the keys of one to four flats and sharps; they include the four modes of common time, three modes of triple time, and two modes of compound time. Robbins's source may have been Jacob French's *Psalmodist's Companion* (Worcester: Leonard Worcester for Isaiah Thomas, 1793), which similarly includes nine four-part lessons in different keys and modes. While only lessons II and VIII are identical (or nearly so) between the two collections, each of Robbins's exercises is written in the same key signature and mode of time as French's.

54. "Passages, where Syncopation takes place, are better explained by the Instructor, than by words; for this reason, an explanation is here omitted." *Village Harmony*/14, p. 9.
55. Hartwell, p. 9.
56. Robbins's treatment of concords and discords, pp. 13–14, is virtually identical to that found in the first five editions of *The Worcester Collection,* whose earlier source, according to Kroeger, "Worcester Collection" (p. 655), was Tans'ur's *Royal Melody Compleat,* p. 12. Robbins's next section, entitled "Scale of Semitones," coincides with the next section in *The Worcester Collection,* whose source is Read's *American Singing Book,* pp. 8, 18, according to Kroeger (pp. 657–658). Robbins's immediate source may have been Belcher's *Harmony of Maine,* which prints *The Worcester Collection*'s introduction.
57. Ingalls's chart separates the "perfect cords" (unisons and fifths) from the "imperfect cords" (thirds and sixths) and "discords" (seconds, fourths, and sevenths). While Robbins's chart divides the intervals only into concords and discords, his text makes a similar distinction between perfect and imperfect "cords."
58. His suggestion is to "invert" the names of the notes, calling them according to the cadence for which they are preparing. When fa is consistently raised by sharps, call it mi and the notes above and below it (fa and la) accordingly. When mi is consistently lowered by flats, call it fa, and the notes above and below it (sol and mi) accordingly. *Hallowell Collection,* p. 6.
59. Britton, pp. 195–198. He cites Holyoke's *Columbian Repository* ([1803]) as one that does.
60. The theoretical introductions written by Japheth Coombs Washburn between 1813 and 1826 do not differ significantly in content and method of presentation, although the rudiment sections of his middle and late tunebooks are more detailed and contain more practice exercises than the abbreviated introduction printed in his earliest tunebook.
61. For no apparent reason, the material in these tunebooks, like that in his first one, is not divided into lessons and uses the earlier terminology of "cliff" and "mi" (instead of "clef" and "me").
62. He uses "point of addition" instead of "point" and "point of diminution" instead of "figure 3."
63. Previously, he wrote that the beat in the second mode of common time was "a little quicker" than in the first mode; here, he says the beat for the second mode is three-quarters of a second, compared to a second per beat in the first mode. In addition, the third mode of common time is no longer quicker than the second mode, as in his 1805 and 1808 tunebooks, but has one second to a beat (the same as the

first mode, although the minim is the unit instead of the semibreve). There are other differences in relative tempi in the other modes.

Notes for Chapter XII

1. See Chapter I for definitions of the principal genres of American psalmody. See Davenport, "Maine's Sacred Tunebooks," pp. 405–426, for tables which show how many tunes of each genre and nationality are in each tunebook.
2. The one earlier Maine tunebook, Supply Belcher's *Harmony of Maine* (1794), is similarly restricted to tunes by Belcher. See Chapter VI for more information on this collection.

   As has been suggested previously, Maxim may have chosen to include tunes by a variety of composers in his later works to provide a larger volume with greater appeal to potential purchasers.
3. Crawford, " 'Ancient Music,' " pp. 225–255.
4. Maxim, *Northern Harmony*/2, p. [2].
5. Compared to NH05, NH08 contains eighteen additional tunes with extension and seventeen fuging-tunes, but only ten more plain tunes.
6. A third edition of Maxim's *Northern Harmony* was published in 1810, but no copies have been located. It would be interesting to know if Maxim's views had changed any by 1810. The extant, but incomplete, copies of the fourth and fifth editions (1816 and 1819) suggest that each succeeding edition contained a smaller percentage of fuging-tunes and American tunes.
7. See Chapter II for a summary of the political events of this era. Restrictions on the shipping trade had an effect not only on the coastal and river towns but also on the new inland settlements, whose residents were dependent on shippers to obtain goods they could not grow or make.
8. Those not owning tunebooks may have used manuscript compilations, consisting of favorite tunes copied out by hand.
9. *Parish Harmony* sold for 50 cents a copy, about half the price of many of the larger books. *Chorister's Companion* was 75 cents per copy. *Hallowell Gazette,* I/40 (November 23, 1814), p. 3; III/2 (January 10, 1816), p. 3.
10. Crawford, " 'Ancient Music,' " pp. 244–245.
11. Washburn, *Parish Harmony,* p. [3].
12. *Ibid.*
13. Maxim and Washburn, *Northern Harmony*/4, p. [2].
14. He expresses an aversion to "the volatile and fugeing style which has characterised so much of our modern compositions," in Hartwell, p. [3].

15. Fuging-tunes were apparently becoming less frequent in church services in southern Maine at least. An address delivered to a musical society in North-Yarmouth in 1812 noted that "we cannot but rejoice that fuging tunes are hopefully going out of use in divine worship. However pleasing and suitable they may be in singing companies for amusement, they are far from being desirable, in a mixed congregation of devout worshippers, and in our opinion, the sooner they are *entirely* done with there, the better. In all religious societies which have the best music, they are laid aside." Mitchell, p. 8.
16. Washburn, *Parish Harmony,* p. [3].
17. While several of the Maine tunebooks include as many anthems as Hartwell's, none contains as many set-pieces. The five anthems are for four different occasions (Fast Day, funerals, ordinations, and Thanksgiving); several of the twelve set-pieces also refer to particular occasions. One is for Independence Day, another is an ode "Introductory to a Sacred Concert," and still another is a Masonic ode, presumably intended for Masonic gatherings. Nine of the extended pieces are by American composer Oliver Holden, while at least six are by Hartwell himself.
18. In Massachusetts, the reform movement effected change quickly, rather than gradually. Crawford, " 'Ancient Music,' " p. 237.
19. Although the statistics for NH19 reflect an incomplete copy, lacking approximately half the contents, I expect that ratios derived from a complete copy would be fairly similar in terms of nationality.
20. See Chapter XII, note 51, for more information on these similarities.
21. Japheth Coombs Washburn, *The Temple Harmony* (Hallowell, ME: E. Goodale & J. C. Washburn, Esq., 1818), p. [2].
22. *Ibid.*
23. The fifty-eight fuging-tunes in TH18 and TH20 may be classified as follows, by mode and meter: nine major mode and fifteen minor mode in Common Meter, six major and seven minor in Short Meter, nine major and five minor in Long Meter, three minor in Hallelujah Meter, two major in Particular Meter, one minor in Long Particular Meter, and one minor in Short Particular Meter, for a total of twenty-six in major mode, thirty-two in minor mode.
24. The Methodist style originated with tunes written for the English Methodists in the mid-eighteenth century. Many such tunes were included in such collections as the Magdalen Collection and the Lock Hospital Collection, which were written for English hospital chapels. Nicholas Temperley, *The Music of the English Parish Church,* 2 vols. (Cambridge: Cambridge University Press, 1979), I, pp. 210–211.

25. [Martin Madan], *A collection of psalm and hymn tunes never published before . . . To be had at the Lock Hospital* (London: Lock Hospital, [1769]).
26. For example, Aaron Williams, *The Universal Psalmodist* (London: the author, 1763; second edition, London: Joseph Johnson, 1764).
27. *The Tocsin* (Hallowell, ME), May 10, 1796, p. 3. Handel himself, incidentally, is represented by twelve tunes in the same collection, as befitting a volume endorsed by the Handel Society of Maine.
28. McKay and Crawford, p. 229.
29. Richard J. Wolfe, *Early American Music Engraving and Printing* (Urbana: University of Illinois Press, 1980), pp. 189–192.
30. Crawford, " 'Ancient Music,' " pp. 228–229, 237.
31. *Hallowell Collection,* p. [iii].
32. Endorsement by Manly Hardy in Little, *Wesleyan Harmony,* p. [3].
33. Crawford, " 'Ancient Music,' " pp. 239–240.
34. Many of the tunes which are unattributed are not found in the earlier Maine tunebooks, suggesting that they may represent a new repertory popular in the 1820s or new tunes by Washburn (see Chapter VIII, note 66).
35. At least the first part of UNION HYMN, for example, appears to be based on Billings's SAVANNAH. Not all of Billings's tunes lack attributions, however; nine tunes are attributed to Billings in TH26.
36. These proportions are similar to those noted for seven of the eight editions of *The Worcester Collection*. Except for the third edition of *The Worcester Collection,* where Particular Meter texts are most numerous, the other editions feature more Common Meter texts than any others, followed by Long Meter, Particular Meter, and Short Meter texts, in that order. Kroeger, "Worcester Collection," pp. 237–238.
37. Seven of the ninety-two tunes (8 percent) are in Particular Meter; forty-two tunes (46 percent) are in Common Meter.
38. The Methodist Hymn Book, originally entitled *A Collection of Hymns for the Use of the People Called Methodists,* was first published in London in 1780 and was soon adopted for the singing of Methodist congregations. The 525 hymns which it contained were taken from previous publications of John and Charles Wesley and were written primarily by members of the Wesley family. Benson, pp. 236–237. Henry Little, in the preface to *Wesleyan Harmony* (p. [3]), notes that there are about 250 Particular Meter hymns in the Methodist Hymn Book.
39. HC17 contains only slightly fewer Particular Meter than Long Meter texts, while HC19 contains the same number of texts in Long and Particular Meters. A European connection has been suggested as a possible cause for the greater proportion of Particular Meter

settings in a non-Maine tunebook: the third edition of *The Worcester Collection*. Karl Kroeger suggests that the inclusion of more Particular Meter settings in this edition than in other editions of the work may have been due to the continental European background of the edition's compiler, Hans Gram, who would have been familiar with the variety of poetic meters used in the Lutheran and Reformed churches. Kroeger, "Worcester Collection," p. 237 n. 33.

40. One would have to examine the corpus of European psalmody to determine if, in fact, three-voice settings were more common among European composers. There are several reasons why composers might arrange a tune for three voices. Eighteenth-century composers accustomed to writing instrumental trio sonatas may have wanted to approximate a similar texture in a choral composition by writing two high melodic lines accompanied by a bass line. Biblical precedent may also have been a factor. Not only was the number three considered perfect (because of its association with the Trinity), but David appointed three singers in his temple (see I Chronicles 15:19).

41. The three-voice settings in WH20, for example, represent a variety of styles, with fewer than a quarter of them containing the features that Crawford (*Core Repertory,* p. xiv) describes as characteristic of tunes in the Methodist-inspired "decorated duple" style. Nearly half of the three-voice settings in WH20 are in triple meters. In most cases, the melody is written for the middle (tenor) voice, rather than the top voice.

42. AUGUSTA was printed in the sixth through tenth editions of *Village Harmony* (1803–1810), TURNER in the seventh through ninth (1806–1808). As a fuging-tune, TURNER was probably omitted from the tenth edition of *Village Harmony* to make room for the core of "ancient tunes" in a simpler style which were becoming an important part of the collection. As a tune with extension, AUGUSTA was allowed to remain. See Crawford, "'Ancient Music,'" pp. 244–245.

43. Declamatory duple tunes are usually in 2/2 time, with half-note motion disrupted by quarter notes. Usually made up of two contrasting sections, such tunes frequently feature more vigorous motion, often in the form of repeated quarter notes, and/or textural change in one of the sections (usually the second). Crawford, *Core Repertory,* pp. xiv–xvi.

44. The text is Isaac Watts's Psalm 50, a Particular Meter text (10.10.10.10.11.11.) which was frequently set by American psalmodists. See Chapter XIII for a discussion of Robbins's setting, which was reprinted in the seventh through tenth editions of *Village Harmony* (1806–1810) as well as in NH05 and NH08.

45. The tunes printed in all the Group I tunebooks except OH02 are COMPLAINT, CONFIDENCE, *CORONATION, DEANFIELD, *DENMARK, DEVOTION, *ENFIELD, GRAFTON, HINSDALE, *JORDAN, *LENOX, *LISBON, *MILFORD, MOUNT-VERNON, *NEW JERUSALEM, NEWBERG, NEWPORT, NORTHFIELD, PENNSYLVANIA, PSALM FIFTIETH (by Robbins), SMITHFIELD, and SUMNER (by Maxim). Starred tunes are Core Repertory tunes.
46. See Chapter III, p. 00 and note 108, for a definition of the Core Repertory.
47. The only two European tunes, DENMARK by Martin Madan and MILFORD by Stephenson, are among the Core Repertory. More than half of the shared tunes are fuging-tunes.
48. The tunes printed in all the Group II tunebooks are *AYLESBURY, *BANGOR, *BUCKINGHAM, CHINA (by Swan), *COLCHESTER, *LISBON, *LITTLE MARLBOROUGH, *MEAR, MORETON, *OLD HUNDRED, PARIS, *PLYMOUTH, PLYMPTON, POLAND, *PUTNEY, *ST. MARTIN'S, SUFFOLK, *SUTTON, *WANTAGE, and *WELLS. Starred tunes are Core Repertory tunes.
49. The 114 tunes found in all three Group III tunebooks include 29 by Maine composers (24 by Maxim, 3 by Washburn, and one each by Belcher and Robbins), 23 by other Americans, 58 by Europeans, and 4 by composers of unknown nationality. The Core Repertory tunes are ALL SAINTS, ANGELS' SONG, BATH, CANTERBURY, COLCHESTER-NEW, DENMARK, DUNSTAN, ENFIELD, HABAKKUK, HOTHAM, IRISH, JORDAN, LISBON, MAJESTY, MEAR, MIDDLETOWN, OLD HUNDRED, PORTUGAL, ST. ANN'S, ST. GEORGE'S, ST. MARTIN'S, SHERBURNE, SUTTON, WELLS, WESTON FAVEL, and WINTER.
50. An ad for NH19 states that the edition contains 280 pages. *Hallowell Gazette,* IX/40 (October 2, 1822), p. 3. The extant copy of NH19 in the Library of Congress ends with page 142 and is defective since it lacks pp. 129–138 and contains two different sets of pages numbered 121–128 (one of the sets is identical to pp. 273–280 in TH18 and TH20). Washburn's TH18 and TH20 were somewhat larger than NH19, with 301 and 309 pages, respectively.
51. Pages 17–32, 49–112, and 139–142, which encompass 105 tunes, are the same in each of the three tunebooks. In addition, pages 121–128 of NH19, containing 6 tunes, are identical to pp. 273–280 of TH18 and TH20. Three other tunes shared by the editions, but on different pages, are LISBON, OHIO, and ANGELS' SONG, located on pp. 42, 47, and 120 in NH19, and on pp. 149, 250, and 129 in TH18 and TH20.
52. Except for COLUMBUS (located on page 11 in both NH16 and NH19), all the tunes common to both NH16 and the Group III collections are on different pages in the Group III tunebooks than in NH16, ruling

out the possibility that large chunks of NH16 were simply reprinted, unchanged, for the later Maxim and Washburn editions.

53. Tunes found in all Group II and III collections are CHINA (by Swan), *COLCHESTER, *LISBON, *MEAR, MORETON, *OLD HUNDRED, PARIS, *ST. MARTIN'S, *SUTTON, and *WELLS. Starred tunes are Core Repertory tunes.
54. Crawford, *Core Repertory,* p. xli. See *Core Repertory,* p. 81, for an edition of the tune.
55. Crawford, " 'Ancient Music,' " p. 253.
56. Tunes printed in all eleven tunebooks are ARUNDEL, BARBY, *CANTERBURY, CASTLE STREET, *COLCHESTER, DEVIZES, GREEN'S 100TH, *HOTHAM, *IRISH, *MEAR, *OLD HUNDRED, OPORTO, PECKHAM, *ST. ANN'S, SHOEL, SILVER STREET, SUNDAY, *SUTTON, and *WELLS. Those found in ten of the eleven collections are *AYLESBURY, *BATH, BLENDON, *BRAY, BRISTOL, DARWENT, DOVER, FERRY, JORDAN, NEWCOURT, PLEYEL'S HYMN, PLYMPTON, RANDALL, *ST. MARTIN'S, *ST. THOMAS', *WANTAGE, WATCHMAN, and *WINDSOR. Starred tunes are Core Repertory tunes; underlined tunes are among the 101 ancient music favorites common to the Massachusetts reform collections and identified by Crawford in " 'Ancient Music,' " p. 253. In most cases, the tunebook not containing the pieces common to the other eleven is the incomplete copy of NH19; a complete copy would probably include these tunes.
57. Another third are triple-meter tunes, with the remaining tunes consisting of dactylic tunes, decorated duple tunes, and other duple tunes. These styles are described in Crawford, *Core Repertory,* pp. xii–xvi.
58. NH05 does not include any of the thirty-seven tunes, while NH08 includes just one (WELLS), and CH05 just five (IRISH, MEAR, OLD HUNDRED, WELLS, and BLENDON).
59. PH13 contains nine of them, CC15 fourteen, and NH16 twenty-nine.
60. None of the other five tunes appears in Maxim's two earliest books, either. WELLS is the only one of the six to be printed in Maxim's next book, NH08. Since Maxim felt American tunes were more pleasing to Americans, he included very few European tunes in his collections. See *Core Repertory,* pp. 154–155, for a printed edition of the tune.
61. Crawford, *Core Repertory,* p. lxxvii.
62. Still, each has its own characteristics; they represent different styles. While WELLS is a dactylic tune, OLD HUNDRED is a classic example of the common-tune style, SILVER STREET is an unusual duple tune, and the other four are triple-time tunes.

63. About 240 tunes are attributed to Williams or his collections; 260 are attributed to Maxim, with an additional 164 unattributed but believed to be by Maxim. Other European composers or collections whose tunes are most frequently reprinted in Maine tunebooks are *Harmonia Sacra,* Dr. Madan, Handel, Harrison or his collections, and Tans'ur or his collections (in that order). It is difficult to specify the exact number of printings actually attributable to each, since the same tune often receives different attributions in different collections (Tans'ur in one, Williams's Collection in another, for example).
64. None is found in Maxim's OH, NH05, and NH08, although it is conceivable that tunes actually by Williams may be attributed to someone else. Only in NH16 and NH19 did Maxim include tunes attributed to Williams, perhaps because by this time, tunes from Williams's collections were so popular that selecting them was unavoidable.
65. Three other Maxim tunes, TURNER, MACHIAS, and NEW-DURHAM, just missed making the list of most frequently printed American tunes; each was published in nine Maine tunebooks.
66. Crawford, *Core Repertory,* p. lxiv.
67. American composers with more total printings in Maine tunebooks than Swan (34) are Abraham Maxim (424), Japheth Coombs Washburn (149), William Billings (90), Daniel Read (69), Charles Robbins (60), and Oliver Holden (59). These numbers include unattributed tunes assumed to be by these composers.
68. Both are printed in Little's *Wesleyan Harmony,* first and second editions.
69. See Chapter VIII for more details.
70. Sterling E. Murray, "Timothy Swan and Yankee Psalmody," *Musical Quarterly,* LXI/3 (July 1975), p. 450.
71. Even more popular for musical settings was the first verse of Watts's Psalm 50, Second Part, set at least 54 times by 46 different composers between 1770 and 1820, according to Karl Kroeger in "Settings of Isaac Watts's Psalm 50 by American Psalmodists," *The Hymn,* XLI/1 (January 1990), pp. 19–27. See Chapter XIII for a discussion of two Maine settings: Charles Robbins's PSALM FIFTIETH and Edward Hartwell's TRIBUNAL.

Notes for Chapter XIII

1. Other Maine composers whose tunes appear in the Maine tunebooks include Turner resident Daniel Cary (or Carey) and several relatives of the Maine compilers: A. Washburn, N. Robbins, and S. Hartwell. There are also tunes attributed to individuals whose

identities remain unknown but who may have lived in Maine (for example, Bonney, Bradbury, Elles, Meservey, and Reynolds). The Maine connection for these five composers is suggested in Britton, Lowens, and Crawford, pp. 665, 666, 669, 675, and 678. See also Cooke, "American Psalmodists," I, pp. 91–92 n. 64.

2. The forty-six plain tunes listed for Maxim in Part III include seven which were first printed as tunes with extension or fuging-tunes but were later altered to become plain tunes: AUGUSTA (1), FARMINGTON, HATFIELD, MACHIAS, NEW-CASTLE, NEW-DURHAM, and NOBLEBOROUGH (2). They have been counted only once, under the original genre, in Table 6. Similarly, Washburn's NEW-PLYMOUTH, printed as a fuging-tune in all but one printing, has been tallied only as a fuging-tune in Table 6.
3. Maxim's tunebooks contain a large number of tunes lacking an attribution other than "Original." In most cases, I have assumed these tunes are by Maxim himself. See Part III for more information.
4. As discussed in Chapter VIII and Part III, the number of tunes by Washburn may be understated, since a number of unattributed tunes in the last editions of *Temple Harmony* may be his.
5. Hartwell, p. [3].
6. Analysis and complete musical examples of two set-pieces and two anthems by Maine composers can be found in Davenport, "Maine's Sacred Tunebooks," pp. 508–528. The pieces are INDEPENDENCE by Hartwell; INDEPENDENT ANNIVERSARY and ANTHEM FOR A DAY OF PUBLIC THANKSGIVING by Robbins; and ANTHEM FOR THANKSGIVING by Maxim.
7. Since none of Hartwell's tunes seems to have been reprinted in other tunebooks, such a criterion cannot be used for his music; however, see Chapter IX, note 30, for a reference to several of his tunes which were copied in a manuscript collection.
8. See Crawford, "William Billings and American Psalmody." Certain Particular Meter settings, such as Robbins's PSALM FIFTIETH, for example, may have been printed in a number of books because they fit the need for a tune in that meter.
9. In Example 1, the penultimate bass note has been changed from A, an apparent printing error in TH20, to C, which replaces it in TH21.
10. The same tune (FALMOUTH) is named PORTLAND in the sixth through tenth editions of *Village Harmony* (1803–1810). Portland was incorporated in 1786 from a part of the town of Falmouth.
11. Three-voice settings account for only about a sixth of the tunes by Robbins and Washburn and about a third of the tunes by Maxim and Hartwell.
12. Maxim and Washburn do not state in their tunebook prefaces whether men or women should sing the tune; however, Maxim

(*Northern Harmony,* p. 10) implies it should be men. He indicates that the tenor is the second staff from the bottom (or the middle staff in three-voice settings), and that is where the melody is usually notated. Unless otherwise noted, references to the melody in the following discussion refer to the tenor part.

13. For contrary motion, see, for example, the second phrase (mm. 5–7) of AUGUSTA and the third phrase (mm. 10–12) of FALMOUTH; for parallel motion, see the third phrase (mm. 7–11) of AUGUSTA.
14. Crawford, *Core Repertory,* p. xiii.
15. For an explanation of the "modes of time" (time signatures which also signified a given tempo), see Chapter XI.
16. For examples of the simpler type of triple-time tune, see BATH and PORTSMOUTH in Crawford, *Core Repertory,* pp. 17, 108.
17. For example, in mm. 5 and 6 of AUGUSTA, the long syllable is sung to slurred dotted quarter, eighth, and half notes, rather than a single whole note, on the first and second beats of these measures. Two slurred quarter notes sometimes substitute for half notes on the third beats (see mm. 6, 8, and 9).
18. In addition, each wrote two tunes in which there is a meter change, with part of the tune in triple and the other part in duple meter.
19. For example, while Crawford categorizes all the triple meter tunes into a single category ("triple-time tunes"), he separates the duple-meter tunes into four types: "common-tune style," "decorated duple," "declamatory duple," and "dactylic tunes." Crawford, *Core Repertory,* pp. xii–xvi.
20. The text for FALMOUTH comes from Watts's Lyric Poems; AUGUSTA's text is verse 8, Hymn 3, of Watts's Hymns, Book I. Between 1770 and 1820, American composers set more than 800 psalms and hymns by Watts, who has been called "the father of the English hymn." Karl Kroeger, "Settings of Isaac Watts's Psalm 50 by American Psalmodists," *The Hymn,* XLI/1 (January 1990), p. 19.
21. In FALMOUTH, the tenor melody in m. 10 is repeated at a lower pitch level in mm. 11 and 12; the tenor melody in m. 14 is repeated at a lower pitch level in m. 15. The other three voices are only sequential in mm. 10 and 11.
22. Word painting in the music of William Billings is discussed in an article of that title by Karl Kroeger in *American Music,* VI/1 (Spring 1988), pp. 41–64.
23. This compositional technique is described in Karl Kroeger, Introduction, in *The Complete Works of William Billings,* I, pp. xviii-xix. The tenor melody was composed first, followed by the bass, the treble (the top voice), and finally the counter (the voice above the tenor and below the treble).
24. The rules for composition set forth by William Tans'ur, an eigh-

teenth-century English parish-church composer, in such books as *The Royal Melody Compleat* (1755), seem to have served as guidelines for William Billings and other eighteenth- and early nineteenth-century American psalmodists who did not have European training. Tans'ur apparently copied the rules from John Playford, *An Introduction to the Skill of Musick,* twelfth edition, "Corrected and Amended by Mr. Henry Purcell" (London, 1694). Karl Kroeger, Introduction, in *The Complete Works of William Billings,* III, pp. xxxix–xl.

Tans'ur's rules (which are reprinted in *The Complete Works of William Billings,* III, p. xl) are primarily concerned with various types of melodic motion (oblique, similar, and contrary) and with maintaining concords (thirds, fifths, sixths, and octaves), except in passing and as suspensions. Parallel fifths and octaves are acceptable if they are covered by a higher part. The only rule pertaining to harmonic considerations is that the bass must rise a fourth or fall a fifth (i.e., from the dominant to the tonic) at final cadences. No mention is made of voice spacing or crossing.

25. To avoid confusion between end-note superscripts and chord inversion superscripts, I will indicate chord inversion symbols in parentheses. The symbol for first inversion triads will appear as "(6)," for example, while the symbol for second inversion triads will be "(6–4)."
26. For example, in AUGUSTA, each of the phrases (except the second) begins on a tonic chord. The second and third phrases end on the dominant, the others on the tonic.
27. *The Complete Works of William Billings,* III, p. xl, Rule II.
28. For example, in m. 8 of FALMOUTH, the Bb in the tenor and the B-natural in the bass each make sense from a linear perspective, with the Bb as a neighbor tone to the A and the B-natural as an appoggiatura to the C. Although the cross-relation produces a momentary dissonance (on a weak beat), consonance returns with the following chord.
29. For example, the third is omitted from the chords ending the first two phrases, while the fifth is omitted from the final chords of the last two phrases.
30. Karl Kroeger (in "Psalm 50," pp. 19–27) has surveyed the 54 American settings of Watts's Psalm 50.
31. *Ibid.,* pp. 24–25. Hartwell and Robbins may have composed their major-mode tunes to provide an alternative to the minor-mode Psalm 50 settings printed in their tunebooks: Ingalls's PENNSYLVANIA in Robbins's book and Blancks's OLD 50TH, or LANDAFF, in Hartwell's.
32. It was printed in the first two editions of Maxim's *Northern Har-*

mony (NH05 and NH08) as well as Robbins's own CH05 and the seventh through tenth editions of *Village Harmony* (1806–1810).

33. Hartwell's setting appears to be the last published setting of Psalm 50 by an American composer in the 1770–1820 period. Kroeger, "Psalm 50," p. 26 n. 29.
34. *Ibid.*, pp. 23–24, 25.
35. In m. 22, to the words "Lift up your heads," the tenor ascends to its highest pitch in the tune (a').
36. Billings does the same thing in his setting called WRENTHAM. Kroeger, "Psalm 50," p. 22.
37. The seventh resolves downward in mm. 3–4 and 25, but not in mm. 15–16.
38. For example, the cross-relation in mm. 14–15 of Robbins's PSALM FIFTIETH is understandable: the tenor's C# is a smooth way of moving from C and D, even though it clashes with the treble's C-natural. Passing dissonances are acceptable under Tans'ur's rules. Other dissonances resulting from converging lines in the same tune are found in mm. 3 (beat 4), 19 (beat 3), and 20 (beat 4). Since the dissonant notes fit smoothly into the individual lines, they are probably not printing errors. On the other hand, the cross-relation in TRIBUNAL, m. 16, is more problematical; voice-leading does not account for the G# in the counter, which forms a dissonance when combined with the tenor's G-natural.
39. Parallel fifths and octaves are permitted when covered by a higher part, a condition not existing in m. 13 of PSALM FIFTIETH, where treble and counter voices form parallel fifths. The parallel octaves between counter and tenor in mm. 21–22 are allowable, though, since they are covered by the treble.
40. Worst, citing the lack of chromatic modulations in New England psalm- and hymn-tunes, refers to the use of secondary dominants or half-cadences on the dominant as "quasi-modulations." John W. Worst, "New England Psalmody, 1760–1810: Analysis of an American Idiom" (Ph.D. dissertation, University of Michigan, 1974), p. 77.
41. Robbins, for example, modulates from the principal key of F major to the dominant key (C major) at the end of the second phrase (m. 8) and the relative minor (d minor) at the end of the fourth phrase (m. 16). After each of the modulations, however, the next phrase begins with the original tonic chord (F major), nullifying the modulation. Hartwell modulates from C major to the dominant key (G major) at the end of the third phrase, but like Robbins, returns immediately to the tonic key to begin the fourth phrase.
42. Kroeger, "Psalm 50," pp. 20–22, 25 n. 8.
43. For example, the second and sixth phrases of PSALM FIFTIETH,

LANDAFF, and WRENTHAM have similar contours, ascending to a high point and then descending.

44. Like Billings, Robbins gives an extra beat to the word "sounds" in the phrase "The trumpet sounds." In his setting, the key (F major) is the same, and his phrases have similar melodic contours to Billings's.
45. For example, he sets the first word of the third phrase ("From") as an upbeat rather than a downbeat so that the following word ("east") can be on a strong beat. Robbins, on the other hand, maintains nearly the same rhythmic patterns throughout each of the first four phrases, resulting in the placement of unimportant words such as "The" and "From" on downbeats.
46. Although the length of the first note differs in the first and third phrases, the phrases are otherwise rhythmically identical. Sacred tunes often began on a whole note, or "gathering note," allowing the singers an opportunity to tune the initial chord.
47. The first two phrases (mm. 1–9) form an extended antecedent phrase, followed by an extended consequent phrase comprised of the next two phrases (mm. 10–18). Not only are the large antecedent and consequent phrases rhythmically symmetrical, but the cadential chords also contribute to the effect; the antecedent phrase ends on the dominant (m. 9), the consequent on the tonic (m. 18). The final two phrases (mm. 19–29), as mentioned previously, are linked together by the cadential subdominant chord (m. 24) which leads from the fifth to the sixth phrase. The effect of this organization is three larger phrases (1–9, 10–18, and 19–29), rather than six unrelated sections.
48. As a setting of two verses of text instead of one, KNOXVILLE is a fairly typical Maxim tune with extension, almost half of which set two verses. Twenty of his tunes with extension set two verses of text, twenty-four set just one. His two-verse settings often have Common Meter texts (four-line stanzas with syllable lengths 8.6.8.6.).
49. Unless otherwise noted, the form of all the tunes has been determined on the basis of the tenor melody.
50. Measures 6 to 10 are scored for just treble and bass, measures 11 to 15 for all four voices. Oliver Holden's popular tune CORONATION ("All hail the pow'r of Jesus' name") may have served as a model. Its structure is similar, although not identical, to ACCORD's; following an opening homophonic section, the middle voices are tacit for a phrase, then all voices join in for the balance of the second section, which is repeated.
51. The same text, with meter identified as 8.7.8.7.4.7., appears in a setting entitled JORDAN in Little's *Wesleyan Harmony*.

52. The ascending, stepwise patterns set to "he is willing" are similar, but not identical.
53. Crawford, *Core Repertory,* p. xiv. Only a small number of Maxim's tunes (a total of seven) are written in this style.
54. KNOXVILLE was printed in the sixth through tenth editions of *Village Harmony* (1803–1810) in addition to twelve Maine tunebook editions.
55. In some of the later printings, including TH20 and TH26, it is notated in the third mode of common time (2/2).
56. See, for example, mm. 16–24, where the upper voices move in sixths while the bass remains somewhat static.
57. Crawford, *Core Repertory,* pp. xiv–xvi.
58. Another Robbins tune with extension exhibiting even more striking contrast between the two halves is CONSONANCE. Not only is the second half more declamatory than the first, through the use of repeated quarter notes, but there is a change of meter. The first half (seven measures) is in triple time with a flowing dotted rhythm, and slurred melismas. The second half (eight measures, repeated) is in duple meter with a largely syllabic setting.
59. For example, although Charles Robbins wrote more tunes with extension than any other genre, his most reprinted tunes were a plain tune (PSALM FIFTIETH) and four of his fuging-tunes (ALBANY, DELIGHT, ELEMENT, and INNOCENCE). Most of his other tunes seem to have been printed just once, in his own tunebook (1805).
60. Since Edward Hartwell wrote only two fuging-tunes and generally did not approve of the fuging style, his two fuging-tunes cannot be considered representative of his overall repertory and style and will receive little mention here.
61. In addition to being printed in nine Maine tunebooks (see Part III), TURNER was published in the seventh through ninth editions of *Village Harmony* (1806–1808), in *Union Harmony,* second and fourth editions (published in the Canadian province of New Brunswick, 1816, 1840), and in retrospective collections from the late 1830s to the 1870s, including numerous editions of *Father Kemp's Old Folks Concert Music* (see Chapter XIV).
62. Post-1830 printings of ELEMENT include those in the retrospective *Ancient Harmony Revived,* second and third editions (1848, 1850), and D. H. Mansfield's *American Vocalist* (1849). ELEMENT was the only Robbins tune included in the New Brunswick tunebook, *Union Harmony* (third edition, 1831).
63. In Example 11, the last treble pitch, apparently printed incorrectly as fourth-space Eb in *Northern Harmony,* has been corrected to C, the final pitch in other printed versions. The title is not hyphenated

in PH13. The versions printed in Washburn's tunebooks omit the repeat signs and first and second endings.

64. The text for TURNER is verse 5 of Hymn 34, Book II. ELEMENT's text is verse 4 of Psalm 46, first part. The source for NEW-PLYMOUTH's text is Book I, Hymn 67, verse 1.
65. Maxim and Robbins each wrote only one three-voice fuging-tune: TROY and RESOLUTION, respectively. All of Washburn's fuging-tunes are set for four voices.
66. The fugal sections of fuging-tunes are usually referred to as "fuges" (not "fugues," since they are not fugues in the classical sense). They were so called in the eighteenth and early nineteenth centuries, and the term was carried over into the twentieth century.
67. Robbins wrote thirteen fuging-tunes, but one, INNOCENCE, has two fuges: one at the beginning and one in the middle.
68. Although Robbins's MARSHFIELD has a complete setting of all four phrases of text in the initial homophonic section, it ends on a dominant chord before the fuging section, so the fuging part is not optional, for tonal reasons.
69. One of these tunes, NOBLEBOROUGH, is transformed into a plain tune in Washburn's TH26 because the fuging-chorus is not printed.
70. The small D (note of transition) in the treble adds the seventh to the dominant chord.
71. For example, the third is probably omitted from the first chord in ELEMENT because of the difficulty of tuning the third; the fifth is perhaps omitted from the second triad because none of the voice lines could smoothly incorporate an E.
72. The first phrase, for example, ends with a tonic triad lacking the third, probably because of the voice-leading. If the tenor had moved to C# in measure 5 to fill out the triad, the shape of its line would have been adversely affected.
73. Statements that the progressions do not follow tonal principles are not intended as criticism, since these composers were not concerned with such principles.
74. See, for example, m. 2, beat 3.
75. For example, beats 3–4 of m. 2 and the first beat of m. 3, ostensibly III(6–4), VII, i in f minor would be I(6–4), V, vi in Ab major. The latter progression, utilizing a deceptive resolution, would not be unusual in conventional harmony.
76. The sequence III, VII (or VII(6)), i, V, i is the foundation for mm. 5–6, 11–13, and 14–16 (beginning with beat 3 of m. 14). A similar pattern is found in the first phrase, mm. 2–4 (beginning with beat 3 of m. 2): III(6–4), VII, i, V, i. These phrases emphasize the tonic and dominant of the relative major, then the tonic and dominant of the minor key in which the tune is based.

77. Kroeger, "Word Painting," pp. 44–45.
78. Worst, pp. 255–256.
79. Of the representative tunes, KNOXVILLE by Maxim was a rare exception in having two identical phrases (the first and third).
80. Worst, p. 256.
81. Crawford, *Core Repertory,* xi–xvi.
82. Cheney, p. 184.

Notes for Chapter XIV

1. In Woodstock, Vermont, for example, the fuging-tune did not fall from favor for church use until about 1814; fuging-tunes were sung at the dedication of the Brattleboro (Vermont) meetinghouse in 1816. Keene notes that the "better music" movement, promoted by Lowell Mason and others in Boston, arrived in rural Vermont later than in the eastern urban centers, partly because of transportation difficulties between 1790 and the mid-nineteenth century. Keene, pp. 18, 21, 25, 50.
2. While singing schools began in Massachusetts in the 1720s, the first Maine singing schools may have been organized as late as the 1780s. See Chapter IV for more information.
3. For example, the Old York Historical Society possesses manuscript subscription lists for singing schools held in Cape Neddock (now Cape Neddick, part of the town of York) in 1850, 1856, 1857, and 1863. The Androscoggin Historical Society has a broadside advertising a singing school to be opened in Lake Hall, North Auburn in 1851. Parlin (p. 17) recalls the large singing schools (a hundred scholars) held in East Winthrop in the late 1830s.
4. Of course, many Massachusetts musical societies predated those in Maine. The Old Stoughton Musical Society in Stoughton, Massachusetts, for example, was founded in 1786.
5. Edwards provides extensive coverage of the numerous nineteenth-century Maine musical societies. See, for example, pp. 42–62, 69–103, and 113–121.
6. A Portland compiler, Benjamin Sweetser, wrote the following: "It is a well known, acknowledged, and lamentable fact, that the good *old European,* and American music (as it was,) is so changed, modified, and mutilated, in modern publications, that the composer himself, were it not for the air, which has suffered less by the mutilation, would hardly know his own production." Benjamin Sweetser, Jr., *Cumberland Collection of Church Music* (Portland: William Hyde, 1839), p. [iii].
7. Edwards does not mention this society, which was no doubt mod-

elled after the earlier Billings and Holden Society of Boston. My knowledge of the organization is limited to a reference in Stephen Blum, "The Fuging Tune in British North America," in *CanMus Documents I,* proceedings of a February 1986 conference (Institute for Canadian Music, University of Toronto, 1987), p. 119. Blum cites a *Boston Courier* review of a Bangor Billings and Holden Society concert which featured almost a hundred singers. The review is reprinted as "Old Fashioned Singing" in *The World of Music* (Claremont, NH), IV/24 (1847), p. 94, according to Blum, p. 140 n. 2.

8. A collection of the tunes was published as *Father Kemp's Old Folks Concert Music* (Boston, 1860 and later editions). For more information, see Judith T. Steinberg, "Old Folks Concerts and the Revival of New England Psalmody," *Musical Quarterly,* LIX/4 (October 1973), pp. 602–619.
9. "It is but doing justice to the subject and to the public, in having them [the tunes we were accustomed to hear in our infancy] corrected and put in a proper state and form for use." Stoughton Musical Society, *Stoughton Collection of Church Music,* fourth edition (Boston: Marsh, Capen & Lyon, 1831), p. [3].
10. The principal modification of the Maxim tunes consists of the addition of a figured bass.
11. [Smith Hinkley and Christopher T. Norcross], *Songs of Sion, or Maine Collection of Sacred Music* (Charleston, ME: Hinkley & Norcross, 1830). No compiler's name appears on the title page, but Hinkley and Norcross are named as the proprietors, as well as the publishers, in the copyright notice; the book was printed by Glazier, Masters & Co. in Hallowell. Charleston is about twenty-five miles northeast of Palmyra, where Abraham Maxim lived until his death in 1829.
12. Stoughton Musical Society, *Stoughton Collection of Church Music*/4.
13. Sweetser, *Cumberland Collection of Church Music.*
14. *Ancient Harmony Revived,* second edition, revised and enlarged (Hallowell, ME: Masters, Smith & Co., Printers, 1848).
15. *Ancient Harmony Revived,* third edition, revised and enlarged (Boston: Perkins & Whipple, 1850).
16. *Ancient Harmony Revived,* sixth edition, revised (Boston: Oliver Ditson, 1855) [cover says fifth edition, title page says sixth edition; copy at Bagaduce Music Lending Library, Blue Hill, ME].
17. Probably misattributed to Belcher; usually attributed to Law.
18. The same tune is entitled HYMN THIRTY-FIFTH in Robbins's *Columbian Harmony* (1805).
19. While the harmonization was by Maxim, the original tune was not.

20. *Songs of Sion,* p. [3]. Some new pieces were included as well. Since the compilers of Maine tunebooks published in the first three decades of the century made only minor alterations to the older tunes, the Charleston compilers must have been responding to other New England collections, such as *The Boston Handel and Haydn Society Collection,* rather than to the Maine tunebooks.
21. The unattributed tunes are presumably the "considerable number of new pieces" referred to in the advertisement (*Songs of Sion,* p. [3]). These tunes of unknown provenance constitute 35 percent of the collection, with European tunes making up another 63 percent, and American tunes only 2 percent. It is possible, and likely, that many of the unattributed tunes are by Americans and that some may be by Maine residents.
22. *Songs of Sion,* p. [3]
23. Of the 175 tunes, only 2 are fuging-tunes. Plain tunes comprise 68 percent of the collection, while tunes with extension amount to 28 percent.
24. Benjamin Sweetser, Jr., *Cumberland Collection of Church Music* (Portland: William Hyde, 1839).
25. David Paine, *Portland Sacred Music Society's Collection of Church Music* (Portland: William Hyde; Colman & Chisholm, 1839).
26. Sweetser, p. [iii].
27. He also includes "many pieces, hitherto unpublished." Sweetser, p. iv.
28. Maxim died in 1829, ten years before the publication of Sweetser's book; however, Sweetser may have been preparing his tunebook for some time and may have contacted Maxim for a new tune during the early stages. ALBANY may have been one of the tunes in the manuscript sixth edition of *Northern Harmony* which Maxim reportedly had in his pocket the day he died. Although the attribution provides only Maxim's last name, it is unlikely that ALBANY is by Abraham Maxim's younger brother, John, whose tunes occasionally appear in collections in the 1840s (including *Ancient Harmony Revived*). Attributions for John's tunes usually include his first name, probably to distinguish him from his better-known brother. In addition, all the other Maxim tunes in Sweetser's collections are printed in Maine tunebooks of the period 1800–1830 and appear to be by Abraham Maxim.
29. Paine, pp. [iii]–[iv].
30. The first complete presentation in Maine of Haydn's oratorio, *The Creation,* was a performance by the Portland Sacred Music Society on April 24, 1837. On September 26, 1838, the society presented Handel's *Messiah* for the first time in Maine. Edwards, pp. 69, 71, 75.

31. Based on the advertisement, the compiler's allegiance belongs not so much to Lowell Mason, compiler of *The Boston Handel and Haydn Society Collection,* as to Charles Zeuner, whose works appear to have served as a model. The advertisement notes that one should not expect the chant tunes to compare "for sublimity and originality of character, with those of Mr. Zeuner, (to whom must be awarded the credit of successfully introducing this new and pleasing style of Church Music;)." Paine, p. [iii]. The German-born Zeuner (1795–1857) came to this country in 1830. He was organist for the Boston Handel and Haydn Society from 1830 to 1837 and president of the organization in 1838 and 1839 before moving to Philadelphia. Many of his compositions are included in Lowell Mason's collections as well as in his own, which include *American Harp* (1839) and *Ancient Lyre* (1848). Perkins and Dwight, I, pp. 102–103, 116–117, 120–121.
32. In addition to the tunes by Paine, there are tunes by the Portland brothers Francis and Ferdinand Ilsley. Cole (p. 115) also identifies several other prominent Portland musicians whose tunes are attributed only with initials: Edward Howe, Jr., Charles Noyes, George Churchill, Joseph Kingsbury, Nathaniel Deering, and Silas Allen.
33. Paine, p. [iii].
34. Portland served as the first capital of Maine from 1820 to 1832, when Augusta became the capital because of its more centralized location. In 1832, Portland, with a population of 13,000, was incorporated as a city. Cole, pp. 6–7. Regarding the quality of the performances by the Portland Sacred Music Society, see the reviews quoted in Edwards, pp. 69–75. In spite of the quality of Portland musicians, Boston musicians were still frequently imported as soloists or orchestral players for large-scale productions in Portland.
35. Other Maine sacred music collections mentioned by Edwards (pp. 111–112), but which I have not personally examined, are C. C. Burr, *Social Melodies* (Portland and Boston, 1841), and John Edgar Gould, *The Modern Harp and Songs of Gladness* (n.p., 1840). Another Maine tunebook named by Edwards is Daniel H. Mansfield, *The American Vocalist* (Boston: William J. Reynolds & Company, 1849). A retrospective collection, Mansfield's book includes nine Maxim tunes and one each by Robbins (ELEMENT) and Bonney (LEWISTON), probably a Maine composer.
36. The first two editions were published by Masters, Smith & Co., one of the successors to Ezekiel Goodale's printing company. Goodale's former employee, Andrew Masters, was one of the partners. Later editions of the tunebook were published in Boston.

37. Chase, p. 136.
38. "And we offer no other apology for sending forth our Aged Harmony to contend with the almost indefinite number of singing books that flood our country with their scientific, cold and heartless chords that make no lasting impression of devotional feelings." *Ancient Harmony Revived*/3, p. [2].
39. *Ibid.*
40. Chase (p. 136) rightly notes that another indication of the trend toward secularization of religious music was the emphasis on the quality of the performance, rather than the spirit of the heart, among choirs trained by Lowell Mason.
41. *Ancient Harmony Revived*/3, title page. The collection by Bangor clergyman Daniel Mansfield, *The American Vocalist* (p. [i]), includes Maxim in a similar list: "From the compositions of Billings, Holden, Maxim, Edson, Holyoke, Read, Kimball, Morgan, Wood, Swan etc. and eminent American authors now living."
42. See Table 8 for the Maine tunes included in the *Stoughton Musical Society's Collection.* Cheney, in *The American Singing Book* (1879), includes a representative Maxim tune, TURNER. Three tunes by Maxim (TURNER, BUCKFIELD, and PORTLAND) were printed in various editions of *Father Kemp's Old Folks Concert Music* (Boston: Oliver Ditson & Co., [1860], 1874, 1917) and *Father Kemp's Old Folks Concert Tunes* (Boston: Oliver Ditson & Co., 1889, 1936).
43. Humbert (1767–1849) was a Loyalist who was born in New Jersey; he settled in New Brunswick (Canada) in 1783. John Beckwith, "Tunebooks and Hymnals in Canada, 1801–1939," *American Music,* VI/2 (Summer 1988), pp. 193–234.
44. The second edition of *Union Harmony* was printed in Exeter, New Hampshire, by C. Norris & Co., the same firm which printed the tenth edition of *Village Harmony* (1810), Washburn's *Parish Harmony* (1813), and Hartwell's *Chorister's Companion* (1815).
45. According to Temperley's analysis, 37 percent of the tunes are fuging-tunes; 59 percent of the ultimate tune sources are American. Nicholas Temperley, "Stephen Humbert's 'Union Harmony,' 1816," in *CanMus Documents I,* p. 62.
46. Humbert, *Union Harmony*/2.
47. Stephen Humbert, *Union Harmony: or British America's Sacred Vocal Musick,* third edition (Saint John, New Brunswick: Stephen Humbert; printed in Boston: James Loring, printer, 1831).
48. Stephen Humbert, *Union Harmony: or British America's Sacred Vocal Music,* fourth edition (Saint John, New Brunswick: Stephen Humbert, 1840).
49. A. Washburn is probably Japheth's older brother, Abisha. See Chapter VIII, note 25.

50. Humbert gives a different text and the title LOCH LOMOND to Washburn's tune NEW-PLYMOUTH.
51. Stephen Humbert, *Union Harmony: or British America's Sacred Vocal Musick,* second edition (Saint John, New Brunswick: Stephen Humbert; Norris & Co., printers, 1816), p. [3].
52. Blum, p. 137. Although Humbert includes a small block of tunes specifically for use at Methodist services, Temperley ("Union Harmony," pp. 75–84, 89) suggests that he seems to have intended the book more for singing school than for church use. Humbert taught singing schools.
53. See Chapter V.
54. My examination of the (Saint John) *New Brunswick Courier,* vols. I–XIII (1811–1823), turned up very few mentions of Maine in any connection. Maine port towns, such as Portland, Castine, and Bath, were sometimes named in the "Marine Journal" section (listing ship arrivals and departures).
55. See, for example, Harvey Strum, "Smuggling in Maine During the Embargo and the War of 1812," *Colby Library Quarterly,* XIX/2 (June 1983), pp. 90–97.
56. Humbert himself would not have condoned smuggling; he was head of a commission organized to seize by force American vessels engaged in offshore smuggling. D. Jay Rahn, "Humbert, Stephen," in *Encyclopedia of Music in Canada,* ed. Helmut Kallmann, Gilles Potvin, and Kenneth Winters (Toronto: University of Toronto Press, 1981), p. 438.
57. Wayne M. O'Leary, "The Maine Transatlantic Salt Trade in the Nineteenth Century, *American Neptune,* XLVII/2 (Spring 1987), pp. 93–97.
58. Some of the Maine tunes which are printed in the third or fourth editions of *Union Harmony* also appear in other tunebooks; however, HANOVER, WARD, and WHITEFIELD are printed only in the fourth edition of *Northern Harmony* and the first two editions of *Temple Harmony,* not in any other extant Maine tunebooks from 1800 to 1830, implying that one of Washburn's tunebooks was the probable source.
59. Beckwith (p. 195) notes that *Union Harmony* was a tunebook from which other publications borrowed. According to Blum, pp. 142–148, Maine fuging-tunes which first appeared in *Union Harmony* were later reprinted in the following Canadian collections: Zebulon Estey, *New Brunswick Church Harmony* (Saint John, 1835); *The Harmonicon,* second edition (Pictou, 1841); George W. Linton, *The Vocalist* (Toronto, 1867); and *The Choir,* third edition (Halifax, 1887).
60. Hamm, p. 170; Edwards, pp. 108–109.

61. Edwards, pp. 103–107.
62. *Ibid.,* pp. 107–108.
63. *Ibod.,* pp. 121–140.
64. Quartets seem to have replaced choirs in some churches by mid-century, however.
65. Many Maine musical societies, formed in the 1830s or later, are discussed in Edwards, pp. 88–102. They include such groups as the Cumberland Musical Association, the Hallowell Harmonic Society, the Penobscot Musical Association, the Franklin County Musical Association, and the Somerset Sacred Music Society, among others. Two national figures active as leaders of the Penobscot Musical Association, organized in 1848, were George F. Root and Nathaniel D. Gould. Edwards, pp. 95–96.
66. *Ibid.,* p. 89.

Notes for Part III

1. As mentioned in Chapter XIII, no original tunes attributed to Henry Little have been found.
2. According to Britton, Lowens, and Crawford, a few tunes by Maxim, Robbins, and Washburn were printed in tunebooks dating from 1810 or before, including the sixth through tenth editions of *Village Harmony*. My Table 8 provides a sampling of their tunes which were reprinted after 1830 in various retrospective collections; Table 9 lists those printed in the New Brunswick *Union Harmony* editions.
3. Nicholas Temperley graciously checked the Hymn Tune Index at the University of Illinois for the unattributed "Original" tunes I assume to be by Maxim or Washburn. He confirmed that the tunes in question were first printed in Maxim or Washburn tunebooks and that they are not attributed to other composers in any tunebooks indexed for the Hymn Tune Index. Two tunes unattributed in the Maine collections are attributed to Maxim in a non-Maine source (see notes 11 and 12 below). While not proving that Maxim and Washburn wrote the unattributed "Original" tunes in their collections, Temperley's findings suggest that they are the most likely candidates.

   The fourth edition of *Northern Harmony* presents a special problem since it was co-edited by Maxim and Washburn. Are the fifteen unattributed "Original" tunes by Maxim or by Washburn? My theory is that all but HARLEM, which is attributed to Washburn in his *Temple Harmony,* are by Maxim. Five can be traced to Maxim in other sources. The other nine are stylistically more like Maxim's works than like Washburn's. In addition, nearly all of Washburn's tunes (including sixteen labelled both "Original" and "Washburn") appear to be identified as such in this edition. The same cannot be said of Maxim's.

4. Maxim's notations are in the Massachusetts Historical Society's copy of *Northern Harmony,* second edition (1808). I am grateful to Brenda Lawson, Curator of Manuscripts at the Massachusetts Historical Society, for providing me with information on the handwritten attributions and to Nym Cooke for first alerting me to the flyleaf inscription.

   In this lengthy inscription, Williams Latham (1803–1883), the Massachusetts lawyer and tunebook collector who purchased the copy from John Maxim, advised that most of the tunes in the book were written by Abraham Maxim. John Maxim wrote the composer's name over the tunes in pencil, Latham in ink. Latham noted that John "well knew" which ones were composed by his brother.

   John Maxim indicates that sixty of the sixty-one unattributed tunes (all but DEANFIELD) were composed by his brother. He is probably correct about DEANFIELD, since it is generally considered to be by Read or Goff. He was apparently wrong in believing that his brother wrote LILY (a tune labelled only as "Original"); it is attributed to West in the fourth edition of *Northern Harmony* (1816).

   He may also be wrong about PELMIRA and INVOCATION, unattributed tunes which Britton, Lowens, and Crawford classify in *American Sacred Music Imprints* (pp. 455, 456) as of unidentified nationality. Swayed by their unwillingness to categorize the tunes even as American, I have not included either among Maxim's compositions, in spite of his brother's assertions. Additional support for this position comes from the fact that INVOCATION is stylistically unlike Abraham Maxim's known works. As for PELMIRA, Abraham Maxim designated the tune only as "Never before published in the Northern Harmony," not as "Original."

   With the exceptions of LILY, INVOCATION, and PELMIRA, all the tunes noted by John Maxim as having been written by his brother have been listed in the following index as Maxim tunes: a total of fifty-seven tunes. The two anthems first appeared in the Maxim tunebook containing only his own tunes (*Oriental Harmony,* 1802), thirty-five other unattributed tunes were designated as "Original" in the first edition of *Northern Harmony* (1805), and twenty were marked "Original" in the second edition (1808). Some of the tunes can be traced to Maxim through printed attributions in later sources.

5. For example, there may have been Maxim tunes which first appeared in the nonextant third edition of *Northern Harmony*. If

reprinted in the fourth edition, they would not include the term "Original" because of the prior printing. Unless they were attributed to Maxim in at least one source, though, they would not be assigned to Maxim in my index. Possible tunes of this type are BEAUTY, BRAINTREE, HEBRON, ILLUMINATION, and MEDFORD, which are unattributed but not marked as "Original" in the fourth edition of *Northern Harmony.*

6. See Chapter VIII, note 66.
7. Maxim apparently uses the term "Original" only once per tune: as a way of indicating first printings. Washburn, though, identifies the same tunes as "Original" in TH20 as in TH18, apparently because the collections were the same except for the seven tunes added at the end of TH20.
8. If one or both of the tunes of the same name were unattributed, one might infer that they must be by different composers, on the premise that a composer would not assign the same name to two different tunes. Maxim's practices, however, sometimes contradict this assumption. For example, he must have written both of the EXETERs and NOBLEBOROUGHs since both of the duplicate-named tunes are attributed to him in print. Accordingly, where two tunes of the same name appear to be by Maxim, I have listed both as his.

   Washburn seems less likely to use the same name twice. There are two WHITEFIELDs attributed to Washburn, but one of the titles appears to be a misprint. The index of TH20 lists WAKEFIELD on page 186 and WHITEFIELD on page 154, but the two different tunes are both titled WHITEFIELD in the body of the tunebook. Later printings of the tune (in TH21, TH23, and TH24) give the former tune its correct title of WAKEFIELD.
9. PITTSTON is not printed in any of the Maine tunebooks, but appears in the sixth edition (1797) of *The Worcester Collection of Sacred Harmony.*
10. LA PLATA is unattributed in the pre-1830 Maine tunebooks but is attributed to Maxim in Sweetser's *Cumberland Collection of Church Music* (1839).
11. While unattributed in the Maine tunebooks, PRODIGY is attributed to Maxim in the index of Azariah Fobes, *The Delaware Harmony* (Philadelphia: W. M'Culloch, 1809).
12. TRINITY is unattributed in the Maine tunebooks but is attributed to Maxim in Fobes's *Delaware Harmony* (1809).
13. Frank J. Metcalf, compiler, *American Psalmody; or, Titles of Books Containing Tunes Printed in America from 1721 to 1820* (New York: Charles F. Heartman, 1917; repr. New York: Da Capo Press, 1968).
14. Allen Britton, Irving Lowens, and Richard Crawford, *American*

Sacred Music Imprints, 1698–1810: A Bibliography (Worcester: American Antiquarian Society, 1990).

15. The printed sources were confirmed by direct inquiry.
16. Some of them, like the Bagaduce Lending Library and the Bangor Theological Seminary Library, do own other tunebooks or later Maine collections, such as *Ancient Harmony Revived*. Others, like the Maine State Museum and the Fogler Library at the University of Maine–Orono, possess some interesting Maine hymnals dating from the early nineteenth century.

BIBLIOGRAPHY

Tunebooks and Musical Collections

Ancient Harmony Revived, second edition, revised and enlarged. Hallowell, ME: Masters, Smith & Co., Printers, 1848.

Ancient Harmony Revived, third edition, revised and enlarged. Boston: Perkins & Whipple, 1850.

Ancient Harmony Revived, sixth edition, revised. Boston: Oliver Ditson, 1855.

Belcher, Supply. *The Harmony of Maine.* Boston: Isaiah Thomas & Ebenezer T. Andrews, 1794.

Brown, Bartholomew, A.M., and others. *Bridgewater Collection of Sacred Musick,* third edition. Boston: Thomas & Andrews; J. West & Co., 1810.

Cheney, Simeon Pease. *The American Singing Book.* Boston: White, Smith & Co., 1879; repr. New York: Da Capo Press, 1980.

The Core Repertory of Early American Psalmody, ed. Richard Crawford. Madison, WI: A-R Editions, 1984.

The Cumberland Melodist; or, A Choice Selection of Plain Tunes. Philadelphia: William M'Culloch for John M'Carrell (Shippensburg, PA), 1804.

[Crouch, W.?]. *The North-Western Harmony and Musician's Companion,* 2 vols. Manuscript Collection at Brown University.

Father Kemp's Old Folks Concert Music. Boston: Oliver Ditson & Co., [1860], 1874, 1917.

Father Kemp's Old Folks Concert Tunes. Boston: Oliver Ditson & Co., 1889, 1936.

French, Jacob. *The Psalmodist's Companion.* Worcester: Leonard Worcester for Isaiah Thomas, 1793.

The Hallowell Collection of Sacred Music. Hallowell, ME: printed and published by E. Goodale, 1817.

The Hallowell Collection of Sacred Music, second edition. Hallowell, ME: printed and published by E. Goodale, 1819.

Hartwell, Edward. *The Chorister's Companion.* Exeter, NH: C. Norris & Co. for the author, 1815.

[Hinkley, Smith, and Christopher T. Norcross]. *Songs of Sion, or Maine Collection of Sacred Music*. Charleston, ME: Hinkley & Norcross, 1830.

Holyoke, Samuel. *Vocal Companion*. Exeter, NH: Norris & Sawyer, 1807.

Humbert, Stephen. *Union Harmony: or British America's Sacred Vocal Musick,* second edition. Saint John, New Brunswick: Stephen Humbert; Norris & Co., printers, 1816.

———. *Union Harmony: or British America's Sacred Vocal Musick,* third edition. Saint John, New Brunswick: Stephen Humbert; printed in Boston: James Loring, printer, 1831.

———. *Union Harmony: or British America's Sacred Vocal Music,* fourth edition. Saint John, New Brunswick: Stephen Humbert, 1840.

Ingalls, Jeremiah. *The Christian Harmony; or Songster's Companion*. Exeter, NH: Henry Ranlet, for the compiler, 1805; repr. New York: Da Capo Press, 1981.

Little, Henry. *The Wesleyan Harmony*. Hallowell, ME: E. Goodale, 1820.

———. *The Wesleyan Harmony,* second edition. Hallowell, ME: Goodale, Glazier & Co., 1821.

Lyon, James. *Urania*. Philadelphia: n.p., 1761; repr. New York: Da Capo Press, 1974.

Mansfield, Daniel H. *The American Vocalist*. Boston: William J. Reynolds & Co., 1849.

Mason, Lowell. *The Choir: or Union Collection of Church Music,* second edition. Boston: Carter, Hendee & Co., 1833.

[Mason, Lowell]. *The Boston Handel and Haydn Society Collection of Church Music*. Boston: Richardson & Lord, 1822; repr. New York: Da Capo Press, 1973.

Manuscript tunebook of tenor part. Patterson Papers, 1650–1930. Collection 1, Maine Historical Society, Box 33/4.

Maxim, Abraham. *The Northern Harmony*. Exeter, NH: Henry Ranlet, for the compiler, 1805.

———. *The Northern Harmony,* second edition. Exeter, NH: Norris & Sawyer, 1808.

———. *The Northern Harmony,* fifth edition. Hallowell, ME: E. Goodale, 1819.

———. *The Oriental Harmony*. Exeter, NH: Henry Ranlet, 1802.

Maxim, Abraham, and Japheth C. Washburn. *The Northern Harmony,* fourth edition. Hallowell, ME: E. Goodale, 1816.

The Middlesex Collection of Church Music: or, Ancient Psalmody Revived. Boston: Manning & Loring, 1807.

Old Colony Musical Society. *Old Colony Collection of Anthems,* second edition, 2 vols. Boston: James Loring, [1818].

Old Stoughton Musical Society. *The Stoughton Musical Society's Centennial Collection of Sacred Music*. Boston: O. Ditson, 1878; repr. New York: Da Capo Press, 1980.
Paine, David. *Portland Sacred Music Society's Collection of Church Music*. Portland: William Hyde; Colman & Chisholm, 1839.
Robbins, Charles. *The Columbian Harmony; or Maine Collection of Church Music*. Exeter, NH: printed at the music-press of Henry Ranlet, for the author, 1805.
———. *Drum and Fife Instructor*. Exeter, NH: C. Norris & Co., 1812.
The Salem Collection of Classical Sacred Musick. Salem, MA: Joshua Cushing, 1805.
Shumway, Nehemiah. *The American Harmony*. Philadelphia: John M'Culloch, 1793.
Stiles, John W. Manuscript (secular) music book, 1807. Manuscript 131, Old York Historical Society, York, ME.
Stoughton Musical Society. *Stoughton Collection of Church Music*, fourth edition. Boston: Marsh, Capen & Lyon, 1831.
Sweetser, Benjamin, Jr. *Cumberland Collection of Church Music*. Portland: William Hyde, 1839.
The Village Harmony: or New-England Repository of Sacred Musick, fourteenth edition. Boston: West & Richardson, [1817].
Washburn, Japheth Coombs. *The Parish Harmony, or Fairfax Collection of Sacred Musick*. Exeter, NH: C. Norris & Co. for the author, 1813.
———. *The Temple Harmony*. Hallowell, ME: E. Goodale & J. C. Washburn, Esq., 1818.
———. *The Temple Harmony*, second edition. Hallowell, ME: Goodale, Glazier & Co., 1820.
———. *The Temple Harmony*, third edition. Hallowell, ME: Goodale, Glazier & Co., 1821.
———. *The Temple Harmony*, fourth edition. Hallowell, ME: Goodale, Glazier & Co., 1823.
———. *The Temple Harmony*, fifth edition [?]. [Hallowell, ME]: [Goodale, Glazier & Co.], [1824 or 1825].
———. *The Temple Harmony*, sixth edition. Hallowell, ME: Glazier & Co., 1826.

Newspapers

American Advocate and General Advertiser. Hallowell, ME. 1823–1824; December 30, 1826; January 6, 1827.
Biddeford Daily Journal. Biddeford, ME. January 10, 1894.
Boston Transcript. Boston. February 8, 1894.
The Christian Intelligencer and Eastern Chronicle. Gardiner, ME. 1829–1830.

Eastern Argus. Portland. 1824–1825, 1829–1830.
Eastport Sentinel and Passamaquoddy Advertiser. Eastport, ME. 1819–1820.
Gazette of Maine/Hancock Advertiser. Buckstown (now Bucksport), ME. 1805–1809.
Hallowell Gazette. Hallowell, ME. 1814–1827; December 12, 1863.
Hallowell Register. Hallowell, ME. January 3, 1885.
Herald of Liberty. Augusta. 1810–1815.
Kennebec Journal. Augusta. 1825; May 3, 1844.
New Brunswick Courier. Saint John, New Brunswick. 1811–1823.
The Orb. China, ME. 1833–1836.
Portland Gazette. Portland. 1802–1806; 1822–1824.
The Tocsin. Hallowell, ME. 1796–1797.

Public Records

China Family Records, 1800–1891. Reel 118, Maine State Archives.
City of Calais Cemetery Records.
Commonwealth of Massachusetts. *Record of Civil Commissions, 1806–1816*. Manuscript records at the Massachusetts Archives.
Cumberland County (ME) Register of Deeds. Vol. 31, pp. 165–166; vol. 32, p. 261.
District Court Records, District Court for the Eastern District, Washington County in Machias (ME). Vol. 4, Docket 526, pp. 176–177.
Hall, Mabel Goodwin, ed. *Vital Records of Hallowell, Maine, to the Year 1892*, 6 vols. Auburn, ME: Merrill & Webber Co., 1924–1929.
Heads of Families at the First Census of the United States Taken in the Year 1790, Maine. Washington, DC: Government Printing Office, 1908.
Heads of Families at the First Census of the United States Taken in the Year 1790, Massachusetts. Washington, DC: Government Printing Office, 1908.
Hoffman, D. *Bucksport Vital Records, Vol. I*. [Bangor]: Cay-Bel Publishing Co., [1980?].
Jackson, Ronald Vern, ed. *Massachusetts 1800 Census Index*. Bountiful, UT: Accelerated Indexing Systems, 1981.
Jackson, Ronald Vern, and Gary Ronald Teeples, eds. *Maine 1830 Census Index*. Bountiful, UT: Accelerated Indexing Systems, 1977.
———. *Maine 1840 Census Index*. Bountiful, UT: Accelerated Indexing Systems, 1978.
———. *Maine 1850 Census Index*. Bountiful, UT: Accelerated Indexing Systems, 1978.
Jackson, Ronald Vern; Gary Ronald Teeples; and David Schaefermeyer,

eds. *Maine 1800 Census Index*. Bountiful, UT: Accelerated Indexing Systems, 1977.
———. *Maine 1810 Census Index*. Bountiful, UT: Accelerated Indexing Systems, 1976.
———. *Maine 1820 Census Index*. Bountiful, UT: Accelerated Indexing Systems, 1976.
Kennebec County (ME) Register of Deeds. Vols. 4, 6, 8, 9, 10, 11, 12, 14, 17, 18, 22, 23, 24, 29, 30, 31, 32, 36, 38, 45, 51, 54, 56, 57, 59, 60, 61, 62, 63, 66, 69, 71, 75, 81, and 90.
Lapham, W. B. "Hallowell Records," in *Collections and Proceedings of the Maine Historical Society,* second series (Portland, 1895), VI, pp. 94–100.
Lincoln County (ME) Register of Deeds. Book 21, pp. 187–188.
Maine Direct Tax Census of 1798.
Maine Old Cemetery Association. *Cemetery Inscription Project.* Volumes at the Maine State Library, Augusta.
Massachusetts Soldiers and Sailors of the Revolutionary War, 17 vols. Boston: Wright & Potter Printing Co., 1896–1908.
Oxford County (ME) Register of Deeds. Vol. 25, pp. 203–204.
Population Schedules of the Fifth Census of the United States, 1830. Washington, DC: National Archives, 1946. Microcopy no. 19, roll 47.
Population Schedules of the Fourth Census of the United States, 1820. Washington, DC: National Archives, 1959. Microcopy no. 33, roll 35.
Population Schedules of the Seventh Census of the United States, 1850. Washington, DC: National Archives, 1963. Microcopy no. 432, roll 273.
Population Schedules of the Sixth Census of the United States, 1840. Washington, DC: National Archives, 1967. Microcopy no. 704, roll 151.
Population Schedules of the Third Census of the United States, 1810: Maine. Washington, DC: National Archives, 1960. Microcopy no. 252, roll 11.
The Public Statutes at Large of the United States of America, from the Organization of the Government in 1789, to March 3, 1845. Boston: Charles C. Little & James Brown, 1846, vol. V.
Records of the Plantation of Canaan and the Town of Canaan (Skowhegan), 1783–1821, parts I and II. Typescript. Maine State Library, Augusta.
Records of the Town of China.
Records of the Town of Wayne, Maine. Reel 524, Maine State Archives.
Resolves of the General Court of the Commonwealth of Massachusetts . . . [1812–1814, 1817–1819]. Boston: Russell, Cutler & Co., or Russell & Gardner, 1812–1814, 1817–1819.
Resolves of the General Court of the Commonwealth of Massachusetts . . . [1819–1824]. Boston: True & Greene, 1824.
Somerset County (ME) Probate Court Records. Vol. 16, pp. 509–510; vol. 17, pp. 108–109; vol. 18, p. 34; vol. 19, pp. 31, 194.

Town of Buckfield Vital Records, Marriages and Intentions, 1804–1858. Reel 90, Maine State Archives.

Town of Woodstock Vital Records, 1814–1895. Reel 558, Maine State Archives.

United States District Court, Maine District. Bankruptcy petition no. 2363, filed by Japhet [*sic*] C. Washburn on October 27, 1842.

Vital Records of Calais, Maine, 1840–1905. Reel 96, Maine State Archives.

Vital Records of Carver, Massachusetts, to the Year 1850. Boston: New England Historic Genealogical Society, 1911.

Vital Records of China, Maine. Reel 117, Maine State Archives.

Vital Records of Greene, Maine, 1784–1859. Reel 204, Maine State Archives.

Vital Records of Palmyra, Maine, 1800–1867. Reel 335, Maine State Archives.

Vital Records of Plympton, Massachusetts, to the Year 1850. Boston: New England Historic Genealogical Society, 1923.

Vital Records of Rochester, Massachusetts, to the Year 1850, 2 vols. Boston: New England Historic Genealogical Society, 1914.

Vital Records of Shrewsbury, Mass., to the End of the Year 1849. Worcester, MA: Franklin P. Rice, 1904.

Vital Records of Turner, Maine, 1787–1839. Reel 478, Maine State Archives.

Wayne (Maine) Vital Records, 1773–1900. Reel 524, Maine State Archives.

Webster, Henry Sewall. *Vital Records of Gardiner, Maine, to the Year 1892. Part I, Births.* Gardiner, ME: Reporter-Journal Press, 1914.

———. *Vital Records of Gardiner, Maine, to the Year 1892. Part II, Marriages and Deaths.* Boston: Stanhope Press, 1915.

White, Virgil D., transcriber. *Index to War of 1812 Pension Files.* Waynesboro, TN: National Historical Publishing Co., 1989.

Other Primary Sources (Books, Essays, Manuscripts, and Pamphlets)

Allen, William. "Now and Then," in *Collections of the Maine Historical Society,* first series, 10 vols. Portland: published for the society, 1876, VII, pp. 267–289.

Barrows, Horace Aurelius. Horace Barrows Papers. Manuscript Collection 19, Maine Historical Society, Boxes 1 and 2.

Book of the South Parish Church [Hallowell, Maine], 1794–1909. Churches, Book 162. Hubbard Free Library, Hallowell, ME.

Bradley, Caleb. Diaries, 1799–1861. Manuscript Collection 844, Maine Historical Society.

Bray, Oliver. *An Oration on Music: pronounced at Fryeburg, before the Hans-Gram Musical Society on their first anniversary, October 10, 1811*. Portland: Arthur Shirley, 1812.

Burrill, Thomas. *History of Central Lodge, No. 45, China, Maine* [December 27, 1823, to September 15, 1875]. Unpublished manuscript. Personal collection, Margaret Clifford, China, ME.

China [Maine] Academy. *Catalogue of the Officers and Students of China Academy, November, 1822*. Hallowell, ME: Goodale, Glazier & Co., Printers, [1822]. Broadside Collection, American Antiquarian Society.

Coffin, Rev. Paul. "Memoir and Journals (1760–1800)," in *Collections of the Maine Historical Society,* first series, 10 vols. Portland: published for the society, 1856, IV, pp. 239–405.

Dana, Daniel, A.M. *An Address on Sacred Musick, Delivered at a publick meeting of the Rockingham Sacred Musick Society in Hampton, October 6th, 1813*. Exeter, NH: Charles Norris & Co., 1813.

"The Diary of Mrs. Martha Moore Ballard (1785 to 1812)," in Charles E. Nash, *The History of Augusta*. Augusta: Charles E. Nash & Son, 1904, pp. 229–464.

The Diary of William Bentley, D.D., Pastor of East Church, Salem, Massachusetts, 4 vols. Salem: Essex Institute, 1907; repr. Gloucester, MA: Peter Smith, 1962.

Diary of William Sewall (1797–1846), 1817 to 1846, ed. C. E. Goodell. Springfield, IL: Hartman Printing Co., 1930.

The East Somerset County Register, 1911–12. Auburn, ME: compiled and published by Chatto & Turner, [1912].

Emerson, Samuel, A.M. *An Oration on Music Pronounced at Portland, May 28, 1800*. Portland: E. A. Jenks, 1800.

Fisher, Elijah. Manuscript diary, 1796–1837, Elijah Fisher Papers. Manuscript Collection 55, Maine Historical Society, Box 1/3.

[Gilman, Samuel]. *Memoirs of a New England Village Choir, with Occasional Reflections*. Boston: S. G. Goodrich, 1829; repr. New York: Da Capo Press, 1984.

Goodwin, D. R. *Memoir of John Merrick, Esq., Prepared for the Maine Historical Society*. N.p.: Henry B. Ashmond, 1862.

Gould, Nathaniel D. *Church Music in America*. Boston: A. N. Johnson, 1853; repr. New York: AMS Press, 1972.

Hale, David. Papers of the Hale family of Turner, Maine, 1792–1851. Manuscript Collection of the Maine Historical Society, Misc. Box 4/3.

King, William. William King Papers, 1760–1834. Manuscript Collection 165, Maine Historical Society, Boxes 6/10, 16/12, 18/6, and 18/9.

Little, Henry. "An Account of Bucksport in 1827, by Henry Little," *Bangor Historical Magazine,* VI/1–3 (July-September 1890), pp. 42–45.

Long, Peirce, ed. *From the Journal of Zadoc Long, 1800–73*. Caldwell, ID: Caxton Printers, 1943.

Manley, Abbie Sewall. *Collected Manuscripts Connected with the Sewall family of Augusta*. Copies in the Maine State Library.

Manning, Samuel. *Two Dialogues, in which are stated, first, Arguments for and against the use of musical instruments in the public worship of God . . .* Windsor, VT: printed by Alden Spooner for the author, 1807.

Manual of the [South] Congregational Church, Hallowell, Maine, 1790–1873. Hallowell, ME: Masters & Livermore, 1873.

The Massachusetts Register and United States Calendar for the year of our Lord 1809. Boston: John West; Manning & Loring, n.d..

The Massachusetts Register and United States Calendar for the year of our Lord 1811. Boston: John West & Co.; Manning & Loring, n.d..

The Massachusetts Register and United States Calendar for the year of our Lord 1812. Boston: John West & Co.; Manning & Loring, n.d.

The Massachusetts Register and United States Calendar for the year of our Lord 1818. Boston: James Loring; West & Richardson, n.d.

The Massachusetts Register and United States Calendar for the year of our Lord 1820. Boston: James Loring; West, Richardson & Lord, n.d.

[Maxim, Abraham]. *The Gospel Hymn-Book*. N.p.: n.p., 1818.

Minutes of the Lincoln Association, Holden at St. George, Sept. 20 and 21, 1815. Hallowell, ME: N. Cheever, 1815.

Mitchell, Hon. Ammi R. *An Address on Sacred Music, delivered before the "Beneficent Musical Society," in the county of Cumberland, August 25, 1812, on their second anniversary, at the Baptist Meeting-House in North-Yarmouth*. Portland: Hyde, Lord & Co., 1812.

Musical Society in Falmouth. *Constitution, September 1, 1807*. Manuscript Collection S-627, Maine Historical Society, Misc. Box 24/4.

Notes taken from the Records of the First Parish, York, Maine. Typescript. Old York Historical Society, York, ME.

Old Hundred, Order of Performance at Bowdoin College, April 29, 1822. [Brunswick, ME]: n.p., [1822]. Broadside Collection, American Antiquarian Society.

Old South Congregational Church [Hallowell, Maine] Parish Accounts, 1820–1824. File folder at the Hubbard Free Library, Hallowell, ME.

Old South Congregational Church Sabbath School, 1820–1825. Manuscript at the Hubbard Free Library, Hallowell, ME.

Order of Exercises at the Dedication of the Bethlehem Church, in Augusta, October 18, 1827. [Augusta, ME]: n.p., [1827]. Broadside Collection, American Antiquarian Society.

Order of Exercises at the Installation of Rev. Edward Mitchell, as colleague with Rev. John Murray, over the First Universal Society in

Boston, September 12, 1810. [Boston]: n.p., [1810]. Special Collections, Bowdoin College, Brunswick, ME.

Order of Exercises at the Ordination of Rev. Darvin [i.e., Darwin] Adams, Camden, Maine. [Belfast, ME]: n.p., [1828]. Broadside Collection, American Antiquarian Society.

Order of Exercises at the Ordination of the Rev. George Shepard, March 5, 1828. [Hallowell, ME]: n.p., [1828]. Collections of the Hubbard Free Library, Hallowell, ME.

Parlin, W. Harrison. *Reminiscences of East Winthrop*. East Winthrop, ME: Banner Publishing Company, 1891.

Parsons, Isaac. "Some Account of New Gloucester," in *Collections of the Maine Historical Society,* first series, 10 vols. Portland: Maine Historical Society, 1847, II, pp. 151–164.

Perley, Jeremiah. *The Debates, Resolutions, and Other Proceedings of the Convention of Delegates, assembled at Portland on the 11th, and continued until the 29th day of October, 1819, for the purpose of forming a constitution for the State of Maine to which is prefixed the Constitution taken in convention*. Portland: A. Shirley, 1820.

Pew Records of the South Parish Church, Hallowell, 1794–1838. Churches, Book 163. Hubbard Free Library, Hallowell, ME.

Porter, J. W. "A Register of the Names of the Members of the Methodist Episcopal Church, in Orrington Circuit, A.D. 1819," *Bangor Historical Magazine,* I/2 (August 1885), pp. 22–26.

Records of the First Baptist Church in China, 1801–March, 1852. Typescript copy in the possession of Mrs. William Foster, church clerk.

Records of the First Church of Wareham, Mass., 1739–1891, transcribed and indexed by Leonard H. Smith, Jr. Clearwater, FL: n.p., 1974.

Records of the First Unitarian Church in Hallowell, 1824–1857. Churches, Book 53. Hubbard Free Library, Hallowell, ME.

Robbins, Benjamin. Three diaries, August 2, 1810–August 17, 1816. Manuscript Collections, Maine Historical Society.

Sewall, Henry. Henry Sewall Diaries, 1784–1794. Typescript. Maine State Library.

Sewall, Rev. Jotham. *A Memoir of Rev. Jotham Sewall, of Chesterville, Maine*. Boston: Tappan & Whittemore, 1853.

Stinchfield, Ephraim. Ephraim Stinchfield Papers, 1777–1830. Manuscript Collection 44, Maine Historical Society.

Subscription Lists for Cape Neddock Singing Schools, 1850–1863. Manuscript Collection 422, Old York Historical Society, York, ME.

Thomas, Isaiah. Isaiah Thomas Papers. Special Collection, American Antiquarian Society, Box 8, Folder 1.

Walker, Tobias. Diaries in the Walker Family Collection. Manuscript Collection 234, Maine Historical Society.

Washburn, Japheth C. Letter to A. H. Abbott, Esq., January 14, 1850. Personal collection, Margaret Clifford, China, ME.

———. Letter to O. W. Washburn, Esq., October 25, 1841. Personal collection, Margaret Clifford, China, ME.

Webb, Nathan. *Reminiscences of Portland.* N.p.: n.p., c. 1875.

Weston, Eben. *The Early Settlers of Canaan* (written for the *Somerset Reporter,* 1890–1892). Typewritten copy by Kathleen A. Martin. Skowhegan Free Public Library, Skowhegan, ME.

Willis, William. *Journals of the Rev. Thomas Smith, and the Rev. Samuel Deane.* Portland: Joseph S. Bailey, 1849.

Dissertations and Theses

Arndt, John Christopher. "The solid men of Bangor: Economic, Business and Political Growth on Maine's Urban Frontier, 1769–1845." Ph.D. dissertation, Florida State University, 1987.

Britton, Allen P. "Theoretical Introductions in American Tune-books to 1800." Ph.D. dissertation, University of Michigan, 1949.

Buechner, Alan. "Yankee Singing Schools and the Golden Age of Choral Music in New England, 1760–1800." D.Ed. dissertation, Harvard University, 1960.

Bushnell, Vinson C. "Daniel Read of New Haven (1757–1836): The Man and His Musical Activities." Ph.D. dissertation, Harvard University, 1978.

Cohen, Marcie. "The Journals of Joshua Whitman, 1809–1811: An Analysis of Pre-Industrial Community in Rural Maine." M.A. thesis, College of William and Mary in Virginia, 1985.

Cole, Ronald Fred. "Music in Portland, Maine, from Colonial Times Through the Nineteenth Century." Ph.D. dissertation, Indiana University, 1975.

Cooke, Nym. "American Psalmodists in Contact and Collaboration, 1770–1820," 2 vols. Ph.D. dissertation, University of Michigan, 1990.

Davenport, Linda Gilbert. "Maine's Sacred Tunebooks, 1800–1830: Divine Song on the Northeast Frontier." Ph.D. dissertation, University of Colorado-Boulder, 1991.

Genuchi, Marvin C. "The Life and Music of Jacob French (1754–1817), Colonial American Composer." Ph.D. dissertation, State University of Iowa, 1964.

Klocko, David G. "Jeremiah Ingalls's 'The Christian Harmony: or, Songster's Companion' (1805)." Ph.D. dissertation, University of Michigan, 1978.

Kroeger, Karl. "The Worcester Collection of Sacred Harmony and Sacred Music in America, 1786–1803." Ph.D. dissertation, Brown University, 1976.

McCormick, David Wilferd. "Oliver Holden, Composer and Anthologist." S.M.D. dissertation, Union Theological Seminary in the City of New York, 1963.

Nitz, Donald A. "Community Musical Societies in Massachusetts to 1840." D.M.A. dissertation, Boston University, 1964.

Noble, John O., Jr. "Messengers from the Wilderness: Maine's Representatives to the Massachusetts General Court, 1760–1819." Ph.D. dissertation, University of Maine, 1975.

Owen, Earl McLain, Jr. "The Life and Music of Supply Belcher (1751–1836), 'Handel of Maine.'" D.M.A. document, Southern Baptist Theological Seminary, 1969.

Plachta, Adele E. "The Privileged and the Poor: A History of the District of Maine, 1771–1793." Ph.D. dissertation, University of Maine, 1975.

Reynolds, Frieda B. "The Music of Supply Belcher." M.M. thesis, Chicago Musical College, Roosevelt University, 1968.

Steel, David W. "Stephen Jenks (1772–1856): American Composer and Tunebook Compiler." Ph.D. dissertation, University of Michigan, 1982.

Wilcox, Glenn C. "Jacob Kimball, Jr. (1761–1826): His Life and Works." Ph.D. dissertation, University of Southern California, 1957.

Willhide, J. Laurence. "Samuel Holyoke: American Music Educator." Ph.D. dissertation, University of Southern California, 1954.

Worst, John W. "New England Psalmody, 1760–1810: Analysis of an American Idiom." Ph.D. dissertation, University of Michigan, 1974.

General Books (Secondary Sources)

Ahlstrom, Sydney E. *A Religious History of the American People*. New Haven: Yale University Press, 1972.

Allen, Rev. Stephen, and Rev. W. H. Pilsbury. *History of Methodism in Maine*. Augusta: Press of Charles E. Nash, 1887.

Allen, William. *History of Industry, Maine,* second edition. Skowhegan, ME: Smith & Emery, Printers, 1869.

Atlas of Somerset County, Maine. Houlton and Skowhegan, ME: George N. Colby & Co., 1883.

Attwood, Stanley Bearce. *The Length and Breadth of Maine*. Orono: University of Maine at Orono Press, 1977.

Bailey, William B. *A Heritage and a Trust: China Baptist Church, 1801–1964*. Typescript, May 1964. Brown Memorial Library, China.

Bandel, Betty. *Sing the Lord's Song in a Strange Land: The Life of Justin Morgan*. Rutherford, NJ: Fairleigh Dickinson University Press, 1981.

Banks, Ronald F. *Maine Becomes a State: The Movement to Separate Maine from Massachusetts, 1785–1820*. Middletown, CT: Wesleyan University Press, 1970.

Bartlett, J. Gardner. *Gregory Stone Genealogy*. Boston: published for the Stone Family Association, 1918.

Benson, Louis F. *The English Hymn: Its Development and Use in Worship*. New York: George H. Doran Co., 1915; repr. Richmond, VA: John Knox Press, 1962.

Berry, Ira. *Sketch of the History of the Beethoven Musical Society, of Portland, Maine, 1819–1825*. Portland: Stephen Berry, Printer, 1888.

Bigelow, Gladys M., and Ruth M. Knowles. *History of St. Albans, Maine*. N.p.: Gladys M. Bigelow & Ruth M. Knowles, 1982.

Black, Henry Campbell. *Black's Law Dictionary,* fifth edition. St. Paul, MN: West Publishing Co., 1979.

Blanding, Edward Mitchell, compiler. *The City of Bangor*. Bangor: Bangor Board of Trade, 1899.

Bliss, William Root. *Colonial Times on Buzzard's Bay*. Boston: Houghton, Mifflin & Company, 1888.

Bourne, Edward E. *The History of Wells and Kennebunk*. Portland: B. Thurston & Company, 1875.

Bouvier, John. *Bouvier's Law Dictionary,* 2 vols., new edition revised by Francis Rawle. Boston: Boston Book Co., 1897.

Brigham, Clarence S. *History and Bibliography of American Newspapers, 1690–1820*. Worcester: American Antiquarian Society, 1947.

Britton, Allen; Irving Lowens; and Richard Crawford. *American Sacred Music Imprints, 1698–1810: A Bibliography*. Worcester: American Antiquarian Society, 1990.

Buck, Alice F. *Bucksport . . . Past and Present*. N.p.: n.p., 1951.

Burrage, Henry S. *History of the Baptists in Maine*. Portland: Marks Printing House, 1904.

Butler, Ben, and Natalie S. Butler. *Farmington's Musical Heritage—from Belcher to "TDX"*. Farmington, ME: Knowlton & McLeary Co., 1975.

Butler, Francis Gould. *History of Farmington, Franklin County, Maine: 1776–1885*. Farmington, ME: Knowlton, McLeary, and Co., 1885; repr. Somersworth, NH: New England History Press, 1983.

The Centennial Celebration of the Settlement of Bangor, September 30, 1869. Bangor: Benjamin A. Burr, Printer, 1870.

Chase, Gilbert. *America's Music from the Pilgrims to the Present,* revised third edition. Urbana: University of Illinois Press, 1987.

China Historical Society. *Japheth Coombs Washburn and His Descendants: Four Generations of Service to the Town of China* [Remembrance Day booklet]. Typescript, 1981.

Clark, Calvin Montague. *History of the Congregational Churches in Maine,* 2 vols. Portland: Congregational Christian Conference of Maine, [c. 1935].

Clawson, Mary Ann. *Constructing Brotherhood: Class, Gender, and Fraternalism*. Princeton, NJ: Princeton University Press, 1989.

Coburn, Louise Helen. *Skowhegan on the Kennebec*, 2 vols. Skowhegan, ME: Independent-Reporter Press, 1941.

Corliss, Augustus W., ed. *Old Times of North Yarmouth, Maine*. [North Yarmouth, ME]: n.p., 1877–1885; repr. Somersworth, NH: New Hampshire Publishing Company, 1977.

Cox, H. Russell, and David L. Swett. *History of Orrington, Maine*. N.p.: Cay-Bel Publishing Co., 1988.

Crawford, Richard. *Andrew Law, American Psalmodist*. Evanston, IL: Northwestern University Press, 1968.

Daniel, Ralph T. *The Anthem in New England Before 1800*. Evanston, IL: Northwestern University Press, 1966.

Dow, Sterling T. *Maine Postal History and Postmarks*. Lawrence, MA: Quarterman Publications, 1976.

Drisko, George W. *Narrative of the Town of Machias*. Machias, ME: Press of the Republican, 1904.

Dumenil, Lynn. *Freemasonry and American Culture, 1880–1930*. Princeton, NJ: Princeton University Press, 1984.

Edwards, George Thornton. *Music and Musicians of Maine*. Portland: Southworth Press, 1928.

Evans, Charles. *American Bibliography, 1638–1820*. Chicago: Columbia Press, 1903–1955.

Farnam, Charles H. *History of the Descendants of John Whitman of Weymouth, Mass*. New Haven: Tuttle, Morehouse & Taylor, Printers, 1889.

Fassett, Frederick Gardiner, Jr. *A History of Newspapers in the District of Maine, 1785–1820*. Orono: University Press, 1932.

Foote, Henry Wilder. *Three Centuries of American Hymnody*. Cambridge, MA: Harvard University Press, 1940.

French, Rev. W. R. *A History of Turner, Maine, from Its Settlement to 1886*. Portland: Hoyt, Fogg & Donham, 1887; repr. Bowie, MD: Heritage Books, 1986.

Goen, C. C. *Revivalism and Separatism in New England, 1740–1800*. New Haven: Yale University Press, 1962.

Goodale, Leon A. *Notes on the Lives of Edward and Sarah Temple Goodale, Pioneer Settlers of Shrewsbury, Massachusetts, 1738–1786*. [Worcester]: mimeographed, [1948]. Located at the American Antiquarian Society.

Goodwin, John Hayes. *Daniel Goodwin of Ancient Kittery, Maine, and His Descendents*. N.p.: n.p., 1985.

Greenleaf, Jonathan. *Sketches of the Ecclesiastical History of the State of Maine*. Portsmouth, NH: Harrison Gray, 1821.

Greenleaf, Moses. *A Statistical View of the District of Maine*. Boston: Cummings & Hilliard, 1816.

———. *A Survey of the State of Maine, in Reference to Its Geographical Features, Statistics and Political Economy*. Portland: Shirley & Hyde, 1829.

Griffin, Joseph. *History of the Press of Maine (with 1874 Supplement)*. Brunswick: Press of J. Griffin . . . Charles H. Fuller, Printer, 1874.

Griffith, Henry S. *History of the Town of Carver, Massachusetts: Historical Review, 1637–1910*. New Bedford, MA: E. Anthony & Sons, Printers, 1913.

Grow, Mary M. *China, Maine: Bicentennial History, Including 1984 Revisions,* 2 books. Weeks Mills, ME: Marion T. Van Strien, [1984?].

Hamm, Charles. *Music in the New World*. New York: W. W. Norton & Company, 1983.

Hatch, Louis Clinton. *Maine: A History,* 5 vols. New York: American Historical Society, 1919.

History of Litchfield and an Account of Its Centennial Celebration, 1895. Augusta: Kennebec Journal Print, 1897.

History of the Town of Wayne, Kennebec County, Maine, from Its Settlement to 1898. Augusta: Maine Farmer Publishing Co., 1898.

Horsman, Reginald. *The Frontier in the Formative Years, 1783–1815*. New York: Holt, Rinehart & Winston, 1970.

Horwitz, Richard P. *Anthropology Toward History: Culture and Work in a Nineteenth-Century Maine Town*. Middletown, CT: Wesleyan University Press, 1978.

Howe, Timothy. *History of the Town of Turner from the First Grant, in 1765, to the Close of 1843*. Manuscript written in 1843; typescript by Samuel D. Rumery in 1927; housed at the Maine Historical Society.

Ireland, Genevieve Rogers Weeks. *A Compilation of Data on the Early History and People of Palmyra, Maine*. Shrewsbury, MA: the author, 1980.

Johnson, H. Earle. *Musical Interludes in Boston, 1795–1830*. New York: Columbia University Press, 1943; repr. New York: AMS Press, 1967.

Keene, James A. *Music and Education in Vermont, 1700–1900*. Macomb, IL: Glenbridge Publishing, 1987.

Kilby, William Henry. *Eastport and Passamaquoddy*. Eastport, ME: Edward E. Shead & Company, 1888.

Kingsbury, Henry D., and Simeon L. Deyo, eds. *Illustrated History of Kennebec County, Maine*. New York: H. W. Blake & Co., 1892.

Knowles, Ruth McGowan. *Warren's Four Towns: St. Albans, Hartland, Palmyra, Corinna*. N.p.: Ruth McGowan Knowles, 1988.

Knowlton, Rev. I. C. *Annals of Calais, Maine, and St. Stephen, New Brunswick*. Calais, ME: J. A. Sears, 1875.

Lapham, William Berry. *History of Woodstock, Maine*. Portland: Stephen

Berry, Printer, 1882; repr. Somersworth, NH: New England History Press, 1983.

Lilly, Georgiana Hewins, state chairman, Genealogical Records, 1932–1933. *Historical and Genealogical Data Presented to Maine Historical Society by Maine Chapters, Daughters of the American Revolution.* Typewritten, 1932–1933; housed at the Maine Historical Society.

Little, George Thomas. *The Descendants of George Little, Who Came to Newbury, Massachusetts, in 1640.* Auburn, ME: published by the author, 1882.

Littlefield, Ada Douglas. *An Old River Town.* New York: Calkins & Company, 1907.

Lorenz, Ellen Jane. *Glory, Hallelujah! The Story of the Campmeeting Spiritual.* Nashville, TN: Abingdon, 1980.

Lovell, Daisy Washburn. *Glimpses of Early Wareham.* Wareham, MA: Wareham Historical Society, 1970.

Lowen, Irving. *Music and Musicians in Early America.* New York: W. W. Norton & Co., 1964.

Macdougall, Hamilton C. *Early New England Psalmody: An Historical Appreciation, 1620–1820.* Brattleboro, VT: Stephen Daye Press, 1940; repr. New York: Da Capo Press, 1969.

McKay, David P., and Richard Crawford. *William Billings of Boston: Eighteenth-Century Composer.* Princeton: Princeton University Press, 1975.

McLellan, Hugh D. *History of Gorham, Maine,* compiled and edited by Katharine B. Lewis. Portland: Smith & Sale, 1903.

MacNutt, W. S. *New Brunswick, A History: 1784–1867.* Toronto: Macmillan of Canada, 1963.

Marini, Stephen A. *Radical Sects of Revolutionary New England.* Cambridge, MA: Harvard University Press, 1982.

Mathews, Mitford M., ed. *A Dictionary of Americanisms on Historical Principles,* 2 vols. Chicago: University of Chicago Press, 1951.

Memories of Hallowell. II. Churches. Scrapbook no. 41, Hubbard Free Library, Hallowell, ME.

Merrill, Georgia Drew, ed. *History of Androscoggin County, Maine.* Boston: W. A. Fergusson & Co., 1891.

Metcalf, Frank J. *American Psalmody; or, Titles of Books Containing Tunes Printed in America from 1721 to 1820.* New York: Charles F. Heartman, 1917; repr. New York: Da Capo Press, 1968.

———. *American Writers and Compilers of Sacred Music.* New York: Abingdon Press, [1925]; repr. Russell & Russell, 1967.

Millet, Rev. Joshua. *A History of the Baptists in Maine; together with brief notices of societies and institutions, and a dictionary of the labors of each minister.* Portland: Charles Day & Co., 1845.

Mitchell, Daggett, Walton, and Lawton, compilers. *The Town Register,*

1907: Bucksport, Orland, Orrington, Verona. Brunswick, ME: H. E. Mitchell Co., 1907.

Monroe, Ira Thompson. *History of the Town of Livermore* . . . Lewiston, ME: Lewiston Journal Printshop, [1928].

Morris, Edward S. *Maine Civil Officer: A Complete Guide for Justices of the Peace* . . . , revised and corrected by Hon. Ether Shepley. Portland: Bailey & Noyes, 1861.

Morris, Gerald E., ed. *The Maine Bicentennial Atlas: An Historical Survey*. Portland: Maine Historical Society, 1976.

Mower, Walter Lindley. *Sesquicentennial History of the Town of Greene*. [Auburn, ME]: n.p., 1938.

Nason, Emma Huntington. *Old Hallowell on the Kennebec*. Augusta: Burleigh & Flynt, 1909.

North, James W. *The History of Augusta, Maine*. Augusta: Clapp & North, 1870; repr. Somersworth, NH: New England History Press, 1981.

Notes, Historical, Descriptive, and Personal, of Livermore in Androscoggin (formerly in Oxford) County, Maine. Portland: Bailey & Noyes, 1874.

Noyes, R. Webb. *A Bibliography of Maine Imprints to 1820*. Stonington, ME: Mr. and Mrs. R. Webb Noyes, 1930.

Page, Annie F. *Historical Sketch of the South Congregationalist Church (Old South Church) of Hallowell*. Hallowell, ME: Register Press, 1900.

Palmyra 175th Anniversary, 1807–1982. [Palmyra, ME: Town of Palmyra], 1982.

Pemberton, Carol Ann. *Lowell Mason: His Life and Work*. Ann Arbor: UMI Research Press, 1985.

Perkins, Charles C., and John S. Dwight. *History of the Handel and Haydn Society,* 2 vols. Boston: A. Mudge, 1883–1913; repr. New York: Da Capo Press, 1977.

Pichierri, Louis. *Music in New Hampshire*. New York: Columbia University Press, 1960.

Pilsbury, Rev. W. H. *History of Methodism in East Maine,* Book II. Augusta: Press of Charles E. Nash, 1887.

Printer File Cards for Franklin Glazier, Ezekiel Goodale, and Andrew Masters. American Antiquarian Society, Worcester, MA.

Remich, Daniel. *History of Kennebunk from Its Earliest Settlement to 1890*. N.p.: n.p., 1911.

Ridlon, G. T., Sr. *Saco Valley Settlements and Families*. Portland: G. T. Ridlon, Sr., 1895.

Rowe, William Hutchinson. *Ancient North Yarmouth and Yarmouth, Maine, 1636–1936: A History*. Yarmouth: Southworth-Anthoensen Press, 1937.

Sesquicentennial Palmyra, Maine, 1807–1957. [Pittsfield, ME: Pittsfield Advertiser, 1957].

Skillin, Glenn. *Bibliography of Printing in Maine Through 1820*. Unpublished typescript.

Snell, Katherine H., and Vincent P. Ledew. *Historic Hallowell*. [Augusta]: Kennebec Journal Print Shop, 1962.

Sonneck, Oscar G. T. *A Bibliography of Early Secular American Music (Eighteenth Century)*, revised and enlarged by William Trent Upton. 1945; repr. New York: Da Capo Press, 1964.

———. *Francis Hopkinson and James Lyon*. Washington, DC: McQueen, 1905; repr. New York: Da Capo Press, 1967.

Stevenson, Robert. *Protestant Church Music in America: A Short Survey of Men and Movements from 1564 to the Present*. New York: W. W. Norton & Co., 1966.

Taylor, Alan. *Liberty Men and Great Proprietors: The Revolutionary Settlement on the Maine Frontier, 1760–1820*. Chapel Hill: University of North Carolina Press, 1990.

Temperley, Nicholas. *The Music of the English Parish Church*, 2 vols. Cambridge: Cambridge University Press, 1979.

Temperley, Nicholas, and Charles G. Manns. *Fuging Tunes in the Eighteenth Century*. Detroit: Information Coordinators, 1983.

Thurston, David. *A Brief History of Winthrop, from 1764 to October 1855*. Portland: Brown Thurston, 1855.

Ulrich, Laurel Thatcher. *A Midwife's Tale: The Life of Martha Ballard, Based on Her Diary, 1785–1812*. New York: Alfred A. Knopf, 1990.

Vroom, Mildred M. *Exeter Publishers and Their Works, 1774–1865*. Exeter, NH: n.p., 1933; slightly revised, 1955. Typescript copy, Exeter Public Library.

Walton, George W. *History of the Town of Wayne, Kennebec County, Maine, from Its Settlement to 1898*. Augusta: Maine Farmer Publishing Company, 1898.

Ward, Andrew H. *History of the Town of Shrewsbury, Massachusetts, from Its Settlement in 1717 to 1829*. Boston: Samuel G. Drake, 1847.

Washburne, Breton P. *The Washburn Family in America*. N.p.: n.p., 1983.

Wheeler, George Augustus, M.D., and Henry Warren Wheeler. *History of Brunswick, Topsham, and Harpswell, Maine*. Boston: Alfred Mudge & Son, Printers, 1878.

Wiggin, Frances T. Frances T. Wiggin Papers, 1950–1983. Collection 364, Maine Historical Society, Box 5/7.

———. *Library of the Maine Historical Society. Lists of Music by Maine Composers and Compilers and Music with Portland Imprint*. Typescript, Maine Historical Society.

———. *Maine Composers and Their Music, Book II. A Biographical Dictionary*. Portland: Maine Historical Society, 1976.

Williamson, Joseph. *A Bibliography of the State of Maine from the Earliest Period to 1891,* 2 vols. Portland: Thurston Print, 1896; repr. Somersworth, NH: Maine State Library and New England History Press, 1985.

Williamson, William D. *The History of the State of Maine from Its First Discovery, A.D. 1602, to the Separation, A.D. 1820, Inclusive,* 2 vols. Hallowell, ME: Glazier, Masters & Co., 1832.

Willis, William. *The History of Portland, from 1632 to 1864*. Portland: Bailey & Noyes, 1865; repr. Somersworth, NH: N. H. Publishing Co. and Maine Historical Society, 1972.

Wolfe, Richard J. *Early American Music Engraving and Printing*. Urbana: University of Illinois Press, 1980.

———. *Secular Music in America, 1801–1825: A Bibliography,* 3 vols. New York: New York Public Library, 1964.

Wright, H. B., and E. D. Harvey, *The Settlement and Story of Oakham, Massachusetts,* 2 vols. N.p.: n.p., 1947.

Articles and Essays (Secondary Sources)

Adams, John W., and Alice Bee Kasakoff. "Wealth and Migration in Massachusetts and Maine: 1771–1798," *Journal of Economic History,* XLV/2 (June 1985), pp. 363–368.

Allis, Frederick, Jr. "The Maine Frontier," in *A History of Maine: A Collection of Readings on the History of Maine, 1600–1970,* ed. Ronald F. Banks. Dubuque, IA: Kendall/Hunt Publishing Company, 1969, pp. 123–135.

Beckwith, John. "Tunebooks and Hymnals in Canada, 1801–1939," *American Music,* VI/2 (Summer 1988), pp. 193–234.

Blum, Stephen. "The Fuging Tune in British North America," in *Can-Mus Documents I* (Proceedings of a February 1986 conference organized by the Institute for Canadian Music, University of Toronto). Toronto: Institute for Canadian Music, 1987, pp. 119–148.

Brown, Richard D. "The Emergence of Urban Society in Rural Massachusetts, 1760–1820," *Journal of American History,* LXI/1 (June 1974), pp. 29–51.

Butler, Joyce. "Cochranism Delineated: A Twentieth-Century Study," in *Maine in the Early Republic: From Revolution to Statehood,* ed. Charles E. Clark, James S. Leamon, and Karen Bowden. Hanover, NH: University Press of New England, 1988, pp. 146–164.

———. "Rising Like a Phoenix: Commerce in Southern Maine, 1775–1830," in *Agreeable Situations: Society, Commerce, and Art in Southern Maine, 1780–1830*. Kennebunk, ME: Brick Store Museum, 1987, pp. 15–35.

Candee, Richard M. " 'The Appearance of Enterprise and Improvement':

Architecture and the Coastal Elite of Maine," in *Agreeable Situations: Society, Commerce, and Art in Southern Maine, 1780–1830*. Kennebunk, ME: Brick Store Museum, 1987, pp. 67–87.

Cooke, Nym. "Itinerant Singing Masters in the Eighteenth Century," in *Itinerancy in New England and New York* (Annual Proceedings, Dublin Seminar for New England Folklife, 1984), pp. 16–36.

Crawford, Richard. " 'Ancient Music' and the Europeanizing of American Psalmody, 1800–1810," in *A Celebration of American Music: Words and Music in Honor of H. Wiley Hitchcock,* ed. Richard Crawford, R. Allen Lott, and Carol J. Oja. Ann Arbor: University of Michigan Press, 1990, pp. 225–255.

———. "Holden, Oliver," *The New Grove Dictionary of American Music,* 4 vols., ed. H. Wiley Hitchcock and Stanley Sadie. London: Macmillan Press, 1986, II, pp. 408–409.

———. "Holyoke, Samuel," in *The New Grove Dictionary of American Music,* 4 vols., ed. H. Wiley Hitchcock and Stanley Sadie. London: Macmillan Press, 1986, II, p. 414.

———. "Lyon, James," in *The New Grove Dictionary of American Music,* 4 vols., ed. H. Wiley Hitchcock and Stanley Sadie. London: Macmillan Press, 1986, III, p. 132.

———. "Preface" to reprint of James Lyon's *Urania*. Philadelphia: n.p., 1761; repr. New York: Da Capo Press, 1974.

———. "Psalmody," in *The New Grove Dictionary of American Music,* 4 vols., ed. H. Wiley Hitchcock and Stanley Sadie. London: Macmillan Press, 1986, III, pp. 635–643.

———. "Set-piece," in *The New Grove Dictionary of American Music,* 4 vols., ed. H. Wiley Hitchcock and Stanley Sadie. London: Macmillan Press, 1986, IV, p. 197.

———. "William Billings (1746–1800) and American Psalmody: A Study of Musical Dissemination," in *The American Musical Landscape*. Berkeley: University of California Press, 1993, pp. 111–150.

Davenport, Linda G. "American Instruction in Sightsinging, Then and Now," in *Bulletin of Historical Research in Music Education,* XIII/2 (July 1992), pp. 90–111.

Hubka, Thomas C. "Farm Family Mutuality: The Mid-Nineteenth-Century Maine Farm Neighborhood," in *The Farm* (Annual Proceedings, Dublin Seminar for New England Folklife, 1986), pp. 13–23.

Kroeger, Karl. "The Church-Gallery Orchestra in New England." Unpublished manuscript.

———. "Isaiah Thomas as a Music Publisher," *Proceedings of the American Antiquarian Society,* vol. 86, part 2 (1976), pp. 321–341.

———. "Introduction," in *The Complete Works of William Billings,* 4 vols. Boston: American Musicological Society and Colonial Society of Massachusetts, 1981–1990, I, pp. xiii-lxiii; III, pp. xi-xlvii.

———. "Performance Practice in Early American Psalmody," in *The Complete Works of William Billings,* 4 vols. Boston: American Musicological Society and Colonial Society of Massachusetts, 1981–1990, IV, pp. xxxiii-lxiv.

———. "Settings of Isaac Watts's Psalm 50 by American Psalmodists," *The Hymn,* XLI/1 (January 1990), pp. 19–27.

———. "Word Painting in the Music of William Billings," *American Music,* VI/1 (Spring 1988), pp. 41–64.

Larkin, Jack. "The View from New England: Notes on Everyday Life in Rural America to 1850," *American Quarterly,* XXXIV/3 (1982), pp. 244–261.

Marini, Stephen A. "Religious Revolution in the District of Maine, 1780–1820," in *Maine in the Early Republic: From Revolution to Statehood,* ed. Charles E. Clark, James S. Leamon, and Karen Bowden. Hanover, NH: University Press of New England, 1988, pp. 118–145.

Meisel, Maribel. "Gram, Hans," in *The New Grove Dictionary of American Music,* 4 vols., ed. H. Wiley Hitchcock and Stanley Sadie. London: Macmillan Press, 1986, II, p. 275.

Merrill, Nancy. "Henry Ranlet: Exeter Printer, 1762–1807," *Historical New Hampshire,* XXXVII/4 (Winter 1982), pp. 250–282.

Mitchell, Stewart. "Mitchell, Nahum," in *Dictionary of American Biography,* 22 vols., ed. Dumas Malone. New York: Charles Scribner's Sons, 1928–1958, XIII, pp. 58–59.

Murray, Sterling E. "Timothy Swan and Yankee Psalmody," *Musical Quarterly,* LXI/3 (July 1975), pp. 433–463.

O'Leary, Wayne M. "The Maine Transatlantic Salt Trade in the Nineteenth Century, *American Neptune,* XLVII/2 (Spring 1987), pp. 83–107.

Rahn, D. Jay. "Humbert, Stephen," in *Encyclopedia of Music in Canada,* ed. Helmut Kallmann, Gilles Potvin, and Kenneth Winters. Toronto: University of Toronto Press, 1981, p. 438.

Sammons, Mark J. " 'Without a Word of Explanation': District Schools of Early Nineteenth-Century New England," in *Families and Children* (Annual Proceedings, Dublin Seminar for New England Folklife, 1985), pp. 78–90.

Sears, Donald A. "Music in Early Portland," *Maine Historical Society Quarterly,* XVI/3 (Winter 1977), pp. 131–160.

Steinberg, Judith T. "Old Folks Concerts and the Revival of New England Psalmody," *Musical Quarterly* LIX/4 (October 1973), pp. 602–619.

Strum, Harvey. "Smuggling in Maine During the Embargo and the War of 1812," *Colby Library Quarterly,* XIX/2 (June 1983), pp. 90–97.

Temperley, Nicholas. "Stephen Humbert's 'Union Harmony,' 1816," in

CanMus Documents I (Proceedings of a February 1986 conference organized by the Institute for Canadian Music, University of Toronto). Toronto: Institute for Canadian Music, 1987, pp. 57–89.

Personal Correspondence

Ayer, Glendon. Letter to Linda Davenport, August 18, 1990.

Camick, Barbara J., Assistant to the Grand Secretary, Grand Lodge of Massachusetts. Letter to Linda Davenport, November 1, 1990.

Gage, Wallace M., Grand Historian, Grand Lodge of Maine. Letter to Linda Davenport, October 6, 1990.

Kaplan, Richard C., Reference Archivist, Massachusetts Archives. Letter to Linda Davenport, December 4, 1990.

Newcombe, Glendon H., Secretary of Kennebec Lodge No. 5, Hallowell, Maine. Letter to Linda Davenport, September 6, 1990.

INDEX

NOTE: Parents, siblings, spouses, in-laws, and children of the Maine psalmodists are only listed by name in this index if they were composers themselves; otherwise, references to them are included in the subheading "relatives of," under the psalmodist's name. Tunebooks are referenced under the compiler's name unless one is not indicated, in which case they are listed by title. The entries for the Maine compilers (Hartwell, Robbins, Maxim, and Washburn) list general items first, followed by tunes discussed in the text, and then their tunebooks. Tune titles are indicated by the use of all capital letters.

ABOUT THE AUTHOR

LINDA GILBERT DAVENPORT, a native of Augusta, Maine, has Maine roots going back many generations. Her ancestors Elijah and Josiah Gilbert were early-nineteenth-century contemporaries of psalmodist Abraham Maxim in Turner, Maine. Dr. Davenport received her undergraduate degree in music education from the University of Maine–Orono and taught music for several years in the Orono, Maine, public schools. Her master's thesis on the music of the contemporary Penobscot Indians was based on fieldwork in Old Town, Maine. She earned her M.M. degree from the University of Illinois and her Ph.D. from the University of Colorado–Boulder, where she was a research assistant at the American Music Research Center. Prior to beginning her doctoral studies, she taught at Mesa State College in Grand Junction, Colorado. She currently teaches at Lewis and Clark Community College in Godfrey, Illinois. Her articles have been published in several professional journals and read at regional meetings of the American Musicological Society and a national meeting of the Sonneck Society for American Music.